PARADISE PLUNDERED

PARADISE
PLUNDERED

Fiscal Crisis and

Governance

Failures in

San Diego

**Steven P. Erie,
Vladimir Kogan,
and Scott A. MacKenzie**

STANFORD UNIVERSITY PRESS
Stanford, California

Stanford University Press
Stanford, California

Printed in the United States of America on acid-free, archival-quality paper

Library of Congress Cataloging-in-Publication Data
Erie, Steven P., author.
    Paradise plundered : fiscal crisis and governance failures in San Diego /
Steven P. Erie, Vladimir Kogan, and Scott A. MacKenzie.
        pages cm
    Includes bibliographical references and index.
    ISBN 978-0-8047-5602-0 (cloth : alk. paper)—
    ISBN 978-0-8047-5603-7 (pbk. : alk. paper)
        1. Finance, Public—California—San Diego.   2. San Diego (Calif.)—
Politics and government.   I. Kogan, Vladimir, 1985– author.   II. MacKenzie,
Scott A. author.   III. Title.
HJ9205.S28E75 2011
336.794'985—dc22
                                                                        2011015039
Typeset by Newgen in 10/13.5 Sabon

To Clarence N. Stone, mentor and friend

Contents

Tables and Figures

Tables

Figures

Preface

The early twenty-first century has not been kind to California's reputation for good government. With a dysfunctional state government and a soaring budget deficit, the state has become the butt of late-night television jokes. Things have fared even worse for local governments. The City of Bell, a small immigrant community located in Los Angeles County, earned national notoriety for allegations of massive corruption and fraud by city officials. The nearby City of Vernon, in the words of the speaker of the California State Assembly, is "a situation where a handful of individuals are able to use an entire city as their own personal fiefdom."[1]

In actuality, the Golden State's governance flaws, whether chronic and seemingly irresolvable budget deficits or public corruption, reflect worrisome national trends with origins in the 1970s and 1980s. Growing voter distrust with government and a demand for services but not new taxes to pay for them, a sharp decline in enlightened leadership and effective civic watchdogs, and dysfunctional political institutions ranging from term limits to an initiative process gone awry have all contributed to the current governance malaise.

Some jurisdictions appeared immune to systematic governance disorders. Until recently, such was the case with San Diego, California, America's eighth-largest city. Lauded by antitax activist Howard Jarvis for its fiscal stewardship and nationally praised as a governance exemplar, this sunny beach town entered the last decade of the twentieth century proudly proclaiming itself "America's Finest City." However, the new millennium has not been kind to paradisiacal San Diego. In a few short years, the town's reputation went from Futureville to Enron-by-the-Sea.[2] A pension scandal blossomed into a huge pension liability. With a large and seemingly intractable budget deficit, the city teetered toward bankruptcy. A number of public officials resigned from office or went on trial, charged with corruption and fraud. Horrific wildfires revealed the paucity of public services. Paradise, it seems, had been plundered.

This is a study of San Diego's myriad civic woes. This project began as a political biography of an understudied Sunbelt city. As events unfolded, we sharpened the focus to the City of San Diego's fiscal crisis and governance failures. San Diego, we believe, is a harbinger for dysfunctional state and national trends related to political culture, leadership, and institutions. The project also can be traced to our active involvement in local civic affairs, ranging from debates about the strong-mayor system to thorny issues involving pension and budget policy, redevelopment, water-supply reliability, and airport development.

Many people have assisted us along the way. Most of all, we wish to thank Kathleen Ames, Cheryl Boudreau, and Laura Tate for their love, support, and patience during the many hours of research and writing. We also want to thank Harold Brackman and Rumman Chowdhury for their able research assistance. Scholars and practitioners kindly read—and improved—earlier drafts of the manuscript. Erik Bruvold, Nico Calavita, Norma Damashek, Jameson Doig, Iris Engstrand, Earl Fry, Larry Herzog, Dennis Judd, Sandy Lakoff, Phil LaVelle, Paul Lewis, Scott Lewis, Roger Showley, Abraham Shragge, Glen Sparrow, Mike Stepner, Clarence Stone, Ken Sulzer, and Todd Swanstrom offered valuable comments and suggestions. We are also grateful to the many individuals we interviewed who so generously gave of their time and effort. Project support was furnished by the University of California, San Diego's Academic Senate Committee on Research.

Finally, we wish to thank an extraordinary mentor and friend, Clarence Stone, who has contributed so much to the study of urban politics. A dedication is small reward for the encouragement, insight, and wisdom Clarence so generously imparts.

Steven P. Erie
Vladimir Kogan
Scott A. MacKenzie
La Jolla, California
February 2011

PARADISE PLUNDERED

I   *Overview and Historical Development*

1　America's Finest City?

Welcome to San Diego, California's second largest city, where blue skies keep watch over 70 miles of beaches and a gentle Mediterranean climate means paradise every day.

—*San Diego Convention and Visitors Bureau,*
Neighborhood Guide[1]

In the popular imagination, San Diego is a sunny seaside paradise. Touted as one of the nation's top leisure-vacation destinations, San Diego aggressively markets itself for an idyllic climate, pristine beaches, a dazzling array of world-class tourist attractions, beachfront resorts and luxury spas, and a vibrant downtown district. Although "the beach is a way of life," golf is "serious business" here, with more than ninety courses offering stunning ocean views, desert sun, or mountain vistas. Local boosters trumpet the "immense options" for business—such as an innovative high-tech industry—as well as pleasure in a place that proudly proclaims itself "America's Finest City."[2]

Yet there is a grim and increasingly visible civic reality to San Diego not depicted in slick marketing brochures. It consists of a chronic municipal fiscal crisis, exacerbated in recent years by a pension scandal and multibillion-dollar pension deficit; severely underfunded public services and infrastructure; grandiose plans for big-ticket civic projects divorced from straitened fiscal realities; and a privatized downtown and bay front, the product of poorly crafted and inadequately monitored public-private redevelopment partnerships underwritten by hundreds of millions of dollars of public investment. Paradise, it appears, has been plundered.

The result of San Diego's civic mismanagement is the making of an American Potemkin village[3]—an impressive privatized facade with a dark public-sector underbelly—featuring a gleaming new downtown and bevy of tourist attractions but saddled with billion-dollar pension liabilities and deficient public services. With civic energies and resources focused on building downtown "legacy projects," such as a new city hall, a central library, an expanded convention center, and possibly a new football stadium, pressing neighborhood improvements and regional initiatives, ranging from improved fire protection to a new airport, have faltered. The appearance of prosperity well serves the interests of the remnants of a once-potent local growth machine, which includes real estate developers, professional sports team owners, the tourist industry, organized labor, public agencies, business groups, and self-interested politicians seeking legacy projects and reelection.[4]

San Diego's civic woes have tangled roots. As far back as the 1970s, the city was an early and eager advocate of limiting taxes and living beyond its means. City officials raided the pension and other revenue streams to pay for big-ticket items while providing a semblance of public services that tax-averse residents demanded but did not want to pay for. At the same time, voter-approved initiatives at the state level, the culmination of a nationwide tax revolt, erected crippling barriers to local governments' ability to raise new revenues. These changes also empowered small but impassioned minorities to block future efforts to raise taxes, thus exacerbating the tenuous financial position of cities like San Diego. To go along with its "free lunch" political culture, San Diego scores unexpectedly low on social capital metrics, with residents displaying low levels of trust in local government and high levels of political ignorance and apathy. As a former local reporter observed, "To win over San Diegans, you have to let them sit back and do nothing and then congratulate them for doing it."[5] Low social capital makes collective action and public monitoring of government performance more difficult.[6]

At the elite level, the capacity to resolve civic challenges diminished as the old business leadership faltered and San Diego became a quintessential branch-plant town. New policy entrepreneurs on the scene have pursued self-interested, single-issue agendas. They include professional sports team owners, real estate developers, and public-sector unions. Aiding and abetting the new policy entrepreneurs are semiautonomous "shadow governments," such as the Centre City Development Corporation, which oversees redevelopment efforts downtown, and the San Diego City Employees' Retirement System, which manages local pension funds.

Another factor contributing to weakened civic capacity has been a sharp decline in the monitoring and effectiveness of civic watchdogs, ranging from the local media to good-government groups.[7] Though hardly unique among the nation's big cities in terms of these troubling civic trend lines, San Diego has been a leader of the pack.[8]

Paradise Plundered dissects San Diego's fiscal crisis and related governance challenges and considers their root causes and likely consequences. In doing so, we hope to provide cautionary lessons for the many communities that are now emulating "the San Diego way." In explaining local government's performance lapses and failures, we emphasize three broad explanatory factors: (1) civic leadership and capacity, (2) political culture, and (3) political institutions. The primary focus is on the City of San Diego and its policy making during the period from 1990 to 2010. We analyze five policy spheres that together encompass the exercise of the city's primary public powers, each with distinct governance arrangements: the city's pension system, municipal finance, public service and infrastructure provision, planning, and redevelopment. We also examine how the city's past has shaped the present, regional and binational infrastructure and governance challenges facing the border metropolis, and prospects for the future. Throughout, we benchmark San Diego with other large cities, particularly in California.

From Futureville to the Most Screwed-Up City in America

After the North American Free-Trade Agreement, the Mexican connection is bound to grow. That and other changes—economic, demographic, cultural—are transforming a place which used to have a reputation as a sleepy navy town, a California cul-de-sac with a great climate and a nice zoo. Nowadays, San Diego can tout itself, without sounding ridiculous, as "the first great city of the 21st century."

—*"Futureville," Economist, 1996*[9]

Most folks probably have certain images in mind when they think of San Diego. A gentle breeze blowing off the Pacific. . . . Well-fed folks lining up putts on country-club greens. Money oozing from the wireless and biotech juggernauts up and down the coast. How, then, to square this idyllic vision . . . with the scandals that have sprouted in California's second-largest city faster than wildflowers after a desert rain? There's so much slime in this town that civic leader George Mitrovitch, president of the City Club of San Diego, calls it "the most screwed-up city in America."

— *"Stay Classy, San Diego! It's Wealthy, Sunny, Beautiful—and Possibly the Most Dysfunctional Big City in America,"* Fortune, 2005[10]

Modern San Diego came of age during and after World War II. In the postwar era, the defense industry brought growth and prosperity, but it collapsed when the Cold War ended, sending unemployment soaring. San Diego embraced the widely held mantra that low taxes, low debt, a small public sector, and business-friendly regulations are the most crucial factors for attracting new businesses and keeping local industries globally competitive.[11] This formula appeared to work. By the late 1990s, San Diego had reinvented itself, with new high-tech industry and foreign trade joining real estate and tourism as pillars of a diverse and apparently healthy economy. In a study of regional innovation, the urban scholar Richard Florida rated San Diego the nation's third-best "creative class" city on the basis of a new model of urban economic development tapping technology, talent, and tolerance.[12]

Beneath the accolades, however, serious problems were festering: woefully underfunded public services and infrastructure, a large and growing low-wage service sector, inadequate schools, and one of the nation's least affordable housing stocks. San Diego's public sector was undernourished and overburdened. Relative to its size (1.3 million residents), the city's police and fire departments ranked among the nation's smallest. Their equipment was aging and deficient. During the disastrous 2003 Cedar Fire, which killed fifteen people and destroyed more than two thousand homes, San Diego firefighters had no helicopters to help contain the conflagration.

In the 1990s, as San Diego recovered from defense cutbacks and a deep recession, the city doubled down, joining other cities in the competition for convention traffic, Super Bowls, and giveaways to professional sports team owners. Raiding pension funds swollen by the bull market of the 1990s was one of the few ways San Diego could pay for big-ticket items like the 1996 Republican national convention and balance its books without raising taxes. Despite San Diego's relatively low tax burden, the *T* word remains anathema to residents in this military and retirement mecca. This has resulted in little money for public services and basic infrastructure improvements essential to a sound economy. After public pensions were boosted, many blamed organized labor for the city's financial woes.

Having plugged its immediate budget deficit with money meant for municipal pensions, San Diego's elected officials chose to lavish scarce public resources on downtown redevelopment and professional sports stadiums. The capstone project of San Diego's "Downtown Renaissance,"[13] which paired the Petco Park baseball stadium for the Padres with ancillary development in the once-moribund East Village, has been widely hailed as a public-private partnership worthy of emulation.[14] This and other projects, their proponents argued, would spur private investment downtown and create new jobs, affordable housing, and public improvements. Critics, however, have pointed to the city's inability to conduct meaningful oversight and to extract public benefits from its substantial investments in downtown and bay-front redevelopment.[15]

California's other big cities appeared to be better prepared to cope fiscally. After Proposition 13 passed in 1978, many cities raised new revenues by imposing utility-users' taxes, increasing business taxes, and charging higher user fees. The Los Angeles Department of Water and Power, for example, found "surplus" revenue to balance the city's budget.[16] Had San Diego emulated these cities, its General Fund revenues would have been much higher, capable of financing essential services and infrastructure without raiding its pension funds. Instead, San Diego became a poster child for the state's tax revolt and the penurious effects of Proposition 13's fiscal straitjacketing of local government.[17] With the onset of the 2008 recession, even fiscally creative cities like Los Angeles faced yawning budget gaps and growing demands from some residents to scale back pensions.[18] In San Diego, the downturn brought the city to the verge of bankruptcy.

Civic Meltdown

The irony is that, before 2003, San Diego was lauded as one of the nation's best-governed cities and held up as a model for the new millennium with its low-tax, business-friendly government; its downtown renaissance; and its environmentally sensitive planning.[19] On the eve of the 1996 Republican national convention, San Diego was praised by *Economist* as "Futureville" for its vibrant high-tech economy; rapidly growing Mexican trade; and lean, efficient municipal government, with the lowest ratio of city employees to population among the nation's fifty biggest cities.[20] The urbanist Joel Kotkin hailed San Diego as an exemplar of a "'Republican' form of urban governance . . . that could make [the GOP] a majority party well into the next century":[21]

> [P]rivate-sector activism constitutes a critical component of making smaller and less expensive government work. . . . This political model, first developed by Republican Progressives in the early 20th century, adapts the best private-sector accounting and hiring practices to city government. Such governments tend to see themselves as a utility that serves the public rather than as a vehicle for political patronage and re-distribution of wealth.[22]

Kotkin also claimed that San Diego "has benefited from what it fortunately does not have: no vast municipal welfare state, no entrenched urban underclass, no powerful municipal employee unions to skew spending priorities, and no industrial union tradition to make its labor force rigid."[23] Evidently, San Diego's Republican progressive political tradition had shallow roots. Even as Kotkin was celebrating the city's center-right consensus, the city was already having trouble managing newly assertive public-employee unions.

Within a few short years of these sunny prognostications, San Diego earned national notoriety as one of the most ineptly managed cities, with a brink-of-bankruptcy pension deficit, multiple bribery and corruption scandals, resignations of key city officials, and charges of gross fire-safety unpreparedness in the wake of major wildfires destroying thousands of homes. San Diego's metamorphosis from civic archetype to national laughing stock was swift. By 2004, as the city's pension scandal unfolded, the *New York Times* proclaimed that "Sunny San Diego Finds Itself Being Viewed as a Kind of Enron-by-the-Sea," and *Governing* magazine called the city "Paradise Insolvent."[24] In 2005, with corruption scandals erupting amid civic turmoil, *Fortune* called San Diego "possibly the most dysfunctional big city in America."[25] The *Washington Post* reported "a serious vacuum of power" in a "former beacon of good government now dimmed by federal corruption probes, deep deficits and election controversies."[26]

According to the *Los Angeles Times*, "one local television station . . . banned use of San Diego's longtime slogan—'America's Finest City'—until further notice, deeming it too 'arrogant and cynical' for a municipality in the throes of national humiliation. The leading local newspaper raised the editorial question: 'Can San Diego sink any lower in the eyes of the world?'"[27] "If you want to study municipal failure," San Diego City Attorney Mike Aguirre observed, "you can't do better than come here."[28]

Mounting Challenges

By 2010, a sizable $2.1 billion unfunded pension liability—projected to increase to $2.6 billion by 2015—placed San Diego's shaky municipal finances in dubious company with once-bankrupt Orange County and once nearly bankrupt New York City.[29] Ballooning pension payments were severely straining General Fund outlays for critical public services like fire protection, police, parks, streets, and libraries. Long considered a model "reform" city, early-twenty-first-century San Diego, according to the *Chicago Tribune*, exceeded political machine–era Chicago in the number of local public officials indicted for or convicted of bribery and corruption.[30] Randy "Duke" Cunningham, a local congressman, was convicted in one of Capitol Hill's worst bribery scandals in recent history. Three city council members were indicted for accepting illegal payments from a strip club owner and were forced to resign. Ongoing criminal investigations into the pension debacle led to the indictment of several members of the city's retirement board. In the face of scandal and investigations, city hall became a revolving door, with the mayor, city manager, and auditor-controller all abruptly resigning.

In the wake of these calamitous events, it was apparent that civic priorities were misplaced. With strong, local antitax sentiment and seemingly feckless political leadership, vital public services remained underfunded and impoverished. Despite experiencing disastrous wildfires in 2003 and 2007, the city had barely two-thirds of the fire stations needed to meet national accreditation standards. Its aging water and sewer infrastructure required billions of dollars in replacement pipes and upgrades. Instead, San Diego continued to seek waivers from the Federal Clean

Water Act while dumping millions of gallons of partially treated wastewater into the Pacific Ocean. With key public officials opposed or sitting on the sidelines, voters rejected plans to build a new airport to relieve congested Lindbergh Field. The town's major newspaper even labeled San Diego "America's Cheapest City," chiding residents for their love of public services but hatred of higher taxes, both of which contributed to the financial chaos.[31] With no new revenues and growing pension outlays, San Diego faced a chronic, long-term, structural-deficit budget crisis.

These vexing civic failures belie San Diego's long history of notable accomplishments. The creation of one of the nation's largest cities on a geographically isolated scrabble of semiarid land with limited local water supplies was no small feat. Although the natural harbor, scenic coastline, temperate climate, and nearby mountains were impressive natural endowments, it took concerted collective action to build this idyllic, if troubled, paradise. Early visionaries planned and built iconic Balboa Park and the world-renowned San Diego Zoo. Energetic civic leaders successfully lobbied for a reliable water supply and to reinvent San Diego as "Navy Town U.S.A." Like many other Sunbelt cities, San Diego's twentieth-century growth was underwritten by the federal government in the form of large-scale military investments. Massive public investments built on the region's impressive natural endowments.[32]

Therein lies the paradox at the heart of San Diego's storied past and troubled current circumstances: the city and region were built and sustained by big government. Even in the early twenty-first century, the military—payroll and defense procurement contracts—still accounts for a significant share of the region's economy. The State of California, through investments in two large public universities, pumps hundreds of millions of dollars more into the regional economy and has fueled a significant number of business spin-offs. As a creature of big government, San Diego never had to fully pay its own way. The region grew accustomed to someone else—particularly the federal and state governments—paying for critical public services and infrastructure, ranging from aqueducts to fire protection. Today, however, San Diego's public dialogue is dominated by conservative critiques of big government and a celebration of laissez-faire capitalism and rugged individualism—notwithstanding a still-hearty appetite for public services coupled with a strong aversion to paying taxes.

When Governance Fails

Semper vigilans (Ever vigilant).
   —*Official motto of the City of San Diego*

The fiscal crisis that has paralyzed the City of San Diego for much of the past decade is just one dimension of a larger failure of the local public sphere. Equally debilitating is the neglect of basic infrastructure, a problem that is decades in the making and that rivals the city's unfunded pension liability in its size. Unlike the pension liability, which exists primarily on the balance sheets of the city and its retirement system, local residents feel the consequences of the city's infrastructure deficit every day. San Diego does not have enough police officers to protect its citizens from crime. Its fire department lacks the personnel to respond to emergencies quickly, and its aging equipment is inadequate for its day-to-day activities, let alone to fight the catastrophic wildfires that have twice threatened core neighborhoods in the past ten years.

San Diego's wastewater system is out of compliance with federal laws passed more than thirty years ago. In the interim, the city has compiled one of the poorest records of sewage spills of any big city in the country. Imported water constitutes more than 90 percent of the city's supplies. Nonetheless, the city continues to dump most of its reclaimed water into the Pacific Ocean. San Diego's library system is hemorrhaging, with too few librarians to staff the local branches and too little money to pay for books, computers, and maintenance. The city's roads continue to decay, with more than 50 percent of roads in poor condition. Among the nation's largest cities, San Diego's roads are the seventh worst.[33] The city's lone commercial airport is undersized, near capacity, and already requires local residents to rely on airports outside the region.

Considered against this backdrop, the city's decisions to pour ample money, including loans backed by future revenues, into downtown redevelopment appear downright irresponsible. The resources devoted to upgrading the convention center and building a new downtown ballpark for the San Diego Padres—projects that, regrettably, yielded few public benefits to local taxpayers—extend beyond the property tax increment harvested by the Centre City Development Corporation. Local public officials have opted to supplement those funds with loans, land,

and development rights that continue to affect the city's General Fund. Equally bizarre are pie-in-the-sky proposals for a new central library, a second convention center expansion, a modern city hall campus, and—more recently—a downtown stadium for the San Diego Chargers.

In short, the modern political history of San Diego has been marked by persistent and systematic governance failures, of which the city's fiscal crisis is just one stark example. Urban practitioners and scholars agree that the most appropriate criterion for assessing the quality of local governments is by their ability to govern—to effectively mobilize both public and private resources to achieve collective goals. The focus on governance recognizes that urban areas today confront incredibly complex social and political challenges that often exceed the capacities of both local government and key stakeholders such as the business community.[34] Contemporary urban problems can be tackled only through sustained cooperation between the public and private sectors that strategically deploys the resources of each to bring about desired policy outcomes. Governance failures occur when public and private actors fail to coordinate to advance welfare-enhancing policies and, alternatively, when civic elites succeed in channeling the powers of government to benefit narrow, private interests at the expense of the broader city interest. San Diego over the past twenty years exemplifies both types of failures.

The informal coalitions between elected officials and local private-sector leaders that define the governing capacity of cities have been described by urban scholars as "regimes." Clarence Stone's influential study of Atlanta first popularized regime theory as a tool to describe and classify cities on the basis of the identity of actors who participate in their governing coalitions. Within this framework, San Diego most resembles many other cities with limited governing capacity and weak regimes. Historically, declining regimes have most often emerged in the former industrial capitals of the Frostbelt, such as Detroit and Cleveland.[35] However, traditional explanations for urban decline, which focus on shrinking populations, deindustrialization, and suburbanization, cannot explain the widespread governance failures in San Diego, a growing Sunbelt city where service industries and tourism have long overshadowed manufacturing as the primary source of jobs and where the urban core has peacefully coexisted with single-family suburbs within the city's municipal boundaries.

In many ways, this book builds on the work of regime theorists such as Clarence Stone and Stephen Elkin. Like these scholars, we focus on local politics as a source of social production rather than social control. Governing San Diego is about the power to achieve public objectives rather than the exercise of power over its citizens.[36] However, our study departs from this theoretical approach in important respects. As Gerry Stoker has argued, regime theory is a tool that should be used "to explain a process rather than to predict an outcome."[37] Too often, however, description and explanation are conflated—for example, progressive regimes are those with progressive public policies, and weak regimes are denoted by the incidence of fiscal or other civic crises. In contrast, this study not only chronicles the governance failures of San Diego but also seeks to identify their primary causes—key factors that vary across cities and can be used to explain and predict policy outcomes.

In addition, although we focus on the central role of political and business elites—the primary actors in regime theory—in setting the political agenda and mobilizing public support for civic initiatives, our analysis also places ordinary voters at the heart of San Diego's governance problems. Although effective leaders can and often do move public opinion, our account recognizes that voter preferences and the broader political culture greatly constrain the strategies and options available to public-sector and private-sector leaders. As Royce Hanson has argued in his study of Dallas, political culture can create a "logic of appropriateness" that defines the parameters within which political debates are held, public decisions are made, and conflicts are resolved.[38] In San Diego, the voice of the voters is amplified through political institutions—including the frequent use of the initiative process and voter-approval requirements added to the state constitution in the late 1970s—that not only structure the interactions between public officials and the business community but also define the relationship between elected officials and their constituents.

More generally, our account stresses the microfoundations of urban governance, a term borrowed from economics that emphasizes individuals, rather than the city, as the primary unit of analysis. Throughout, we pay particular attention to the motives of individuals—whether voters, elected officials, or business owners—and the strategies available to them to achieve their goals. By rejecting alternative accounts of urban politics based largely on theories of economic determinism, this book emphasizes the political choices of San Diego's civic leaders and its citizens, and it pays close attention to the alternative paths not followed and the resultant outcomes.[39] In San Diego, systematic governance failures have been an unintended, but largely predictable, by-product of these decisions.

Explaining Governance Failures

The roots of the city's failures are not in the necessity of earning its keep but in how that impulse gets translated into action.

—*Stephen L. Elkin,* City and Regime in the
American Republic, *1987*[40]

How can San Diego's local governance failures be explained? We have spent several years researching this question—culling through countless primary documents; compiling detailed statistics measuring local inputs and outputs; interviewing former city officials and other informed observers; and reading hundreds of news accounts, local histories, and academic analyses. Several recurring explanatory themes emerged from the secondary sources we consulted and were echoed by those we interviewed who had firsthand knowledge of the policy decisions analyzed in this study. We have organized these themes into three broad explanatory categories: leadership, political culture, and political institutions. These form our primary explanatory variables in the chapters that follow.

Leadership

The first category, leadership, is perhaps easiest to describe but its impact hardest to measure or explain. Unlike Atlanta or Dallas and many other cities, contemporary San Diego lacks cohesive and effective business leadership. This was not always the case. Powerful business moguls like John D. Spreckels, who invested in regional water and transportation systems, shaped the city's early trajectory. Later, a well-organized business community led a concerted campaign to lure the U.S. Navy to San Diego. In the years following World War II, local defense contractors such as Reuben Fleet, bankers, hoteliers, and real estate developers provided the city with a critical mass of civic-minded business leaders concerned about San Diego's future. In the late 1950s, many of these leaders organized San Diegans Inc., which was instrumental in drafting early plans for the city's downtown revitalization. Like the economist Mancur Olson's "stationary bandit," the pursuit of personal profit encouraged these business leaders to promote needed investment in public services and infrastructure, thus providing critical private-sector leadership necessary to sustain public initiatives with widespread positive spillovers.[41]

Over the past thirty years, however, San Diego's corporate civic leadership has diminished. The savings-and-loan scandals of the 1980s crippled San Diego's financial services sector. The end of the Cold War led to a decline in local defense-related firms and employment. More than anything, however, the decline is a consequence of global economic forces. Today, San Diego's financial services sector consists largely of regional branches of national and multinational megabanks. Similarly, local hotel proprietors compete with international chains, which capture a large share of the region's tourist traffic. More recently, the city's only major daily newspaper—never a strong civic watchdog—was sold to a private equity group located in, of all places, Beverly Hills. In place of Spreckels and Fleet, San Diego's new private-sector entrepreneurs more closely resemble Olson's "roving bandits"—pursuing exceedingly narrow, single-issue agendas that provide few positive spillovers for the entire city. With the decline of civically engaged local business leadership, the politics of extraction have replaced policies promoting public investment.

These changes, not unique to San Diego, have had several effects. First, the absence of corporate civic leadership has removed a strong source of monitoring of local government's performance. Unlike residents who pay little attention to politics, local businesses have an interest in the health of the city by virtue of their role as major employers and property owners. Increasingly staffed by branch-plant managers with few local roots, the region's major corporations today are less inclined to see their fate and the city's as intertwined. As such, their interest in local politics has declined.

Second, as Clarence Stone has argued, corporate civic leadership provides local governments with critical resources needed to accomplish public objectives.[42] Business leaders can serve their communities in many ways, including by serving on local boards, partnering on programs of mutual interest, identifying and mobilizing funding for local initiatives, and contributing information and expertise. This vital component of civic culture has diminished in San Diego and elsewhere.[43] Finally, the deterioration of business leadership has had consequences for downtown development. As the influence of broad-based groups of executives like San Diegans Inc. has declined, redevelopment policy, for example, has become the province of real estate speculators and developers, whose interests are often short term and project specific.[44]

The vacuum left by San Diego's mostly absentee business establishment has not been filled by public-sector officials. In the postwar era, the development of many big cities was profoundly shaped by the activities of political leaders, such as Mayors Richard J. Daley in Chicago and Tom Bradley in Los Angeles, and by bureaucratic entrepreneurs, such as Robert Moses in New York. With the notable exception of Mayor Pete Wilson (1971–1982), San Diego has lacked transformative leadership to achieve collective purposes.[45]

Political Culture

The second category, political culture, describes the general political dispositions of the city's residents. As a navy town swelled by returning veterans after World War II, San Diego's civic identity is shaped in important respects by the military service of many of its citizens. Even today, the city remains home to some of the largest concentrations of veterans in California.[46] Political sociologists have long hypothesized that military service would be closely linked to the political preferences of individuals, as a result of both the transformative experiences of service and self-selection on the part of people who sign up to serve in an all-volunteer military. "In an institution that values conformity and conservatism, and whose core value is national defense, [veterans'] attachment to the contemporary Republican Party seems a reasonable assumption," some scholars have suggested.[47] Although the empirical evidence is mixed, some studies have found a significant conservative tilt in the preferences of veterans.[48]

Political ideology, however, is but one part of the story. Other aspects of the local political culture, like social capital, cut across partisan and ideological lines. Social capital is a concept that scholars use to denote the norms and social relationships embedded in a community that allow people to coordinate their activities to achieve desired ends.[49] More practically, social capital refers, in the words of the political economist Francis Fukuyama, to "the ability of people to work together for common purposes in groups and organizations."[50] The dimension of social capital we focus on here is local residents' trust in government. If local government is to be effective, it must cultivate support for its actions and policies among voters. If voters perceive government as wasting resources or engaging in activities that conflict with their preferences, they will not support the officeholders who are responsible, whether by returning them to elective office or by granting their requests for new revenues and authority.

San Diegans have little trust in local government. Given the city's recent history, voter distrust is perhaps justified. The level of distrust, however, goes beyond residents' appraisals of local government performance. At a basic level, many San Diegans, Republicans and Democrats alike, believe that local government ought to do as little as possible; they prefer allowing the private sector to take the lead. They believe that local government officials waste much of the money they receive in taxes and that government spending can be cut dramatically without consequence to the quality of public services they receive. Mark Baldassare described the sentiments of many San Diego voters well in noting the disconnect among suburban voters in their support for initiatives limiting tax increases and their desire to maintain or even increase spending on public services.[51] In short, local voters want to pay less for the services they receive and blame elected officials or municipal employees when deficits arise or services are cut.

High voter distrust of local government animates local politics in San Diego and has shaped responses to the pension scandal, fiscal crisis, and other policy challenges. Public officials accept voters' antipathy to tax increases at face value and strive to avoid programs and policies that would require them. Nonetheless, these same officials recognize that cuts to public services enjoyed by middle-class voters will be unpopular. These competing pressures provide a context for understanding efforts to tap municipal pensions for budget relief.

What kind of politicians succeed in such an environment? Urban sociologist Terry Clark coined the term *new fiscal populism* to describe a breed of public officials who flourish under conditions of voter distrust of local government. Such politicians win office by advertising their fiscal and managerial credentials. Their combination of fiscal conservatism and social liberalism appeals to voters who want to keep the costs of government low while avoiding extreme positions on social issues like affirmative action and the environment.[52] The current San Diego mayor, Jerry Sanders, a former police chief who pledged to play hardball with municipal employees and reversed his opposition to gay marriage, is very much a new fiscal populist. Unfortunately for Sanders and other mayors in this vein, even as voters have asked politicians to wring ever-greater efficiencies from local government, their appetite for public services has not slackened one bit.

In San Diego, the tenuous fiscal situation is exacerbated by the actions of opportunistic politicians in the new fiscal populist mode. These politicians attempt to stoke rather than deflect voter anger with accusations of governmental fraud, waste, and mismanagement. In San Diego, conservative fiscal populists have presented voters with a simple narrative whereby greedy public employees and powerful public-sector unions are entirely responsible for the pension deficit and the need for massive budget cuts.

Political Institutions

The third category, political institutions, refers to the extent to which the structures of local government align the career incentives of public officials with the long-run interests of voters. San Diego entered the 1990s with a regime whose institutions reflected the legacies of Sunbelt-style reform. A critical aspect of this legacy was a fragmented public sphere that featured weak deliberative and executive capacities. The deliberative capacities of local government were concentrated in a city council composed mainly of amateurs who relied on the city manager for information and resources. The council's deliberative capacities were also shaped by the adoption of district elections in 1988 and term limits in 1990. The unelected city manager controlled the regular departments of city government, but executive authority was spread out among myriad special-purpose governments, including independent boards overseeing airports, the port, the convention center, downtown redevelopment, and the municipal pension system.

Designed in the old reform tradition, these boards were controlled by experts—usually individuals with a deep and personal involvement in the policy areas they were overseeing and whose interests often diverged from those of the broader San Diego electorate.[53] Fragmentation helped insulate these policy arenas from political interference but simultaneously made it exceedingly difficult for elected public officials to mount a coordinated response to crises like the pension scandal in 2004 and the global economic downturn in 2008 or to bring policy into closer alignment with voter preferences when they strayed too far.

Like other California cities, San Diego entered the 1990s with a more limited range of fiscal tools than is available to many cities elsewhere. Under Proposition 13, local governments must attain approval from two-thirds of voters before raising most taxes. Subsequent court decisions and additional voter-approved initiatives (Proposition 62 in 1986 and Proposition 218 in 1996) established that any local taxes, whether for general or specific purposes, require a vote of the people. Constraints on local taxation have led public officials throughout California to adopt other mechanisms for financing government activity. After Proposition 13, many turned to revenue bonds, a form of borrowing in which future revenues secure the debt obligation. Cities have also used a litany of fees and charges for admission to city-owned facilities (e.g., museums), parking, business licenses, and franchises (e.g., telecommunications). Each of these revenue sources has the virtue that it does not require a vote of the people. But they typically provide less flexibility to local governments than taxes on local property, sales, or hotel occupants do.

We argue that San Diego's misplaced priorities reflect in part the workings of a political system that fails to align the interests of public officials with the citizens they represent. First, the high bar for raising local revenues empowers small minorities and makes the status quo, however intolerable, difficult to change. Second, fragmentation of political authority among the regular branches of government and a host of unelected boards and commissions militates against a coordinated response to local problems and further strengthens the hand of small but influential interest groups. Third, the switch to district elections after 1988 has encouraged members of the city council to cultivate narrow constituencies while neglecting citywide needs. Finally, the imposition of term limits for elective offices reduced the time horizon of elected officials, who became far more willing to sacrifice long-term stability in exchange for short-term gains.[54] Term limits also eliminated whatever institutional memory existed on the council, thus giving special interests a distinct information advantage.

Our argument, in a nutshell, is that the deficient policy outcomes recently experienced in San Diego, including the pension scandal that brought the city to the edge of insolvency and political collapse, are an outgrowth of deterioration along these three critical dimensions. San Diego's extreme outcomes cannot be explained with reference to a single area of public activity or civic infrastructure. They required a systematic breakdown in the fundamental supports of local democracy. Local governments function best when private-sector investment supplements their efforts; when local residents, media, the business community, and other interest groups monitor their activities; and when political institutions align the career interests of public officials with the interests of a majority of constituents. Local governments function poorly when one of these conditions is not met. Where most of these conditions are lacking, as in San Diego, local governments hardly function at all.

In San Diego, local government failure has taken at least two particular forms. First, there are public policies that favor private interests at the expense of the public good. Such policies include financing strategies that provide money for new, but not old neighborhoods; shift money from the General Fund to downtown redevelopment; and earmark scarce local revenues for tourism marketing, environmental mitigation, and other special uses. They also include governance strategies that stack decision-making bodies—for example, the boards of the quasi-public downtown redevelopment corporation, retirement system for municipal employees, and private conservancy to manage Balboa Park—in favor of special interests.

Second, there are public policies that privilege short-term considerations over long-term health and stability. The back loading of costs approved in successive deals to underfund the pension system and the supply-side logic of financial plans for big projects like Petco Park are just the most notable examples. Policies that require political actors to give up something now in return for something later cannot be made because most actors have limited shelf life; those with significant longevity do not believe that the something later will ever materialize.

Urban Governance in a New Era

There is a San Diego brewing in every community.
—*San Diego City Councilman Carl DeMaio, 2008*[55]

Given the social, economic, and political changes currently transforming American cities, we believe that San Diego's experience holds important lessons for understanding the evolution of urban governance at the start of the twenty-first century. Although we expect few other cities to experience as extraordinary and swift a decline as San Diego, recent research has documented evidence of significant deterioration in civic capacity along the three key dimensions that we examine in this study.

Across the country, the continuing pressures of globalization and suburbanization have accelerated the decline of corporate leadership in civic affairs. In many regions, mergers and acquisitions by global corporations are replacing local executives with managers who lack personal ties to their communities and possess few career incentives to participate in local public policy debates. Among local business leaders who remain engaged, their attention is shifting from the central city to broader regional and metropolitan initiatives designed to foster economic competitiveness.[56] Given the historic nadir in private-sector unionization rates, regional labor federations are becoming increasingly dominated by the construction trades and government employee unions, which is creating growing conflicts between these groups' responsibility to represent the interests of their workers and labor leaders' broader roles as community watchdogs and governing coalition partners.

Even as they lose their historical partners in the business community, public officials are facing new challenges that undermine their capacity to govern. Two institutional innovations first popularized in California—municipal term limits and constitutional tax-and-expenditure limitations—have become common in many other parts of the country in part because of growing public distrust of local government. Currently, nearly half of America's largest cities limit the tenure of their chief executives or legislators.[57] Following the passage of California's

Proposition 13 in 1978, almost every state has moved to adopt statutory or constitutional restrictions on the taxing powers of local governments.[58] In addition, stronger federal civil rights protections and successful demands for incorporation by previously excluded minority groups have been responsible for the growing use of district-based city council elections in historically reformed cities, thus weakening the electoral link between citywide interests and public officials.

Although San Diego's fiscal crisis has ample local plot lines, its basic story about how pension mismanagement leads to political scandal and financial ruin is likely to replay across the country in the coming years. In this sense, San Diego's turmoil serves as the proverbial canary in the coal mine for state and local governments across America, which have only begun to realize the financial impacts of the generous promises made to retiring employees in the context of pension investment losses suffered during the nation's 2008 economic crisis. Although San Diego has felt the financial and political consequences of its pension mismanagement earlier than most governments, because it relied on the pension fund to backfill city budgets sooner and to a larger extent than most, its experience is by no means unique.

State and local governments currently owe an estimated $2.37 trillion in retirement benefits to their workers. Many of these entities, like San Diego, have had to manage large cutbacks in federal funding and state and local revenue constraints imposed by voters. As a result, pension funds across the country have formed attractive targets for state and local governments seeking temporary budget relief. The City of Chicago faces significant deficits in the eight funds it manages for municipal workers. In New Jersey, chronic underfunding of the state pension fund has created a liability estimated at anywhere from $24 billion to $54 billion.[59]

In 2003, the federal government estimated that pension funds for state and local government workers faced a funding gap of $278 billion. More recently, an analysis by Barclays Global Investors found that the underfunding problem was closer to $700 billion. In this context, the pension scandal and ensuing financial crisis in San Diego is likely to be a harbinger of pension wars looming in many cities and states across the country. How San Diego has responded to these growing challenges amid declining business and political leadership provides important lessons for local governments now finding themselves in similarly difficult straits.

Organization of the Study

A city is a body of fate, but unfortunately the world cannot be persuaded that San Diego is anything other than a sunny congeries of tourist attractions. . . . Historically, it seems San Diego cannot represent itself, and is barely represented by others. In history and literature, though America's seventh largest city at the millennium, it scarcely registers.

> —*Mike Davis, Kelly Mayhew, and Jim Miller,* Under the Perfect Sun, 2003[60]

Despite national media attention to its civic woes, no longer bland-and-benign San Diego—California's second-largest city, and, as of 2010, the nation's eighth-biggest city—has received little scholarly attention.[61] Unlike New York or Boston in the Northeast, Chicago in the Midwest, Atlanta in the South, and Los Angeles and San Francisco on the West Coast, San Diego is little researched and understood. Whereas Sunbelt cities of comparable size, like Phoenix, Houston, Dallas, and Las Vegas, can boast of one or more comprehensive urban political histories, San Diego is still awaiting its first scholarly political biography.[62] Though among the least studied of major American cities, San Diego's recent civic troubles can offer valuable lessons for cities experiencing pension and budget deficits, public service and infrastructure deficiencies, and other governance challenges.

Based on extensive field research and the authors' involvement in local civic affairs,[63] *Paradise Plundered* explores San Diego's intertwined fiscal crisis and governance failures in the context of twenty-first-century regional and binational transformation. How did this ostensible paradise endowed with "splendid assets"—a mild and stable year-round climate and a "bold natural endowment" of mountains, mesas, canyons, and sea[64]—and boasting a high-tech knowledge-based economy and reputation as a world-class tourist destination become a veritable Potemkin village, beset with seemingly intractable fiscal, public service, infrastructure, and planning problems? In answering this question, the next seven chapters tell three interrelated stories.

First, in Chapter 2, we trace San Diego's growth trajectory from the 1800s to 1990. We examine the city's early rivalry with Los Angeles, its development as a navy town, and its more recent evolution into a high-tech, tourist-oriented boomtown. Throughout, we focus on the role of leaders in shaping the city and region—from early-twentieth-century businessman John D. Spreckels to Mayor Pete Wilson in the 1970s and 1980s. Like other Sunbelt cities, San Diego's post–World War II regime was characterized by strong business leadership, weak labor and minority groups, and compliant politicians advocating low taxes. However, by the 1970s the old regime was faltering. Unlike cities such as Dallas or Atlanta, San Diego became a quintessential branch-plant town, where business leaders have little interest and involvement in local public affairs.

Second, Chapters 3–6 examine San Diego's major fiscal, public service, planning, and redevelopment challenges. In Chapter 3, we trace the roots of the city's pension debacle and budget crisis to voters' approval of Proposition 13, which sharply reduced local property taxes and erected new barriers to raising revenues in the future. In San Diego, more so than elsewhere, this fueled the development of "creative" financing techniques to raise revenue without having to seek voter approval. In Chapter 4, we benchmark San Diego's fiscal performance against other California cities and document the growing underfunding and deterioration of its basic public services and infrastructure. San Diego, with its early and extensive raids on municipal pensions, represents a cautionary tale for other communities now experiencing pension deficits and fiscal stress.

Chapter 5 explores the sharp disconnect between San Diego's soaring ambitions for costly new public monuments and the reality of inadequate project funding. Over the past several years, public officials unveiled plans for a new city hall and downtown central library. A mayoral task force endorsed a $750 million convention center expansion, and a proposal has surfaced for a publicly subsidized Chargers football stadium downtown. Despite the city's gaping budget shortfalls, such projects continue to garner serious consideration.

Chapter 6 examines redevelopment policy making. Although San Diego is heralded for its apparent downtown renaissance, the city is also notorious for its generosity and lax oversight with respect to redevelopment. We compare the benefits and costs of San Diego's nonprofit corporation model for downtown revitalization relative to Los Angeles and San Francisco, which use citywide redevelopment agencies. We also critically evaluate the widely celebrated public-private partnership underwriting Petco Park and ancillary development in nearby neighborhoods, as well as the city's experience with two military-base reuse projects.

Third, in Chapter 7, we look more broadly at regional and cross-border infrastructure and governance challenges and failures. The San Diego region faces a host of thorny infrastructure issues, ranging from inadequate port and airport facilities to growing water-supply reliability concerns. For infrastructure, San Diego relies on single-purpose special districts that magnify the parochial voices of suburban and rural jurisdictions at the expense of the central city. San Diego remains in the shadow of Los Angeles and heavily depends on L.A.'s superior port, airport, rail, and water systems. There are also cross-border issues, ranging from illegal immigration to escalating drug-related violence in neighboring Tijuana. San Diego is the nation's busiest border crossing. Nonetheless, there is a long-standing debate over whether the two economies and societies can and should be better integrated.

Finally, in Chapter 8, we reexamine the leadership, political culture, and institutional forces that have shaped San Diego's fiscal crisis and governance failures. In doing so, we consider the lessons to be gleaned from San Diego's recent experiences, its current policy options, and its prospects for the future. Among the leading policy choices are the wholesale privatization of city services and even bankruptcy. We believe San Diego's quandaries and culprits deserve careful scrutiny. In the early twenty-first century, the city has become one of the nation's leading examples of fiscal mismanagement, poor governance, and misplaced policy priorities. As the federal government, states, and cities search for ways to close cavernous budget deficits, pay for underfunded pensions and over-burdened public services, and reorder their priorities, they would do well to study prosperous and seemingly idyllic San Diego as a cautionary tale.

2 Never, Never La-La Land
Growth and Governance Challenges, 1800s–1990

San Diego is now the largest and thinnest populated county in the state; yet it could be made the richest, most populous. A little wise statesmanship and masterly activity is all that is necessary to make everybody rich, happy and contented.

—San Diego Herald, *before ceasing publication in April 1860*[1]

The English historian Lord Acton once wrote that "history [is] . . . not a burden on the memory, but an illumination of the soul."[2] The sentiment is apt for San Diego. San Diego has a long and rich history, its claims to Futureville notwithstanding. This history is informative for understanding the challenges now facing the city and region. In particular, the major factors contributing to San Diego's current woes— residents' unwillingness to raise taxes, the lack of strong political leadership, the erosion of business elites' cohesiveness and capacity, and poorly formed and performing political institutions—have historical roots and antecedents. Equally important is San Diego's long-standing rivalry with its northern neighbor, Los Angeles, located 120 miles away. Against the backdrop of this history, the pension crisis, infrastructure deficit, and other municipal woes appear to be a natural evolution from, rather than an abrupt break with, the past.

From the 1800s to World War II, San Diego's main challenge was too little growth. San Diego was outmaneuvered by Los Angeles in the early competition for growth and development of infrastructure to support manufacturing activity. San Diego's consolation prize was the U.S. Navy, the pursuit of recreation and tourism as a major development strategy, and subordinate regional status. While Los Angeles built infrastructure crown jewels—world-class municipal water, power, harbor, and airport facilities—that fueled its early industrialization and rapid growth, San Diego emphasized quality-of-life concerns. Its amenities-oriented crown jewels consisted of Balboa Park, the San Diego Zoo, Mission Bay, and pristine local beaches. These divergent investment strategies resulted in markedly different growth trajectories. By 1940, the City of Los Angeles's population had soared to 1.5 million; San Diego's population stood at 200,000.

Since World War II, however, San Diego has experienced rapid growth, which has given rise to new challenges. From 1940 to 2008, San Diego's population increased by 650 percent—to 1.3 million residents—whereas the City of Los Angeles (notwithstanding prodigious suburban growth) grew at a slower rate, to 3.8 million residents. By the 1980s, San Diego's sprawling growth had spawned antigrowth groups like Prevent Los Angelization Now! challenging the hegemony of the local growth machine. Nonetheless, lacking the transportation and water infrastructure to support its burgeoning population, San Diego chose throughout most of the twentieth century to heavily rely on the superior facilities of Los Angeles. From the distant past to the present, San Diego's development has been fundamentally shaped by its rivalry with L.A.

This chapter examines the historical forces shaping the development of modern San Diego and its current fiscal, infrastructure, and governance quandaries. Given that San Diego is understudied and little understood, we use a "thick description" narrative approach to provide needed historical context for the city's major growth and governance debates, the key actors involved, the strategies pursued, and the outcomes that resulted.[3]

We consider five major eras of San Diego's development from the early 1800s to 1990. First, we explore the fierce nineteenth-century competition between Los Angeles and San Diego for infrastructure development (e.g., railroad, harbor, water), regional growth, and hegemony. San Diego's infrastructure deficiencies reflect a long-standing pattern of inadequate civic leadership, governance arrangements, and public investments.

Second, we explore the heavy-handed reign of business mogul John D. Spreckels and the failure of Progressive Era reform efforts, from 1900 to 1917. Although the era featured notable accomplishments such as the development of Balboa Park, Spreckels and his allies thwarted political and planning reforms and retarded public infrastructure development.

Third, we examine the building of Navy Town U.S.A. and the local military-industrial complex, from 1917 to 1945. Bringing the military to San Diego was a major achievement, the result of strenuous and effective lobbying by determined public officials and a cohesive business community. The massive military presence strengthened the region's conservative political culture. It also weakened local governance capacity as San Diego ceded control of critical land-use, infrastructure, and fiscal authority to Washington, D.C.

Fourth, we consider the postwar challenges of downtown revitalization, suburban sprawl, municipal corruption, and the incubation of a high-tech economy, from 1945 to 1971. In this era, city hall was controlled by a Sunbelt-style, business-led growth machine dedicated to low taxes. The course of events was powerfully shaped by another business mogul, C. Arnholt Smith. Yet taxpayer protests over underfunded new development, major planning and growth conflicts, and a corruption scandal weakened business rule.

Finally, we critically evaluate iconic Mayor Pete Wilson and his mayoral successors, focusing on new and consequential approaches to public finance, governance, and planning, from 1971 to 1990. Arguably, many of the city's current pension, budget, and governance difficulties can be traced to the Wilson administration (1971–82), which championed fiscal conservatism, an underfunded growth management plan, and a "shadow" government for downtown revitalization. Subsequent mayors embraced Wilson's policies. In this era San Diego became a quintessential branch-plant town.

In the Shadow of Los Angeles

When I proposed the Tenth Avenue [marine] terminal, I was told it would be impossible to compete with Los Angeles for commercial shipping—that we should be content with keeping this a Navy port and yachtsman's paradise. . . . We're going to have to fight Los Angeles for every inch of industrial development for years to come. . . . Los Angeles wants us as a satellite, and not an independent industrial complex.

—*San Diego Unified Port District Director John Bate, 1963*[4]

In contradistinction to the urban theorist Edward J. Soja's famous postmodern formulation—"It all comes together in Los Angeles"[5]—

stands San Diego. Until well into the twentieth century, San Diego was a perennial also-ran to its Southern California neighbor and rival Los Angeles. Site of the first landfall (in 1542) and first settlement (in 1769) by Europeans in Alta California, San Diego lacked the wherewithal to translate early settlement into regional predominance relative to Los Angeles.[6]

The reasons for this failure appear rooted in a history that predates San Diego's emergence as an American city. Unlike L.A.—a pueblo, or town, from the start—Spanish and then Mexican San Diego was founded around the dual nuclei of mission and presidio, or military garrison. These two centers of authority sometimes competed, yet they shared an authoritarian ethos not always congenial to civic engagement or private enterprise. At its inception, San Diego was an embattled colonial outpost—cut off from eastward supply by steep mountain passes, threatened by interior Native American bands, and made vulnerable to seaward attack by its natural harbor. When San Diego finally sought to shift from presidio to pueblo, its model was Los Angeles.[7]

San Diego County was incorporated in 1850 by California's first legislature as the state's first county, and the town of San Diego became the locus of a new, increasingly Anglo merchant class. Dreaming of harbor development, railroad acquisition, and real estate profits, San Diego's newcomers planned a townsite, built a wharf, and persuaded the army to add a depot and post. Despite lofty ambitions, the struggling New Town, San Diego's current downtown, went bankrupt in 1852. Shortly thereafter, and until 1889, it was governed by an archaic board of trustees, elected irregularly and granted only limited municipal lawmaking powers by the state before 1876. After the Civil War, the board of trustees petitioned the state legislature to allow it to convey public lands to the federal government to build a naval depot and "harbor of refuge." Los Angeles retaliated by lobbying successfully to have the mail delivered to L.A. by stagecoach from Arizona through the San Gorgonio Pass, rather than to San Diego through the Jacumba Pass.[8]

Dashed Railroad Dreams

Los Angeles and San Diego both rode an economic roller coaster as they fiercely competed to become the region's terminus of a transcontinental railroad. The major difference was that L.A. achieved early, decisive success in 1876 by linking with the Southern Pacific Railroad, whereas San Diego repeatedly experienced a boom-bust cycle of frustrated railroad expectations, never fully reaching its goal. In 1854, San Diego organized and granted nine thousand acres of public land to the San Diego & Gila, Southern Pacific, and Atlantic railroads to link along the thirty-second parallel with the antebellum Southern transcontinental line that was never built because of the Civil War. This would be the first of many attempts by the city to attract private investment with public land giveaways.

The plans for New Town harbor development—to be located several miles south of Old Town, San Diego's original settlement at the foot of Presidio Hill—by local entrepreneurs disappeared into dust. From the 1850s onward, the local population ebbed and flowed with dreams of railroad development. Little else attracted early settlers to the place. According to Thomas Whaley, a newcomer from New York, writing home in 1855: "We all think about the great railroad and believe that it must terminate here. And if it does I have enough land to make me as rich as any man can wish to be. For this alone, I am induced to remain in this dreary place, the inhabitants of which (many of them) are from the rough-scruff of creation."[9]

In 1869, John C. Fremont's Memphis, El Paso, and Pacific Railroad made illusory promises to San Diego New Town builder Alonzo Horton that fueled a short boom. In 1880, negotiations commenced for a new regional railroad to become part of the Atchison, Topeka, and Santa Fe Railroad's transcontinental system. Service on the local connector began in 1883, and the first transcontinental train arrived in San Diego in 1885. But the financially strapped Santa Fe soon moved its offices and shops inland to San Bernardino, to be better positioned to compete with the Southern Pacific in L.A., thereby disappointing hopes for a permanent San Diego terminus. To add insult to injury, the Santa Fe routed most of its traffic to San Diego through L.A. and joined the Southern Pacific in a citrus pool fixing freight rates that made it more expensive to ship San Diego produce to New York than to import it from Sicily. A San Diego delegation that went to L.A. in 1900 to meet, hat in hand, with the Southern Pacific's imperious Collis P. Huntington received no better treatment.[10]

The boom of the 1880s—when San Diego experienced a fivefold population increase (to sixteen thousand compared with Los Angeles's fifty thousand residents) and a hundredfold increase in the price of city lots, as well as the introduction of electric lights and streetcars—soon turned into a bust. During the depressed 1890s, San Diego's population stagnated, and local entrepreneurs saw investments in harbor development undercut by the nightmarish prospect of Los Angeles's new San Pedro harbor.[11]

Finally, there was the early-twentieth-century denouement of San Diego's railroad ambitions. In 1919 local business mogul John D. Spreckels—scion of the San Francisco sugar-refining fortune—drove in the golden spike completing the San Diego & Arizona Railway. Spreckels's railroad was not a legitimate transcontinental terminus but an ill-starred, short-haul line connecting San Diego to the Southern Pacific's route from New Orleans to L.A. and San Francisco.[12] Los Angeles reformers united with *Los Angeles Times* publisher Harrison Gray Otis—a political reactionary but civic patriot—to end economic and political domination by the powerful Southern Pacific Railroad, notoriously known as the "Octopus." A few years later, San Diego reformers put the best face on the success of John D. Spreckels in fastening the Octopus's tentacles even tighter around their city's future. Spreckels was the Southern Pacific's secret, self-styled confidential agent. The mirage of railroad independence Spreckels had carefully cultivated evaporated when the Southern Pacific formally acquired the troubled San Diego & Arizona Railway in 1933. Passenger service was phased out entirely by 1951 and freight service after Hurricane Kathleen in 1976.[13]

Civic Failures

The usual explanations for formative San Diego's dashed railroad dreams revolve around bad timing, dubious railroad finances, and the chronic machinations of the Southern Pacific Railroad. The Southern Pacific appeared intent on protecting its core investments in San Francisco by stifling the potential threat of any combined harbor-railroad development by San Diego that might compete with the Bay Area—five hundred miles more distant from New York by sea than San Diego. Still-landlocked Los Angeles, just beginning to create a man-made harbor, seemed the lesser threat. Geography also served as a contributing factor. Southern California's two most level, traversable mountain passes to the east—the San Gorgonio and Cajon passes—pointed directly to L.A., in contrast with the steeper Jacumba Pass directly east of San Diego. But geography was not the whole story.[14]

Although these explanations have merit, another factor—a failure of municipal leadership and civic will—also played a key role. For the Santa Fe Railroad to connect to San Diego, local boosters ultimately offered public land grants rather than L.A.'s 1870s-era $602,000 voter-approved bond subsidy—equaling 5 percent of Los Angeles County's assessed valuation, which in 2010 would be valued at more than $50 billion—that was given to the Southern Pacific to connect it to San Francisco. San Diego repeatedly pled poverty when it came to paying in hard cash or bonds, a very different situation from L.A. taxpayers' collective willingness to assume heavy public indebtedness for needed infrastructure.[15]

As local merchant Ephraim W. Morse put it in a letter to a railroad promoter, "You blame the San Diego people for not doing anything. This is very true. Nothing has been done, literally nothing. The reason with most of us is we are too poor to experiment."[16] San Diego's mix of enticements to the railroads was decidedly skewed toward public land grants and private stock subscriptions—not municipal bond financing. In San Diego, scheming railroad promoters divided and ruled over competing local interests, ultimately building only a north-to-south spur line to L.A. rather than an enduring transcontinental terminus.[17]

Harbor and Water Quandaries

Not only railroad subsidies but also other needed infrastructure projects—including harbor development and a municipal water supply—reflected San Diego's deficient civic leadership, governance arrangements, and public investments. Los Angeles's epic "Free Harbor Fight" before and after 1900 to develop the San Pedro–Wilmington public harbor and to wrest control of the tidelands from the Southern Pacific actually had an earlier parallel in San Diego—but with a quite different result. In 1868, after the state legislature authorized the sale of certain swamps and tideland, local developers Alonzo Horton and Ephraim W. Morse moved to put within pueblo limits, protected from private sale, the remaining tidelands, including eighteen miles of waterfront. But the board of trustees later voted to convey five miles of tidelands to San Diego City Attorney

Charles P. Taggart, who was the local Republican political boss, and his business partner.[18]

Ultimately, the California Supreme Court ruled that the tidelands belonged to the state and that the San Diego trustees had no authority to grant them to private individuals. There was a stark contrast, however, between how Los Angeles and San Diego approached tidelands development. Los Angeles successfully lobbied for the right of municipal control of the tidelands to wrest them from the grasp of the Southern Pacific. In contrast, the San Diego board of trustees tried to assert municipal control over the disposition of tidelands for the purpose of relinquishing them to aggrandizing private interests. At the same time, the trustees proceeded to auction large parcels of pueblo or common lands to cronies at low prices. The trend toward private sales of the common patrimony resulted in the loss of more than three-quarters of the forty-eight thousand acres of pueblo lands originally owned by the city. Finally, in 1890, San Diego voters called a halt to the giveaways.[19]

Regarding water supply—a critical concern in semiarid Southern California—San Diegans in 1896 voted to issue $1.5 million in water bonds. The bond was opposed by the Municipal Ownership Club, which saw it as an attempt by Spreckels-backed interests to derail public ownership of the water system. The local company, which owned the flume delivery system, refused to sell out to the city. Spreckels's business partner, Elisha S. Babcock, wanted to make the City of San Diego pay dearly for his Otay Water Company. He used his influence to defeat a more generous offer to sell San Diego water from a rival company. The San Diego result again sharply contrasted with L.A.'s determined and systematic moves to municipalize water provision, culminating in the public purchase of the Los Angeles City Water Company in 1902. San Diego did not succeed in municipalizing its water system until 1913, and then at a high price exacted by Spreckels.[20]

Stillborn Progressivism in Spreckelstown, 1900–1917

[Alonzo] Horton built a town and [John D.] Spreckels would build a city.
—*Richard F. Pourade, The Glory Years, 1964*[21]

The prime beneficiary of San Diego's turn-of-the-century discomforts was the real estate, water, and transportation magnate John D.

Spreckels—the dark star around which all of early-twentieth-century San Diego revolved in subservience, resentment, or both. Spreckels was the son of sugar magnate Claus Spreckels and the proprietor of a lucrative firm representing sugar plantations in the Hawaiian Islands. In 1887, Spreckels's sleek pleasure schooner, *Lurline*, docked in San Diego. Desperate San Diegans petitioned the "Sugar King of the Sandwich Islands" to launch a steamship line to connect them to New York. Impressed by the pace of real estate development, Spreckels invested in the wharf and in much, much more.[22]

Laying tracks linking his wharf for coal bunkers with the Santa Fe Railroad, Spreckels then built a local traction empire, buying local horse, steam, and cable-car systems. By 1900, he controlled most of the south side of downtown to the waterfront, acquiring a local bank to finance his subdivisions and a private water company to slake San Diegans' thirst. Spreckels quickly became the largest landowner in San Diego, accounting for 10 percent of all local property tax assessments. He bought the *Union* newspaper in 1890 and later the rival *Tribune*, and became a dominant voice in local Republican politics as a standpatter opposing the party's more progressive elements. Progressive Governor Hiram Johnson denounced him—along with *L.A. Times* publisher Harrison Gray Otis—as among California's "militant, marauding millionaire publishers." His influence over what L.A. reformer Meyer Lissner called "a one-man town" extended until after World War I.[23]

The Failure of Local Progressivism

The Progressive reform movement in California went into hyperdrive with the 1907 San Francisco graft trials; the formation of the statewide Lincoln-Roosevelt League; the 1909 Los Angeles municipal reform sweep; and reformer Hiram Johnson's 1910 gubernatorial victory. In San Diego, a fragile movement slowly blossomed as reformers mobilized against what they saw as "a concrete case of despotism" characterized by "government *of* the machine, *by* the machine, and *for* the machine." The 1905 election of reform Mayor John L. Sehon and the streamlining of the city council, followed by San Diego's 1909 switch from a mayor-council to a city commission governance system, and newfound voter willingness to fund public projects like Balboa Park, a 1,200-acre parcel of land overlooking downtown, were political landmarks. The reform tide peaked and receded with merchant-philanthropist George W. Marston's unsuccessful 1913 and 1917 mayoral campaigns, the cooptation of reform politicians like Sehon, and the 1915 repeal of commission government. Electoral battles—often pitting the old guard of Spreckels-backed GOP boss Charles Hardy, tied to the Southern Pacific's statewide political machine, against local reformers such as Marston and *San Diego Sun* publisher E. W. Scripps—were visible manifestations of deeper political fault lines over planning, growth, and governance.[24]

Reformer Marston, whose hero was Robert F. LaFollette, fired the first reform salvo in 1902 by paying to bring Samuel Parsons Jr., New York City's head landscape architect, to San Diego to design what later would be named Balboa Park. In 1907, Marston broadened the initiative by orchestrating the hiring of Boston-area planner John Nolen, whose 1908 "City Beautiful" blueprint, *San Diego: A Comprehensive Plan for Its Improvement*, envisioned a neoclassical Renaissance makeover emphasizing the advantages that "nature has presented to . . . [San Diego] as a free gift." The plan featured a comprehensive park system, grand boulevards, and a public plaza and civic center extending to the harbor, which he wanted to make into San Diego's "front yard instead of backyard." Nolen's grand vision, however, was stillborn because of opposition by Spreckels's interests wanting growth along the lines of the traditional town grid.[25]

In 1909, Marston, in disgust, went on a long European vacation. He returned in 1910 for what proved to be the Waterloo of San Diego's Progressive Era planning movement. That year, local developer D. C. Collier emerged as director general of the proposed Panama-California Exposition in San Diego—scheduled to open in 1915 in conjunction with the Panama Canal and supported by $2 million in stock subscriptions and $6.2 million in municipal bonds and other public improvements.[26]

Initially opposed to San Diego's Panama-California Exposition as a diversion from the city-planning movement, Marston reluctantly accepted chairmanship of the Building and Grounds Committee. He retained the services of John C. Olmsted and Frederick L. Olmsted Jr., sons of New York Central Park designer Frederick Law Olmsted, to transform Balboa Park into "Central Park West." Spreckels worked behind the scenes to undermine the Olmsteds' plan in favor of a built-up Balboa

Park that would stimulate the development of adjoining real estate subdivisions; he also was intent on building a streetcar line through the park's eastern edge to land he owned in University Heights.[27]

To get his way, Spreckels staged a coup. First, he tried to strip the Park Commission of authority over the exposition, which he wanted to vest entirely in an insulated board dominated by his allies. Then in 1911, he increased pressure by resigning from the Exposition Corporation and withdrawing his corporate support. This resulted in a new Park Commission majority controlled by Spreckels. Believing that Spreckels's plan "would ruin the park by putting the exposition in the middle of it," the Olmsted brothers indignantly resigned, as did their sponsor Marston. Thanks largely to Spreckels's baleful influence, historian Matthew F. Bokovoy writes, "San Diego would never become a 'City Beautiful.'"[28]

In 1913 the reformer George Marston ran for mayor. Though initially favored to win, Marston was a casualty of the same growing class polarization that cost L.A. Progressives control of city hall after 1911. The difference was that San Diego Progressivism was narrowly based and shallowly rooted, and less able to withstand electoral reverses. Marston was an enlightened employer whose department store catered to a working-class clientele. In 1911, however, he made the mistake of building a new store with nonunion labor. More serious, his conservative businessman opponent, Charles F. O'Neill, portrayed Marston as an effete reformer with a "garden city" agenda out of touch with working people, despite Marston's assurances that an amenities-oriented "city beautiful" would "pay in dollars and cents." With Marston splitting the liberal-left vote with a socialist candidate, O'Neill finished first in the primary and went on to win the general election.[29]

In 1917, Marston made a second try at the mayor's office. This time, he faced Louis J. Wilde, a banker-businessman fresh from L.A. who promoted Los Angeles–style industrial development. Though endorsed by much of the old-line elite, who resented the upstart Wilde, Marston lost again by a larger margin. "Smokestack" Wilde routed "Geranium George" in a campaign where San Diegans seemingly voted for new industry (smokestacks) over cultivating tourists and retirees (geraniums).[30] One of the principal casualties of Marston's defeat was the nascent local progressive planning movement that had produced the Nolen Plan of 1908.

"No Pots of Gold"

San Diego benefited from the 1911 California Tidelands Act giving municipalities greater control over their harbors. It made progress in its quest to become the terminus of a national highway reaching Southern California through Yuma. San Diego also made a successful "pueblo rights" riparian claim against landowners north of the San Diego River. In 1924 local voters approved the El Capitan Dam project, a reservoir project in central San Diego County, and two years later the city filed for 112,000 acre-feet of Colorado River water, compared to L.A.'s earlier filing for 1.1 million acre-feet. In 1926, the year that Spreckels died, San Diego welcomed back the planner John Nolen, who successfully advanced a new urban development blueprint "to recover lost ground," tied to Marston's interest in the historic preservation of Presidio Hill and the creation of Presidio Park, a project even Spreckels had supported.[31]

Yet these apparent achievements reflected the weaknesses of San Diego progressivism and governance relative to L.A.'s more robust variety, institutionalized in potent semiautonomous municipal bureaucracies like the Department of Water and Power and the Harbor Department. San Diego was largely a free rider when it came to the passage of the 1911 Tidelands Acts—pushed primarily by L.A. and Oakland. San Diego's assertion of pueblo water rights also was an imitation of L.A.'s pioneering strategy in this area.[32]

Furthermore, San Diego was three times blocked by Spreckels-backed interests from purchasing the Cuyamaca Water Company, whose principal owner, Ed Fletcher, joined with a local irrigation district to delay completion of the El Capitan Dam and stymie San Diego from using water rights to force annexation of surrounding thirsty communities—the way that "imperial" Los Angeles had swallowed up smaller neighboring communities. And the San Diego electorate—after voting three to one to pay for the El Capitan Dam—booted out of office the city's allegedly spendthrift political leaders. These included City Councilman Fred Heilbron, whose later proposal for the city to join the L.A.-based Metropolitan Water District was rejected on the advice of the city's consulting engineer John R. Freeman. A hidebound professional contemptuous of L.A. water czar William Mulholland, Freeman declared: "For the people of San Diego to expect to take water from the Colorado River—it would be like finding the pot of gold at the end of the rainbow." San Diego years before had ceded to L.A. control of the League of the Southwest, established to lobby for Colorado River projects.[33]

With its debt limit almost reached by the $4.5 million bond approved to build the El Capitan Dam, San Diego had no gold left for any other municipal water improvement projects between 1924 and 1939. Local voters twice rejected bonds to finance an independent Colorado River aqueduct. The criticism of Los Angeles was for building too much water capacity to meets its growth needs; the criticism of San Diego was for building too little.[34]

Navy Town U.S.A.

I picked up 311 selected employees and brought them to San Diego, paying their moving expenses. We left all the bad Radicals there in Buffalo.
—*Reuben H. Fleet, 1935*[35]

Neptune and Vulcan

World War I brought a sea change, in every sense, to San Diego. It signaled the gradual weakening of the political power of John D. Spreckels. Spreckels preferred to milk the federal government for $5 million for North Island—located at the north end of Coronado Peninsula on San Diego Bay, and later serving as a naval air station and aircraft carrier homeport—rather than lead the charge to get the navy. It also marked the first arrival on the scene of Reuben H. Fleet, who served locally with the Army Signal Corps but after the war moved to Buffalo, where he founded Consolidated Aircraft. Rechristened after a merger as Convair, the company relocated to San Diego before World War II.

In an era demarcated by two world wars, the San Diego regime changed from Spreckelstown to Fleetsville. Yet the reigning scepter in Fleetsville was held not by Reuben Fleet and the future aerospace industry but by the U.S. Navy and San Diego's enduring maritime-industrial complex. The fundamental fortunes buoying the city were military and nautical—not civilian and aeronautic. Fatefully, San Diego became a navy town transformed permanently by a martial marriage of Neptune, monarch of the waves, to Vulcan, god of the fiery forge. Smokestacks came to San Diego via navy-ship boiler rooms.[36]

San Diego's martial-maritime ambitions stretched back to its post–Civil War pretensions as a naval harbor of refuge; the fortification of its harbor entrance and a coaling station during the Spanish-American War; and the stopover of Teddy Roosevelt's Great White Fleet in 1908. The World War I consummation, which came just in time to pull the city out of a prewar economic slump, had an unlikely political sponsor in a rock-ribbed Republican town. Congressman William Kettner—a power in the chamber of commerce, Wilsonian Democrat, and friend of U.S. Navy Undersecretary Franklin D. Roosevelt—was elected in 1912 largely because of the split between Progressives and old-guard Republicans. As a member of the House Rivers and Harbors Committee, Kettner cheered from Washington when San Diegans in 1915 overwhelmingly voted to transfer five hundred acres of submerged land to the navy for a proposed U.S. Marine Corps base. As historian Roger Lotchin notes, "Like the potlatch givers of the Pacific Northwest, the San Diegans always offered some impressive gifts to their [navy] guests."[37]

Early in 1917, Kettner's efforts to solidify San Diego's maritime future were partially rebuffed by the navy's Helm Commission, which recommended San Diego for a naval air training base but Los Angeles for a submarine base. Navy Secretary Josephus Daniels, however, later recommended San Diego for both aviation and submarine bases. Kettner staged a coup when a major shipyard moved from Los Angeles to San Diego. This paved the way for the postwar tidal shift when L.A. gave up its home port status for the Pacific Squadron so that it could better pursue commercial harbor development.[38]

By 1918, San Diego was a military town, thanks largely to Kettner and the local chamber of commerce, whose energetic seducing of admirals contrasted with its lassitude in courting industrialists. In the early 1920s, naval expansion continued with the completion of the Naval Hospital in Balboa Park and the commissioning of a naval supply depot and a naval training station and U.S. Marine Corps base. In 1935, all of North Island came under navy jurisdiction. By 1939, there were eight local naval and marine bases on four thousand acres. The military had become San Diego's leading employer.[39]

San Diego's fervent navy embrace would prove to be a Faustian bargain. The city got the growth it wanted but at the cost of sizable public land and other giveaways. San Diego also ceded control of critical land-use, harbor, and airport decisions to a Washington, D.C.–based military entity. By the end of World War II, the federal government would control nearly 40 percent of the region's land, severely depleting local tax bases and local government revenues. For much of the twentieth century, San Diego would have two reigning mayors—one in city hall and the other representing the U.S. Navy.

Wartime Growth Challenges

Four days before Pearl Harbor, Reuben Fleet sold Consolidated Aircraft to escape wartime taxation. Reorganized and rechristened as Convair in 1943, it announced plans to bring ten thousand workers, mostly from the Midwest and South, to San Diego. Manufacturing employment in San Diego increased from four thousand in 1935 to seventy thousand in 1943, and the value of industrial output soared from $35 million to $1 billion. Convair alone delivered thirty-three thousand aircraft during the war.[40]

Between 1940 and 1944 San Diego's combined military-civilian population doubled to 480,000. As workers, soldiers, and sailors flocked in, the number of streetcar rides increased almost fivefold between 1939 and 1943, and the federal government was forced to divert buses from other cities to San Diego. Because of surging water demand, the city nearly went bankrupt. As for city planning, the Nolen Plan was overwhelmed as orderly growth became a casualty of war. By 1942, separate, permanent housing had been found by only half the city's new families—with the other half doubling up; sharing beds in shifts; or occupying hotels, trailers, and even park accommodations.[41]

The federal government aggravated matters by locating defense plants and emergency housing on isolated sites that overstretched the city's existing infrastructure stock and increased congestion. On the plus side, twenty thousand new homes were built by the end of 1942 with $15 million in federal money for sewers and other improvements. The navy, having ordered the newly created San Diego County Water Authority's 1946 shotgun marriage with the L.A.-based Metropolitan Water District and its Colorado River Aqueduct, agreed to pay 70 percent of the cost. The federal government also modernized Lindbergh Field, San Diego's major airport. Fiscally, though, the war was far from an unalloyed godsend. As noted, forty percent of the county was owned or occupied by the federal government, and thus not subject to local taxation. The military preempted most of the harbor it did not already control. Although the federal government paid for some housing, it provided little for needed public facilities such as schools.[42]

New Challenges and New Directions, 1945–1971

Where once the *San Diego Union* had noted that San Diegans congratulated themselves that their City was not like Los Angeles, it now complained that there were those in Los Angeles who looked upon San Diego as being lethargic, and what they meant was that it is a nice City, nice climate, but does San Diego as a City know, or care, where it is going? A contingent of twenty-five San Diegans representing San Diegans, Inc., the Chamber of Commerce, the Convention and Tourist Bureau, and the City government went to Los Angeles [in 1960] to see where it was going.
    —*Richard F. Pourade,* City of the Dream, *1977*[43]

From the Old to the New Economy

San Diego emerged from World War II with city hall controlled by a Sunbelt-style, business-led growth machine based on low taxes and a "reform" council-manager form of government approved by voters in 1931. In terms of postwar growth strategies, the paradigmatic local polarity pitting a "geraniums" amenities orientation against "smokestacks" industrialization persisted. The geraniums platform received an electoral mandate when voters in 1945 approved $2 million in bonds for Mission Bay, which was formally dedicated as an aquatic park in 1949. Supported by federal money for San Diego River flood control, Mission Bay park development continued apace into the 1950s but with an increasingly commercial turn. In 1958, the city council unanimously overrode the objections of the Mission Bay Committee and approved a public-private partnership master plan for the bay that featured boat landings, picnic areas and playgrounds, hotels and motels, and commercial development. In 1960, the Department of Parks and Recreation assumed control of four-thousand-acre Mission Bay, preparatory to voter approval of $12.6 million additional bond money that floated SeaWorld, which opened in 1964.[44]

On the side of smokestacks, the Korean War, during which the United States resolved the competition between advocates of new supercarriers and supersonic bombers by deciding to build both, inaugurated the golden age of San Diego's military-industrial complex. Acquired by General Dynamics (GD) in 1953, Convair opened a new factory, increasing its floor space by more than sixteen times in six years. In late 1957 the first of the Convair Division's Atlas missiles—produced at the huge Kearney Mesa plant—was fired successfully from Cape Canaveral. Producing fighter jets as well as missiles, Convair tipped the balance in San Diego's economy to aerospace manufacturing employment, which by 1958 exceeded military employment by 50 percent.[45]

Although GD's management was generally enlightened, it nevertheless made San Diego a branch company town subject to the whims of absentee ownership. Sociologist William Domhoff, for example, found that San Diego had the lowest membership by corporate managers in local elite institutions among the seven cities he studied. Meanwhile, the geographer Allan Pred discovered that San Diego had the highest percentage of employment in branch plants controlled by firms headquartered elsewhere among fifteen major western cities.[46]

The capstone of the era was, appropriately, space age related. Founded in 1956 by John Jay Hopkins and Frederic de Hoffman, GD's General Atomics Division opened its Torrey Pines research center on four hundred acres of city-donated pueblo land in 1959, a year before Jonas Salk accepted adjoining city land to develop the Salk Institute for Biological Research. The nucleus of San Diego's scientific-academic complex, however, was formed by the new campus of the University of California, San Diego (UCSD). In 1955 General Atomics chair John Jay Hopkins helped secure UCSD with the promise of a $1 million corporate subsidy offered to the University of California Board of Regents. In 1956, San Diego voters approved the grant of one thousand acres of pueblo land for the La Jolla campus. Urged on by Roger Revelle of Scripps Institution of Oceanography, the preeminent ocean and earth sciences research center, which became part of the University of California in 1912, the regents adopted a plan for a major university.[47]

San Diego's aerospace sector, however, went from boom to "bust town," as *Time* magazine put it, in 1962, when Convair shut down its assembly lines for fighter and commercial passenger jets. The Atlas missile was gradually replaced by the solid-fuel, Seattle-produced Minuteman. From a World War II peak of forty-four thousand employees, Convair was reduced to a skeletal four-thousand-person workforce by the early 1960s. San Diego's port economy also floundered as plans for a second, southern deepwater entrance through the Tijuana Estuary, modeled on Houston's Ship Canal, were sunk by opposition from both the Mexican government and the U.S. Army Corps of Engineers. The giant cargo ships of the container revolution of late-twentieth-century global maritime commerce would largely bypass San Diego, just as the city's short, single-runway Lindbergh Field failed to fully meet the area's jet-age needs.[48]

If the new high-tech economy taking shape around GD's General Atomics and UCSD was the wave of the future, the 1960s-era growth debates in San Diego were still mired in the past. The era's great debate arrayed, on the one side, proponents of industrialization looking for ways to prolong the glory days of Fleetsville. Their ranks included port director John Bate, whose model was Los Angeles—"the most diversified industrial city in the country." Bate lauded L.A. for attracting Kaiser Steel and for its "Jobs and Growth Campaign," bankrolled by local entrepreneurs. Foiled in their efforts to obtain rezoning for industrial purposes of ten thousand acres of privately owned South Bay land annexed by the city, these supporters of an unfettered smokestacks agenda retaliated by pushing 1960s-era ballot propositions weakening the Planning Commission and all but abolishing the Planning Department.[49]

Downtown Versus Suburban Development

The main opposition to efforts to further industrialize San Diego's bay front was a coalition headed by Planning Director Harry Haelsig and San Diegans Inc. (SDI), an influential downtown redevelopment planning group launched in 1959. Despite SDI's later role in the genesis of Horton Plaza–centered downtown commercial revitalization, it originally focused on creating a central core of public space and civic buildings housing government offices. Championing planned growth, SDI worked to soundly defeat the 1960s-era antiplanning ballot initiatives, although its ally, Haelsig, was ultimately sacked by the city council and mayor for his efforts.[50]

SDI won an early victory with the creation of a community concourse, built under the administration of Mayor Charles Dail using money from the city's pension fund (thereby avoiding a public bond vote) to house a new city hall, auditorium, and civic theater. The new civic center, dedicated in 1964, won for San Diego a designation from the National Municipal League as an "All-American City." Unfortunately, the anticipated downtown commercial renaissance was slow to follow. Except for vice traffic, the urban core was typically deserted after sundown. Ranking fifth among cities in downtown building activity in 1958, San Diego went downhill thereafter. Part of the reason was that urban renewal efforts in San Diego were hobbled by local fears of federal government intrusion and the imposition of open-housing mandates benefiting racial minorities.[51]

As supporters of industrialization and downtown revitalization fought to a standstill, the real victors were suburban developers. The defeated 1963 mayoral candidate Murray Goodrich—a dealer in surplus aircraft parts—was a true believer in heavy industry as a savior for San Diego's depressed economy. Not so the hotelier Charles H. Brown, whose real priority was aggrandizing Mission Valley at the expense of downtown. Located five miles northeast of downtown and featuring working farms and agricultural open space along the banks of the San Diego River, Mission Valley symbolized for many San Diegans the region's "geranium" heritage. In 1958, however, the dike was broken when the city council unanimously overrode the Planning Department and approved the building of a shopping center in Mission Valley, joining Brown's Town & Country Hotel, the pioneer commercial beachhead dating from 1953. Linked by interconnecting state and federal highways, suburban development first spread east and north from Mission Valley—to include planned communities like Rancho Bernardo and Rancho Peñasquitos—and then up and down the coastal strip. Centrifugal forces also led the *San Diego Union-Tribune* in 1973 to relocate its headquarters to Mission Valley.[52]

Fighting against the prophecy of downtown civic leader Arthur Jessop that planning had "died in San Diego," community planning groups protested as the city council, plied with developer money, ginned up spot-zoning ordinances that overrode existing land-use limits. In the 1960s voters twice defeated proposals placing the Planning Department under the city manager. After rejecting a general plan in 1965, voters finally approved one in 1967. The city council soon breached the new plan to make possible C. Arnholt Smith's downtown Westgate hotel and Brown's Hotel Circle project in Mission Valley. The council then placed the Planning Department under the thumb of the City Manager Walter Hahn, who was driven into retirement in 1971 by charges, which he indignantly denied, that he was in the pocket of developer interests.[53]

Mr. San Diego

At the apex of the local power elite stood C. Arnholt Smith, a former hotel clerk anointed "Mr. San Diego" by the local Rotary Club in 1968, who had diversified his holdings from the tuna industry to steel plants, banks, hotels, airlines, taxicabs, advertising, and the San Diego Padres professional baseball team. Smith's labyrinthine empire consisted of interlocking shell corporations, defrauding each other in Ponzi-scheme fashion—an Enron-style conglomerate before its time.[54]

Municipal corruption—smoldering since the 1950s with vice and bunko squad scandals and allegations of sweetheart tax assessments for political favorites—blew the roof off San Diego politics in the late 1960s. City hall was presided over by Mayor Frank Curran, a waffling centrist Democrat, and compliant city council members who were the willing enablers of Smith and his henchmen, including Agua Caliente racetrack owner and hotelier John Alessio and Yellow Cab taxi executive Charles Pratt. Pratt's campaign largesse to politicians and lavish gifts to the police provided reform District Attorney Ed Miller—a Smith nemesis elected in 1970—with the opening he needed to indict, though not convict, Mayor Curran and eight other members of the city council who had voted unanimously in 1967 to give Yellow Cab a 22 percent fare increase against the advice of an independent expert. Much of the pressure for reform came from the outside, exerted by an L.A.-based federal-state task force resented by San Diego locals as carpetbaggers that Miller had organized while he was still U.S. attorney.[55]

Denial became particularly difficult after the chief prop of Smith's pyramid scheme, the U.S. National Bank, collapsed in 1973, a mega-collapse bigger than all other U.S. bank failures from 1933 until that time combined. The collapse was caused by a large amount of bad loans to other companies that Smith controlled. The remnants of San Diego's proudly independent financial colossus were purchased at a corporate garage-sale price by San Francisco's Crocker Bank. The collapse of U.S. National followed hard on the charging of Smith, one of San Diego's strongest Nixon boosters, with securities and tax fraud. Smith was ultimately convicted of embezzlement and tax fraud.[56]

Charges that San Diego was a "little Newark of corruption" and "Mafia watering hole" frequented by vacationing gangsters were sensational. Even so, according to some observers, San Diego's real alchemy, which parlayed developer campaign contributions into political access and influence, never did receive grand jury scrutiny, much less result in indictments or convictions. Throughout the 1960s and early 1970s, the local growth machine continued unchecked, with new suburbs cropping up miles away from the city's historical and ever-deteriorating center.[57]

The results of such activities were palpable. In the 1960s, the city's population grew from six hundred thousand to seven hundred thousand. Because of aggressive annexation, three hundred square miles—three times the city's area circa 1950—came within municipal boundaries. As Mike Madigan, former aide to Mayor Pete Wilson, noted, "The annexation policies in place . . . were far-sighted. They allowed San Diego to control its own destiny."[58] Yet taxpayers complained of having to pay for the infrastructure costs of poorly planned new development. The aggravations of sprawl, compounded by embarrassing scandals, created strong momentum for a shift in political leadership as well as a recalibration of city government to make elected officials—the mayor and city council—more powerful and accountable while reducing the autonomy of the appointed city manager.

New Approaches: Mayor Pete Wilson and His Successors, 1971–1990

People look at Pete Wilson's mayoralty as the golden age. Wilson had a broad vision. He surrounded himself with talented people who were able to carry out their mission.

—*Former San Diego Acting Planning Director
Michael Stepner, 2007*[59]

The Wilson Era

As geriatric Mr. Smith went to jail, a scandal-plagued, growth-stretched metropolis propelled young-man-in-a-hurry Pete Wilson into San Diego's mayoralty. According to reporter Harold Keen, San Diego's transition from the Smith to the Wilson era was partly the consequence of a power struggle won by the young Turks who had backed the successful 1970 campaign by former U.S. Attorney Ed Miller, a Democrat, for district attorney. Leading the rebels were Richard T. Silberman, a former Convair executive, and Robert O. Peterson, founder of Jack in the Box, who teamed up to make a fortune in fast food and then seized control of San Diego's First National Bank. In the 1970s, they would function as potent behind-the-scenes power brokers, along with such luminaries as real estate broker Malin Burnham and the bankers Gordon Luce and Kim Fletcher, all GOP stalwarts, and the new owner of the Hotel del Coronado, Larry Lawrence, a maverick Democrat like Peterson and Silberman. During the Wilson era, the conventional wisdom was that, for the first time, local business elites, both old and new, took a backseat to an elected political leader.[60]

Pete Wilson graduated from Yale and then Boalt Hall Law School at the University of California, Berkeley, before moving to San Diego, where he was elected to the state assembly at the age of thirty-four. He rose quickly in the legislature, emerging as a Republican moderate who sponsored environmental legislation that became a model for the successful 1972 state coastal protection initiative. During the 1971 mayoral campaign, Wilson railed against unchecked growth, in particular unfinished developments in the Mira Mesa area. He threatened developers with a construction moratorium unless they paid for schools and other infrastructure. In the fall, Wilson defeated both the remnants of the old-line Smith GOP regime and the labor-supported Democratic mayoral candidates. Four years later, Wilson returned to the controlled growth theme, warning, "We don't want to be another sprawled-out Los Angeles monster." Despite being outspent two to one, Wilson resoundingly defeated Lee Hubbard, a cement contractor. Returning with Wilson were several city council allies, including Democrats Maureen O'Connor and Leon Williams.[61]

Supported by the Sierra Club, Wilson delivered environmentalists real victories by purging the Planning Commission of pro-growth stalwarts and blocking development in the Tijuana flood-control channel. But Wilson's pet Charter Revision Commission failed to secure voter approval of a "strong mayor" reform that would have given the mayor a veto over council actions and shifted powers from the city manager to the Mayor's Office. In practice, however, Wilson proved a formidable mayor. He made the best of the city's embarrassing loss of the 1972 GOP convention by marketing "unconventional" San Diego as "America's Finest City." He effectively reduced the city manager to a political nonentity while forcing through the council a new governance system with the mayor (a council member) as kingpin in control of the council agenda, committee assignments, and city board appointments.[62]

In building his disparate political coalition, Wilson used the city budget as his political war chest, making decisions that laid the foundation for future fiscal difficulties. In particular, Wilson made extensive use of earmarking of city funds to reward two pillars of his coalition: environmentalists and civic boosters. In 1972, the city created a special fund that set aside a portion of its franchising revenue to pay for environmental preservation. Wilson also backed efforts to set aside some of the city's hotel taxes for tourism promotion. Working to build a reputation as a fiscal hawk and to create a favorable business climate, Wilson cut the city's property tax rate and eliminated a separate pension tax—decisions that were locked in by the passage of Proposition 13 in 1978. Wilson's tax cuts set the stage for the city's later fiscal crisis. The elimination of a dedicated pension-fund tax mechanism meant that employee benefits would vie with city services in annual budget deliberations.[63]

The mayor also empowered new semiautonomous governance structures, such as the San Diego Transit Corporation and the Centre City Development Corporation (CCDC), both chaired in their formative periods by Wilson's éminence grise, Dick Silberman. Wilson also supported regional government initiatives, including the city's participation in the countywide Comprehensive Planning Organization, the forerunner of the San Diego Association of Governments. Fronteras 1976, later known as Fronteras de las Californias, was a Wilson-era project seeking better cross-border relations.

Arguably, Wilson's greatest accomplishment was a comprehensive growth management plan adopted in 1975—difficult to achieve in a conservative community. According to former city planner Michael Stepner, as late as the 1960s "San Diegans thought planning represented a communist plot."[64] Based on an earlier study, Wilson's plan was structured into five tiers.[65] Tier 1 included the downtown area; the plan advocated active government participation in redeveloping downtown. Tier 2 contained the older urbanized areas; here the market would provide in-fill development. According to Mike Madigan, "Tier 2 probably constitutes the greatest failure of the plan. At the time, we did not understand the design and infrastructure needs of these areas."[66]

Tier 3 comprised urbanizing communities such as Mira Mesa and Rancho Bernardo. Tier 4 identified future urbanizing areas. Tier 5 was reserved for permanent open space. According to Madigan, "the goal was to preserve community separation and protect the canyons, coastal bluffs and lagoons in the area."[67] Although many hailed the plan as visionary and the template for modern San Diego development, critics like former state Senator Jim Mills argued that "the plan did not succeed in making development pay for itself. Subsequent development has since cost the taxpayers enormous amounts to finance infrastructure and public services." Mills believed that Wilson's policies created a serious mismatch between the city's growth plans and the ability to provide adequate public services and infrastructure financing.[68]

Downtown Redevelopment

In terms of downtown revitalization, Mayor Wilson felt that the city needed a separate entity, independent of traditional local government institutions, which could respond quickly to market forces. The Centre City Development Corporation (CCDC), a nonprofit corporation, was chartered in 1975 to fast-track Horton Plaza redevelopment—a San Diegans Inc.–supported project conceived in 1969. Local civic pride had been tempered by the reality that San Diego's historical core had degenerated into a skid row and vice district. From the nucleus of Horton Plaza Park, the proposed project was expanded to fifteen square blocks, including a new federal courthouse, hotels, housing, and office buildings.

In 1972 the city council approved the redevelopment plan; two years later the developer Ernest Hahn won a competition with a proposal for Horton Plaza's centerpiece—a million-square-foot retail complex—that Hahn urged should be supplemented by mass transit, new housing, and a convention center. The CCDC's chair Silberman lauded San Diego's planned new downtown for "the attributes of Nice, the commercial potential of London . . . [and] the advantages of Newport and Balboa."[69]

In 1976, two additional project areas—the Marina residential zone, south and west of Horton Plaza, and the Columbia office zone, to the northwest—were added. The Gaslamp Quarter Association was formed in 1974 to promote "historic preservation." The Gaslamp Quarter Planned District Ordinance was passed in 1976, but the quarter did not become an official redevelopment project until 1982. Much less progress was made by Chicano activists in Barrio Logan, south of downtown, who had seen their neighborhood cut in two by Interstate 5 and further decimated by construction of the San Diego–Coronado Bridge. Although opponents of bulldozer-style redevelopment were largely silent—because San Diego had no history of federal urban renewal and the Horton Plaza project was supposed to be paid for by CCDC tax-increment financing— the city also lacked any recent tradition of shopping or living downtown to inspire support. As planning experts Bernard J. Frieden and Lynne B. Sagalyn would later put it, "The problem in San Diego was to create a downtown rather than bring one back to life."[70]

Wilson pursued a substantive policy triad—downtown redevelopment, a new convention center, and a binational airport in Otay Mesa—that bore the imprint of a pair of planning authorities, University of Missouri's Robert H. Freilich and Massachusetts Institute of Technology's Kevin Lynch. Two legs of this tripod—a new convention center and a new airport—fell by the wayside, but Horton Plaza tortuously moved toward its grand opening in 1985, by which time U.S. Senator Wilson had moved on to Washington.[71]

Horton Plaza developer Ernest Hahn also launched the University Towne Centre shopping mall project in University City near UCSD. Opponents viewed the controversial project as a sinister quid pro quo between Wilson's endorsement of University City—contradicting the mayor's distaste for additional, large-scale development on San Diego's periphery—and Hahn's entry into the downtown redevelopment sweepstakes. Hahn did not sign a final contract until 1977, and almost immediately the statewide voter passage of Proposition 13 in 1978 undercut the initial plan to finance Horton Plaza at the same time that Hahn was having difficulty finding department stores willing to anchor the project. An $11 million bond issue, floated to refinance an earlier $8 million issue, went into technical default when Proposition 13 cut property tax reserves set aside for debt service; the city had to apply for a state loan to help make principal and interest payments. In 1979, Hahn claimed that Horton Plaza was "on a hairline, as it relates to the practicality of the project." Hahn decided to sell his development company but proceeded with Horton Plaza, which took another four years to complete, for $140 million (including $40 million in public funds).[72]

Did the respective roles played by Mayor Wilson and developer Hahn in downtown revitalization fit the conventional wisdom of public leadership and private support? Wilson aide Mike Madigan concedes that "downtown development under Wilson was heavily influenced by discussions with Ernie Hahn."[73] Former state Senator Jim Mills goes even further: "Hahn was calling the shots downtown. . . . Both Horton Plaza and the trolley system were done because Hahn wanted them done. Wilson's chief accomplishment involved doing what Hahn wanted him to do."[74]

Downtown housing development was slow going, although San Diego did win praise for changing its zoning rules to encourage single-room occupancy downtown. The Wilson administration, however, flatly refused federal public housing assistance. In the Marina district, private housing projects were slowly finished, block by block, in the 1980s and 1990s. The innovative San Diego trolley system—made possible by state Senator Jim Mills's creative financing legislation—was also slow to get out of the station. The purchase of the defunct Arizona & Eastern rail line for $18 million made possible the construction of the first line, which ran from downtown to the Mexican border. All in all, Wilson's program brought people and resources back to downtown. Unfortunately, too few people were living there well into the 1990s.[75]

Changing Tack

During his second administration, Mayor Wilson began to receive heat from key backers such as local bankers Kim Fletcher and Gordon

Luce. Fletcher had lauded Wilson in 1974 for applying "the brakes on uncontrolled growth" and saving San Diego from the experience of Los Angeles and Orange County, but by 1976 Luce demanded that Wilson "broaden his thinking on the controlled growth issue." Changing tack, Wilson first opposed and later supported the navy's plan, fought by environmentalists and citizen groups, to build a new hospital in Balboa Park. He also supported the sale of city pueblo lands by noncompetitive bidding to Signal Companies Inc., to entice the company to relocate its headquarters to San Diego. More significant, he shifted positions to support the massive new North City West residential and commercial project east of Del Mar.[76]

Wilson's 1979 mayoral opponent, Democrat Simon "Sy" Casady, accused him of sweetheart deals for developers, down zoning of older neighborhoods to the detriment of low-income residents and minorities seeking affordable housing, shortchanging blue-collar North Park, and ignoring entirely the southeastern San Diego ghetto. Burnishing his credentials as a champion of law and order against both violent criminals and striking public employees, Wilson crushed his liberal opponent, positioning himself for his successful 1982 U.S. senatorial run against Democratic Governor Jerry Brown.[77]

The Sorcerer's Apprentices

Back home in San Diego, Pete Wilson's apprentices—among them, Maureen O'Connor and Roger Hedgecock, the Del Mar city attorney and darling of the environmentalists, who broke with Wilson over development on the northern outskirts of the city—struggled to master the politics of land use in San Diego during the 1980s. The growth genie—let out of the bottle during the 1950s and 1960s—had been partly tamed during the 1970s by Wilson's mixed, managed-growth wish list. Buffeted by progrowth and antigrowth forces, post-Wilson political leaders looked to put a lock back on Pandora's box.

After Wilson's ascension to Washington, Councilwoman O'Connor—a moderate Democrat, Wilson protégé, and close friend of *Union-Tribune* publisher Helen Copley—lost the 1983 race to fill out the mayor's remaining term in a political upset to Hedgecock, by then a member of the San Diego County board of supervisors. Hedgecock's political rise was largely orchestrated by Del Mar council members Nancy Hoover and Tom Shepard, who, by the early 1980s, had graduated to new roles—Hoover as the mistress and partner of financier J. David Dominelli and Shepard as San Diego's hottest political consultant and fund-raiser.

Dominelli was a scam artist who convinced investors he was an expert in complex financial instruments. He used the money he received from new investors to maintain a lavish lifestyle and, when necessary, to pay off previous investors. Just before J. David & Co. was toppled by federal investigators, after bilking clients for an estimated $80 million, an employee told the FBI: "They're buying the mayor's job. They're corrupting the place and they are doing it in the name of good government." Dominelli's fool's gold was funneled into the Hedgecock campaign through Shepard's consulting firm. Hedgecock deserved credit for crafting a brilliant populist campaign that portrayed O'Connor as the captive of "Downtown fat cats" and Copley's *Union-Tribune*. Like his predecessors, he also promised to stop the Los Angelization of San Diego.[78]

The principal issue, if there was one, was the candidates' positions regarding a harborside convention center. Hedgecock supported a 1983 ballot initiative, masterminded by Shepard, to build on the old Navy Field property near Harbor Drive a $191 million convention center financed by the Unified Port District from revenues generated by the port's management of tourism and harbor real estate. Noncommittal regarding the convention center, O'Connor rejected the new "niche" strategy for maritime development in favor of the older mixed-industrial approach favored by the labor unions supporting her. During his short tenure as mayor, Hedgecock prevailed on this issue and beat back an attempt to strip the mayor's office of the power, previously won by Wilson, to control the council's agenda and committee assignments.[79]

During the 1984 campaign to elect a mayor to a full term, there were criminal indictments of Dominelli, Hoover, and Hedgecock for laundering $375,000 in campaign contributions during the prior 1983 election. Although the chamber of commerce demanded Hedgecock's resignation, the mayor defeated savings-and-loan executive Richard Carlson. After an initial hung jury, Hedgecock's second trial ended in his conviction for thirteen felony counts of perjury and conspiracy. Hedgecock was forced to resign in 1985, after which he became an influential right-wing radio talk-show host specializing in inciting the locals against illegal immigration. He never served his twelve-month sentence after the California Supreme Court threw out all but one conspiracy conviction, for which he paid a fine and served three years' probation.[80]

Maureen O'Connor succeeded Hedgecock, winning the 1985 and 1988 mayoral elections. O'Connor proved a liberal-minded but politically ineffectual mayor, losing most of the powers to control the council that Wilson had instituted and Hedgecock had defended, and failing to push through term limits, charter reform, and campaign-finance-reform charter amendments. In 1988, however, voters narrowly approved district elections, setting the stage in the 1990s for a Democratic and labor-friendly city council majority in a once heavily Republican city.

In 1991, *Financial World* magazine ranked San Diego ninth on a list of the ten best-run cities, but the ranking stressed administrative basics—not mayoral leadership. O'Connor's first term was overshadowed by growth wars that began in earnest in 1985 after a study revealed that growth in new areas was exceeded by a factor of nine by growth in older neighborhoods, which needed $1 billion in infrastructure repairs and investment. San Diegans for Growth Management pushed through Proposition A banning further development of the urban reserve without prior voter approval. The council then passed an interim growth-control ordinance allowing the construction of only eight thousand homes within city limits for eighteen months. In 1988, the voters rejected four growth control measures that went down in the face of a $3 million negative ad blitz financed by developers. A fifth measure, proposed by the county board of supervisors, that mandated a regional growth strategy to be developed by the San Diego Association of Governments—the metropolitan planning organization—passed.[81]

In 1986, columnist George Will came to town to laud local entrepreneurial zeal. The 1980s witnessed notable electronics and biotech start-ups including Qualcomm, founded in 1985 by UCSD engineers and computer scientists. Urban development scholar Joel Kotkin was soon to tout San Diego for not "reaching for mass and a wide spread of industries" and instead having "captivated its elites with the notion of creating a qualitatively better 'clean' city economy, conspicuously free of smokestacks, lunch pails, and low-cost housing." Yet by the late 1980s, San Diego's military-industrial sector was poised on a precipice. In 1989 the local real estate boom peaked. After the Cold War ended, a deep local recession ensued, with massive aerospace and military job cutbacks.[82]

By 1990, fifteen top local corporations had been taken over, had moved, or faced the threat of acquisition. Despite efforts to lure and incubate high-technology businesses, San Diego remained a quintessential branch-plant town. San Diego–based Imperial Savings was in the hands of federal regulators, and Gordon Luce's Great American Bank—the fifth-largest thrift in the nation—was about to collapse. Local military facilities such as the Naval Training Center and the Miramar air base faced the Damocles' sword of the Base Realignment and Closure Commission, with several rounds of base closings scheduled for the 1990s. And in 1989 power broker Dick Silberman, married to San Diego Mayor Susan Golding, was arrested for laundering drug money. The young Turk who had helped topple C. Arnholt Smith ended up the same ignominious way. A bridge named after Silberman had to be renamed as a corruption scandal dethroned yet another San Diego kingpin.[83]

The 1980s appropriately ended, as San Diego's modern history had begun, with the long-standing regional rivalry with Los Angeles. In 1988 San Diego Gas & Electric Company's (SDG&E) board voted to merge with L.A.-based Southern California Edison, whose size and power dwarfed that of SDG&E. For local critics, "it was another step toward the 'Los Angelization' of San Diego . . . and local leaders wanted none of it."[84] In the end, San Diegans succeeded in blocking the proposed utility merger. Ironically, SDG&E later would merge with the L.A.-based Southern California Gas Company, forming Sempra Energy, with the proviso—insisted on by San Diego leaders—that the new headquarters would be located in San Diego. San Diego's love-hate relationship and rivalry with Los Angeles would continue into a fourth century. *Plus ça change, plus c'est la même chose.*[85]

What's Past Is Prologue

The Pete Wilson era marked the end of good decisions in San Diego. These included the zoo, Mission Bay, Sea World, and UCSD. In the earlier era there was cronyism and a potent mix of self-interest and community interest. The city was led by businessmen with deep roots, and a stake in San Diego . . . who made money on city projects, but they also produced substantial community benefit. As this business elite died off, they were not replaced. Into this leadership vacuum stepped self-interested, project-focused developers. . . . Post-Wilson mayors and councilmembers have been followers not leaders.

—Bruce Henderson, former city councilman[86]

San Diego's development into one of the nation's ten-largest cities was a remarkable, if improbable, achievement. Isolated geographically and lacking the fertile soil and water supplies that attracted settlers elsewhere, the city and region have historically lacked the resources to spur growth. The city's initial growth spurt was almost wholly the work of private entrepreneurs, men from other places, like Spreckels, who recognized the opportunities to enrich themselves by speculating in local real estate. The city's earliest water, power, and transportation facilities were built by such private agents to make these real estate investments lucrative.

In the early twentieth century, San Diego's leading citizens organized a concerted campaign to attract a different type of external actor, the U.S. Navy. Local officials made good use of their most abundant resource, pueblo land, to entice the military to locate bases and training centers and, ultimately, the entire Pacific Fleet, in San Diego. Federal largesse helped pay for much-needed water and transportation infrastructure, although rapid population growth spurred demand for housing and services that the local public sector was ill prepared to meet. As with Spreckels, the navy's interest in San Diego was a mixed blessing. When what the navy wanted conflicted with local needs or desires, San Diego officials frequently found navy officials to be unyielding.

Participation by private entrepreneurs and the U.S. Navy in San Diego's growth coalition helped spur the city's twentieth-century development but proved imperfect substitutes for the diverse manufacturing-based economy developed in cities such as Los Angeles. Despite notable accomplishments such as the bringing of the U.S. Navy to the region, San Diego's business community generally looked anemic next to the robust business classes in New York, Chicago, Atlanta, Dallas, and Los Angeles.[87] San Diego also failed to develop strong and independent public bureaucracies, whether for the development of port, airport, and water infrastructure or for planning. As a result, its governance arrangements lacked the developmental capacities supplied by semiautonomous harbor, water and power, and, later, airport departments in Los Angeles. The activities of L.A.'s proprietary departments, protected by charter provisions and supported by numerous voter-approved municipal bonds, provided a much-needed counterweight to private-sector pressures. Rather than empower local government, tightfisted San Diego voters preferred to keep their public servants on a very short leash.

That leash became even shorter with passage of Proposition 13 in 1978. San Diego's fiscal position, never strong to begin with, was weakened by Wilson's popular property tax cuts. But neither Wilson nor his successors were willing to scale back their ambitions for downtown redevelopment, let alone reign in fast-growing development in the suburban periphery. So local officials developed alternative sources of fiscal slack, setting up a shadow redevelopment corporation in CCDC and treating the municipal pension fund as a cash reserve. In all these efforts, they could count on support from the *Union-Tribune*, the city's conservative leading newspaper, which consistently put a happy face on local events. And even when the news was bad, editors, politicians, and citizens alike could take comfort in the fact that at least they were not Los Angeles.

II   *Fiscal Crisis and Governance Challenges, 1990–2010*

3   Paradise Insolvent
From Pension Scandal to Fiscal Crisis

San Diego is a Ponzi scheme. They built a statue to Pete Wilson. They should've built it for Ponzi, that's the essence of San Diego.

—Former San Diego City Attorney Mike Aguirre, 2009[1]

From Seaside Paradise to Enron-by-the-Sea

Since 2002, the City of San Diego has been consumed by a financial crisis that has brought it to the brink of insolvency. At the heart of the crisis is an underfunded retirement system for municipal employees, which the city has shorted for years to balance its annual budget. In the 1980s and the 1990s this chronic underfunding was masked by robust stock market returns that kept the retirement system flush with cash. But following the 2000 burst of the dot-com bubble; the terrorist attacks of September 11, 2001; and the ensuing recession, a perfect storm of underfunding, increased benefits for city workers, and lower-than-expected investment returns placed San Diego's retirement system, and the city as final guarantor, at the edge of a financial abyss. What started as a $10 million accounting trick had mushroomed into an unfunded liability of more than $1 billion by June 2003—equal to more than one-third of the assets held by San Diego's pension system and several times the size of the city's total payroll.

San Diego's pension crisis quickly ballooned into a full-blown fiscal and political scandal paralyzing city government. In 2003, it was revealed that city officials had misled creditors about the extent of the pension liability in bond offerings for a new downtown ballpark and other projects. The city's auditor, KPMG, refused to issue an opinion on

San Diego's annual financial reports. With no official financial accounting to rely on, San Diego found itself shut out of the public bond market. In 2004, the Securities and Exchange Commission opened an investigation into the city's troubled finances. Comparing the city to the largest corporate bankruptcy in American history, *New York Times* headline writers described San Diego as Enron-by-the-Sea, a moniker that quickly grew to symbolize the scale of the crisis and the public humiliation faced by those who had contributed to it. Having lost the confidence of local residents, Mayor Dick Murphy resigned in July 2005.

This chapter examines San Diego's pension scandal and the fiscal crisis that occurred in its wake. Although the aim of the city's various pension chicaneries was to increase the level of public services while sparing residents the cost of higher taxes, the schemes' unraveling has wrought devastation for San Diego's municipal finances. In the summer of 2009, the pension system's actuary estimated that the city's unfunded liability would grow to $2.6 billion, nearly three times the size of the city's regular budget. This figure did not include $1.3 billion in unfunded health-care benefits for city employees. Because a significant portion of the city's pension and retiree health-care benefits are paid out of the General Fund, the source of money for most essential city services, these unfunded liabilities have threatened San Diego's ability to provide basic public services and finance needed infrastructure maintenance and improvements.

Benchmarking San Diego

[P]olitics and the political context of economic scarcity are central to understanding the urban fiscal condition. Surprisingly, the political dimension of the urban fiscal crisis, has, in fact, been considered last and least, even by political scientists.

—*Ester Fuchs,* Mayors and Money, *1992*[2]

Cities, like families, experience financial difficulties from time to time arising from a number of factors. Sometimes, these come in the form of external shocks—such as economic recessions, declining intergovernmental aid, or state-imposed constraints on revenue collection. These are experienced broadly across many cities, and individual municipalities generally have little capacity to change them. Other factors are structural—including population loss, poverty, an aging housing stock, and low market values for taxable properties—and vary widely across cities. Unfortunately, these factors are also difficult for local governments to alter in the near term. Still other factors are internal, attributable to cities' policies or the activities of their elected officials. These include decisions to offer benefits to residents that cannot be sustained by existing revenues, and fiscal mismanagement, where public officials allow a city's financial position to deteriorate through poor decisions or neglect.[3]

When trying to both explain and predict municipal fiscal stress, scholars have tried to measure the financial difficulties facing cities, focusing on private employment, per capita income, and levels of municipal debt and taxation. They have developed detailed explanations of how fiscal stress waxes and wanes according to the different factors cited here.[4] In the late 1970s, for example, scholars observed that cities with aging housing stocks and large numbers of residents in poverty were having the greatest trouble maintaining services at an acceptable cost to residents, especially where suburbanization had separated large cities from the region's more affluent residents. In the 1980s and 1990s, the difficulties of urban centers were tied to large reductions in federal aid and declining tax bases as a result of continued out-migration and voter-imposed constraints on revenue collection.[5]

Less attention has been paid to financial crises, where local governments lose access to credit markets and, as a result, are in danger of defaulting on loan obligations or not meeting current expenses. Such episodes are rare among large municipalities. In 1975, the City of New York lost its credit lifeline when banks refused to continue lending money to the city on a short-term basis to cover payments on past loans and operating expenses. The state ultimately intervened, setting up new agencies that guaranteed the city's loans and imposed tighter constraints on its finances. In 1978, a standoff between the mayor and local banks caused the City of Cleveland to go into default after the banks refused to refinance $14 million in bonds. In 1990, banks refused to provide the City of Philadelphia with loans to cover its immediate expenses. Over a three-year period, the city passed a sales tax increase, froze employee benefits, and cut services to residents. In 1994, Orange County became the largest municipality to declare bankruptcy after county officials sustained losses of $1.6 billion in its investment pool. In 1996, a federal corruption probe revealed an enormous budget shortfall in the City of Miami, which pre-cipitated a collapse in its credit ratings. As in the New York case, the state intervened by setting up an oversight board to control the city's finances.[6]

San Diego's fiscal crisis ranks among the most serious in U.S. history. The experiences of other large local governments, in particular New York and Orange County, indicate that no single factor can explain all crises and that the path to recovery varies substantially. In the case of New York, for example, scholars have pointed to structural causes, including growing poverty and job losses, as well as lingering fallout from the oil crisis in the early 1970s. Political scientist Martin Shefter, in contrast, attributes New York's crisis to overspending by political au-thorities eager to build support among the city's myriad special interests, especially its increasingly powerful municipal employee unions. San Di-ego experienced no such structural upheaval, nor can its woes be tied to external shocks. As in New York, municipal employee unions were active players in San Diego's financial crisis, although city pension costs represented only the most proximate trigger, rather than the root cause, of the fiscal crisis.

On its face, the Orange County bankruptcy offers a more compel-ling comparison. Like San Diego, Orange County faced enormous fiscal pressures arising from voter-imposed constraints on revenue collection. Like San Diego, tightfisted voters in Orange County were loath to relieve these pressures through increases in taxes, fees, or other revenues. In both places, citizens harbored doubts about the capacities of local government. In Orange County, elected officials counted on strong returns from the investment pool in the same way that San Diego officials tapped "surplus earnings" from its municipal pension fund—which was deeply invested in the stock market—to balance the budget. When the crisis hit, there was no help coming from state government, in contrast to New York, Cleve-land, and Miami. Despite these apparent similarities, Orange County and San Diego chose very different responses to the crisis.

In Orange County, public officials immediately opted for a Chap-ter 9 bankruptcy filing; a new executive officer was appointed to oversee the process. The county sold off its risky assets, removed those tainted by the scandal, and negotiated a settlement with participants in the county pool. When voters rejected a tax increase to pay off the investment losses, a plan that combined staff and services cuts with borrowing was quickly implemented. By June 1996, the county had sold its bond offering, ending the crisis. The entire process lasted eighteen months.

By contrast, San Diego's decadelong fiscal crisis has only grown worse. With ballooning pension payments consuming an ever-larger share of the budget, public officials have continued to struggle to close the city's structural budget deficit. Business and civic leaders, who stood by for decades as the city diverted money from its pension fund to pay regular city expenses, quickly mobilized to oppose efforts to increase revenues, using the pension scandal to their political advantage. By late 2010, the city was no closer to a permanent solution than when the crisis began.

In San Diego, the pension scandal was born of the basic desire to put off until tomorrow choices that are unpleasant today. The unpleasant choice was whether to cut desired benefits and services or raise taxes to pay for them. Institutional constraints, in particular California's voter-imposed spending and borrowing limits, contributed. These, however, were not unique to San Diego. More important were internal factors, such as the city's fragmented political system that encouraged parochial behavior, and a political culture characterized by widespread distrust of local government and voter unwillingness to raise taxes. Underfunding the pension allowed local officials to temporarily avoid making the fundamental choice created by voter insistence on both low taxes and generous public services. The decision to simultaneously increase retirement benefits made the final reckoning all the more severe.

America's Cheapest City

San Diego has been the victim historically of a libertarian political culture. Where else in California do you have five Republicans sitting on the county board of supervisors? San Diego is just a very conservative place and very anti-tax as well.

—*Former San Diego City Manager Jack McGrory, 2007*[7]

Although the news of San Diego's financial problems first attracted national attention in 2004, the origins of the crisis can be found at least three decades earlier. In the 1970s, an ill-timed local property tax cut motivated by a larger statewide tax revolt permanently froze the city's below-average tax rates for years to come. Rather than respond to growing fiscal stress by creating new revenue sources or reducing public services, San Diego's elected public officials resorted to a series of creative financing schemes designed to shift the burden of paying for public services from the city's citizens or to simply hide it altogether. Although underfunding of the city's public employee pension system represented the most bold and daring of these tactics, it followed a long series of ruses and stratagems used by San Diego officials to provide constituents with government services without ever asking them to pay the full cost.

Howard Jarvis's Antitax Utopia

If all cities were as well run as San Diego, we wouldn't need Proposition 13.
—*Antitax crusader Howard Jarvis*[8]

San Diego emerged from World War II with a city hall controlled by a Sunbelt-style growth machine based on suburban expansion; low taxes; and business-friendly, reform-style government. During the tenure of Pete Wilson, who served as mayor between 1971 and 1982, the city adopted a master plan that laid out a template for population growth and development, and Wilson also took up the cause of reshaping the city's political structure by pushing a failed initiative to expand the powers of the mayor. On fiscal matters, however, Wilson continued to toe a conservative fiscal-hawk party line, reducing the city's property tax rate shortly after taking office. Coming at a time of historical real estate appreciation that was driving up property tax bills, the cut proved politically popular.[9]

The political logic of Wilson's tax cut was rooted in a taxpayers' revolt brewing across the state. News reports highlighting the plight of senior citizens on fixed incomes provided popular momentum for a series of efforts to restrain local government taxation powers. Seniors faced the prospect of losing their homes because they were unable to pay ballooning property taxes caused by a real estate boom and a rapid increase in assessed valuations. The most famous of the reforms was Proposition 13, a ballot initiative advocated by antitax crusader Howard Jarvis and passed by voters in 1978. The initiative capped total property taxes at 1 percent of the 1975 assessed valuation and limited future increases. Prior to Proposition 13, cities, counties, and other local government agen-

TABLE 3.1   Property tax revenue of the ten largest California cities before and after Proposition 13

City	1977–78 property tax revenue (dollars per capita)	1978–79 property tax revenue (dollars per capita)	Change (%)
Oakland	$96.34	$35.38	−63
Long Beach	$82.71	$32.25	−61
Sacramento	$74.78	$32.31	−57
San Jose	$48.54	$22.32	−54
Santa Ana	$57.39	$27.73	−52
Los Angeles	$103.41	$50.65	−51
Fresno	$71.33	$35.95	−50
Huntington Beach	$71.85	$35.93	−50
San Diego	$55.99	$31.71	−43
Anaheim	$40.19	$23.75	−41

SOURCE: California State Controller, *Financial Transactions Concerning Cities of California* (Sacramento: California State Controller, n.d.).

cies had set their own tax rates, which in the aggregate usually exceeded the 1 percent cap; these were precisely the taxes that Wilson had cut.

Although Proposition 13 affected all municipal governments in California, Wilson's tax cuts left San Diego particularly vulnerable because of the way state lawmakers chose to divide the smaller property tax pie among competing local governments—cities, counties, and special-purpose districts such as schools. Emergency legislation passed after the ballot measure gave each local government the same proportion of total local property taxes that it had received before passage of Proposition 13. The effect of the legislation was to reward localities with the highest tax rates before Proposition 13 and to punish conservative cities like San Diego, which collected fewer property taxes, by giving them a smaller share of property tax revenues. "Ironically, Proposition 13 paralyzed San Diego while rewarding cities like San Francisco for their fiscal profligacy," noted a senior Wilson aide.[10]

Although there is no doubt that San Diego received a smaller percentage of local property taxes than other cities, a close analysis of the city's financial position before and after Proposition 13 suggests that the Wilson tax cuts were less pivotal in setting the stage for the city's financial squeeze than is generally believed.[11] Table 3.1 reports per capita property taxes collected by California's ten largest cities in the years immediately

TABLE 3.2   Per capita general revenue of the ten largest
California cities, fiscal year 1977–78

City	1977–78 general revenue (per capita)
Oakland	$473.76
Long Beach	$439.63
Los Angeles	$428.80
Fresno	$394.74
Sacramento	$349.37
Santa Ana	$302.81
San Jose	$302.59
San Diego	$291.64
Anaheim	$276.05
Huntington Beach	$268.98

SOURCE: California State Controller, *Financial Transactions Concerning Cities of California* (Sacramento: California State Controller, n.d.).

before and after Proposition 13. It indicates that San Diego did collect significantly less in property taxes than the majority of California's ten largest cities before the passage of the tax-limitation measure.[12] For example, in the fiscal year that began in July 1977, the year before Proposition 13 took effect, San Diego collected slightly less than $56 in property taxes per resident, compared to the nearly $72 average for the other nine cities. Among the largest cities, only San Jose and Anaheim collected less. After Proposition 13, San Diego's share of property taxes fell to $31.71 per resident, a marked decrease but not much less than the amount received by most other major cities in the state. Only Los Angeles, with a per capita haul of more than $50, collected significantly more.

Although the reduction in property taxes certainly hurt city finances, the more important impact of Proposition 13 was its limit on all other forms of taxes, requiring voter approval for all proposals to increase taxes to pay for specific city services. As indicated by Table 3.2, which compares the general revenues of California cities, San Diego collected just $291.64 in general revenue per person in the year that ended in June 1978, the month voters passed Proposition 13. Most other major cities collected at least $300 per resident, whereas Long Beach, Oakland, and Los Angeles all received more than $400 per resident. These three cities collected millions of dollars in utility users' taxes, a revenue source used by many other major California cities but not by San Diego. Although Proposition 13 did not cut these other taxes that cities used to balance their budgets, it did institute a new two-thirds supermajority vote requirement for future attempts to increase them. The effect was to freeze San Diego's low tax base until such time that voters decided taxes ought to be raised.[13]

The Post–Proposition 13 Runaround

Perhaps the most important insight that can be gained from the passage of Proposition 13 is that blunt initiatives lead to the development of other ways of getting things done. These other ways are usually more complex, more expensive, and typically are not discussed in public forums in ways that are intelligible to the public and elected officials. The world is full of very bright and ingenious people who delight in ways of circumventing poorly drafted initiatives.

—*Public finance scholar Jeffrey Chapman, 1998*[14]

In the wake of Proposition 13, and the state's growing clout over local revenue allocation decisions, California cities responded in different ways to fiscal scarcity. In Los Angeles County, for example, several cities instituted new utility users' taxes or raised existing ones. Some cities created new redevelopment programs, which under state law allowed them to capture a greater percentage of new property taxes, and others wooed major retailers to increase the amount of sales tax flowing into local coffers. San Diego exemplified the latter two approaches, pursuing an aggressive redevelopment agenda and working hard to attract new retail. However, local public officials strenuously avoided any remedy that would require them to ask voters to approve new taxes.[15]

Elected officials' desire to avoid public votes to raise taxes has meant that San Diego residents have continued to receive for free many municipal services provided on a cost basis in other areas. Since 1919, for example, city residents living in single-family homes have enjoyed free trash pickup. Although numerous city task forces have recommended that San Diego institute a trash collection fee like most other cities, a move that would bring tens of millions of dollars into the public treasury, the city council has refused, worried about the political backlash from approaching voters for more money.[16] Because successfully passing new tax increases—and amending the city charter to permit trash collection fees—would require city council members to publicly campaign for higher taxes, such proposals have represented a political third rail for San Diego elected officials. "I went to the council 24 times with refuse collection [fees]," recalled former City Manager Jack McGrory. "Each time, the city council said no."[17]

Instead, in the aftermath of Proposition 13, Mayor Wilson and the city council expanded the dubious practice of using pension fund earnings to ease the stress on the city's day-to-day budget, adopting several practices that put the long-term solvency of the pension fund at risk.[18] Most damaging was the diversion of investment earnings to pay for programs and services that local officials desired but were loath to fund through higher taxes. In 1980, the city council passed a resolution defining all pension fund investment returns in excess of 8 percent as surplus earnings. The resolution directed the San Diego City Employees' Retirement System (SDCERS) to use 50 percent of the earnings to pay enhanced retirement benefits. The other half was used to reduce the city's annual pension contribution, freeing up city revenues for other purposes.

The additional benefits were distributed to retirees via a "waterfall"—a thirteenth check on top of the regular monthly payments. These checks provided relief to retirees suffering from double-digit inflation and rising health-care costs. The waterfall allowed local officials to increase retiree benefits without raising money to pay for them. Most important, the practice provided the template for future pension schemes: convince pension board members to underfund the system by pledging some of the savings toward benefit enhancements.[19]

The waterfall was problematic in several respects. First, the 8 percent rate of return assumed by SDCERS was a target it expected to meet over a period of many years. High returns in one year would be needed to balance out low returns in others. Taking surplus earnings out of the system left the pension fund vulnerable to economic downturns. Second, unusually high investment returns created an embarrassment-of-riches problem for local officials. To avoid paying out hundreds of millions of dollars, city officials reportedly used their influence on the pension board to manipulate the fund's annual earnings (e.g., by directing fund managers to sell off assets that were losing money). When this method failed, city officials sought to cap the amount of the thirteenth check.[20]

Around the time that Wilson discovered the pension system as a prime source of additional city funds, Ron Saathoff assumed the leadership of Local 145, the union representing San Diego's firefighters. Possessing boundless energy, political savvy, and a detailed understanding of municipal finance, Saathoff became a force in local politics. Saathoff, however, was not an ideologue. He preferred to work with the business community and public officials to increase benefits and improve working conditions. In 1981, Saathoff assumed the firefighters' seat on the pension board and quickly became a headache for city officials. The thirteen-member board had traditionally been a rubber stamp for city initiatives. With Saathoff on the board, any new deals between the city and the retirement system would entail concessions to city workers.[21]

The House That Jack Built

Harry Mathis, a member of the [city] council who represented La Jolla years ago, called the city manager to say he had forgotten to ask for a brush-fire truck in the budget. [City Manager Jack] McGrory said he would put the truck in the appropriations ordinance. Back then as now, you could surreptitiously add and delete items, because nobody read the budget. Mathis owed McGrory after that.

—*Former Taxpayers Association Executive Director Scott Barnett, 2007*[22]

The early practice of raiding the pension system to fill gaps in the city budget grew over time to become a central tenet of San Diego's public policy in times of dire fiscal need. By the early 1990s, three events conspired to exacerbate the city's fiscal stress by fundamentally changing the nature of budgetary politics in San Diego. First, California voters pledged more funding for public schools in 1988 with the passage of a constitutional amendment known as Proposition 98, which set aside roughly 40 percent of the state budget for local school districts and community colleges. To provide the new money, state lawmakers shifted a portion of local property taxes to schools, reducing the amount of tax revenue available to the city. Second, the fall of the Soviet Union and the ensuing recession battered the local defense industry, a key element of the San Diego economy. To offset the effects of the downturn and to encourage investment, elected officials cut business taxes in the city, thus further increasing the strain on public finances.[23]

Third, a voting-rights lawsuit filed in 1988 by the Chicano Federation charged that the city's at-large election system unlawfully diluted the voices of black and Latino voters. The challenge and a subsequent voter-approved ballot initiative led to the creation of eight city council districts, with the mayor—still a member of the council—remaining as the only legislator elected on a citywide basis. This change empowered minority groups and the local Democratic Party by lowering the bar for representation on the council from a citywide to a districtwide majority. The creation of geographic electoral constituencies, however, gave city council members an incentive to prioritize district services over broader issues. The new district focus diverted council members' attention from long-term, citywide challenges, such as San Diego's darkening fiscal picture.[24]

Susan Golding, a pro-choice Republican who supported affirmative action and environmental protection, was the first mayor of San Diego to be elected after the switch to district elections. Having narrowly defeated an antigrowth opponent in the 1992 mayoral election, Golding emerged as a dynamic presence in city hall, more interested in getting things done than in balancing the city's books. Although her predecessor, Maureen O'Connor, had dissipated much of the de facto power that Pete Wilson had accumulated, Golding proved adept in forging a council majority behind her business-friendly agenda. Intent on building a record for higher office, Golding pushed a series of high-profile projects, including the expansion of the city's convention center and a new ballpark for the San Diego Padres. At Golding's urging, the city council also adopted an ordinance requiring new city revenues to be earmarked to hire more police.[25]

Although a recession in the early 1990s had sharply reduced the city's revenues, Golding would not consider raising taxes. Nonetheless, she needed additional revenues to pay for the convention center and other projects. In 1994, she came up with a solution, proposing that San Diego take a pension "holiday" and not make its annual required contribution to the pension system. Ultimately, her proposal was rejected.[26]

While Golding was busy building legacy projects and preparing for a bid for higher office, other council members were focused on delivering district goodies, especially after local voters passed a term-limits initiative in 1992. In this context, the main responsibility for budget management fell to the appointed city manager, Jack McGrory. An ex-marine, McGrory served as the city's chief executive between 1991 and 1997. McGrory had worked for the city since 1975 and knew more about its capabilities than anyone. As city manager, he quickly developed a reputation for budget wizardry. According to local budget lore, McGrory required city departments to hand over a portion of their budgets to be kept in an opaque network of reserve accounts made undecipherable by the city's byzantine budget system.[27] "Jack was the only one of us who actually understood that document," former Councilman Juan Vargas said of the budgets prepared by McGrory. "It was like Da Vinci looking at a drawing of one of his flying machines."[28]

When individual council members needed money for a pet project, they came to see McGrory, and he unlocked the da Vinci code. When Mayor Golding needed money to host the 1996 Republican convention in the city, she went to see McGrory, and he made it happen. According to veteran newsman Gerry Braun, members of the city council "didn't like how he squirreled away money where no one could find it. But when the time was right, and he presented the money to them like a gift, all was forgiven."[29]

McGrory, in turn, blamed elected officials for weak leadership and their unwillingness to consider new taxes. "Every city manager tried to pull rabbits out of a hat to make the budget work. . . . Political officials put gigantic handcuffs on the manager for developing a reasonable budget," he recalled. "People look at San Diego's high standard of living and think that it must have large revenues and taxes going to the city. That is simply not the case. We were told to never put utility and tax in the same sentence. I told the council every year about the need for new revenues."[30] With the council forswearing new taxes, the difficult job of balancing the budget fell to McGrory.

San Diego's Fiscal Time Bomb

The pension fund was long used to get around the city council and public votes to fund capital projects. The city manager would meet with the pension's actuary. They would adopt mechanisms to reduce the city's contribution. The city's budget had numbers that members of the pension board had never even seen.

—*Ron Saathoff, head of Local Firefighters Union 145 and former member of the board of SDCERS, 2007*[31]

McGrory's task in the 1990s was daunting. The fiscal constraints on local government were tightening. The local economy was still reeling from the post–Cold War recession. Neither the city council nor local voters had any appetite for new taxes. Mayor Golding had directed McGrory to revamp San Diego's aging Jack Murphy Stadium and to finance the 1996 Republican National Convention while keeping existing city programs intact. Meanwhile, the retirement system was reaping record returns.

Like most local governments, San Diego provides pension benefits to employees through a defined-benefit plan. Defined-benefit plans pay monthly allowances to employees who retire after a prespecified minimum number of years or go on disability. The level of benefits is determined by a formula negotiated between the city and its employees, and funded by contributions from both.[32] From an administrative standpoint, a defined benefit plan ought to be easy to manage. Using actuarial tables and employment data, a sponsor can predict what its future payments will be. On the basis of assumptions about investment returns, pension fund administrators can collect and use contributions to acquire interest-bearing assets that will yield an amount equal to the plan's liabilities. In the early 1990s, the fund's total assets exceeded $1 billion, more than the benefits owed to future retirees. The solution was obvious. In 1994, McGrory sought approval for a $10 million reduction in the city's annual pension contribution. Although this proposal was nixed by the retirement system's outside legal counsel, the city's mounting budget problems created a need for a new plan to satisfy both the fund's administrators and board members like Ron Saathoff.[33]

Making a Deal

With respect to Manager's Proposal 1, I would do the same deal again. The pension was 105 percent funded three years after I left. When the market crashed, the correct decision was to limit, not expand benefits as the city decided to do.

—*Former City Manager Jack McGrory, 2007*[34]

In 1996, the City of San Diego and SDCERS reached agreement on a plan known as Manager's Proposal 1 (MP-1). The basic outline of the deal was simple. The city received a $110 million break on its annual contribution over ten years. A trust fund used to pay for retiree health care was eliminated, with SDCERS agreeing to pick up health-care costs using its surplus earnings. Of the $110 million in savings, approximately $71 million was used to retroactively upgrade benefits for current workers and retirees. The new benefits included an increase in the "waterfall" check and a change in calculations that resulted in more generous monthly pension payments.[35] The city also implemented a program for the purchase of service credits that would allow employees to buy extra years of service. With enough credits, an employee with twenty years of service, for example, could retire with benefits equivalent to an employee with twenty-five years. The city promised to revert to the old system of making its entire annual contribution by 2007.

City Attorney Michael Aguirre, elected in 2004, cites MP-1 as the start of a secret conspiracy to pass on pension debt to future taxpayers. In reality, MP-1 was debated and approved by the city council and pension board in the light of day. The *San Diego Union-Tribune* reported on the plan's details and the concerns of those it affected. Outside counsel hired by the city signed off on the deal. So, too, did the outside counsel hired by SDCERS to replace the law firm that had scuttled McGrory's 1994 deal.[36]

There was ample enthusiasm for MP-1 among city workers and their representatives at SDCERS. The agreement, however, placed pension administrators in an awkward position. The contribution schedule from the city, which would replace the actuarially calculated bill, immediately reduced funding levels by 5 percent. In 1996, the retirement system was 93.5 percent funded—that is, the system had assets equal to 93.5 percent of its projected liabilities—with an unfunded actuarial accrued liability of $96.3 million. Although MP-1 promised the city short-term savings, the enhancements in pension benefits offered in exchange would be in place for perpetuity, with no clear plan to pay for them. The agreement, as originally proposed, would result in a substantially reduced funding ratio and greater liabilities that would have to be made up for with future contributions.

To sell pension administrators on MP-1, McGrory included a novel trigger clause. If the system's funding ratio ever fell to less than

82.3 percent (10 percent below its 1996 level), the city would make a lump-sum payment the following year to bring the system back up to the 82.3 percent floor. With the stock market booming, there was ample reason to believe that the funding ratio would remain stable.[37]

Problems with the agreement and the process that produced it were legion. First, the entire arrangement arguably violated state law as well as the city charter. The charter instructs the city to make its annual required contribution, and state law gives city workers the right to an actuarially sound pension. Second, the logic of the agreement was faulty. MP-1 was adopted because the city was having trouble meeting its current obligations. However, the benefit hikes that were included seemingly to get the deal passed would make the city's future fiscal situation doubly difficult. Third, nothing in the agreement prevented the city or the board from reneging on the deal in future negotiations. Finally, although members of the board were legally bound to safeguard the fiduciary interests of the retirement system, conflicts of interest made this virtually impossible. Board members representing city workers stood to gain from the benefit hikes. The city's representatives needed the agreement to close a $10 million hole in the 1997 budget.

McGrory left the city in 1997. He was succeeded by Michael Uberuaga, a city manager from Huntington Beach who had little knowledge about San Diego. Under Uberuaga and a conflicted board, the financial position of SDCERS rapidly deteriorated. One cause was the increasing retirement obligations approved with MP-1. Surplus earnings were tapped to pay cost-of-living adjustments to protect the value of retirees' benefits. The purchase of service credits, intended to be cost neutral, were systematically underpriced. Older workers took advantage of the program to buy years of service and increase their benefits. When SDCERS calculated the cost of the program in 2002, it found that it had increased liabilities by $77.7 million, causing a 2 percent reduction in the funding ratio. In addition, SDCERS was struggling with rising health-care premiums.[38]

In 1998, SDCERS was sued by a group of retirees who claimed that calculations of their pension benefits had improperly excluded vacation and sick leave. The plaintiffs sought across-the-board increases in their pension benefits. The city council agreed to settle the case in 2000 and directed SDCERS to do so without allowing the funding ratio to dip below 90 percent. The $84 million owed to retirees was omitted in its next calculation of the funding ratio, which nonetheless dropped from 94.4 percent to 90.3 percent.[39]

Pulling the Trigger

Murphy realized that the ballpark was a net loss for the city. He was looking for cover and guys like Ron Saathoff agreed to provide it. The *Union-Tribune* also provided political cover. In exchange, the unions received pension benefits and salary increases. But the money to pay for these was not there. That was how we ended up with Manager's Proposal 2. That deal was an impetus for [city] employees to look the other way.

—*Bruce Henderson, former city council member, 2007*[40]

Local elections in 2000 installed a new mayor, Dick Murphy, and replacements for four termed-out councilmen. Murphy was worried about local finances. In April 2001, he appointed the nine-member Blue Ribbon Committee on City Finances to study the issue. The committee was assisted by the city auditor and comptroller, whose focus was to ensure the report said nothing that would jeopardize the upcoming sale of the city's ballpark bonds. Its work was largely completed by September 2001, but a final report was delayed until late February 2002. Worse, the final report declared the city to be "fiscally sound." Delaying and then whitewashing the report prevented speculation about shaky local finances from scuttling the ballpark bond offering, which closed on Valentine's Day 2002. Had the problems with the retirement system been publicly aired, the ballpark likely would not have been financed.[41]

Bad news steadily accumulated during the first six months of 2002, starting in February, when SDCERS announced that its funding ratio had decreased from 97 percent to 89.9 percent between June 2000 and June 2001. The system's unfunded liability ballooned from $69 million to $284 million. This was before the 2001 recession. Investment losses during the 2001 calendar year were $42 million. These losses were particularly worrisome given the city's reliance on pension earnings for funding a variety of city expenses and benefits. Investment losses continued to mount in the first quarter of 2002. In March, the mayor and city council were told that the funding ratio was approaching the 82.3 percent trigger in MP-1. By April 2002, SDCERS was informing the city that, absent a dramatic turnaround, the funding ratio reported in June 2002 would almost certainly fall below 82.3 percent, thus forcing the city to make a hefty lump-sum payment.[42]

By spring 2002, the implications of breaching the 82.3 percent floor were clear. Lawrence Grissom, the pension system's administrator, sent an e-mail to the city manager's office estimating that the funding ratio would hit 80 percent by June 2002. This estimate did not include the additional burden created by the city's earlier legal settlement with retirees. To restore funding to 82.3 percent, a onetime lump-sum payment of at least $75 million would be needed. This was fiscally infeasible and politically unthinkable, so both the city and SDCERS changed their interpretation of MP-1 to mean that hitting the trigger would require that the city simply begin making its full annual required contribution instead of maintaining the 82.3 percent floor. Under this interpretation, the city would owe the retirement system an additional $20 million to $26 million in 2003. Given the deteriorating fiscal conditions the city was facing, even this contribution would be difficult to make.

Meeting in closed session, the mayor and city council agreed to the broad outlines of a solution. Much like MP-1, it exchanged short-term pension relief for the city for retroactive increases in benefits for public employees. The trigger would be lowered to 75 percent. Were the trigger breached, the city would ramp up its contribution over five years to reach the full actuarial contribution rate rather than make an onerous payment the following year. The city would again improve the formula used to calculate pension benefits.[43] To sweeten the deal for Saathoff, a presidential-leave provision was adopted that would combine the city and union salaries of union presidents when calculating their benefits. Because only Saathoff received both, he alone would benefit from the provision.

Uberuaga approached the pension board with a formal offer, Manager's Proposal 2 (MP-2), in June 2002.[44] As with MP-1, the problem with MP-2 lay in getting SDCERS administrators to sign off on underfunding. Rick Roeder, the actuary for the pension, had reluctantly blessed MP-1 because it included a minimum funding ratio. He believed that MP-1 required the city to maintain the system at 82.3 percent, not just resume making its full annual required contribution. Now the floor was being dispensed with, and there was no guarantee that a lower trigger would not be eroded later on. In July and November, the pension board voted again to approve MP-2. Bowing to what seemed inevitable, Roeder signed off on the deal.[45]

Unlike MP-1, MP-2 was negotiated almost entirely behind closed doors. The city's representatives and Saathoff were intimately involved in drafting the proposal, but other board members were apparently unaware of key provisions. The *Union-Tribune* published no stories, although the process unfolded over several months and was tied to ongoing labor negotiations. Indeed, when MP-2 finally came before the city council in November 2002, its provisions were broken up and placed on the consent agenda, meaning that they would be voted on without debate.[46]

The details of MP-2, and ultimately the woeful state of the retirement system, were brought to light through the efforts of Diann Shipione, a financial consultant appointed to the board of SDCERS in 2001 by Mayor Murphy. Shipione was married to attorney Pat Shea, who headed the board of the San Diego Convention Center and helped resolve the Orange County bankruptcy in the mid-1990s. Shipione opposed MP-2 from the start and spoke against the proposal at the November board meeting. Shipione pulled the components of MP-2 from the city council's consent agenda and read a written statement in open session. The statement denounced MP-2 as a corrupt product of the board's city and union representatives. She criticized the mayor and the board for agreeing to a proposal that would delay most of the burden created by underfunding and benefit enhancements until 2009, by which time every elected official present would be termed out of office.

The council ignored Shipione and voted eight to one to approve the deal. It even agreed to indemnify members of the pension board from prosecution for approving their own underfunding. For her troubles, Shipione was ridiculed by her fellow board members and SDCERS administrators. In responding to her accusations, the new City Manager Lamont Ewell wrote that "[Shipione] has omitted, slanted and misrepresented the facts related to these matters." The Kroll Report, a lengthy document investigating the pension scandal, cited the city's "cursory and dismissive response" to Shipione's claims as a low point in its management of pension funding issues.[47]

In December, Roeder informed the board that the funding ratio had dropped to 77 percent by July 2002, much less than the 80 percent estimate on which MP-2 was premised. The unfunded liability mushroomed from $238 million to $720 million during the 2001-02 fiscal year. In a private e-mail to another pension board member, Acting City Auditor and Comptroller Terri Webster warned that the deteriorating funding ratio had become a "fiscal time bomb" for the city. With investment losses mounting, SDCERS was, for the first time, unable to pay for the thirteenth check out of surplus earnings. Worse, Roeder estimated that the system's health-care liability amounted to an additional $1.1 billion. If left unaddressed, the city's annual required contribution, which excluded the waterfall, legal settlements, and health-care liabilities, would grow to 30 percent of payroll by 2009. The *Union-Tribune* finally picked up on the story, running a front-page article stressing investment losses as the cause of the turmoil.[48]

In January 2003, two former city employees filed a class-action lawsuit against the city for illegally underfunding the retirement system. Roeder delivered a formal report on the state of the retirement system to the mayor and city council the following month. The *Union-Tribune*'s coverage of the event shifted the focus from investment losses to the underfunding, benefit increases, and health-care liability perpetuated by MP-1 and MP-2. Murphy directed the city manager to develop solutions but then put off the issue. By then Michael Conger, the attorney handling the class action lawsuit, was engaged in a full-court press against the city.[49]

By July 2003, Murphy could no longer avoid the pension fallout. Instead of acting, however, he stalled for time, announcing support for the creation of the Pension Reform Committee to study the retirement system. The committee was not impaneled until September; its members, including several carryovers from the mayor's previous Blue Ribbon Committee on City Finances and his campaign treasurer, did not begin work until October. Murphy and the council chose to defer action until receiving the final report. In the meantime, the city continued its current practice of shorting its annual contribution to the pension system.

Unfortunately, the effects of the pension scandal had spread beyond the city's control. Conger had found discrepancies in disclosure documents approved by the city to market its bonds to investors. In the bond disclosures, the city was asserting that state law required it to fund its retirement system at the actuarially determined rate. This assertion, which implied that the city's pension system was on solid footing, was a clear misrepresentation. Shipione learned about the disclosures and informed her employer, UBS Financial Services, which happened to be underwriting the city's $505 million bond to improve its sewer systems. With UBS refusing to price the bonds, the city pulled back its offering. In December, Roeder delivered his most ominous report to date. The pension fund, valued at $2.5 billion, had an unfunded liability of more than $1.1 billion.[50]

In January 2004, the city revealed that accounting errors had led it to understate the amount of its pension obligations in official documents. Moody's Investors Service responded to this news and Roeder's report by lowering the city's fiscal outlook. In February, Murphy warned that the city would need to consider tax increases, service cuts, and the sale of the city's real estate assets to close the $1.1 billion pension gap. Efforts to settle the damaging class-action lawsuit against it had gone nowhere. Finally, the U.S. Attorney's Office in San Diego and the Securities Exchange Commission (SEC) opened a federal investigation into the city's finances.[51]

Even with all of these troubles, Murphy ran first in the mayoral primary in March. Shortly thereafter, he announced that the city had reached a settlement agreement with retirees. Under the terms of the agreement, the city agreed to pay SDCERS $130 million in 2005 (compared to the $95 million it paid in 2004) and the full annual required contribution starting in 2006. As security, SDCERS received deeds to $375 million in city property. The agreement ended the practice of further underfunding the retirement system. Unfortunately, it did nothing to address the $1.1 billion, and growing, unfunded liability.[52]

Voting for Change

Dick Murphy was constitutionally incapable of being mayor. He did not take good advice, when offered. Unfortunately, the Chamber [of Commerce] encouraged him to run again because they were afraid of Donna Frye. You can't have revolutionaries in government. Frye is a bomb thrower.

—Mike Madigan, former assistant to Mayor Pete Wilson, 2007[53]

The fall campaign of 2004 was among the most tumultuous in the city's history. The ballot included several propositions dealing with the retirement system. Proposition G changed the city charter to make underfunding the pension illegal. Proposition H altered the composition of the retirement board to give independent appointees with financial investment experience a majority of seats relative to city employees. Also on the ballot was a proposition to change the city's government to a so-called strong mayor-council system. Under the new plan, the mayor would no longer sit on the city council but, replacing the city manager, would be responsible for the budget and day-to-day operations of city government.

Meanwhile, a law firm hired in February 2004 to look into problems with the city's financial disclosures and to represent the city before the SEC issued a scathing report. The report concluded that the accounting and disclosure errors acknowledged by the city were the result of confusion and dysfunction. For Murphy's critics, the report was a clear whitewashing of local officials' complicity in contributing to and then covering up the eroding state of the retirement system. The auditor KPMG refused to issue an opinion on the city's financial statements. Standard & Poor's Rating Services suspended its ratings of San Diego, formally shutting the city out of the municipal bond market.[54]

By September, Murphy was outpacing his primary opponent, County Supervisor Ron Roberts, in the mayoral race. Roberts had offered tepid support for bankruptcy, a nonstarter with San Diego's business community. Moreover, Roberts had his own pension sins to atone for. The San Diego County Employees Retirement Association, the county equivalent of SDCERS, had a pension deficit of $1.4 billion (not counting $800 million in outstanding pension obligation bonds) and a funding ratio of 75 percent, as a result of both investment losses and benefit hikes. In late September, the populist city council member Donna Frye formally entered the race as a write-in candidate. Frye, a golden-haired, husky-voiced surf-shop owner, was the lone member of the council to oppose MP-2. Facing mounting pressure, Murphy escalated his proposals, endorsing the sale of $600 million in pension obligation bonds recommended by the Pension Reform Committee.[55]

When the dust cleared, Frye's write-in campaign had scored a slim victory over Murphy: 160,805 to 157,459. Unfortunately for Frye, more than 5,500 voters who had written her name on their ballots neglected to darken the oval beside it as required by city law. The votes were thrown out and Murphy was declared the winner. San Diego voters, however, had registered a preference for reform. Proposition F, the so-called strong-mayor provision, passed with 51.4 percent of the vote.

But the result of the November elections failed to register with the board at SDCERS. Less than three weeks after the election, the board met in secret to plot the ouster of whistle-blower Diann Shipione. Board members voted to exclude her from future closed-session meetings and wrote a letter to Murphy seeking her removal from the board. Fresh off a comfortable reelection victory in his city council race, Scott Peters, who voted for both the faulty bond disclosures and MP-2, criticized Shipione for disclosing damaging information about the city's financial position.[56]

The days of quiet consensus, however, were over. Although the 2004 elections produced no turnover on the city council, the voter-approved propositions initiated a process of reform that would change the city's financial practices and bring to power a new city attorney. Attorney Michael Aguirre narrowly defeated Assistant City Attorney Leslie Devaney, 50.4 percent to 49.6 percent. Unlike his predecessor, Aguirre, a self-styled populist, believed that the city attorney worked for the people of San Diego, not for its elected officials. While almost everyone else in city government was pausing to take a breath after the recent elections, Aguirre went right to work. In mid-January, the City Attorney's Office released its first report on the pension crisis. Its first paragraph was a shot across the bow of the political establishment:

> The San Diego City Attorney is investigating possible abuse, fraud and illegal acts by San Diego City officials and employees. The scope of this investigation will extend to all possible illegal acts and will expand as necessary based on findings made during the investigation, in other words, the City Attorney's office will pursue all evidence of possible illegal acts no matter where they may lead.[57]

Over the following four years, Aguirre would be a central figure in pension reform efforts.

A Mad Juggler's Circus

We're going to be living with this problem for a generation. If we don't get this problem turned around, the quality of life as we know it in San Diego will drop significantly.

—*City Attorney Michael Aguirre, July 2005*[58]

The chaotic 2004 election was an appropriate overture to the events of 2005, a year that marked the end of the political careers of two mayors and brought city government to a virtual standstill. Although Mayor Murphy had survived Donna Frye's spirited insurgent campaign, the lack of confidence expressed by local voters gave him little leverage with which to tackle San Diego's mounting fiscal problems. The firm responsible for auditing the city's official financial reports for 2003, KPMG, had rejected the $4 million investigative report commissioned by the city. Until the city could satisfy the firm that the people and practices responsible for the pension deficit and improper bond issues had been fully investigated, the city would continue to be locked out of the credit markets.

In February, Aguirre declared war on Murphy and the city council. He accused local officials of violating federal securities laws and of concealing the scheme to trade pension underfunding for benefit hikes. To assuage KPMG's concerns, the city authorized the private law firm hired to investigate the city's fiscal practices to conduct additional interviews, hired a new city auditor, replaced its outside counsel, and appointed a three-person audit committee to review the law firm's report and recommend solutions. The audit committee was headed by former SEC Chairman Arthur Levitt. Levitt and the other two members were associates of Kroll Inc., a private consulting firm. The city council also pledged its complete cooperation with the ongoing probe by the U.S. attorney and the SEC, voting to waive its attorney-client privilege and urging the pension board to do the same.[59]

Unfortunately, neither Murphy nor the council could compel SDCERS to cooperate. The same board that had tried to oust Diann Shipione after she blew the whistle on MP-2 voted in February to withhold crucial documents. Fortunately for Murphy, Proposition H, which changed the composition of the pension board to give independent members a majority, was scheduled to take effect in mid-April. If the current board would not cooperate, then perhaps a new board with seven new mayoral appointees would be more amenable. Murphy released a list of his appointees in February. Conspicuously absent from the list was Shipione, the one board member most responsible for revealing the sorry state of the retirement system. Her tenure would end when the new board assumed control on April 15. On April 16, the new board met for the first time and promptly refused to waive its attorney-client privilege.[60]

The pension board's inaction was the final straw. Aguirre called on the mayor to resign. Two days later, *Time* magazine published an article that named Murphy, Philadelphia Mayor John Street, and Detroit Mayor Kwame Kilpatrick the three worst mayors in the United States. For Murphy, a proud, quiet man, the notoriety clearly stung. On April 26, he announced his resignation, and a special election was scheduled for July. Murphy's looming departure created a political vacuum in city government. Michael Zucchet, a council member and deputy mayor elected in 2002, was scheduled to temporarily replace Murphy. Unfortunately, Zucchet and two other council members, Ralph Inzunza and Charles Lewis, were already facing federal extortion, conspiracy, and fraud charges in the so-called Strippergate scandal. They were accused of accepting bribes from a local strip-club owner in exchange for relaxing laws prohibiting dancers from touching the patrons.[61] Murphy officially stepped down on July 15, thus making Zucchet acting mayor. Zucchet and Inzunza were convicted on July 18.[62] Two hours later, the remaining six members of the council appointed Toni Atkins, who had approved the improper disclosures and underfunding, as mayor pro tem. Unfortunately, the July 26 mayoral special election to choose Murphy's replacement failed to produce a majority for any of the candidates. The top two finishers, Donna Frye and former Police Chief Jerry Sanders, would square off in a November 8 runoff, with the winner taking office on December 5.

The lengthy absence of a duly elected mayor meant that there was no effective leader to give direction to the array of internal investigations, legal proceedings, and other pension-related problems facing the city. In May, Murphy and Ewell had proposed a budget that, while making the annual required contribution, was $127 million less than the full costs, including health benefits, of the retirement system. Murphy's resignation was followed by the departures of four high-ranking city officials involved in crafting MP-2. Three of them were subsequently indicted by the county district attorney for violating California's conflict-of-interest law, although the state supreme court would eventually dismiss the charges. The council repeated its demand that the pension board waive the attorney-client privilege and cooperate fully with the SEC and U.S. attorney. The board continued to refuse and instead asked the city to foot the legal bills of board members caught up in the legal investigations.[63]

With Murphy gone and the council rudderless, the Office of the City Attorney stepped in to fill the void. In April, Aguirre declared the benefits granted by MP-1 and MP-2, and the waterfall provision adopted in 1980, to be void. He called for a compromise solution whereby the city would use taxes and other revenues to increase funding for the pension and municipal employees would give up some of the illegally conferred benefits.[64]

Repeated attempts by the council, including a threat by Scott Peters to place SDCERS in receivership, failed to induce cooperation from the pension system's board. The council also withheld approval of the board's annual budget until the end of June but had no formal control over its funding. Members of the pension board rebuffed the audit committee, which recommended firing the system's actuary. When the board refused to release documents subpoenaed by a federal grand jury, Aguirre sued to have himself appointed as legal counsel to the retirement system. At the same time, Aguirre filed a second lawsuit seeking to have the benefits granted in MP-1 and MP-2 nullified. The outcome of these lawsuits would dramatically impact the city's fiscal and political outlook.[65]

Shootout at Pension Gap

I did not disagree with much in the Kroll Report. I did not find it offensive or a whitewash. But a report is what you do when you do not want to do anything about the problem. We had the Aguirre reports, the [law firm's] report. In the Orange County bankruptcy, we did no reports. We were too busy fixing the problem. There was no money for reports.

—*Former mayoral candidate Pat Shea, 2009*[66]

In February 2005, the city hired Kroll to complete an investigation into the causes of the pension scandal, with an initial contract of $250,000. By August 2006, when the firm finally released its report, it had extracted more than $20 million from the city. While the city council and its well-paid consultants dithered, the Office of the City Attorney was conducting its own investigation, pursuing lawsuits against those involved in underfunding and developing strategies to deal with the crisis. Indeed, through much of 2005, Aguirre acted as if he, and nobody else, was the representative of the public will. In August 2005, when the council was in recess and the city manager was on vacation, he released a fifteen-point recovery plan. It advocated dealing directly with the SEC, with the city accepting responsibility for misrepresenting its financial condition. Aguirre again recommended that the city cease to recognize the benefits granted in 1996 and 2002, and pursue a settlement with retirees who were already receiving the benefits. Finally, he proposed placing before voters several ballot initiatives that would raise taxes to pay for legal pension benefits, require voter approval for any new pension benefits, and change the composition of the pension board to exclude city employees from serving.[67]

Needless to say, Aguirre's proposals went nowhere. He had alienated whatever support he had on the city council by accusing members of breaking the law in voting for underfunding and improper bond offerings. In targeting the benefits granted in MP-1 and MP-2, he incurred the enmity of thousands of city employees, many of whom showed up to heckle Aguirre wherever he went. His attempts to intimidate SDCERS caused board members and administrators only to dig in. Indeed, only after receiving a court order from a federal judge did the board finally vote to turn over documents to investigators. The city attorney was also fighting an uphill battle in the courts. In October 2005, a state judge ruled against Aguirre, thus crippling the city's attempt to have the benefits overturned. In March 2006, a different judge rejected Aguirre's attempt to take over the legal affairs of the pension fund.[68]

As Aguirre battled with the courts, the attention of local officials and residents was fixed on yet another mayoral election. Like the 2004 campaign, the runoff between Frye and Sanders featured dueling pension proposals. Frye proposed a half-cent increase in the sales tax to close the funding gap and pledged to negotiate an agreement with city employees to rein in costs. If that failed, she supported a council ordinance to rescind the 1996 and 2002 benefits. Sanders's recovery plan focused on cost cutting. As did Frye, Sanders supported Aguirre's lawsuit to overturn the benefits. Failing that, Sanders proposed cutting the local workforce by 10 percent, imposing salary freezes and furloughs for remaining employees, outsourcing many public services to private contractors, and closing off the pension system to new hires.

Predictably, the editorial board of the *Union-Tribune* derided Frye's plan, calling the tax hike a political nonstarter that "defies the good common sense of San Diego voters." Sanders's so-called common-sense approach was received more favorably even though its opposition to new revenues and focus on future costs did nothing to directly address the existing pension liability. The paper also joined Sanders in distorting Frye's record, painting her as an advocate of underfunding the pension, even though she had been the only member of the city council to vote against MP-2. On November 8, Sanders defeated Frye by 54 percent to 46 percent. In the end, Sanders's attacks on city employees resonated with voters' discontent over the growing fiscal crisis. Sanders would be the first mayor to serve under the city's new strong-mayor form of government, which voters had approved the previous November. In addition to dealing with the pension scandal, Sanders would have to manage this difficult transition.[69]

The Politics of Muddling Through

It [the annual pension contribution] really dictates the level of services that this city will be able to continue to provide. If it's a very high number, then we obviously have to make cuts so that we can afford to make that correct payment.

—*Mayor Jerry Sanders, 2006*[70]

The challenges facing Mayor Sanders as he assumed office in December 2005 were unprecedented in the history of San Diego. The new strong-mayor system did give the mayor new powers, including control over the municipal budget. Sanders, however, had pledged to tackle the pension mess without raising taxes. Politically, this was the safe approach in tax-averse San Diego. In practice, this campaign promise has weighed down efforts to reduce the unfunded liability. During his first few months in office, the mayor moved cautiously. In February 2006, he proposed borrowing $100 million to help stabilize the pension fund. Since the city was locked out of the credit markets, Sanders put up $100 million awarded in a recent tobacco settlement as collateral.[71]

In April, Sanders released his first budget proposal and a plan to borrow an additional $674 million to pay down half of the $1.4 billion pension liability.[72] The Sanders budget and the borrowing plan assumed a quick restoration of the city's credit rating. With Kroll still investigating the city's pension system and the 2003 and 2004 audits still unfinished, the mayor's budget had $374 million in funding that might not materialize. This and other shortcomings were pointed out in a report by the independent budget analyst, who reported to the city council and whose office was created when San Diego voters approved the strong-mayor plan. Under Andrea Tevlin, the analyst's office documented San Diego's progress on the pension and brought unprecedented clarity to a budget process that had been little more than smoke and mirrors under McGrory.[73]

While Sanders and Tevlin were working out procedures for San Diego's new budget process, SDCERS was undertaking its own reform efforts. In October, the same board that had voted for underfunding and then covered it up commissioned a separate investigation. In January the system's consultant released its report, blaming the underfunding agreements on the cozy relationship between board members and city officials but largely exonerating SDCERS administrators. Following a national search for a new chief executive, SDCERS hired David Wescoe, a local investment manager with no ties to MP-1 or MP-2. The board also hired a new actuary and changed the way it calculated its costs and the pension liability. Ultimately, the concept of surplus earnings was eliminated, and the costs of both the pension benefits and retiree health-care benefits were made more transparent.[74]

On the heels of Aguirre's legal defeats in late 2007, the *Union-Tribune* ran a devastating story tallying the costs of Aguirre's various lawsuits and airing stories from former employees about his odd behavior. Aguirre would spend the rest of his tenure in an uphill and ultimately losing battle for reelection. In November 2008, voters rendered a final verdict, replacing Aguirre with an opponent who believed the city attorney had vastly overstepped his authority.[75]

Two Steps Forward, Two Steps Back

Until and unless a court of law grants the City authority to retroactively rescind these benefits, my plan is to propose a new pension plan for future City employees beginning next fiscal year, and to seek collective bargaining agreements that are more advantageous to San Diego taxpayers. I believe that with continued belt-tightening and fiscal discipline over a period of years, our long-term obligations can be managed, especially as the City's revenues naturally increase over time. I do not believe it is appropriate to ask the voters to tax themselves to pay for these benefits.

—*Mayor Jerry Sanders, 2007*[76]

By late 2006, it was clear that the city was stuck with the pension benefits it had approved in MP-1 and MP-2. Unfortunately, successive mayors and city councils had never developed a revenue source to pay for them. The city had two choices: borrow enough money to smooth out the pain or make up what the city owed its employees with large cuts elsewhere in the municipal budget.

In October 2006, Kroll finally released the results of its investigation of the pension system. The report found that the city violated numerous federal securities laws and Internal Revenue Service regulations but was largely silent on which officials, if any, were legally responsible. The firm issued 121 mostly technical recommendations for reforming the city's financial practices but offered little advice on how to address the current liability. Alarmingly, that liability was growing. In October, city officials acknowledged that the unfunded pension liability had reached $1.76 billion, despite the $550 million the city had put in over the previous three years. San Diego was more underwater than ever before.[77]

Constrained in his ability to address the past, Sanders instead focused on the future. The mayor adopted the findings of the Kroll Report and worked to implement the report's recommendations. In November 2006, the city settled with the SEC, agreeing to cease and desist from future securities violations. That same month, Sanders issued a five-year plan to put the city back on a firm financial footing. The plan included eliminating or not filling 570 vacancies and cutting an additional 130 positions each year for the following three years.[78]

One area in which the mayor has been especially aggressive is in negotiating new contracts with the city's labor unions. In March 2008, Sanders issued a proposal seeking to implement a hybrid pension plan, with some workers shifting to a defined contribution plan. The proposal also sought an increase in the retirement age for non-public-safety workers. When the council and unions balked, Sanders threatened to place his plan on the ballot. In July, the city and its white-collar union agreed on a two-tiered retirement plan for municipal employees. Existing employees would keep all of the benefits passed with MP-1 and MP-2. However, all new city employees would have to pay a greater share of their retirement contributions. The cap on how much each employee could receive after retirement was also lowered. Unfortunately, because the new two-tier plan targeted only future benefits, it did little to close the existing deficit in the pension system, which was growing rapidly because of ongoing investment losses. Although the Sanders plan promised to provide some savings, these were dwarfed by the growth in the city's pension bill.[79]

In 2007, KPMG was completing its long-awaited audits of the city's finances, and by May 2008, Standard & Poor's Rating Services restored the city's credit ratings and assigned it a "positive" outlook. The agency cited the financial and managerial reforms implemented by city officials and the release of its financial statements for fiscal years 2003–06. This and other announcements cleared the way for the city's return to the municipal bond market. In January 2009, the city successfully sold a $157.8 million water revenue bond, its first offering since the onset of the pension crisis in 2003.[80] By then, however, the global financial crisis had produced punishing investment losses for the city's pension system. By July, the city's unfunded liability had mushroomed to a harrowing $2.1 billion and was projected to continue growing in the years to come.[81]

A Burgeoning Fiscal Crisis

The City of San Diego is facing a structural budget deficit. Over the past six fiscal years the City has endured significant budget reductions, employed the use of one-time solutions, and sharply scaled back new programs or program enhancements in order to balance annual budgets. Unless clear, decisive, and long-term solutions are implemented, municipal services will continue to erode in the future.

—*Independent budget analyst Andrea Tevlin, 2008*[82]

In his first state-of-the-city address, delivered in January 2006, Mayor Jerry Sanders laid the blame for the city's fiscal problems at the feet of San Diego's previous administrations. "As best as I can tell, the operating philosophy around City Hall involved one of these three words: delay, deny or deceive."[83] However, it soon became clear that Sanders's efforts to address previous wrongdoing had done little to fix the city's underlying budget problems. In an influential February 2008 report, independent budget analyst Andrea Tevlin argued that the city's continuing fiscal problems were a product of an underlying "structural deficit"—a failure of the city to live within its means by systematically spending more money than it was willing to collect. Although diverting money from the pension system had previously helped the city make its ends meet, the growing pension liability had become a central cause of the problem. Pension payments, a legacy of the pension underfunding and a result of the more recent investment losses, continued to balloon.

For years, elected officials sought to hide the structural deficit with onetime budget tricks, including sales of public lands, transfers of onetime and restricted funds for general use, and systematic underbudgeting of expected expenses. Unfortunately, the city was running out of onetime fixes. Sanders's five-year budget outlook, released the same year, echoed Tevlin's assessment. The plan projected budget deficits in each of its five years—ranging from $20.6 million to $68.3 million each year—even after making optimistic assumptions that the city would sell more lands, offer no salary increases for most employees, and hold the line on retiree health-care costs.[84] As the consequences of the global financial crisis became clear in 2009, Sanders increased his projection of the annual deficit to more than $150 million, in a General Fund budget of about $1.2 billion.[85]

The city's chronic structural deficit stemmed from two underlying causes. First, the pension underfunding and the granting of unfunded benefits of the 1990s and early 2000s had pushed significant liabilities into the future, a loan that came due when the scheme was exposed and invested earnings dried up. Second, conservative political, media, and business leaders seized on the psychological effects of the pension debacle to effectively block attempts to raise new revenue. Led by the *Union-Tribune* editorial board, these leaders argued that citizens should not be asked to pay higher taxes until the city had rolled back the excessively generous benefits granted to employees in exchange for their support to underfund the system, lest the new money be diverted toward employee pensions.

Crying "Pension!"

If you do not deal with the pension, it will affect everything else that the city does. If you did not have an enormous pension deficit, but you just had shortages, people would probably agree to pay more to keep the bathrooms open at the beaches. But people know that every new dollar is subsumed by the pension.

—*Former mayoral candidate Pat Shea, 2009*[86]

Although some officials, like former City Council President Scott Peters, have argued that San Diego has simply followed in the steps of other local governments in diverting pension revenues during the roaring 1990s, the scale of San Diego's trouble put the city in a league of its own.[87] In the fiscal year that ended in June 2009, the city's unfunded pension liability exceeded $2 billion, nearly four times the city's total annual payroll. Table 3.3, which compares San Diego's unfunded liability with that of its peers, makes clear the magnitude of the city's predicament. Although recent financial losses have hurt public pension funds across the country, in San Diego those losses only compounded decades of underfunding that have left the city with the largest pension deficit, in relative terms, among large California cities. As a result, San Diego was contributing more than thirty cents for every dollar in wages paid to city employees into the pension system in 2009, an annual payment that greatly exceeds the bills in most other big California cities.

The unusually large pension payment has been due, in part, to an aggressive repayment plan to close the pension gap adopted by the city's pension system. In 2004, the Murphy-appointed Pension Reform Committee recommended that the city adopt a fifteen-year schedule for paying off its debts to the pension system, significantly shorter than the usual thirty-year amortization schedule that many other cities use. At the urging of Mayor Sanders, the pension board adopted a twenty-year schedule in 2007.[88] The combined effect of the city's unusually large pension liability and its unusually short repayment schedule has produced a growing crisis in the city's finances. Although the short repayment schedule served as a positive signal to credit-rating agencies, former City Comptroller Greg Levin said that it also "put more pressure on the city's already pressing financial problems." In fiscal year 2011, the city was set to make a nearly $180 million pension contribution out of a General Fund of slightly more than $1 billion. By 2015, pension actuaries estimated that the sum would rise to nearly $250 million, or more than one-fifth of the city's day-to-day budget.[89]

TABLE 3.3   Public pension burden in the largest California cities, fiscal year 2008–09

City[a]	Pension payment (percentage of annual payroll[b])	Unfunded pension liability[c] (percentage of annual payroll)
San Diego	31	393
Anaheim	29	111
Oakland[d]	26	228
Long Beach	20	23
San Jose	20	204
Santa Ana	17	68
Riverside	17	43
Los Angeles	16	85
Sacramento	15	113
San Francisco	5	0
Fresno[d]	0	0

SOURCES: City of Fresno, Finance Department, *Comprehensive Annual Financial Report: Effective and Responsive Government*, fiscal year ended June 30, 2009, Fresno, CA; City of Oakland, Finance and Management Agency, *Comprehensive Annual Financial Report*, fiscal year ended June 30, 2009, Oakland, CA; City and County of San Francisco, Office of the Controller, *Comprehensive Annual Financial Report*, year ended June 30, 2009, San Francisco, CA; City of Santa Ana, Finance and Management Services Agency, *2009 Comprehensive Annual Financial* Report, fiscal year ended June 30, 2009, Santa Ana, CA; City of Sacramento, Department of Finance Accounting Division, *City of Sacramento Comprehensive Annual Financial Report*, fiscal year ended June 30, 2009, Sacramento, CA; City of Long Beach, Department of Financial Management, *Comprehensive Annual Financial Report*, fiscal year ended June 30, 2009, Long Beach, CA; City of Riverside, City Manager's Office—Finance Division, *Comprehensive Annual Financial Report*, year ended June 30, 2009, Riverside, CA; City of Los Angeles, Office of the Controller, *Comprehensive Annual Financial Report*, fiscal year ended June 30, 2009, Los Angeles, CA; City of Anaheim, Department of Finance, *Comprehensive Annual Financial Report*, year ended June 30, 2009, Anaheim, CA; City of San Jose, Finance Department, *Comprehensive Annual Financial Report*, fiscal year ended June 30, 2009, San Jose, CA; City of San Diego, Office of the Comptroller, *Comprehensive Annual Financial Report*, fiscal year ended June 30, 2009, San Diego, CA.

NOTE: Does not include employee portion contributed by city per collective bargaining agreement.

[a]Includes all local pension plans managed by the cities and/or by the California Public Employees Retirement System.

[b]Total covered payroll is estimated from the most recent actuarial valuation in each city.

[c]Based on data from the most recent actuarial valuation for each city, which is from fiscal year 2007 for Riverside; fiscal year 2008 for Anaheim, Fresno, Sacramento (for two of three plans), and Santa Ana; and fiscal year 2009 for all other cities (including one of three Sacramento plans).

[d]Both Oakland and Fresno have issued pension obligation bonds to prepay a portion of their pension liabilities. The annual repayment cost for these bonds is not included in the table.

In addition to the large pension payments, San Diego also faced two other looming liabilities. Under new accounting rules, the city has been required to estimate the full cost of the health-care benefits promised to its workers after retirement. By late 2009, the health-care liability had grown to more than $1.3 billion, as the city continued to make less than its actuarially calculated contribution. Finally, Mayor Sanders also estimated that the city's backlog of badly deferred maintenance—the up-keep of streets, sidewalks, and city-owned parks and facilities—stood at between $800 million and $900 million.[90]

Even as the city faced these looming liabilities, it struggled to raise sufficient revenues to pay its regular operating expenses. Over the years, a series of analyses from the labor-affiliated Center for Policy Initiatives, a local academic, and a city-hired consultant all concluded that San Diego lagged behind many other California cities in its revenue collections. Unlike most major cities, San Diego did not charge for its refuse collection or have a tax on utility users. It also levied comparatively low taxes and fees on businesses, and its transient occupancy tax—charged on out-of-town visitors staying in San Diego hotels—fell short of other California cities and comparable tourism destinations. Using very conservative assumptions, the city's independent budget analyst estimated that San Diego could raise more than $100 million in additional revenue each year by instituting just a portion of the fees and taxes that most other major California cities already collected. As indicated in Table 3.4, which compares the total revenues collected by the ten largest California cities, San Diego has lagged well behind. As a share of median household income, the city's revenue was near the bottom of the list.[91]

Despite the growing gap between San Diego's liabilities and the revenues available to pay for them, public officials remained reluctant to pursue new revenue sources, arguing that the initiative for new taxes must come from the voters themselves. In addition, the city's fiscally conservative business establishment used the fallout from San Diego's pension controversy to effectively mobilize its supporters to block efforts to raise new revenues. Although the agreements to underfund the pension system were authored by city administrators and approved by the city council, conservative leaders placed the blame squarely at the feet of overweening public-sector labor unions and parasitic public employees. Using the specter of the looming pension liability, they have successfully fought off proposals to increase taxes and urged the city to pursue major concessions in labor negotiations.

In 2004, in the aftermath of the devastating 2003 wildfires that exposed the weakness of San Diego's fire-protection apparatus, the city council proposed two increases in the city's hotel taxes—a fee that would

TABLE 3.4   Revenues of the ten largest California cities, fiscal year 2008–09

City	Revenue per household	Revenue as percentage of median household income
Oakland	$6,192	12.0
Santa Ana	$5,057	9.5
Anaheim	$4,920	8.9
Los Angeles	$4,658	9.6
San Jose	$4,546	5.9
Long Beach	$4,479	8.7
Riverside	$3,943	7.0
San Diego	$3,823	6.4
Sacramento	$3,440	7.3
Fresno	$2,538	5.9
Average[a]	$4,419	8.3

SOURCES: City of Fresno, Finance Department, *Comprehensive Annual Financial Report: Effective and Responsive Government*, fiscal year ended June 30, 2009, Fresno, CA; City of Oakland, Finance and Management Agency, *Comprehensive Annual Financial Report*, fiscal year ended June 30, 2009, Oakland, CA; City of Santa Ana, Finance and Management Services Agency, *2009 Comprehensive Annual Financial Report*, fiscal year ended June 30, 2009, Santa Ana, CA; City of Sacramento, Department of Finance Accounting Division, *City of Sacramento Comprehensive Annual Financial Report*, fiscal year ended June 30, 2009, Sacramento, CA; City of Long Beach, Department of Financial Management, *Comprehensive Annual Financial Report*, fiscal year ended June 30, 2009, Long Beach, CA; City of Riverside, City Manager's Office—Finance Division, *Comprehensive Annual Financial Report*, year ended June 30, 2009, Riverside, CA; City of Los Angeles, Office of the Controller, *Comprehensive Annual Financial Report*, fiscal year ended June 30, 2009, Los Angeles, CA; City of Anaheim, Department of Finance, *Comprehensive Annual Financial Report*, year ended June 30, 2009, Anaheim, CA; City of San Jose, Finance Department, *Comprehensive Annual Financial Report*, fiscal year ended June 30, 2009, San Jose, CA; City of San Diego, Office of the Comptroller, *Comprehensive Annual Financial Report*, fiscal year ended June 30, 2009, San Diego, CA; U.S. Census Bureau, *2009 American Community Survey*, December 14, 2010.

NOTES: To make data comparable across cities, the table includes only revenues from governmental activities, including taxes, service charges, and grants. It does not include revenues from business-type activities, such as municipal utilities.

[a]The average is computed for all cities except San Diego.

be paid by out-of-town visitors, not the city's taxpayers. In both cases the increases were defeated at the ballot box. To buy the support of the tourism industry, the city's first proposal promised to earmark a portion of the new tax toward efforts to market San Diego. Under Proposition 13, the set-aside meant that the measure would require support from two-thirds of voters. To qualify for a lower, simple-majority threshold, the second proposal dropped the earmark, thus pushing the tourism industry to oppose the measure. "At this point, we had the hotel industry against us," recalled former City Council President Scott Peters. "And all they said was, 'Pension, pension, pension!'"[92]

Echoing the views of the hotel owners, the *San Diego Union-Tribune* editorial board urged a no vote on the hotel tax:

> Proponents say the tax increase, which appears as Proposition J, would help pay for police and fire equipment. In truth, any tax hike at this time would be immediately devoured by the voracious demands of the pension system, which already is crowding out spending on virtually any new initiative. . . . [I]t makes no sense whatsoever to raise taxes until the financial crisis spawned by uncontrolled pension costs is brought firmly under control.[93]

In response to a 2009 county grand-jury report urging the city to adopt trash-collection fees, the newspaper again tied its opposition to the pension crisis. The new revenue, its editorial board warned, "would be devoured in an instant by the voracious retirement system, whose out-of-control costs to taxpayers are expected to jump by $100 million in a single year. So, kiss your trash-collection windfall goodbye, City Council, because it just disappeared into the black hole of the pension fund."[94]

In April 2009, a Democratic-controlled city council, elected with strong union support, stunned local observers by unanimously imposing new labor contracts on the city's police officers and blue-collar workers. The contracts promised to save the city $30 million in the next fiscal year by cutting compensation and benefits, what city officials described as the labor group's "fair share." On top of the concessions already made for new hires, the cuts pushed the brunt of pain onto current and future city employees, leaving retirees—who benefited from the previous benefit enhancements—untouched.[95]

Having defeated the two hotel tax proposals, local taxpayers were not asked to pay their fair share. Efforts to raise taxes were dead on arrival, and a long-overdue study recommending adjusting user fees to match the actual cost of city services ran into opposition from anti-tax conservatives like newly elected City Councilman Carl DeMaio. In 2002, DeMaio, the founder of a for-profit market-oriented think tank, presented city officials with an award for running the most efficient city government in California. In 2008, he was elected to the city council on a platform of eliminating widespread government waste and corruption and ending excessive benefits.

The San Diego Way

San Diego's pension scandal grew out of a series of efforts designed to ease budgetary pain during difficult economic times. Faced with the prospect of asking voters to raise taxes or the option of raiding an overflowing pension system, politically savvy officials chose the latter. The underfunding scheme designed by City Manager Jack McGrory was not a secret plot hatched in smoke-filled rooms, nor was it particularly novel. Instead, it built on the city's decades-old practice of diverting pension earnings to ease the strain on city finances.

When a series of court cases and another recession exposed the flaws of MP-1, local officials opted to double down rather than to fold a poor hand. Unlike McGrory's plan, MP-2 was indeed a conspiracy to pass on city debt to future taxpayers, a bargain struck among shortsighted city officials, self-interested unions, and conflicted pension board members. It was put into place with little public debate, including less than passing interest from the local business community or the leading newspaper.

In the wake of the pension scandal, San Diego voters adopted a series of reforms to strengthen the city's internal controls. Between 2004 and 2010, voters considered ten separate amendments to the city charter—San Diego's governing document—designed to eliminate the institutional deficiencies blamed for the city's financial and political problems. All ten were adopted by the electorate, eight of them passing with more than 60 percent of the vote. The reforms, summarized in Table 3.5, helped address crucial weaknesses in the structure of San Diego city government. Collectively, they will make it far more difficult for elected officials to repeat the mistakes of the 1980s, 1990s, and early 2000s—shortsighted policy decisions that have helped bring the city to the brink of ruin. Unfortunately, the reforms have done little to create the political momentum necessary to address the city's structural budget deficit and some, like the ambitious short repayment schedule for the unfunded pension liability, have contributed to the city's growing difficulty in balancing its budget.

Despite voter appetite for reform, none of the political actors involved in crafting the city's disastrous pension deals that have wrought such havoc on San Diego's finances have been held to account. Mayor Murphy and the remaining members of the city council who had ap-

TABLE 3.5   San Diego's era of reform, 2004–10

Year	Measure	Description	Vote share (%)	Passed?
2004	D	Provides a right to access information concerning the conduct of the people's business	82.6	Y
2004	E	Enables the Ethics Commission to retain its own legal counsel instead of being represented by City Attorney	77.1	Y
2004	F	Creates "strong-mayor" form of government for trial periods and a new Office of Independent Budget analyst to advise City Council	51.4	Y
2004	G	Enacts 15-year amortization schedule for unfunded pension liabilities and prohibits city and retirement system from adopting agreements to delay full actuarial funding	53.6	Y
2004	H	Changes composition of retirement board to create independent majority with professional qualifications	64.8	Y
2006	B	Requires voter approval for any increase in retirement benefits for public employees	69.9	Y
2006	C	Allows the city to contract out services traditionally performed by city employees	60.4	Y
2008	A	Exempts public safety services from managed competition	67.9	Y
2008	C	Creates office of independent City Auditor and makes Independent Budget Analyst permanent	63.0	Y
2010	D	Makes "strong-mayor" form of government permanent, creates ninth City Council district, and increases veto-override threshold to two-thirds	60.4	Y

SOURCE: City of San Diego, Office of the City Clerk.

proved MP-2 won reelection in 2004. None of the appointed city officials facing criminal charges for their role in the underfunding stood trial.[96] And employee groups have been allowed to keep the benefit enhancements they received in exchange for supporting the city's schemes, with new hires paying the cost.

The two officials most responsible for bringing to light the scope of the city's problems, City Attorney Mike Aguirre and pension board member Diann Shipione, did not survive the political fallout. Although Aguirre had urged the city to adopt a compromise strategy, his call for new taxes has all but been abandoned by San Diego's opinion leaders, who continue to argue that the city can address its budgetary problems by squeezing employees, selling pension obligation bonds, and privatizing city services. Although initial public outrage over the pension crisis helped propel the progressive populism behind Aguirre's electoral victory and the near election of Donna Frye, by 2010, it was conservative elites who had succeeded in channeling public discontent to attack public employees, block tax increases, and push for the outsourcing of city services. Ironically, although the early pension diversions had been designed to spare San Diego taxpayers from having to choose between fewer services and higher taxes, the ensuing pension scandal only further widened the city's structural deficit and made finding a permanent way to close the growing gap between its revenues and expenditures more difficult.

Paradise Impoverished
Underfunded Public Services

The 18-month budget that the San Diego City Council is likely to enact today will hurt. It cuts deep into good programs that many people cherish. It hits basic, core services that people depend on, like police, fire and lifeguard protection. It will cost some 200 city employees their jobs. And it puts off further efforts to eliminate the structural deficit in city finances for another year.

—San Diego Union-Tribune *editorial board, 2009*[1]

During the 1980s and 1990s, San Diego leaders raided the city's pension system and used its "surplus revenues" to fund services its residents wanted but preferred not to pay for. But by the mid-2000s the pension system had become a net drain on the city's finances, making the task of balancing the budget ever harder. In addition to rising pension payments, the budget crunch was exacerbated by three factors. First, with San Diego's credit rating suspended as a result of securities fraud allegations, public officials found their access to the bond markets effectively blocked. In the absence of bond financing, already-strained public infrastructure, such as decades-old sewers and potholed streets, continued to deteriorate.

Second, reforms adopted in the wake of the pension scandal committed the city to a shorter schedule for paying off the pension liability, including sharp investment losses suffered during the 2008 financial crisis. With revenue falling as a result of the recession, larger pension payments had to be offset by cuts to existing programs. Third, the city's leading conservatives, who had long opposed efforts to raise taxes, were gifted a new rhetorical weapon to block future tax increases. New revenue would do little to improve the quality of city services but would instead be gobbled up by pensions for city workers.

In short, the absence of civic leadership and political will that gave rise to the city's ill-conceived efforts to underfund public pensions grew worse, thereby intensifying the city's political paralysis. Public service levels, already low compared with other major California cities, declined further during the period 2000–2010. In addition, the business community and public employee unions, two groups that anchored the political coalitions that developed the pension underfunding schemes, found themselves bitterly divided, a rift exacerbated by San Diego's new strong-mayor form of government. Business leaders backed the new mayor, Republican Jerry Sanders, who was elected on a platform of fiscal austerity and ruled out new tax increases. Labor leaders found strong allies on the Democrat-dominated city council, which vocally opposed further service cuts.

In this chapter, we chronicle how San Diego's fiscal crisis—the roots of which preceded the pension fiasco but became even worse in its wake—has accelerated the decline of the city's most basic public services. Contrary to claims made by conservative critics, we find little evidence that gross waste and budgetary excess were the primary causes of San Diego's financial collapse. On the contrary, we show that, for decades, funding and service levels for most city services in San Diego have lagged behind other major California municipalities. Already underfunded before the pension scandal, San Diego's public services continued to face further cuts as the fiscal crisis narrowed the options available to close the budget deficit. And with the city's pension payments projected to increase, the gap between San Diego and other cities is likely to grow.

In addition to benchmarking San Diego to other California big cities, this chapter examines in depth the fate of three core city functions—public libraries, fire safety, and sewer infrastructure. These three critical public services have historically fallen under the purview of city government in California, and extensive archival records and existing independent analyses are available. Throughout, we supplement the archival research with interviews from key policy makers and other informed observers.

Bleak Fiscal Realities

The question is what do you short? You can short the pension, which I don't think is going to happen. You could short maintenance. You could short street paving or street sweeping. That's what the budgeting process is. None of it is going to be optimal.

—*City Council President Scott Peters, 2008*[2]

During the late 1990s, healthy increases in city revenues helped disguise a fundamental imbalance in San Diego's budget. The city's population and its fiscal needs were simply growing faster than the money available to pay for them. Indeed, accounting for population growth and inflation, the city's total budget in 2007 was no larger than it had been a decade earlier. Yet decisions made in the 1990s—including the construction of Petco Park and the expansion of the city's convention center— pledged many of the new dollars flowing into city coffers to pay off old debt, which left basic public services, including the maintenance of aging infrastructure, underfunded.

Despite claims that overspending lay at the roots of San Diego's budgetary crisis, an argument championed by conservative city leaders like Councilman Carl DeMaio and the editorial board of San Diego's leading newspaper, the city's public finances over the past four decades have been marked by fiscal austerity, not profligacy. San Diego's total public spending in the early 1970s, as seen in Figure 4.1, was not much different

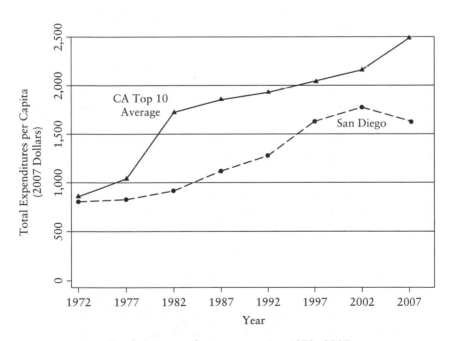

FIGURE 4.1   Total city expenditures per capita, 1972–2007

SOURCES: California State Controller, *Financial Transactions Concerning Cities of California* and *Cities Annual Report* (Sacramento: California State Controller, various years).

TABLE 4.1   Per capita expenditures by function, fiscal year 2007–08

Function	San Diego	Average among 10 largest CA cities
Police	$292.23	$371.27
Fire	$143.44	$168.42
Streets and roads	$85.89	$149.78
Planning	$0.73	$23.85
Sewers	$235.92	$99.02
Parks	$104.65	$96.12
Libraries	$38.73	$38.66

SOURCE: California State Controller, *Cities Annual Report*, Fiscal Year 2007–08 (Sacramento: California State Controller April 20, 2010).

from that of other major California cities.[3] Over the following thirty-five years, however, growth in San Diego's city budget sharply lagged behind its peers. By 2007, real per capita spending had grown more than three-fold among the largest California cities. In San Diego, by contrast, per capita budget outlays had barely doubled. Since the start of the new millennium, as growth in municipal spending accelerated across the state, San Diego expenditures actually contracted in real terms.

Table 4.1, which compares total expenditures by category of public services, depicts the consequences of decades of underfunding. Across many categories of essential services, San Diego's expenditures in 2008 stood markedly lower than spending in other major California cities. As we show here, the one anomaly—San Diego's apparently generous investment in sewer infrastructure—is itself the product of decades of previous underinvestment and has come about because of court mandates. Together, these figures suggest that excessive public spending was not the primary cause of San Diego's budgetary problems. More important, the numbers show how years of inadequate investment in basic city services left the city particularly vulnerable in the wake of cuts made necessary by the global financial crisis and the city's efforts to pay back ballooning retirement system obligations.

Riding the Gravy Train?

Have you heard about the fire captain in the city of San Diego who made $242,138 in one year? How about the city lifeguard who made $138,787? It's all true—and if you thought the city of San Diego's pensions were generous, wait until you see how much some city workers are being paid. . . . In the end, city workers are not the problem. They did not create the current gravy train, but will continue to ride it unless taxpayers demand real reforms. Old guard city politicians and powerful union bosses continue to claim that the pension benefits and salaries are appropriate, if not low. Their only solution is place more burden on San Diego taxpayers by hiking taxes and increase fees. On the other side of the battle stand the reformers led by Mayor Sanders who see that the real problem at City Hall is mismanagement and broken systems.

—*Future City Councilman Carl DeMaio, 2006*[4]

Public debates about San Diego's finances almost always focus on the compensation of city public employees. This is largely driven by simple math—four out of five dollars in the city budget are spent on personnel, a greater share than in other California cities.[5] This figure includes wages, health care, pension contributions, and other fringe benefits. Yet despite the attention attracted by the city's pension system, San Diego has commissioned little analysis to examine the largest share of its total personnel costs—the salaries and wages paid to city employees.[6]

Figure 4.2, which traces trends in San Diego city employment and payroll between 1992 and 2007, the period most closely associated with the ascendancy of organized labor in city politics, provides little evidence to support claims made by critics like Councilman Carl DeMaio. Historically, the city has employed fewer workers at lower wages than other big California cities, and the gap appears to have persisted in recent years. Moreover, after accounting for growth in overall personal income in California, the city's total payroll costs have only shrunk during the fifteen-year period. In 1992, San Diego's total annual payroll stood at slightly less than $61 million in 2007 dollars for every one hundred thousand residents, or 30 percent less than the average among large California cities. By 2007, its payroll expenditures had fallen to less than $55 million for every one hundred thousand residents, 25 percent below the big-city average.[7] Across nearly all city departments, San Diego has consistently hired fewer employees and spent less on their wage compensation than other large California cities.

The payroll statistics offer an important footnote to San Diego's pension controversy. Although various pension enhancements granted to workers as part of the city's two underfunding schemes allow employees to retire earlier and retain a larger share of their preretirement income,

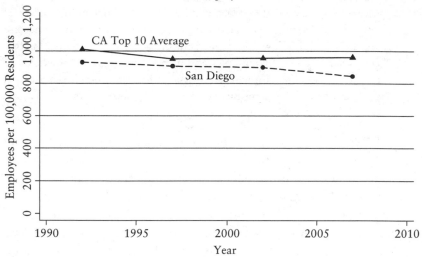

Panel A
Total Employees

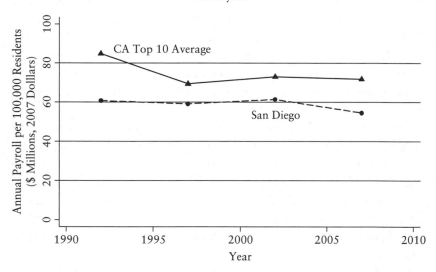

Panel B
Total Payroll

FIGURE 4.2   San Diego city payroll trends, 1992–2007

SOURCES: U.S. Census Bureau, *Government Employment and Payroll,* various years; California Franchise Tax Board, *Adjusted Gross Income Tables.*

the salaries on which the pensions are based appear to be lower in San Diego than in other major California cities. Indeed, San Diego labor leaders have long argued that the city granted pension benefit increases in exchange for concessions made by city employees that lowered the city's immediate wage costs, effectively deferring compensation—and thereby delaying the impact on the city budget—until years later, beyond the time horizons of the elected officials voting on the increases. Of course, labor leaders were willing partners in these bargains. With pension benefits protected by the state constitution, union heads had little reason to worry about the wisdom or financial impact of back loading the compensation of their members.

Paying the Piper

As I write this Letter, I keep recalling the apocryphal question put to Abraham Lincoln's widow, "So, other than that, how did you enjoy the play, Mrs. Lincoln?" Why? Because other than experiencing one of the worst investment years in history, SDCERS had a great FY 2009.

    —*San Diego Interim Pension Administrator*
    Mark A. Hovey, 2009[8]

Although earlier decisions to underfund the pension have contributed to San Diego's deteriorating financial solvency, sharp investment losses have made the challenge considerably more difficult. Plummeting San Diego City Employees' Retirement System (SDCERS) investment performance in 2001 and 2002 raised the specter of a massive lump-sum payment to stabilize the pension system, as required by the original pension deal negotiated by City Manager Jack McGrory in 1996. A second agreement reached in 2002 (City Manager's Proposal 2) allowed the city to avoid the immediate pain, but it did little to erase the large, and growing, pension liability.

Between 1998 and 2003, the city's annual pension contribution nearly doubled from $36 million to more than $70 million.[9] By contrast, city revenues grew by only 31 percent. During this period, the pension payment rose from about 5 percent of the city's General Fund—which is used to pay for basic city services like police, fire protection, libraries, parks, and street repairs—to more than 8 percent. By 2006, the pension payment had more than doubled yet again, to more than $180 million, with one out of every six dollars of the General Fund flowing into the city's pension system.

Aided by a temporary housing bubble and the bumper property tax increases it produced, new revenues helped relieve the growing budget crunch in the early years of Mayor Sanders's administration. When the bubble popped in late 2008, San Diego found itself in its worst financial position in decades. In the twelve-month period ending in June 2009, investment losses wiped out $1 billion—or one-fifth—of the pension system's assets. To offset these losses, the city's required pension payment jumped to more than $230 million in 2010, equal to nearly a fifth of the city's entire regular budget. At the same time, slowing economic activity depressed city revenues, creating a perfect storm that pinched the city budget from both sides. The city's pension payment continued to grow at precisely the moment the city could least afford it.

As illustrated in Figure 4.3, rising pension payments combined with shrinking revenues created a fiscal vise that has continued to squeeze

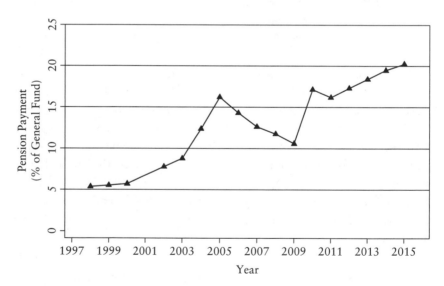

FIGURE 4.3   Pension payment as percentage of the general fund

SOURCES: City of San Diego, *Comprehensive Annual Financial Report,* various years; San Diego City Employees' Retirement System, *Comprehensive Annual Financial Report,* various years; City of San Diego, Office of the Mayor, "FY2012–2016 Five-Year Financial Outlook," February 1, 2011.

NOTES: For years before 2009, the General Fund portion of the pension payment is estimated as 80 percent of the total city contribution. These figures exclude the $90 million payment made from securitized tobacco settlement funds in 2006.

out basic services. In December 2009, the city council approved Mayor Jerry Sanders's plan to close a $180 million budget deficit projected over the following eighteen months through layoffs, further reductions in library hours, and rolling brownouts that shut down fire engines in some of the city's fire stations.[10] Yet within two months, unexpected increases in the city's required pension contribution and decreases in revenue projections opened a new $60 million shortfall in the budget.[11] Elected on a platform of fixing the city's financial mess in 2005 and having repeatedly forsworn tax increases, Sanders was still searching for a long-term solution to put San Diego's financial house in order five years later.

"A Budget with Smiley Faces Stamped on It"

Service levels must be maintained. I have heard from thousands of citizens with strong opinions on our budget priorities, and the consensus is that we cannot sustain further cuts in city services.

—*San Diego Mayor Jerry Sanders, 2009*[12]

As a mayoral candidate, Sanders vowed to take a tough line with employee groups and to use the threat of bankruptcy to extract concessions.[13] In office, however, the mayor found the job far more difficult than anticipated. Sanders's first budget included neither layoffs nor service cuts—two possibilities he said during the campaign that he would consider. Indeed, the budget represented an 8 percent increase in spending. The head of the city's pension reform committee described Sanders's spending blueprint as "a budget with smiley faces stamped on it."[14] A long-term plan released by the mayor at the end of his first year in office identified a budget shortfall totaling nearly $400 million over five years. However, it included few ideas for how to close the deficit.

In his second year, Sanders rolled out a bolder budget blueprint, envisioning the elimination of more than seven hundred city positions. However, because most of the targeted positions were vacant, and almost all other affected employees would be transferred to other open jobs, the plan avoided actual layoffs and thus a showdown with organized labor.[15] In addition, the mayor's budget envisioned increased investment in San Diego's festering but long-ignored needs. For example, the proposal called on the city to begin prefunding retiree health-care benefits and allocated funds to repair sewer and water pipes, begin work on overdue maintenance needs, and help the city comply with federal disability laws. For the most part, however, the plan identified little new revenue to pay for these initiatives, using onetime savings projected from refinancing the city's debt and onetime revenues from the sale of city-owned properties.

Testing the Strong Mayor

The Annual Budget is a contract between the City Council and the Mayor. The Mayor proposes the budget, the City Council approves spending policies, and then the Mayor executes those policies in good faith. Budget and policy changes should always be brought forward to the City Council. Currently, actions and proposals are often being communicated to the City Council at the last minute and without public discussion. Some are not being communicated at all. And, at times, public reports are not being made available, as was the case with the Mayor's recent budget changes.

— *Office of the San Diego Independent Budget Analyst, 2006*[16]

As the first chief executive elected under San Diego's new strong-mayor form of government, Sanders appeared, on paper, to possess much broader budgetary powers than had been available to his predecessors. The new city charter empowered the mayor to propose the first draft of the budget, allowing him to set the agenda in budget negotiations. Although the city council could make changes to the proposal, the mayor's new line-item veto authority empowered him to undo the changes and restore the funding levels in the mayoral plan, subject to a veto override. In practice, however, the strong-mayor form of government actually left the mayor with less control over the city's fiscal blueprint—because the same five-member majority of the city council required to adopt the budget was also sufficient to override the mayor's veto. Civic leaders who designed the strong-mayor proposal had originally supported a supermajority requirement for veto overrides but weakened the provision to gain city council support for the plan, which was necessary to place it on the ballot for voter approval.[17]

With little formal authority, Sanders moved to consolidate his control over the city bureaucracy by concentrating information in the mayor's office. Under a new policy unveiled in late 2006, Sanders forbade city employees from speaking to the press, allowing department heads to conduct interviews only when a member of the mayor's public relations staff was also present. Other directives required city officials to file reports detailing their conversations with the news media and city council members, and ordered all formal requests for public information to go through the office of the mayor.[18] At public meetings, city council members complained that key city reports would be turned over with too little time to read them before casting votes on important city policies. Some also complained of being "frozen out" after casting votes that conflicted with the mayor's preferred policies. "I think the day after the mayor came in, collaboration with the council went out the door," recalled the city's former Comptroller Greg Levin, a Sanders appointee.[19]

Although the conflict continued to grow as the Democrat-controlled city council confronted the Republican mayor over broad city policy, it came to a head over relatively minor budget changes. In October 2006, press reports revealed that Sanders's park director had ended an advanced swimming program at the city's pools. The program cost just $115,000 and affected a handful of constituents, but it had been expressly funded in a line-item included in the budget adopted by the council and signed by the mayor earlier in the year. Within days, council members learned that the mayor's staff had dramatically scaled down another program included in the budget, allowing homeless residents to be hired to clean up litter and graffiti. In neither case was the council alerted of the changes or asked to approve amendments to the city budget.[20]

Sanders argued that his authority as the chief executive gave him direct control over city departments, including the ability to use his discretion in implementing council policy. The cost of the swimming program had grown far more quickly than was estimated in the original budget, thus making it unsustainable, the mayor argued, and collective bargaining agreements gave city workers the right of first refusal to compete for all work, thus putting the homeless program contract in violation of the labor contract. City staff pointed out that similar minor changes had been made routinely under the previous city manager form of government, with little council participation or complaints.[21]

Indeed, there was little disagreement about the changes, which the council likely would have approved. The problem, argued the council's budget analyst, was not the substance of the policy changes but the process through which they were made.[22] For council members frustrated with the mayor's centralization of information, the unauthorized budget changes were the last straw. When Sanders failed to attend a council hearing called to examine the situation, council members interpreted this as yet another in a long series of slights. "I don't understand who the heck thinks they're running this place here, but the last time I checked the legislative body has a role in this operation, and it's darn time some people started figuring this out," an angry councilman, Jim Madaffer, complained at the hearing.[23] Leaving little room for compromise, Sanders continued to maintain that the mayor's executive authority gave him unilateral control over city departments, including the power to order midyear budget cuts. When the council moved to reverse the cuts, Sanders called the vote illegal and promised a veto.

The conflict between the branches escalated when the city council adopted a new policy requiring the mayor to receive council permission for any midyear cuts that reduced service levels in the city. Sanders, who considered the policy an unlawful limit on his mayoral powers and a violation of the city charter, promised to take the measure to the voters. In particular, the mayor worried that the new policy would sabotage his efforts to find budget savings by overhauling city departments and outsourcing city jobs, a key promise he made to voters when he ran for mayor. "I will ask the voters a relatively straightforward question: Which do you prefer, a mayor intent on implementing reforms and maximizing tax dollars, or a city government that fights reforms and is controlled by special interests?" Sanders said after the adoption of the new council policy.[24] Neither side appeared to leave much room for a compromise to avoid a costly election fight.

Behind the scenes, however, Sanders began working on a deal with Council President Scott Peters, a moderate Democrat with mayoral ambitions and an opponent of the new budget policy adopted by the council, to end the standoff. The eventual agreement brokered by Peters struck a middle ground between the mayor and council positions, thus allowing each side to claim victory. The agreement required council approval for any midyear cuts that reduced individual department budgets by more than 10 percent, or if total cuts amounted to at least 3 percent of the overall city budget. Although the mayor could make smaller cuts unilaterally, these would have to be publicized and reported to the council.[25]

Manufacturing Dissent

The relationship between the mayor and council is different from what it used to be. As mayor, you used to need to keep a meaningful relationship with all members of the council. It forced cooperation. The new structure gives incentives for the mayor to fight with the council. The mayor can close a public pool in a member's district if he or she does not cooperate.

—*Jerry Butkiewicz, former secretary-treasurer, San Diego and Imperial Counties Labor Council, 2008*[26]

In 1988, San Diego voters changed the city's electoral system from at-large to district elections. Before 1988, members of the council were nominated in districts but elected by voters citywide. The old system ensured that Republicans, an absolute majority of voters citywide, would retain control of the council, even as the city's minority population grew rapidly. In 1988, a federal court ruled that a system of at-large elections in Watsonville, California, illegally discriminated against Latinos. The implications of the decision for San Diego were clear. The Chicano Federation in San Diego had already sued the city to overturn at-large general elections. In November 1988, voters rendered the lawsuit moot.

Former City Manager Jack McGrory credits the change to district elections with eliminating a citywide focus among elected officials. Members of the council, McGrory and others argue, became more interested in policies and projects focusing on their respective districts.[27] Term limits, imposed by voters on local elected officials in 1990, have enhanced the parochial bent of the council. Members are not around long enough to master the nuances of the budget process or any complex policy.[28]

More dramatically, district elections are associated with the rise of organized labor in San Diego politics. By limiting electoral contests to small geographic subsets of the city, district elections help groups that can deliver boots on the ground. Organized labor helped get out the vote to pass ballot initiatives to expand the convention center and build a downtown ballpark for the San Diego Padres. Having mastered grassroots electioneering, union leaders set their sights on the city council and labor-friendly policy objectives. The ballpark project, discussed in Chapter 6, was the first public-private partnership to require a significant number of union jobs. Other private-sector construction projects requiring city approval were suddenly asked to make pro-worker concessions.

New pension benefits were granted to city workers, even as the city's fiscal position deteriorated. And with the election of Donna Frye in 2002, labor achieved a council majority controlled by Democrats.

Less appreciated is the effect that district elections have had in institutionalizing conflict within the City of San Diego. Prominent conflicts include those between Democrats and Republicans, the poor and working class against the wealthy, and between older and newer areas of the city. Such conflicts intensified with the adoption of Proposition F, the strong-mayor initiative, in November 2004. The reform awarded the mayor control over city personnel and the day-to-day management of the city, as well as responsibility for proposing the budget.

Conflict between the mayor and city council is rooted in what political scientist Bruce Cain has dubbed the "two constituencies" problem.[29] Under the city charter, the eight districts of the city council are apportioned according to population. Thus, each member of the city council represents a subset of the city's residents (i.e., those who live in the district). Table 4.2 describes the characteristics of these eight subpopulations in both 1990 and 2000. Figure 4.4 is a council district map adopted with the 2000 redistricting plan. The 2000 map was adopted by a local citizens' redistricting commission. This body of appointed citizens was created in 1992 to remove authority for drawing districts from members of the city council, several of whom were accused of politicizing the process that resulted in the 1990 plan.

The 2000 redistricting made only minor changes to the districts adopted in 1990. Thus, the eight district constituencies that form the basis of council representation have remained more or less the same for two decades. As Table 4.2 shows, the demographics of these districts vary widely. In 1990, five of eight districts had overwhelming white majorities. Another had a narrow white majority; one a plurality of black and Latino residents; and one, District 8, an overwhelming Latino majority. In 2000, whites maintained a majority in five of these six districts, although Latinos had increased their presence in Districts 3 and 4. Interdistrict differences in income have widened over time. They range from District 1, which includes La Jolla and boasts a median income of $71,000, to Districts 3 and 8, where median income was slightly more than $31,000 in 2000.

These differences are at the heart of many contentious policy debates. Although members of the city council represent subsets of local

TABLE 4.2 Demographic and political characteristics of San Diego city council districts, 1990 and 2000

| District 1990 | POPULATION | | | | HOUSING | | SOCIOECONOMIC STATUS | | PARTISANSHIP |
	Total	White (%)	Black (%)	Hispanic (%)	Single family (%)	Home value (median $)	Household income (median $)	Poverty (%)	Dem. pres. share[a] (%)
1	131,638	78	2	8	63	305,826	50,499	7	39.5
2	134,118	79	5	12	40	297,511	30,831	11	43.0
3	142,304	57	11	23	39	160,392	23,898	19	56.0
4	143,407	21	30	28	72	124,419	31,189	16	59.5
5	142,998	70	3	9	68	203,449	45,548	6	33.6
6	136,946	77	3	12	59	190,349	37,253	8	39.0
7	137,749	73	7	11	64	185,636	35,445	13	41.0
8	141,389	19	9	62	51	125,750	23,769	26	53.0
City	1,110,549	59	9	21	56	189,693	33,910	13	43.5
County	2,498,016	65	6	20	59	187,794	35,028	11	37.3

| District 2000 | POPULATION | | | | HOUSING | | SOCIOECONOMIC STATUS | | PARTISANSHIP | |
	Total	White (%)	Black (%)	Hispanic (%)	Single family (%)	Home value (median $)	Household income (median $)	Poverty (%)	Dem. pres. share[a] (%)	Dem. reg. 2010 (%)
1	157,301	70	1	7	61	369,073	71,307	8	47.8	34.4
2	148,501	77	3	13	41	385,443	42,615	12	52.4	37.5
3	156,827	41	11	35	39	192,857	31,334	24	68.2	53.5
4	153,888	12	25	36	76	143,516	40,254	17	66.6	56.3
5	159,524	59	3	8	72	255,177	69,352	5	43.1	30.2
6	149,307	62	4	17	57	212,129	46,027	12	49.1	37.3
7	146,853	60	8	18	64	223,783	45,973	16	49.2	40.9
8	151,199	14	8	69	54	160,972	31,901	25	65.8	51.0
City	1,223,400	49	8	25	56	230,076	45,825	15	52.9	41.2
County	2,813,833	55	6	27	60	223,363	47,268	13	45.7	35.9

SOURCES: Presidential Vote, San Diego County. Office of the Registrar, 1992 and 2000. Registration, City of San Diego, Office of the City Clerk, Current Registration Report. Population, housing and economic figures, San Diego Association of Governments, Census Profiles, 1990 and 2000.

[a]Percentages reflect the Democratic share of the presidential vote for the 1992 and 2000 general elections.

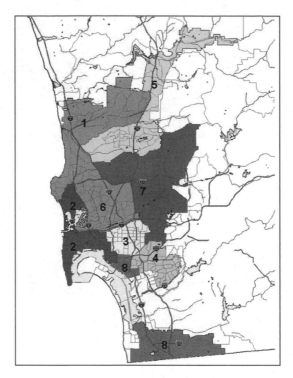

FIGURE 4.4   Map of San Diego city council districts, 2000
SOURCE: City of San Diego 2000 Redistricting Commission.

residents, the mayor represents voters. In 2000, whites comprised 49 percent of all residents. Only 15 percent of San Diegans fell below the poverty line. These figures understate the importance of affluent white voters in citywide elections. Because of differences in registration and turnout, whites constitute a much larger share of San Diego's voting population. Tables 4.3A and 4.3B show the votes by council district of successive mayoral elections from 2000 to 2005. The 2000 election pitted two Republicans, Dick Murphy and Ron Roberts, against each other. Murphy won a narrow victory, including a majority in five of eight districts.

The 2004 mayoral election began as a rematch between Murphy and Roberts. The late entry of write-in candidate Donna Frye, however,

TABLE 4.3A   2000 and 2004 mayoral election results

District	2000				2004				
	Reg. voters	Turnout (%)	Murphy (%)	Roberts (%)	Reg. voters	Turnout (%)	Murphy (%)	Roberts (%)	Other[a] (%)
1	96,628	76.5	55.1	44.9	106,009	73.6	35.9	35.0	29.1
2	87,746	65.1	54.8	45.2	109,336	66.5	30.2	28.4	41.4
3	75,823	62.8	43.1	56.9	79,994	65.4	25.3	25.1	49.7
4	62,474	58.1	40.9	59.1	64,084	59.4	43.1	30.4	26.5
5	97,054	73.3	53.4	46.6	91,072	73.8	38.9	36.7	24.5
6	86,076	71.3	54.8	45.2	88,335	71.5	29.5	27.9	42.7
7	79,485	69.3	57.7	42.3	81,214	68.5	37.4	30.5	32.1
8	47,316	53.2	40.3	59.7	52,155	58.3	42.1	32.9	25.0
Total	632,602	67.6	51.7	48.3	672,199	68.1	34.5	31.0	34.5

SOURCES: San Diego County, Office of the Registrar, various years.

[a]Nearly all votes for other candidates in 2004 were for write-in candidate Donna Frye.

TABLE 4.3 B 2005 special mayoral election results

	PRIMARY					RUNOFF			
District	Reg. voters	Turnout (%)	Frye (%)	Sanders (%)	Francis (%)	Reg. voters	Turnout (%)	Frye (%)	Sanders (%)
1	97,665	46.1	37.3	28.7	27.4	98,711	57.9	40.3	59.5
2	95,764	45.2	45.4	28.1	19.9	96,344	53.6	48.5	51.2
3	69,198	44.4	62.5	19.7	13.0	70,206	53.6	64.5	35.1
4	56,569	32.1	49.6	22.9	22.7	56,903	44.3	52.1	47.5
5	83,367	48.2	31.1	30.5	31.2	83,956	58.5	33.3	66.5
6	80,028	50.7	45.1	25.3	23.0	80,712	58.9	47.0	52.7
7	71,751	47.9	36.5	32.5	24.8	72,159	57.0	40.6	59.1
8	46,163	28.7	49.7	21.3	23.4	46,422	44.4	54.8	44.9
Total	600,505	44.2	43.1	27.0	23.5	605,413	54.5	46.1	53.6

SOURCES: San Diego County, Office of the Registrar, various years.

dramatically altered the pattern of voting. As we describe in Chapter 3, Murphy won a controversial victory after several thousand ballots with Frye's name on them were thrown out. But even with three candidates in the race, the disparities among the eight districts in their support for the leading candidates were greater than in 2000 (twenty-five versus seventeen points). The 2004 election was among the most divided in the city's history, a pattern that would continue in 2005.

The importance of affluent white voters to crafting a citywide coalition can be seen by examining the registration and turnout figures in Tables 4.3A and 4.3B. In 2004, for example, Districts 1, 2, and 5 had by far the most registered voters. These districts, which include San Diego's entire coastline between downtown and the northern boundary, contain the city's most affluent neighborhoods. District 5, currently represented by Carl DeMaio, is a rapidly growing district with much of the region's new suburban development. In 2004, Districts 1 and 2 had twice the number of voters as District 8, San Diego's poorest district and the only one with a Latino majority. Districts 3 and 4, which contain the oldest neighborhoods in the city and have the most minority residents, were second and third to last in terms of registered voters.

These differences in registration are magnified by differences in turnout. In addition to having more voters, Districts 1, 2, and 5 have more reliable voters. That is, registered voters in these districts are more likely to show up on Election Day. In the 2004 election, 74 percent of District 1 and District 5 voters and 66 percent of District 2 voters turned out to vote. Turnout in Districts 3, 4, and 8 was 65 percent, 59 percent, and 58 percent, respectively. In low-turnout elections, like the 2005 special mayoral election, the differences are further magnified.[30] The turnout gap between Districts 5 and 8, for example, was nearly 20 percent. In this election, Frye won a plurality in all eight council districts in the July 2005 primary. But low turnout in San Diego's most Democratic districts kept her from reaching the 50 percent threshold. In the November runoff, large victories in vote-rich Districts 1 and 5 propelled Sanders into office.

The voting patterns in the past few elections point to the dominant strategy for winning citywide races. The key is to rack up victories in the vote-rich affluent areas of Districts 1, 2, and 5. The interests of San Diego's racial minorities and the concerns of its older, deteriorating neighborhoods can be safely ignored because voters in these areas make up too small a share of the citywide electorate. This, combined with the weak state of the local Democratic Party, explains why in a city that gave a majority of its votes to Al Gore in 2000 and an overwhelming victory to Barack Obama in 2008, the Democratic Party failed to field a viable candidate in the 2000 and 2008 citywide mayoral contests.

The political calculus for winning elections to and control of the city council is quite different. Here, the voices of District 8's fifty-two thousand voters count just as much as those of District 5's ninety-one thousand voters. Thus, in 2004, Republicans won 65 percent of the city-wide vote, but Republicans and Democrats split the four council seats. In 2008, Mayor Jerry Sanders won reelection with 54 percent of the vote. That same year, Democrats won three of the four council races, with only DeMaio winning for Republicans in District 5. Democrats have scored important victories in council races by promising voters better public services and by using the superior get-out-the-vote infrastructure of local labor organizations. By contrast, Republicans have dominated citywide races by promising affluent voters that they would close the budget deficit primarily through cuts, thus putting the two branches on a collision course.

Slow Decline: San Diego's Public Libraries

The financial support for libraries can best be described as one of "chronic underfunding."

> —*Zero-based management review of San Diego Public Library, 1998*[31]

With the city council opposed to most significant budget cuts—especially reduction in district-based neighborhood services—Sanders pursued a strategy of finding new savings through workforce attrition. As city workers retired or moved on, their positions would remain un-filled. For many already-underfunded city functions, like San Diego's public library system, the cuts accelerated the steady erosion of service levels. Already under financial strain during the boom years of the late 1990s, the library system's budget continued to shrink as San Diego tackled growing budget deficits, even as the overall size of the library system continued to grow.

Just as the adoption of district elections fundamentally transformed the nature of budgetary politics in San Diego in the early 1990s, the electoral reforms also shifted the locus of policy making on the city council. With their electoral fortunes now tied to the satisfaction of small segments of the city, elected officials redoubled their efforts to improve the quality of district services. Between 1980 and 2000, the city committed hundreds of millions of dollars to capital improvements for San Diego's public library system primarily by expanding its network of branch libraries. During this period, the city opened four new library locations, bringing the total number of branches to thirty-three. In addition, the city rebuilt sixteen other facilities, tripling the size of each.[32]

Yet during much of the 1990s, budget outlays for library system operations actually declined, when accounting for population growth and inflation. Although each library branch remained open for roughly fifty hours each week even as new locations came online, staffing did not keep pace. With fewer than nine librarians for every hundred thousand residents, San Diego lagged well behind other major California cities. In addition, to cover the increased cost of operating new branches, the city continued to shift resources away from the library system's downtown central branch. Between 1977 and 1997, staffing at the central library declined by 20 percent even as the city's population grew by nearly 40 percent.[33]

In 1998, the city commissioned private consultants and local volunteers to review the operations of the library system. The consultants warned that years of "chronic underfunding" had begun to take its toll. Simply to provide basic services, the library budget would need to be increased immediately by 25 percent, their report concluded. They also warned that the problem would continue to grow worse, as the opening of new branches would force the already-underfunded library budget to be divided into ever smaller slices.[34]

The report served as a wake-up call for San Diego library enthusiasts, represented by a group known as the Friends of the San Diego Public Library, which mobilized to qualify an initiative to amend the city charter and guarantee higher funding for the library system. When the group failed to collect the necessary signatures, it appealed directly to the city council, asking it to place a charter amendment on the November 2000 ballot. Although the council refused, elected officials did adopt an ordinance setting new requirements for library operations. The policy included minimum staffing and operating standards at city libraries, requiring branches to remain open for at least forty-eight hours each week. However, the ordinance did not address the critical question of funding, thus leaving the annual library allocation to the discretion of the city council.[35]

Robbing Peter's Branch to Pay for Paul's

The overall library's operating expenditures are not able to satisfy its most pressing needs. This shortfall will get worse, as more branch libraries are constructed for an increasingly diverse population.

—*Zero-based management review of San Diego Public Library, 1998*[36]

In 2000, the council made good on its commitment, adopting a second ordinance requiring allocations for the library system to rise until they totaled 6 percent of the city's day-to-day budget. In practice, however, the new ordinance did little to alleviate the problem of chronic underfunding. First, a library blueprint brokered by Mayor Dick Murphy and Councilman Jim Madaffer two years later committed most of the new funds to pay for continued expansion of the library system rather than enhancing service levels at existing branches. Under the Murphy-Madaffer plan, discussed at greater length in Chapter 5, increased library allocations would be diverted to a separate fund that would be used to pay for building and operating a new central library and additional branch locations. Over the following decade, the plan committed the city to building twelve new branch libraries and upgrading nine others. With most new revenues earmarked for future libraries, increasing the city's library allocation did little to close the funding gap for existing branches.[37]

However, even the Murphy-Madaffer plan would prove optimistic, because the city council never actually appropriated the funds to meet its funding commitment under the 2000 ordinance. Instead of rising, as the council expected in 2000, the portion of the city budget dedicated to the library system actually declined during the mid- and late 2000s. By

2009, only $1 million had been deposited in the dedicated fund for new branches; under Sanders's 2009 midyear budget cut proposal, the $1 million was diverted back to the city's day-to-day budget, and the expansion fund was eliminated.[38]

Although the city did little to increase library funding to close the shortfalls identified in 1998, much less to pay the cost of operating the newly opened branch libraries, actual expansion of the library system continued apace. In 2005, the number of library branches grew to thirty-five, with additional branches under construction, even as funding continued to shrink. Rather than providing additional money to fully fund the expansion, Sanders continued to cut library hours at existing branches to close the growing city budget deficit. By 2008, the city employed fewer librarians than it had in 2000—when the library system had two fewer library branches—and the total number of library employees had fallen 20 percent below its 2003 peak. As Figure 4.5 shows, across the city, hours at existing branches also declined 20 percent, with the average library open for only forty hours each week by 2008.

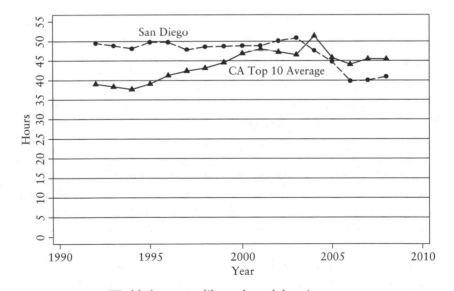

FIGURE 4.5   Weekly hours per library branch location

SOURCES: Institute of Museum and Library Services and the National Center for Education Statistics, *Annual Public Library Survey,* various years.

Despite documenting a history of chronic underfunding, the 1998 consultants' report noted that San Diego still maintained longer library hours than other major cities. A decade later, this was no longer true. Rather than reversing course, efforts to close the city's chronic budget deficit have only accelerated the deterioration of the city's public library system. To pay the cost of operating new branches built under the Murphy-Madaffer plan, even as it cut the overall size of the library budget, the city continued to divert resources from existing branches. To fill the gap, the city encouraged private fund-raising to support local branches. In some parts of the city, like the wealthy area of La Jolla, private donors stepped up to provide significant resources, allowing the La Jolla library to remain open on Sundays. In poorer areas, however, philanthropy did not succeed in protecting local branches from further cuts. Between 1998 and 2008, the city's practice of systematically underfunding the library system only accelerated, contributing to a growing divide in public services between San Diego's haves and have-nots.

Stasis in the Wake of the Most Destructive Fire in California History

The Cedar Fire validated that the [San Diego Fire-Rescue Department] is underfunded, under-staffed and inadequately trained to respond effectively to complex incidents for extended operational periods. SDFD senior management has historically documented that continued budget reductions, deferred apparatus purchases and maintenance, and lack of staffing to keep up with community growth would have serious implications for its ability to respond to emergencies.
    —Cedar Fire 2003 after Action Report, 2004[39]

In late October 2003, raging wildfires fueled by Southern California's powerful Santa Ana winds crossed into San Diego across the city's eastern border. During the next week, the fires burned twenty-eight thousand acres within the city limits and destroyed more than three hundred homes in the worst firestorm (up to that point) in state history. As they set out to battle the flames, San Diego's firefighters quickly confronted a logistical nightmare. Just four days before the start of the fires, the lease on the city's—and the region's—only fire helicopter lapsed, leaving the department with no aerial support. As off-duty firefighters returned to their posts, the department quickly ran out of spare fire engines, forcing many firefighters to travel to the front lines in buses. Of the available reserve apparatuses, many had been stripped of key equipment to outfit the city's regular fleet of vehicles; one of the reserve engines had recently been sold to a city in Mexico. Within days of the start of the fires, the department also ran out of batteries to power its wireless communications equipment—consisting of three incompatible radio systems, each requiring different chargers that many fire rigs simply lacked—leaving some firefighters unable to communicate with their superiors and with one another.[40]

Although a disaster of the magnitude of the 2003 Cedar Fire would likely have overwhelmed any fire department, there is little doubt that San Diego's history of systemic underfunding left the city woefully ill prepared. Just three months before the conflagration, the city's fire chief, Jeff Bowman, and the president of its firefighters' union, Ron Saathoff, met with Mayor Murphy and made a private appeal to increase funding for the department. Years of inadequate budgets had left the department significantly understaffed, and more recent budget cuts had largely brought to an end its program for replacing aging equipment. Indeed, when the fires broke out, nearly half of San Diego's 250 emergency fire-fighting vehicles had exceeded their useful life; one rig was more than forty years old. Bowman warned that, without additional funds, the department would run out of money for basic supplies less than halfway through the fiscal year. Murphy listened patiently but made no commitment to find additional resources.[41]

Uncharred Territory

The City has been unable to keep pace with the growth of San Diego in terms of infrastructure, capital improvements projects, staffing and other critical resources on a citywide basis. The continued erosion of critical needs has resulted in a reduction of service levels that has also affected the Fire-Rescue Department.

—*Commission on Fire Accreditation International, 2005*[42]

Aging, inadequate fire-fighting equipment, the primary problem identified in various post-wildfire reports and analyses, represented just one of several serious deficiencies in San Diego's public safety system. In addition, the city has faced a significant shortage of basic public safety infrastructure, including fire and police stations in its fastest-growing neighborhoods, and a severe lack of firefighters and police officers needed to staff them.

In the wake of California's Proposition 13, San Diego ended its policy of using regular city dollars to construct new public safety facilities. Instead, in the early 1980s, the city council turned to developer fees and special assessments to pay for the construction of basic infrastructure needed to support continued population growth. However, funds raised through these methods proved insufficient to fund both land acquisition and construction costs for new fire stations. In addition, in some cases, the city agreed to exempt developers from the fees if planned housing included fire sprinklers—even though medical emergencies, rather than fires, represented the vast majority of the dispatches involving San Diego firefighters. Older parts of the city, which continued to see significant in-fill development but were not included in the development impact fee and special assessment financing programs, received no new money to pay for continued infrastructure development and expansion.[43]

During the 1980s and 1990s, brisk population growth and the city's 1970s growth blueprint pushed new residents toward the outer perimeters of the city—areas closest to undeveloped brushlands and, thus, facing the highest fire dangers. Unfortunately, construction of new public safety infrastructure did not keep pace. Many of the fire stations planned for the 1980s were not completed until two decades later. In some cases, the planned stations were simply never built, putting additional strain on San Diego's limited existing fire-fighting capacity. Indeed, an external audit commissioned in 2005 found that the coverage areas for nearly one-third of the city's fire stations exceeded nine square miles, a critical threshold needed to ensure timely response. Although national standards called on the department to respond to calls within five minutes 90 percent of the time, the audit found that San Diego's firefighters were responding in fewer than six minutes less than 70 percent of the time. Fire stations in San Diego's newest areas in the northern and eastern parts of the city—those facing the most serious fire risks—were farther apart, covered more territory, and responded more slowly than did older stations.[44]

Although developer fees provided at least partial funding for the construction of new facilities, the city's day-to-day budget remained responsible for funding their annual operating costs. And elected officials showed little interest in providing the necessary funds to hire new firefighters. Between 1990 and 2006, San Diego's population grew by two hundred thousand people and the city added sixty thousand homes. Yet the department's ranks of firefighters increased by just eighty-four. In comparison with other major cities in the country, outside auditors ranked San Diego dead last in its ratio of firefighters to citizens in 2005. Even among other cash-strapped California cities, San Diego has consistently maintained a smaller fire-fighting force than similar jurisdictions.[45]

To provide essential public safety services to a growing city without a sufficient number of firefighters, city officials pursued two related strategies. First, in the late 1990s, the city began a practice known alternatively as adaptive staffing or cross-staffing—which can best be described simply as understaffing. For stations equipped with both a fire engine (holding water and hoses) and a fire truck (carrying tall ladders), the department no longer assigned eight firefighters who could operate both apparatuses simultaneously. Instead, cross-staffed stations, since the late 1990s, have been manned by just four firefighters, who need to alternate between the engine and the truck depending on the nature of the emergency call to which they are dispatched. Second, the city greatly expanded its use of overtime—sometimes mandatory—to backfill vacant positions. Because only employees' base salaries are used to calculate pension benefits, extending working hours for existing firefighters has provided the city with significant cost savings compared to filling empty positions with new hires.[46]

One Step Forward, Two Steps Back

When you have one of the biggest disasters in state history, and it doesn't change the mindset of this community, nothing will. . . . Even if I stayed, nothing would change. I don't think the money will show up for years.

—*Fire Chief Jeff Bowman, 2006*[47]

In the immediate wake of the 2003 wildfire, the prospect of another major disaster appeared to focus the minds of the city's officials. Within months, the city council commissioned an analysis of the unfunded needs of San Diego's public safety departments, which concluded that the fire and police departments would require more than $300 million in additional appropriations over the following five years. Without additional revenues, staff emphasized, the city would make little progress in closing the gap.[48]

However, the call for higher taxes would bring to an end the short-lived consensus about the need to improve fire-preparedness and public safety. With the business community and elected officials divided, San Diego voters rejected two proposals to increase the city's hotel taxes in 2004 to increase funding to the police and fire departments. Mayor Murphy opposed both proposals. In addition, raises for firefighters largely consumed the few additional dollars that found their way into the fire department budget, although the city made halting progress to replace its aging apparatuses and equipment.[49]

Bowman's call to build twenty-two new fire stations to reduce response time and his proposal to increase the number of firefighters by 50 percent was largely ignored. City Council President Scott Peters, who accused the fire chief of "staffing for Easter," called the plans financially infeasible and politically impractical. Even the conclusion by outside auditors that the fire department lacked sufficient staffing and infrastructure to receive national accreditation did little to prompt further city action. As a frustrated Bowman announced his retirement in 2006, the *San Diego Union-Tribune* editorial board noted that "San Diego plainly did not, does not and will not soon have the money to fund the fire department Bowman envisioned."[50]

Although a fire-station master plan completed by his handpicked successor, Tracy Jarman, in 2009 largely echoed Bowman's call to build and operate nearly two dozen new fire stations, at a price tag of $200 million and an increase in annual operating costs of $75 million, the city's deteriorating budget and its growing pension payment have made the plan a long-term aspiration rather than a short-term goal. Indeed, rather than expanding, the size of San Diego's fire department has continued to shrink since Bowman's retirement. Grappling with a large midyear budget deficit in late 2009, the city council adopted Mayor Jerry Sanders's plan to "brown out" fire stations by temporarily reducing staff at stations across the city on a rolling basis to save $11.5 million.[51]

In the summer of 2010, the preventable death of a two-year-old boy made the dangers of the brownouts all the more apparent. With the closest fire engine off duty under the brownout policy, it took emergency personnel more than nine minutes to reach the boy's Mira Mesa home after his parents called paramedics when he began choking on a gum ball. Arriving more than four minutes after the city's five-minute response-time goal, the paramedics were too late to save the little boy's life. Although initial news of the death provided new political impetus to end the brownouts, the city council found no money to bring the off-duty fire engines back online. Indeed, the mayor warned that continued budget deficits would likely force the city to begin layoffs at the city's fire department— which, by 2010, already had fewer firefighters than in the months before the 2003 wildfires.[52]

Sui Generis on Sewers

The city has proved that the minimum that they must do is the maximum that they've ever done. That's the sad fact.

—U.S. District Judge Rudi M. Brewster, 1991[53]

Until the 1940s, San Diego disposed of raw sewage by dumping it untreated into San Diego Bay and the Pacific Ocean. In 1943, the city constructed a treatment plant in Barrio Logan south of downtown after the navy complained that the bay's contaminated waters were corroding vessels and making sailors sick. The city's growing population, however, quickly overwhelmed the facility. In 1963, the city opened a new wastewater facility on the cliffs of Point Loma. Using several massive tanks and a grit screen, the Point Loma Wastewater Treatment Plant was designed to remove 60 percent of dissolved particles found in sewage before discharging the effluent two and a half miles offshore.[54]

The Point Loma facility became the backbone of the region's wastewater system. With the ability to handle 240 million gallons of wastewater per day, the facility made capacity a nonissue. Unfortunately, the technology used to treat San Diego's raw sewage quickly became outmoded. In 1972, Congress passed the Clean Water Act to clean up the nation's polluted waterways. The act required cities to implement a "secondary sewage treatment" process that used microorganisms to remove 85 percent of the dangerous particles contained in raw sewage. It also limited how much of those substances can be discharged from wastewater facilities.[55]

Point Loma, designed for primary treatment, did not meet the new requirements. It also did not meet the less stringent standards of the California Ocean Plan, adopted in 1972 and amended several times since. Improvements at the facility ultimately increased the removal rate of dissolved particles to 75 percent. This satisfied state requirements, but discharges were still much greater than federal limits. In response, San Diego joined with other cities in seeking modification of the Clean Water Act to exempt ocean dischargers. In 1977, Congress added a section to the Clean Water Act that allowed the Environmental Protection Agency (EPA) to grant five-year waivers.

The EPA tentatively approved a waiver for San Diego in 1981. In 1986, the EPA denied a revised version of the city's application, citing potential noncompliance with new California regulations and evidence of changes to the ocean floor around the area of the Point Loma discharge. In February of that year, the city council voted to shelve its waiver application and to begin implementing secondary treatment. These decisions, however, came late in the game. The deadline for compliance was July 1, 1988. With no waiver and no plan for secondary treatment, the city was out of compliance with federal law.

The EPA sued the city, joined later by the Sierra Club. In 1989, the city hired consultants to develop a plan to upgrade Point Loma and build new treatment plants. The plan's $2.5 billion price tag, however, attracted political opposition. Federal grants were available to offset some costs, but the bulk would fall on local ratepayers. Leading the charge against secondary treatment were Bruce Henderson and Bob Filner, two city councilmen from opposite sides of the political spectrum. They argued that upgrading Point Loma would result in rate hikes for repairs that would have little impact on marine life. The council rejected these pleas, voting six to three to spend the $2.5 billion.[56]

Having opted for secondary treatment, the city began settlement negotiations with the EPA. The city and the EPA ultimately agreed on an accord that required the city to begin a massive program to upgrade its wastewater facilities, including construction of six new tertiary treatment plants, distribution of reclaimed water from these plants, upgrades at Point Loma, and a new international secondary treatment plant at the Mexican border. The city agreed to comply with all federal regulations by 2003.

As the federal district court Judge Rudi M. Brewster prepared to begin hearings on the accord, Henderson and Filner were pushing the city council to revisit its 1989 decision. In August 1990, Henderson filed a motion seeking to overturn the agreement between the city and the EPA. By September, Henderson had prevailed with the city council. The city attorney began preparing a legal defense designed to convince Judge Brewster that the Clean Water Act was needlessly restrictive for San Diego. In October, the city council voted to revive its waiver application. The ability to claim credit for protecting ratepayers from federal interference, even if success was unlikely, was irresistible.[57]

Secondary treatment at Point Loma was not the only issue facing San Diego's wastewater system. In 1990, the EPA released its list of polluted waterways. The list included Mission Bay, San Diego Bay, and twelve miles of ocean along the city's shoreline. Some listings stemmed from raw sewage released from Tijuana. Also at fault were the city's dilapidated sewer lines; lackluster maintenance was responsible for numerous spills. In February 1992, the city's chronic neglect was revisited on local residents as another broken pipe caused a massive sewage spill at Point Loma. Several hundred million gallons of raw sewage floated to the surface less than a mile offshore, forcing Governor Pete Wilson to declare a state of emergency in America's Finest City.[58]

In March 1991, Judge Brewster began handing down decisions that would shape San Diego's wastewater system for decades to come. His first act was to fine the city $3 million for more than twenty thousand violations of the Clean Water Act, including its "outrageous record" of sewage spills. In June, Brewster opted to defer acceptance of a settlement between the city and the EPA until January 1993, citing the accord's weak water reclamation requirements. In a victory for Henderson, the judge ordered the city to conduct a pilot test of an alternative chemical treatment process at Point Loma. The city was also directed to extend the facility's 2.2-mile outfall pipe to a distance of 4.5 miles.[59]

Judge Brewster's qualms about the political will of San Diego officials proved prophetic. By May 1992, members of the city council were openly balking at the price tag for six new water reclamation facilities the city had agreed to build. The facilities had not been at issue in Henderson's original motion, but the estimated doubling of the city's $19.24 monthly sewer rate for single-family homes suddenly was. Quietly, city staff was instructed to cut the costs of the project, including postponing water reclamation, eliminating three of the six plants, and forgoing the Point Loma overhaul. The council approved a scaled-down version of its original accord in 1992.[60]

In 1994, the city's hopes to avoid a multibillion-dollar Point Loma upgrade received a boost when Judge Brewster refused to order the city to upgrade to secondary treatment. He instead gave local officials until 1995 to convince Congress to grant San Diego an exemption. The EPA Administrator Carol Browner agreed to work with local officials to resolve the city's now decades-long dilemma. With the EPA on board, Congress passed the Ocean Pollution Reduction Act (OPRA) allowing San Diego to file for a waiver from the Clean Water Act's regulations. In exchange, local officials agreed to build water reclamation plants to handle at least 45 million gallons per day by 2010 and to reduce the volume of solids discharged into the ocean over the waiver's five-year life.[61]

In April 1995, the city submitted its waiver application.[62] In June, the EPA tentatively granted San Diego's request, calling the treatment process used at Point Loma adequate. In September 1996, the city and EPA finally settled their eight-year legal battle. The agreement required the city to make $88 million worth of improvements to local sewer lines and pump stations, in addition to $1.8 billion in previously approved projects. The agreement put off a final decision about secondary treatment at Point Loma. However, even without an upgrade, the mandated projects raised wastewater spending in San Diego well beyond that of other California big cities.[63]

Sewer Crazy After All These Years

Water and sewer rates need to go up. We got an $800 million water bond passed six to three, with Mayor Susan Golding voting no. Every time we put together a bond package or proposed to raise the sewer rates, the council would go nuts.

—*Former City Manager Jack McGrory, 2007*[64]

In early 2000, as the five-year reprieve granted by the EPA was nearing its end, San Diego officials faced a dilemma. During the waiver period, the city made no plans to upgrade Point Loma. Like their predecessors, the current crop of elected officials were counting on a second waiver to save them from raising sewer rates to pay for wastewater infrastructure. Unfortunately, OPRA imposed more stringent requirements on San Diego, requiring the removal of more pollutants from the discharged wastewater. The city also agreed to reduce the volume of solids discharged into the ocean. Over the five-year period, the Point Loma facility performed admirably in meeting the goals.

The San Diego region, however, was growing. The Point Loma facility, already handling approximately 190 million gallons of sewage per day generated by 2 million people and fifteen public agencies, would be unable to reduce total volume indefinitely. In December 1999, Mayor Susan Golding wrote the EPA, urging the agency to let the city out of OPRA's more stringent requirements when its waiver came up for renewal. The EPA, however, believed that the requirements were minimal conditions for renewing the five-year waiver. Supporting the EPA's position were local environmental groups, including the Sierra Club, which had backed the city in 1995. In March 2000, the city sued the EPA.

Fortunately for local officials, change had arrived in Washington. With Bush administration appointees in charge of EPA enforcement, the agency's stance softened considerably. In 2002, the city and EPA agreed to support a second waiver and raise the allowable volume of discharges. The decision pleased new Mayor Dick Murphy: "Approval of the waiver will allow the city to fix its antiquated sewer pipe system, which is a far greater threat to local beaches than bacteria-laden sewer effluent that is diluted by the ocean and doesn't return to the shore."[65] Murphy's assessment of the sewer-pipe system was accurate. In March 2000, as local officials were launching their legal assault on the EPA, state agencies were investigating a weeklong spill from an aging sewer main in Mission Valley that dumped 36 million gallons of raw sewage into the local ecosystem. More than one thousand miles of sewer pipe were past life expectancy. Since the 1996 settlement with the EPA, the city had averaged close to 350 spills per year and was leading the nation in beach and bay advisories. The city was fighting lawsuits filed by San Diego Baykeeper and the Surfrider Foundation over its chronic sewage spills.[66]

Facing mounting fiscal problems and a stalled ballpark project, Murphy had no time to waste on protracted legal battles with environmentalists. The city negotiated an agreement with a coalition of local environmental groups. The coalition agreed to drop its opposition to San Diego's waiver application before the EPA review board. In exchange, the city agreed to work with the Scripps Institution of Oceanography on an independent public review of its ocean monitoring program. The city also agreed to conduct a comprehensive study of potential uses for reclaimed water. Finally, the agreement provided for a pilot test of a new filtration method at Point Loma. If successful, the method could serve as a cost-effective means of upgrading the facility to comply with the Clean Water Act.

The novel agreement, a sign of strength from the local environmental movement, set the agenda on wastewater issues for the following several years. The city honored its end, completing a review of its monitoring program. The water reuse study was completed in 2006, after extensive public outreach and consultation, at a cost of $1 million. Some of its recommendations were far reaching, including expanding the city's recycling program by placing treated water back into the city's reservoirs to augment drinking supplies. The pilot test of the new treatment method at Point Loma found it to be a viable alternative for implementing secondary treatment. The cost of implementing the filtration method, however, is projected to be between $700 million and $1 billion.[67]

Wastewater Redux: Right Back Where We Started

The City's infrastructure is falling into disrepair. The City's water system, wastewater system, streets and storm drains all need critical upgrades to continue to provide reliable service to the citizens of San Diego.
— *Office of the City Attorney, Interim Report No. 13, 2007*[68]

Since taking office in late 2005, Mayor Jerry Sanders has continued the city's reluctant strategy regarding wastewater issues. Sanders accepted the water reuse study but distanced himself from its recommendations. The city's original settlement with the EPA required it to build water reclamation facilities capable of generating 45 million gallons of reclaimed water per day. The city built two facilities, North City and South Bay, but use of reclaimed water has been limited to 8 million gallons per day for irrigation and commercial purposes. The rest of the treated water is dumped into the Pacific Ocean. Local officials have admitted that the city will be unable to meet its legal obligation to use 50 percent of reclaimed water generated at North City. In November 2007, Sanders vetoed a one-year pilot program to supplement the city's supplies with purified water from the city's reclamation plants. The council overrode the veto, but the program, which critics have derided as "toilet-to-tap," was delayed until 2009.[69]

In 2007, Sanders opted to seek a third waiver from the EPA that would continue to exempt Point Loma from secondary treatment requirements. As in 2000, the city failed to convince environmentalists, setting up another costly legal showdown. Facing a deep fiscal crisis and having already raised sewer rates to comply with court-ordered upgrades of its aging pipes, the city had no money for a retrofit. In December 2008, the EPA granted preliminary approval of the city's application but warned local officials that they should not plan on receiving more exemptions. The EPA officials also urged the city to expand its water recycling program. In January 2009, Sanders cut a deal with local environmental groups to avoid costly litigation over the city's waiver application. The groups dropped their opposition to the waiver in exchange for a new study to identify ways for the city to use more recycled water.[70]

In 2007, the city approved a plan to raise sewer and water rates. These increases were necessary to comply with legal settlements to lawsuits stemming from the city's wastewater rate structure and its chronic sewage spills. Before 2004, the city overcharged residents living in single-family residences for sewer services while subsidizing commercial and industrial users. Some of the money raised for wastewater projects was diverted to other uses, a violation of the state constitution. In 2004, the city settled claims related to past sewage spills, paying $1.2 million in damages, and agreeing to upgrade existing pump stations and replace thirty miles of sewer lines.[71]

Under the 2007 consent decree, the city is scheduled to spend $632 million to upgrade sewer infrastructure by 2013, including replacement of 450 miles of aged sewer pipes, upgrades to more than twenty pump stations, and continued implementation of an aggressive inspection and maintenance program. This amount is on top of another $611 million in water capital improvement projects mandated by a California Department of Health order to replace aging pipes and improve treated water storage. Early compliance with the terms of the consent decree has

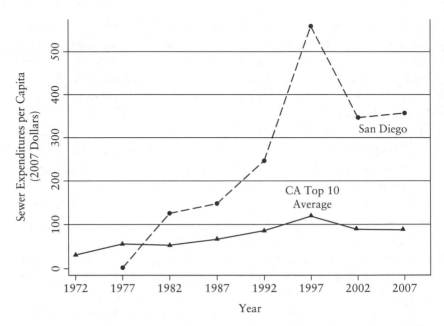

FIGURE 4.6   Per capita spending on sewers in California's ten largest cities
SOURCES: California State Controller, *Financial Transactions Concerning Cities of California* and *Cities Annual Report*, various years.

resulted in a dramatic decrease in sewer spills, from 365 and 238 spills in 2000 and 2001 to 77 and 62 spills in 2007 and 2008.[72] As Figure 4.6 shows, as a result of the federal consent decree and state mandates, San Diego in 2007 was forced to spend more than three times per capita on sewer infrastructure than other big California cities.

Going forward, the city faces powerful obstacles to upgrading its wastewater system to meet its legal obligations, let alone federal standards. First, San Diego's 1.3 million residents are spread over a 324-square-mile area, which gives the city the lowest population density of California's ten largest cities. To serve its dispersed population, the city has to maintain more than 3,000 miles of sewer pipeline—more than twice the 1,437 miles maintained by Los Angeles for a population of 3.8 million residents. Second, the city's poor bond ratings mean higher borrowing costs to finance needed projects. Third, the city is once again on a five-year lifeline with respect to Point Loma. Facing severe budget deficits, San Diego can ill afford the $700 million to $1 billion upgrade.[73] Finally, given the city's straitened circumstances, mandated sewer outlays, paid for with higher sewer fees, encourage elected officials and residents to defer badly needed maintenance on other aging and deteriorating but essential infrastructure such as streets and roads.

The Tipping Point

Our approach has been to cut broadly across the spectrum, to reduce programs, not end programs. But we really fell on our face in demonstrating accountability and evaluating the effects of service cuts. My sense of it has been—and you have to understand that a lot of this is gut feeling just having a finger on the pulse of the financials of the city—we gradually cut so broadly so that we've reached a tipping point where the services are no longer effective, that they're spread broadly without enough administrative support to effectively manage the programs.

—*Former San Diego City Comptroller Greg Levin, 2009*[74]

Since at least the late 1970s, the City of San Diego has provided its constituents with significantly fewer public services than other major cities in California (see Figure 4.1). Over the course of the past decade, that gap has widened, as the city has struggled to balance its budget while funding new obligations, including the repayment of its pension debt and federally mandated efforts to upgrade its wastewater infrastructure. Table 4.4 shows the decline in selected San Diego public service levels, from 2001 to 2010. The 2008 recession, which reduced city revenues even as investment losses further exacerbated the unfunded liability in public pensions, has made balancing the city budget while preserving core public services ever more difficult.

San Diego's new governance structure, which created two coequal branches of government with fundamentally different constituencies and priorities, has also created new barriers to finding a permanent solution to the city's structural deficit. With the city council unwilling to accept deep cuts to existing services, and the mayor unwilling to support new revenues, a default policy of passive and not-so-benign neglect, marked by gradual savings through attrition of city employees, has only contributed to the continued deterioration of all service levels and the quality of San Diego's public infrastructure. "We're doing all of the same stuff,

TABLE 4.4   Selected San Diego public service levels, fiscal year 2001 versus fiscal year 2010

Activity	FY2001	FY2010
Number of customer service centers	15	0
Number of aquatic programs users	712,000	255,380
Number of youth program after-school sites	37	15
Average number of weekly recreation center hours	62.3	40.3
Average number of weekly library hours	48	36
Firefighters per 100,000 population	80	71
Police officers per 100,000 population	166	158

SOURCE: Office of the Independent Budget Analyst, *Review of the Fiscal Year 2010 Proposed Budget*, IBA Report 09-37, April 28, 2009.

we're just not doing it very well anymore," one former city financial official concluded.[75]

By late 2010, it had become clear to both sides that the status quo was simply unsustainable. Reversing his earlier opposition, Mayor Sanders endorsed a proposal developed by his former mayoral opponent, Councilwoman Donna Frye, that promised to pair new revenues with cost-saving reforms. If labor leaders agreed to make significant concessions on the outsourcing of city services and helped the city make cuts to the cost of retiree health care, the proposal called on the city to enact a temporary increase in the city's sales tax, to raise $100 million in new revenue each year. However, as the proposal headed to a vote of the people in November 2010, the likely outcome was marked by great uncertainty if not outright pessimism. Councilman Carl DeMaio, and his only other fellow Republican on the city council, Kevin Faulconer, came out as leading opponents of the plan, dubbing the sales tax increase a "pension tax." "This is nothing more than a desperate attempt, a Hail Mary pass by city politicians and labor unions to grab cash, to push off the necessary reforms that we have to make in the city's budget [and] the pension system," DeMaio argued.[76]

With the business community sitting on the sidelines—both the Chamber of Commerce and the San Diego Regional Economic Development Corporation chose to make no initial endorsement on the sales tax increase—and voters reluctant to raise their own taxes, the same political forces that gave rise to San Diego's pension fiasco have also conspired to keep the city from finding a permanent solution to the fiscal crisis that both predated and was exacerbated by pension underfunding. Ironically, well-meaning institutional reforms have contributed to political paralysis. The strong-mayor form of government, drafted in response to the 2003 Cedar Fire and given new life by the pension scandal, has effectively institutionalized conflict between the mayor and city council. In separating the legislative and executive branches of city government, such reforms, when combined with large discrepancies between district and citywide constituencies, undermine the ability of civic leaders to work toward common purposes.

Eyes Wide Shut
      Grandiose Plans for America's Finest City

Potemkin Village Planning?

It is especially damning that San Diego's inaction intensifies an ominous drift toward a socially, economically, and racially fractured city. If the most important function of local government is the equitable distribution and provision of public facilities and services to its citizens, then San Diego has failed miserably.

> —*Nico Calavita, Roger Caves, and Kathleen Ferrier, "The Challenges of Smart Growth: The San Diego Case," 2005*[1]

Although San Diego's chronic budget deficit has cut deeply into the provision of basic city services, dire fiscal straits have done little to quench the city's thirst for ambitious projects worthy of America's self-styled finest city. These projects have formed the basis for an aggressive campaign to invest more than $1 billion in a series of high-profile, publicly financed megaprojects located downtown, even as infrastructure and public services in outlying neighborhoods have continued to decay. Indeed, since the early 1990s, the city has undertaken one of the most expensive, extensive, and challenging planning efforts in its history. In this chapter, we consider city leaders' inability to reconcile the growing danger of insolvency and the mounting laundry list of neighborhood needs with their desire for mammoth and iconic legacy projects.

On top of budgetary stress, San Diego's quality of life at the start of the new millennium was threatened by substandard public facilities; a changing economic base; and serious environmental challenges, including a dwindling and insecure water supply. For the first time in the city's history, there was little vacant land available for future development.[2] For the most part, however, San Diego's planning strategy did little to address these knotty problems. With city council attention focused on growing budgetary challenges in the city's day-to-day operations, the initiative for long-range planning has been provided by a series of ambitious mayors, intent on using visible achievements to try to build legacies and possibly careers for higher office, and self-interested developers, who have worked to direct city investments to promote their own economic interests. Lower-profile challenges and projects attracting no private-sector champions have largely escaped civic attention.

San Diego's grandiose plans did not emerge from a rational planning process in which public officials take seriously their responsibilities for assessing the city's opportunities, prioritizing needs, and devising prudent and sustainable financing strategies.[3] Instead of delivering a coherent assessment of city needs, San Diego's planning process has been co-opted by prominent business and civic leaders, who can provide the resources necessary to sustain the costly efforts of turning blueprints into reality. Arguably, San Diego residents have been the real losers. Political and economic logic has encouraged city leaders to focus on visible projects whose concentrated benefits are large enough to attract the interest of private-sector participants. The same logic has discouraged support for less visible projects with diffuse public benefits, such as parks, police and fire stations, and basic infrastructure. Even the growing effort to revitalize San Diego's famed but chronically underfunded Balboa Park attracted few powerful and wealthy advocates and presented public officials with little voter appeal.[4]

Planning on the Cheap

In some cities, such as Phoenix and Seattle, officials have settled [debates over new civic facilities] by placing massive bond measures on the ballot and convincing their voters to strive for greatness. But in San Diego, the mere thought of going to the polls sends shivers down the backs of the mayor, the City Council and the city manager's staff. Defeated before they start, they search for creative ways to avoid ballot bond issues.

—*Roger M. Showley, "It's Time to Pour Pride into a New City Hall," 1995*[5]

In many ways, San Diego's policies governing growth and development have been constrained by the conservative preferences of its citizens. Largely because of their aversion to paying up-front costs to fund public investments that promise long-term benefits, the city has forgone upgrades to existing infrastructure and public amenities. Over the past two decades, San Diego voters have approved just one general obligation bond, to upgrade police communication equipment, compared to thirteen bond approvals in Los Angeles, eight in San Jose, and three in Oakland. As Table 5.1 shows, at less than two-tenths of 1 percent of total assessed valuation, the city's outstanding long-term debt is one of the lowest among major California cities, reflecting the paucity of public investments in San Diego.[6]

The city's historical difficulty in securing approval for major bonds has been exacerbated by the passage of Proposition 13 in 1978 and Proposition 218 in 1996, which extended voter approval requirements to most types of taxes and bonds. Table 5.2, which tabulates the number of proposals for new taxes and bonds appearing on the ballot in the City of San Diego and San Diego County from 1995 to 2008, compared to other

TABLE 5.1   Outstanding long-term debt of the ten largest California cities, fiscal year 2007–08

City	Total outstanding debt (millions)	Assessed valuation (millions)	Debt as percentage of assessed valuation
Long Beach	$2,352.68	$45,211.10	5.2
Oakland	$2,009.99	$41,695.47	4.8
Riverside	$880.37	$24,592.91	3.6
Los Angeles	$12,885.80	$411,135.22	3.1
Sacramento	$802.10	$41,866.64	1.9
Fresno	$526.67	$29,858.64	1.8
San Jose	$1,657.53	$123,843.86	1.3
Santa Ana	$186.62	$21,756.43	0.9
San Diego	$264.70	$181,721.10	0.1
Anaheim	$29.95	$34,735.96	0.1

SOURCE: California State Controller, *Cities Annual Report*, Fiscal Year 2007–08 (Sacramento: California State Controller, April 2010).

TABLE 5.2 Local city and county tax and bond propositions, 1995–2008: San Diego relative to other large California cities and counties

	CITY OF SAN DIEGO		OTHER TOP 10 CALIFORNIA CITIES[a]		COUNTY OF SAN DIEGO		OTHER TOP 10 CALIFORNIA COUNTIES[a]	
	Proposed	*Passed*	*Proposed*	*Passed*	*Proposed*	*Passed*	*Proposed*	*Passed*
TAXES								
Business	0	0	4	4	0	0	1	1
Property	0	0	14	7	1	0	6	3
Sales	1	0[b]	0	0	3	1	3	1
Utility	0	0	12	9	0	0	3	3
Miscellaneous	0	0	3	1	3	1	0	0
Transient occupancy	2	0	4	1	0	0	1	1
Total	3	0	37	22	7	2	14	9
BONDS								
General obligation	0	0	15	12	0	0	1	1
Revenue	0	0	0	0	0	0	0	0
Mello/Roos	0	0	2	1	0	0	0	0
Total	0	0	17	13	0	0	1	1

SOURCE: California Data Election Archives, Institute for Social Research, California State University Sacramento.

[a]Figures exclude County and City of San Francisco.

[b]In November 1996, city voters approved a proposition providing for a branch library endowment fund paid for by the city's share of a quarter-cent increase in the county sales tax. The proposition did not go into effect because county voters failed to approve the proposed quarter-cent sales tax increase.

large California cities and counties, illustrates the extent to which San Diego public officials have avoided testing voters' antipathy to tax hikes. Over the thirteen-year period, not a single general obligation, revenue, or Mello-Roos bond—each of which requires voter approval—appeared on the ballot in the City of San Diego or County of San Diego. Similarly, only three proposals for tax increases were put before the voters. Two tax proposals were offered in 2004 and targeted nonresident hotel occupants. The other was offered in 1996 and sought to raise the local sales tax by a quarter of a cent to pay for new branch libraries. None of the three, including a March 2004 proposal to raise hotel taxes to pay for emergency police and fire service, came close to the necessary vote thresholds.

Public officials in other California cities have been much more successful in securing needed voter support for new taxes and bonds. Table 5.2 shows the number of such proposals that were offered and passed in the other ten largest California cities between 1995 and 2008.[7] In these cities, public officials went to the voters thirty-seven times for new taxes, including taxes on local businesses, property owners, and utilities. Voters approved twenty-two (nearly 60 percent) of these proposals; only some of these taxes required two-thirds support, and others needed just a bare majority. These cities' batting average for bonds was even better, with twelve of fifteen general obligation and one of two Mello-Roos bonds (76 percent) approved by voters.

Because Proposition 13 enables a minority of voters to block any initiative that requires additional taxes, large public projects in San Diego have typically been financed in ways that do not obviously add to voters' tax burden. To close the gap between the political demand for new facilities and the constricted supply of public dollars, city leaders invented complicated financing mechanisms designed to thwart the procedural requirements of Proposition 13. In particular, by simply assuming that future growth in city revenue would pay for the cost of massive capital projects, elected officials could promise voters that new construction would neither reduce existing services nor result in higher taxes. As they struggled to finance their wish list of megaprojects, city leaders used this supply-side logic to borrow heavily against San Diego's future revenues, thus putting further pressure on the budget at a time when the city could least afford it.

This chapter considers the intertwined stories behind San Diego's post-1990 plans for civic greatness and the stark reality of its chronic budgetary problems. We examine the contentious politics behind the city's embrace of a smart-growth strategy that envisioned increasing the intensity of development in its oldest neighborhoods and the plan's unraveling in the face of grassroots opposition and daunting financing costs. We also look at the city's frenetic search for money to pay for a series of high-profile downtown projects, including a new central library, a new city hall, two convention center expansions, and a controversial conservancy proposal that raised the specter of privatizing the governance of San Diego's most iconic crown jewel, Balboa Park. Although extravagant public relations and architectural renderings promised to further refine and enhance what increasingly resembled the showy exterior of a Potemkin village, the city's ambitious civic planning agenda did little to address its crumbling fiscal foundation.

New Dreams of Civic Greatness

San Diego has the location and the physical foundation in general for an important, perhaps a great, city. Its people are awake to its needs, and are resolved to meet them.

—*Boston-area planner John Nolen, 1908*[8]

During the first decade of the twentieth century, John Nolen's blueprint for transforming San Diego through carefully planned growth was scuttled in the face of opposition from powerful local actors such as John D. Spreckels. A century later, the city faced a fundamentally different barrier to comprehensive planning: the need to unite a politically and economically divided city behind a single vision for its future. San Diego's modern political leaders shared Nolen's belief that the city had unbounded potential, yet they struggled to overcome skepticism from a tax-averse voting public for whom planning and development had become synonymous with unrestrained growth and the absence of sufficient investment in basic infrastructure necessary to support it.

In the late 1980s, public discontent gave rise to a citizens' revolt that produced new limits on growth via the ballot box and the election of public officials sensitive to vocal opposition to new construction in the city's older neighborhoods. Over the course of the ensuing decade, the city council adopted a variety of emergency measures designed to protect existing neighborhoods and preserve open space, yet city leaders struggled to develop a longer-range plan to guide future growth that could accommodate the conflicting demands of residents and politically powerful developers.[9] Beginning in 1999, city staff began work on an innovative growth strategy championed to boost the city's image and beautify its physical environment through massive infusions of public and private resources. Realizing this ambitious agenda and providing needed funding would become key challenges for San Diego's political leaders.

Building a City of Villages

San Diego needs a well defined strategy for investing finite City resources for the greatest public benefit. This strategy will help to accomplish that objective and ensure the future prosperity of the City and its residents. If successfully implemented, the City of Villages strategy will be a testament to Nolen's original vision of San Diego.

—*Strategic Framework Element, City of San Diego General Plan, 2002*[10]

Mayor Pete Wilson's lengthy term in office (1971-82) substantially altered the trajectory of San Diego's long-term growth. In particular, two planning policies adopted by Wilson and his allies would frame the key planning debates when public officials began a much-delayed update of San Diego's growth blueprint in the late 1990s and early 2000s. The first Wilson policy divided the city into five zones, pushing major development toward the outer edges of the city. The second required that development pay for itself without further burdening the city's already strained public finances.

As discussed in Chapter 2, the 1979 *Progress Guide and General Plan* backed by Wilson split the city into a series of tiers. The urbanized and Centre City areas covered the downtown core and other established neighborhoods. North of Interstate 8, the plan designated planned urbanizing areas in communities like University City, Tierrasanta, and Scripps Ranch that were expected to receive a significant share of future growth. The city's remaining developable land, particularly along the State Route 56 corridor, was set aside as "future urbanizing." Figure 5.1 provides a map of the city divided into the different development tiers. In 1985, a

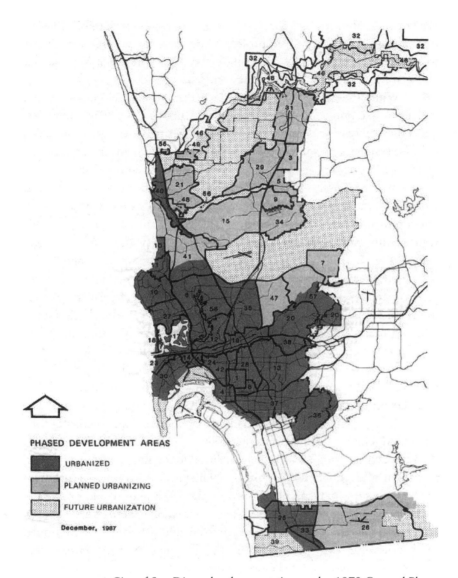

PHASED DEVELOPMENT AREAS

URBANIZED

PLANNED URBANIZING

FUTURE URBANIZATION

December, 1987

FIGURE 5.1   City of San Diego development tiers under 1979 General Plan

SOURCE: City of San Diego, Planning Division, "Guidelines for Future Development," *1979 Progress Guide and General Plan* (San Diego: City of San Diego, 1979), p. 54.

growth-control initiative approved by voters in response to public discontent over a recently approved project made these lands largely off-limits to further development by requiring a citywide vote for any plan that changed the area's land-use designation.[11]

While the Wilson plan envisioned that new development would include ample public amenities, including schools, open space, libraries, and other recreational and cultural facilities, it insisted that the city's existing residents be spared the burden of funding them. Instead, public facilities in newly urbanizing areas would be provided through a combination of special assessments and impact fees levied on developers, who would pass the costs on to future property owners.[12] To encourage in-fill development in existing neighborhoods in the urbanized core, these areas were exempt from the new impact fees, with the city's day-to-day budget expected to pay for the cost of needed infrastructure improvements.

Though largely praised by planners, this basic template came under increasing strain by the late 1980s. Taking advantage of permissive land-use regulations, developers rushed to construct (often poorly designed) multifamily complexes in previously single-family neighborhoods.[13] The city's new system of financing public facilities in newer areas with special benefit assessments was not implemented until 1986, leading to significant lag time between the construction of new housing and the availability of sufficient public facilities. By the late 1990s, demographers projected continued population growth for San Diego, but less than 4 percent of the city's land remained available for new development. City officials deemed the future urbanizing areas largely unsuitable for new construction, setting them aside for conservation as open space. Additionally, although the financing mechanisms envisioned by the 1979 plan would eventually ensure adequate public facilities in newer areas, they were of little help in addressing the needs of already-urbanized neighborhoods that continued to experience growth through in-fill development. Nor did impact fees provide any money to pay the operating costs of new facilities.

With city finances strained after the passage of Proposition 13, older communities received little money to finance new parks, schools, police services, and sewer lines needed to accommodate their growing residential populations.[14] In 2002, the city pegged the public facilities needs of these older neighborhoods at $2.5 billion. Although a general obligation bond would have allowed the city to finance the backlog over a period of many decades, public officials did not believe that they could secure the necessary approval from voters. Residents in newer areas, whose own public services were adequate, had little appetite for higher taxes to fund the needs of older neighborhoods. Increasingly, debates over growth and planning had begun to pit residents of the older, urban core against newcomers on the periphery. According to former City Council President Scott Peters, the politics of growth in San Diego has become "a tale of two cities. . . . I think the divide is between old vs. new."[15]

As the city's leaders prepared for the first major update of the 1979 General Plan, there was widespread agreement that any new growth blueprint would need to provide housing for future residents and meet the needs of existing neighborhoods. In early 2002, planning officials unveiled a proposal that they argued included both components. Called "City of Villages," the document outlined a radically different approach to growth that moved away from new construction on the city's outer edges and instead shifted focus toward environmentally sensitive development in existing neighborhoods. To create new urban "villages"—pedestrian-friendly areas that would combine housing, jobs, public spaces, and commerce—the city would direct future growth into high-density, mixed-use projects in and around the city core. New development would be paired with additional resources for mass transportation and investment in public facilities, to reduce traffic congestion and urban sprawl.[16] One veteran journalist dubbed the plan "density for dollars."[17] Single-family neighborhoods in the city's newer suburbs would be spared the burden of additional growth.

Mayor Dick Murphy quickly adopted the City of Villages concept as his own, scheduling appearances before community planning groups to lobby on its behalf. However, the document remained largely silent on how the city would finance the required infrastructure investment, and Murphy emphatically ruled out tax increases.[18]

"A Never-Never Land Kind of Idea"

At least a year ago, the planning department presented information on the financing needed to improve the infrastructure, most of which would require some political will. Now the plan is more akin to the emperor with no clothes. . . . I've yet to see the city at all interested in providing new clothes for the emperor.

—*San Ysidro Business Association official Judy Elliot, 2004*[19]

Murphy's plan received a chilly reception at community meetings. Planning activists expressed concerns over increasing the intensity of development in existing neighborhoods, which community planner Lisa Ross argued "had become synonymous with overcrowded recreation facilities and schools, crime, and traffic jams." Many also remained skeptical that the city would follow through on its commitment to provide the funding to repave sidewalks and construct public improvements long promised to the city's older communities. Ross dubbed Murphy's plan "a never-never land kind of idea."[20]

As the City of Villages blueprint moved closer to a city council vote, grassroots opposition to the plan continued to grow. A committee of community planners offered a lukewarm endorsement but demanded that the city develop and implement "a realistic financing plan to ensure the provision of [promised but never built] public facilities and services at the time of their need" before moving ahead on any new development.[21] In other words, if the city wanted more intense development, it would have to provide the overdue infrastructure first. Months earlier, a citizens group and consultants tasked with finding the necessary funds calculated that San Diego would need to spend an additional $100 million a year over fifty years to finance the necessary improvements. The group identified a series of fees and taxes that the city could raise to provide the funds—including the imposition of a utility users' tax and a charge for residential trash collection—though all would require a public vote.[22]

In the face of opposition from politically powerful community planning groups and the prospect of a public vote on higher taxes that he was sure to lose, Murphy abandoned his support for the growth blueprint. Seizing on new population projections that predicted fewer-than-expected new residents, the mayor announced that slowing population growth relieved the city of the need to plan for more housing units and demanded that planners remove all mention of increased density in the document.[23] When the city council adopted the outlines of a new General Plan in 2002, the document provided few details about how the city would pay for the $2.5 billion in promised-but-not-yet-constructed public facilities, improvements that would be needed even without the construction of new villages.

Although the city council approved five "pilot" villages in 2004, the future of the City of Villages program remained in doubt. Most of the proposed villages would require at least partial public funding, but the plans included few details about where this money would come from. Critics warned that without significant changes, the pilot projects would take too long and would do little to alleviate opposition to higher density and taxes.[24]

Three years later, the city had constructed or replaced just a fraction of the promised facilities, and turnover among city staff—including the departure of San Diego's planning director—left the program with little institutional memory. Although mayoral candidate Jerry Sanders criticized his predecessor Murphy for ruling out tax increases to pay for the required infrastructure during the campaign, he did little to change course once in office. Explaining the lack of progress on the financing front, a Sanders spokesman argued that "the city government has to prove its worth, its effectiveness, its efficiency, before we can politically ask for increased revenue streams." Other mayoral appointees showed little interest in proceeding with the City of Villages blueprint and blamed their predecessors and community groups for the lack of progress on the pilot villages.[25]

Despite financing hurdles and uncertainty about its viability, the city retained the City of Villages framework as the basic principle behind its new General Plan, the document outlining San Diego's growth strategy for decades to come. The final plan, adopted by the city council in 2008, retained some of the aspirational language from the original blueprint, but also acknowledged the serious challenges facing its implementation. While noting the city's massive infrastructure backlog, the General Plan stated only that San Diego voters would have to choose how to finance the city's public facilities and infrastructure needs. Ominously, it noted that residents voted down recent tax increases. To some senior city staff, the effort represented a clear failure to adequately plan for and invest in the city's future. "The 'City of Villages' process should have been halted early on until the reality of the situation were allowed to sink in with the voting public, the media, the bureaucracy, and most of all, our elected officials," recalled Hank Cunningham, the city's former head of community and economic development. "Instead, this exercise in futility was allowed to plod along under its own volition until it became law in 2008 with adoption of the current General Plan update."[26]

The General Plan represented only the first step in the city's planning efforts by laying out a general foundation for future growth. Its provisions would have to be implemented through detailed community plans to be adopted with considerable participation and consultation from neighborhood planning groups. However, budgetary problems left the city with little money to take even this preliminary step, delaying progress on most community blueprints. In the Otay Mesa, the city's southernmost neighborhood located next to the Mexican border, the city turned to the private sector to help fund a more detailed local growth plan. For years, the Otay Mesa represented a battleground for the city's industrial business interests, who valued the community for its proximity to cross-border trade, and its real estate establishment, who hoped to transform the Otay Mesa into the city's newest residential community.

In a private agreement hashed out between the city's planning officials and leading real estate companies in 2004, the developers agreed to pay to hire the costly architects, engineers, and consultants necessary to complete a new Otay Mesa community plan. In exchange, the city agreed that the version of the plan most favored by developers—which promised to rezone large swaths of Otay Mesa from industrial to residential use— would be among the options that would be presented to the city council. If approved, the rezoning plan would generate a small fortune for the developers by greatly increasing the value of their real estate holdings in the Otay Mesa.[27]

In downtown, the Centre City Development Corporation (CCDC), San Diego's downtown redevelopment arm, took the lead in developing a new community plan. Again, private developers would come to dominate the process and win significant concessions. The final plan, adopted in the face of opposition from the environmental community, greatly increased the allowable density of development, projecting that downtown's residential population would grow threefold by 2030. The blueprint allowed developers to purchase additional density credits by paying into a fund to finance new public infrastructure, at rates critics warned were too low to actually cover the cost of needed improvements. To pay for the remaining facilities, the plan envisaged tapping the city's growing redevelopment budget; however, as we discuss in Chapter 6, few redevelopment dollars have since gone to finance the promised amenities.[28]

"A Storybook Library"

Many are calling it San Diego's most important public building for the next hundred years. . . . Some invoked local landmarks, such as the [train] depot and the County Administration Center, while others reached back to ancient monuments and European models to describe how the library, due for completion in 1999, could set a worldwide standard.

—*Roger M. Showley, "Competing Architects Detail Strategies for Library," 1996*[29]

Two key barriers to the adoption of the City of Villages framework—opposition to new taxes and the competing priorities of San Diego's older and newer communities—also stood in the way of another blockbuster project, the replacement of the city's aging central library. During the 1990s, the battle over the library became entangled in political rivalries and in competing plans and priorities for downtown redevelopment. These threatened a decades-long quest to replace the leaky and decrepit building that had become a symbol of the city's political paralysis.

Built in 1954, San Diego's downtown library failed to keep pace with the city's rapidly growing population and changing building codes. By the mid-1970s, it was clear that the building had grown obsolete and no longer met the needs of the city's library system. Over the ensuing three decades, dozens of commissioned studies urged the replacement of the downtown central branch and noted the general inadequacies of the whole library system, which remained underfunded in comparison with its peers in other cities.[30]

In 1989, voters rejected a $125 million bond measure to replace the central library and expand its branches. Although polls showed that the library system remained very popular among voters, few supported higher taxes to help meet its needs. Voters expressed even less interest in additional investment in the system if the money was tied to the replacement or expansion of the downtown library, which was found to have significantly less public support than local neighborhood branches.[31]

The city's studies gathered dust for the following two years, as other political priorities occupied the attention of elected officials and community leaders. Indeed, few paid attention when the city's Library Commission, a seven-member board appointed to advise the city council on library policy, recommended a new library on Port District–owned land near the waterfront. In 1991, however, Mayor Maureen O'Connor resurrected the Library Commission proposal. Calling for "a storybook library" equipped with the latest technology, O'Connor made the new downtown library a central pillar of her last state-of-the-city address.

Although the mayor offered few details about possible funding sources for the project, she called for the formation of a nonprofit corporation to finance, design, and construct the facility, and announced that she had received $3 million in pledges for the project from local foundations and prominent San Diego families. O'Connor also tapped Mike Madigan, an executive at one of the largest home-building companies in the region and a consummate political insider, to head a separate fundraising committee to drum up additional private money.[32]

Susan Golding, O'Connor's successor, embraced the library proposal—though in a different downtown location—along with a series of other high-profile projects and appointed a separate Madigan-led committee to select a world-class architect to design the new building. Golding also assembled a financing package that would rely on the city's existing hotel tax revenues, private donations, and redevelopment dollars to avoid issuing general obligation bonds and bypassing a public vote on the library project. However, Golding's plan faced opposition from City Councilwoman Judy McCarty, a political rival and the council's chief library advocate. McCarty urged a shift in focus to improving the city's neighborhood branch libraries instead of building an expensive new downtown colossus. "There's no sense doing construction if we can't afford to operate and maintain [the branches]," McCarty argued. "That's a mistake we've made before. If you want new libraries and librarians in them, you will have to pay for them."[33]

Eventually appointed chair of a new regional library authority, McCarty spearheaded two campaigns to raise the sales taxes to improve branch libraries throughout the county. Neither promised to provide money for a new central library downtown. Mayor Golding opposed both ballot measures, arguing that higher taxes were not necessary to

devote additional resources to the library system. The 1996 initiative received support from 60 percent of voters—still short of the two-thirds
required under Proposition 13. A follow-up proposal in 1999 was supported by barely half the electorate, which reinforced widely held beliefs
that not enough San Diego voters would support a library project with
higher taxes to meet the required two-thirds vote threshold. Instead of
identifying new sources of funding, the city council adopted a new ordinance in 2000 that directed the city manager to divert a growing share
of city expenditures into the library system until appropriations for the
libraries totaled 6 percent of the city's budget.[34]

Financing also remained the Achilles' heel of the downtown library effort. An iconic domed structure designed by celebrated local architect Rob Quigley won many plaudits, but few believed that the city
could afford its $118.4 million price tag. The planned library would also
cost nearly twice as much to operate as the old central library, threatening to bust the library system's annual operating budget. With no viable
financing plan in sight, and with part of the Kettner Boulevard location
favored by the Library Commission up for sale, Golding's push for a new
downtown library appeared to be dead in early 1998.[35]

Sensing defeat for the Golding-backed plans, council members
McCarty and Byron Wear wrote to the mayor urging the appointment of
a new task force to study whether a library could be included in the redevelopment district around a planned downtown ballpark for the Padres.
Unlike general obligation bonds, redevelopment bonds backed by future
property tax increments are exempt from the public vote requirement.
Two local architects also urged the city to consider building an annex to
the old central library, a much cheaper option. Golding made clear that
she favored the original location but referred the matter to the Library
Commission, then chaired by Madigan, who had also been hired by the
city to oversee and plan the ballpark project.[36]

Padres' owner John Moores and Madigan lobbied hard for the
proposed library site in the new ballpark district, although they won no
converts on the Library Commission. Commissioners argued that the
area could not support sufficient parking for a new central library and
worried that ball-game traffic and noise would interfere with its operations. Instead, they voiced support for an alternative location just north of
the city's historic train depot; only Madigan voted in favor of situating the

library in the ballpark redevelopment area. However, Golding announced that the city council would have the final say over the location, and city staff released a report concluding that the site favored by the Library Commission would be too expensive to be viable.[37]

Critics accused the city of working behind the scenes to steer downtown investment, including the new library, into the ballpark district to help Moores, who had committed to hundreds of millions in residential and commercial development downtown as part of the ballpark project. They argued that Madigan violated the city's conflict-of-interest laws by not abstaining from the Library Commission vote and noted that the consultant who authored the report critical of the train depot site was also working for the city on ballpark-related projects. The two candidates vying to replace Golding urged the city council to hold off on choosing the location. County Supervisor Ron Roberts suggested that the city could not afford a new downtown library, whereas his opponent— and eventual winner—superior court Judge Dick Murphy favored locating the central library in Mission Valley or the Naval Training Center, a shuttered military base in another redevelopment project area of the city. Bucking criticism, Golding pushed ahead on the vote, steering the council to select the ballpark site.

Once in office, Murphy reversed his opposition to the downtown location but did little to move the project along. Instead, the mayor teamed up with freshman City Councilman Jim Madaffer in an eighteen-month effort to negotiate a grand bargain on library funding. Their final proposal, released in the spring of 2002, paired financing for the downtown library with construction of twelve new branch libraries and the expansion of nine others. To secure the support of the council, the plan also guaranteed each council district a library of at least fifteen thousand square feet, large enough to house a community services center to provide constituency services. "In the past, it was always about 'A main, a main, a main, we need a main.' And the neighborhoods were saying, 'Well what about us?' And there was always this tug of war," Madaffer said. For the first time, the city had found a logroll that pleased both the supporters of a new central library and advocates for expanding its network of local branches.[38]

The expected bill for the Murphy-Madaffer plan totaled $312 million, $149 million for the central library and the rest for the branches. Like Golding, the new mayor and councilman worked with city staff on a funding plan that would avoid the need for a public vote. The final financing schedule envisioned that revenue bonds, to be repaid from future growth in hotel tax revenues, would provide two-thirds of the necessary funding, with the remaining money coming from development impact fees, redevelopment dollars, grants, and private philanthropy. In the short term, the city would tap new money set aside for libraries in the 2000 funding ordinance.[39]

However, the funding for the plan quickly began to unravel. The same day the city council voted to approve the financing blueprint, City Manager Michael Uberuaga called for across-the-board budget cuts to deal with the city's declining revenues. Before the city could sell the necessary revenue bonds, the underfunding of the pension system became public, and San Diego was exiled from the public bond market. To deal with the fallout, public officials diverted funds earmarked for the library to balance the city's budget. By 2009, the city was allocating just 3 percent of its shrinking budget to the library system, half of the amount promised by the 2000 ordinance. More important, the city was spending less in real dollars on the library system than it had when the ordinance was adopted. Mayor Sanders's budget for 2010 cut library funding further and proposed shuttering the Ocean Beach branch library to save money on operating costs—even though the same library had been slated for expansion under the council-approved plan. Confronted with a gaping deficit, Sanders unveiled midyear budget cutbacks in late 2009 that promised to slash hours at libraries across the city, including closing most branches on Sunday.[40]

Despite broad cuts and quickly shrinking service hours in the rest of the system, however, Sanders remained a vocal supporter of the downtown library project. Shortly after taking office, the mayor endorsed an earlier financing plan to cover the central library's projected $185 million price tag. Under the plan, most of the money would come from the city's downtown redevelopment arm and private philanthropists. To cover increased operating costs, the city would also lease out the top two stories of the new library to commercial tenants—an idea abandoned in 2009, when the San Diego Unified School District agreed to contribute $20 million in school bond proceeds to help pay for construction in exchange for the city's agreement to house a charter school in the space. By 2010, with a $20 million state library grant set to expire, San Diego's leading library enthusiasts had raised only half of the private donations needed to pay for the construction costs. Despite being $30 million short and lacking any long-term plan to finance ongoing operations of the new facility, the city broke ground on the project in late 2010.[41]

A New City Hall?

If civic buildings symbolize a city's self-image, then the 1990s may provide a chance to remake that image of self-conscious frugality into one reflective of a self-assertive ambition. To old-timers, this all sounds too familiar.

—*Roger M. Showley, "It's Time to Pour Pride into a New City Hall," 1995*[42]

For boosters, San Diego's public buildings have long represented symbols of the city's unmet potential. Civic greatness, they believe, cannot be achieved without great civic architectural marvels. And no structure is more symbolic than city hall, the headquarters of municipal government. In the mid-1920s, civic reformer and planning advocate George Marston unveiled plans for a picturesque civic complex on the waterfront. Although residents offered support for the plans, they repeatedly rejected the bonds to pay for them. A new city hall on the bay, one component of the Marston plan, was constructed only when the federal government stepped in to provide funding under the New Deal public works programs in the 1930s.[43]

At the end of World War II, city leaders approached voters with a proposal to construct new city offices, to be located just east of the waterfront location or in Balboa Park. The voters again rejected the proposal. Concluding that the electorate would oppose any effort to finance a new civic center, the city council turned to the retirement system for help in 1962, foreshadowing later schemes to use the retirement system to supplement the city budget. Using borrowed money from the pension fund, the city built a downtown concourse that included a modest city hall, concert hall, and convention center—with the cost of the project to be repaid with parking fees.[44]

Unfortunately, by the late 1980s, the concourse had already become less than adequate to meet the city's needs. As the size of its workforce outgrew the office space available in the municipal office building, the city began leasing additional facilities. City hall was also beset by a slew of electrical, mechanical, and structural problems. The price tag for the needed improvements exceeded $10 million, with the city paying millions more each year for the rented office space.

The Importance of an "Ernest" Vision

Mayor Maureen O'Connor endorsed efforts to construct a new civic complex downtown, and she found an ally in Ernest Hahn, the developer of the famed Horton Plaza downtown shopping center. As the chair of the city's downtown planning group, Hahn became the lead cheerleader for the project. As one of the city's largest investors in downtown real estate, Hahn had long been a champion of using public resources to encourage economic development in the area. Despite the rejuvenation fueled by Horton Plaza, large swaths of downtown remained blighted, a problem, Hahn insisted, that could be alleviated only with a government-funded facility on its eastern edge. His plan called for the construction of a new civic center nine blocks east of the existing civic concourse, at Twelfth Avenue and Broadway.[45]

To avoid a public vote, the mayor and council urged city staff to find a way to make the project cost neutral. In particular, project supporters envisioned that the city could sell certificates of participation—a form of debt exempt from constitutional voting requirements—to cover the up-front costs. To repay the debt, the city would use money currently spent on leased office space—the new city hall would be large enough to house all of San Diego's downtown public workers—and revenue generated by renting out its existing headquarters.

Hahn's vision for a new city headquarters in underdeveloped parts of downtown was not shared by other business leaders. San Diegans Inc., an umbrella organization representing downtown merchants, vocally opposed the plan, fearing that moving the existing building would create a "black hole" for crime and destitution in its current location in the heart of downtown. Instead, San Diegans Inc. released its own plan to redevelop the site of the city's existing city hall, an idea the group argued would be more affordable. The plan was opposed by Hahn and his allies.[46]

With the business community divided, the recession of the early 1990s ground plans for a new civic center to a halt. Downtown office vacancies approached 15 percent in 1991, casting a dark shadow over the city's preferred financing model. By taking advantage of the soft market, the city could sign long-term agreements that reduced the amount it paid for office space—and thus realize the savings promised by a new public building. Lack of demand also threatened the revenue that could be generated by leasing out the existing city hall.

With a price tag between $250 million and $350 million, the project remained dormant throughout the mid- and late 1990s. After Hahn's death in 1992, the proposal for moving the city center eastward lost its leading advocate. As a 2000 deadline for meeting the city's own building codes approached, Mayor Susan Golding and her successor, Dick Murphy, expressed support for redeveloping the existing concourse site, although the idea found little traction.[47]

In 2007, Mayor Jerry Sanders again floated the idea of redeveloping the concourse site. Unlike earlier efforts, however, Sanders proposed delegating the job of constructing a new city hall to a private developer as part of a larger overhaul of a four-block area north of Horton Plaza. Like his predecessors, the mayor framed the proposal as an effort to save the city money on expensive office leases. In exchange for helping finance the new complex, Sanders's plan would give a private developer rights to build ancillary commercial projects and reap any resulting profits.[48]

With the mayor's blessing, CCDC moved to award the project to Portland-based developer Gerding Edlen, whose more than $600 million bid was the only one the city received.[49] The firm's proposal for a sail-shaped city hall, equipped with the latest green technologies, won universal praise, although city officials wanted to take no risks. Quietly, CCDC hired political consultants to advise the city about "the most formidable challenges in overcoming resistance from the public." In late 2010, a planned public vote on the project was put on hold as elected officials struggled to build voter support for a sales tax increase to close the city's budget deficit.[50]

Selling San Diego

May the San Diego spirit prevail!
—*Former slogan of the San Diego Convention Center*

While conflicts between developer Ernest Hahn, the downtown business establishment, and the city's tourism industry helped stall progress on a new civic center for more than a decade, concerted efforts to construct a major convention center on the city's waterfront would prove one of San Diego's largest and most successful public projects in the latter half of the twentieth century. The convention center would come to symbolize both San Diego's immense hopes for transforming itself into an emerging world-class city and the substantial constraints imposed by the post–Proposition 13 fiscal straitjacket.

Efforts to build, and later expand, the San Diego Convention Center would help launch the political careers of two mayors—and later contribute to ending the tenure of one of them—highlighting the political utility of big-box public projects for local elected officials. In addition, the delivery of pivotal resources by the private sector that was so crucial to the construction of the convention center would further reinforce the belief among city leaders that private initiative, when harnessed and incentivized via public-sector resources, was the solution to overcoming the city's lack of civic capacity. Above all else, the convention center would become the poster child for arguments that San Diego could carry out massive public works without draining the public treasury.

Wilson's Failure, Hedgecock's Success

The convention center will make San Diego an image of the nation, a major force in the convention business and it will make us a real up-and-coming city competing for business and industry.

   —*Port Commissioner Louis Wolfsheimer, 1987*[51]

Ernest Hahn's plans to open Horton Plaza, a new mall in the heart of downtown's Gaslamp Quarter, had all along assumed that the city would build a new convention center nearby and that the mall would fulfill the shopping needs of out-of-town visitors. With just three hundred thousand square feet of usable space, broken up among two major halls and a theater, the city's old convention center adjacent to city hall on the civic concourse could not compete with a new generation of massive complexes rising up all across the country. Mayor Pete Wilson had directed

CCDC to draw up plans for a new convention center downtown, but voters rejected the proposal in a referendum in 1981.

With Wilson vacating office midway through his third term to serve in the U.S. Senate, his successor, Roger Hedgecock, resurrected the idea of a new convention center as a central pillar of his own mayoral campaign. If he succeeded where Wilson had failed, Hedgecock could burnish his mayoral credentials and buttress his argument for a full four-year term. Hedgecock spearheaded the 1983 campaign for a new convention center, teaming up with the same political consultant who was overseeing his reelection bid the following year. To avoid a repeat of the 1981 ballot defeat, Hedgecock endorsed a proposal by wealthy businessman Doug Manchester that would site the convention center on lands owned by the Port District and would require support only from a simple majority of voters in a symbolic advisory vote.

Manchester had secured long-term leases for large parcels of waterfront land from the Port District and had built the first of several planned hotels there. Under Manchester's plan, some of the leased land would be returned to the Port District for the construction of the convention center. In exchange, Manchester would receive rights to a more prized waterfront parcel nearby and would guarantee the construction of at least two more hotel towers to serve the new convention center. His hotels would, in turn, benefit from the major influx of conventiongoers. The Port District would use the lease revenue generated by the Manchester hotels to recoup its investment in the convention center. The City of San Diego would rent the center from the port at a nominal rate, and use the tax revenues generated by the hotels to pay for its operations.

During the 1983 campaign, Hedgecock assured voters that a state-of-the-art, world-class convention center could be built for $95 million, which would come from the flush Port District rather than from the city. The new convention center would include 250,000 square feet of exhibition space and another 100,000 square feet of meeting space, making the city one of the premier convention destinations in the West.[52] With the city poised to reap the economic benefits of hundreds of thousands of visitors, without the need to pay any of the costs, the advisory measure easily passed with 59 percent of the vote. Hedgecock secured his own reelection victory the following year, defeating Maureen O'Connor, a former city councilwoman serving on the Port Commission who had steadfastly opposed the convention center.

However, the fortunes of both Hedgecock and the convention center would soon turn. A consultant hired by the Port District delivered a sobering report concluding that $95 million would buy a center at least 20 percent smaller than the one promised to voters—indeed, smaller than the existing downtown facility. Constructing the new convention center as planned would cost another $20 million. Embarrassed Port District officials admitted that they had done no independent analysis of the costs before the public vote, relying instead on numbers furnished by Manchester. Using her position as port commissioner, O'Connor publicly assailed Hedgecock, who defended the information that was provided to voters.[53]

Both the San Diego Regional Chamber of Commerce and the Convention and Visitors Bureau came out in adamant opposition to reducing the proposed size of the center to come in under the $100 million mark. "San Diego has time after time in the past shortchanged itself. We're not going to allow that to happen anymore," chamber president Lee Grissom said. The Port District agreed, putting the original specifications out for bid. However, the resulting bids put the total cost of the convention center between $130 million and $150 million, dwarfing the estimate delivered by the port consultant just months earlier.[54]

On top of the public outrage over the projected costs, Hedgecock was facing accusations related to his role in the 1983 referendum. Among a series of alleged campaign finance violations, the Fair Political Practices Commission (FPPC), a bipartisan state commission set up to regulate state and local elections, argued that Hedgecock's political consultant, Tom Shepard, had agreed to work on his mayoral campaign for below cost, in exchange for the mayor's help in obtaining the lucrative contract to run the convention center campaign. Both Hedgecock and Shepard denied the charges, although the mayor was forced from office in 1985 after convictions on conspiracy and twelve counts of perjury connected to the FPPC complaint.[55]

The Port District delayed the start of construction on the complex, hoping to rebid the project after making cost-saving design changes. The second round of bids, however, put the total cost of the convention center at greater than $160 million. In the meantime, Manchester sued the port, arguing that the unnecessary delays had cost his hotels valuable business. The port would eventually pay the litigious hotelier more than $11 million to settle the lawsuit.

Though labeled an obstructionist by Hedgecock and his allies and removed from the Port District board by the city council, O'Connor proved prophetic in her predictions about the continued increases in the cost of building the convention center. She quickly emerged as a leading candidate to replace the disgraced mayor. O'Connor's main opponent, City Councilman Bill Cleator, failed to stake out a coherent position on the convention center issue. An early proponent of the convention center and a general ally of developers, Cleator accused O'Connor of opposing a project that would put San Diego on the map. At the same time, he criticized the Port District for its role in the escalating costs. In the 1986 runoff, O'Connor soundly defeated Cleator.

Fortunately for O'Connor, her inheritance of the troubled convention center project was of limited duration. Following voter approval of the 1983 ballot initiative to build a waterfront convention center, the city council voted to create a nonprofit public corporation, the San Diego Convention Center Corporation (SDCCC), to manage and operate the new facility. SDCCC was governed by an appointed nine-member board of directors; O'Connor would have little control over the board and, as a result, not much influence over policies governing the convention center. The Port District ultimately agreed to fund the entire project at a cost of $164 million, a decision made easier by O'Connor's exit from the Port District board. Construction was completed in November 1989.

Keeping Up with Vegas

The previewing of the San Diego Convention Center went off like an ad-lib regional fair. It was delightful, clean, happy, charming. It was handled beautifully. . . . Here we had the previewing of a building that many citizens had been against, some because the early budgets and schemes were wrong and too many who just were against change of any kind unless it meant more comfort or money for themselves. . . . Congratulations to the Port District, to the architect, to the politicians and to us. . . . I have seen San Diego's future. I feel good!

—*Real estate executive Sanford Goodkin, 1989*[56]

The San Diego Convention Center opened with great fanfare in late 1989. Its performance surprised even its strongest proponents, with bookings and attendance surpassing initial projections. The city, however, was becoming increasingly concerned about the subsidies needed to operate the center. With a recession in the early 1990s paralyzing public finances, the city needed hotel tax revenue from waterfront hotels to offset painful cuts to core city services. For help, officials again turned to the Port District. Although the original deal had required the port to pay for the construction of the center and the city to fund its continued operations, San Diego used its three delegates on the seven-member Port District board—one short of an absolute majority—to secure additional relief. In exchange for a promise from the city's delegation to support port projects in the South Bay, the Port District used $5.6 million of its own money to close the convention center's operating deficit in 1993. Next year, the city requested another bailout, although united South Bay port commissioners rejected the city's request.[57]

The city's management challenges went beyond a temporary budget deficit. Less than two weeks after the convention center opened, the city released a study warning that the center would need to expand to remain competitive in the feverish arms race that was emerging in the national convention market. Hoping to lure major events from one another, convention centers across the country had begun a series of massive expansions, using their new space as a free inducement to win additional market share. The Las Vegas convention center was moving ahead with an expansion that would make it one of the largest facilities in the world. A second study in 1991 echoed earlier findings, noting major deficiencies with San Diego's facility and projecting that the needed expansion would cost at least $111 million.[58]

The decision by the Republican Party to bypass the city as a host for its 1992 national convention, in favor of Houston, cemented in the minds of many convention center boosters the need to commence work on a major addition.[59] To finance the expansion, the city again turned to the Port District, where its plans received a chilly reception. With its accounts far less flush than in the 1980s, the port was reluctant to invest more money in the convention center. Other cities with representation on the Port District board argued that San Diego had received its fair share of port largesse and that it was now time to shift focus to projects along their own waterfronts. In the end, the port agreed to fund up to $47 million of the expansion costs, with the city paying the remainder.[60]

An advocate of major public projects, Mayor Susan Golding threw her support behind the expansion. "If we are to remain competitive and retain our large convention trade . . . we must get on the fast track," the mayor argued shortly after taking office in 1993. "Los Angeles, San Francisco and Long Beach are working hard to capture our share of the market. We can't allow that to happen." Although it had no financing plan in place, the city moved forward with the expansion. Despite rising costs, the Port District continued to reject the city's requests for additional funding.

By 1996, with the convention center designs complete and the expansion ready for construction, there was still little agreement on how to pay the expected cost, which had climbed to $205 million. Issuing a general obligation bond was ruled as not being a viable option. Even the popular 1983 proposal, which carried no direct cost for the city, would have fallen short of the two-thirds vote threshold required by the state constitution. Instead, the mayor directed City Manager Jack McGrory to find an alternative way to finance the construction.

McGrory proposed that the city and Port District come together to create a new joint-powers authority, a legal entity that was bound by neither Proposition 13 nor the debt limitations in the city charter and could thus issue bonds without a direct public vote. In turn, the city and Port District would lease the convention center from the authority at a rate equal to the annual bond payment. Because the city would technically be under no legal obligation to renew the lease each year, it would not be undertaking new debt and thus not need to go to the voters. To make the annual lease payments, McGrory argued that the city could tap its hotel tax revenues, which had again begun to grow as the economy improved. McGrory's plan won unanimous support from the city council and the Port District board.[61]

However, the plan was quickly challenged by local libertarian antitax crusader Richard Rider, who filed a lawsuit accusing the city of violating its charter and state law. Although city officials were confident that they would prevail—indeed, the California Supreme Court eventually rejected Rider's argument—the legal challenge promised to paralyze the expansion for months, if not years. Convention center supporters argued the delay would be fatal to the city's reputation and would result in stag-gering losses in convention trade. In need of a new financing strategy, McGrory proposed that the Port District take the lead on expansion. In turn, the city would lease the additional space at a rate necessary to cover its share of annual bond payments, ranging between $10 million and $15 million, just as it had planned to do with the joint-powers authority. Because the city could refuse to renew the lease at any time, all of the financial risk would be borne by the Port District.

This time, opposition to the McGrory plan came from former City Councilman Bruce Henderson. In late 1997, Henderson financed a drive to call for a voter referendum on the expansion project. Like Rider, Henderson argued that the city had violated the spirit of the law by proceeding with the costly expansion without a public vote. Ahead of the 1998 referendum, San Diego's business establishment, labor unions, and the Convention and Visitors Bureau put together a well-funded campaign that spent more than $700,000. Rather than framing the vote as a referendum on the city's and the port's financing plan, the campaign made the expansion itself the subject. Opponents of the expansion, led by Henderson, raised a little more than $100,000. On Election Day, 60 percent voted in favor of the city's plan, more than the simple majority needed to sustain the city council action.[62]

"Expand or Die"

This facility is the goose that lays the golden eggs for taxpayers. But like that goose, if we don't protect our investment in this facility, the golden eggs will go away.

— *San Diego Mayor Jerry Sanders, 2008*[63]

The timing of the convention center expansion—completed in 2001—could not have been worse. The terrorist attacks on September 11, 2001, paralyzed the American tourism industry and resulted in a sharp downturn for the convention industry. Over the following several years, the number of convention attendees across the country fell to its lowest level since 1993. Surprisingly, however, falling demand did little to slow down the rapid increase in the available supply of convention space nationwide. Indeed, more and more cities unveiled plans to expand their facilities, in an effort to win a larger slice of a convention industry pie that had stopped growing.[64]

The San Diego convention center, which had more than doubled its exhibition space to over half a million square feet, saw its business recover to pre–September 11 levels only in 2005. Even so, within several years, city leaders were mulling a second expansion, expected to double total convention exhibition space yet again to almost 1 million square feet. The city pointed to increasing pressures from a growing number of metropolitan competitors, which threatened to bump San Diego from the list of the ten largest convention destinations in the country, and to the popularity of the city's homegrown Comic-Con event, a comic book and sci-fi festival that had attracted a cult following and was the largest event hosted at the convention center. In 2008, Comic-Con organizers announced that they would be forced to leave San Diego within half a decade unless the convention center grew to keep pace. Despite its large size, the economic impact of Comic-Con was unclear, because many attendees were locals already contributing to the regional economy.

Mayor Jerry Sanders threw his support behind the expansion, appointing a committee made up of seventeen tourism industry officials and other convention center supporters to develop a plan for another expansion of the center. The "expand or die" hysteria, as the *Union-Tribune* described the push for the first expansion, had only grown louder. In late summer 2009, the mayor's committee came out in support of adding additional capacity at the center at a cost of more than $750 million, easily the largest public works project in the city's history. Amortized over three decades, the city's annual bill for the expansion would likely exceed $50 million.

From the start, Sanders had argued that the city's General Fund and its redevelopment budget would not provide any money for the project. The Port District said it, too, would be unwilling to bankroll the expansion, as it had done with the original construction and the last round of additions. Indeed, the Port District had planned to use the land eyed by the convention center to build a new hotel, and insisted that the proposed expansion proceed only if the Port District was able to receive market-rate rent in exchange. In contrast, the city was still paying just $1 a year for its lease on the original convention center facility.

Aside from endorsing the expansion plans, the mayor's task force offered little guidance on how the construction would be financed. The committee expressed support for a publicly run hotel in conjunction with the expansion, which could provide revenues to offset the annual bond payments. In addition, the group pointed to new surcharges on tourist-related amenities like the San Diego Zoo and SeaWorld, and endorsed a tax assessment on hotel occupants. Under Proposition 218, the assessment would require a majority vote among hotel owners before it could be levied. Several major tourism industry officials expressed support for the assessment, although they made clear that their endorsement was conditional on the money going to finance the expansion rather than helping close a growing deficit in the city's General Fund budget.

Balboa Park: Another Century of Magnificence?

Balboa Park is one of the very most beloved institutions in Greater San Diego. Beyond the incalculable natural and cultural value, it is also an economic powerhouse, adding to the wealth of the region through tourism, property value, direct use and health value, environmental savings and more. It is like a goose with a constant stream of golden eggs, but it is a threatened goose which could fail if it is not replenished and revived.

— *Center for City Parks Excellence, 2006*[65]

Even as San Diego laid plans for its second convention center expansion, one of the city's biggest destinations for out-of-towners was facing an existential crisis. The 1,200-acre Balboa Park recreational area that houses the city's world-famous zoo along with dozens of other cultural institutions and serves as an attraction for millions of visitors was one of the biggest victims of chronic fiscal austerity. As part of the city's Parks and Recreation Department, Balboa Park had seen its budget allocation dwindle in recent years even as it confronted a growing list of maintenance and improvement needs.

In 2006, several local foundations with close ties to the institutions located in the park launched an effort to highlight the problems at the park ahead of the celebration to mark the 1915 Panama-California Exposition, the event that put San Diego on the world map and from which modern Balboa Park emerged. Unfortunately, consultants brought in by the foundations painted a dire picture. Not only was the park ill prepared to mark its centennial, but years of underfunding had raised questions about its continued viability as one of the largest public parks in the country. The city had scant resources to clean up a defunct fifty-acre landfill in the center of the park, much less afford an ostentatious campaign to mark the 1915 celebration.[66] Building on the city's experiments with public-private partnerships, such as the 1998 Petco Park agreement (see Chapter 6), the foundations recommended the creation of a private conservancy to raise new funds for the park and take over a significant portion of the management responsibilities from the city.

Challenges in the New Millennium

[L]ike the famous experiment which showed that frogs will ignore the gradual heating of their water until they suddenly succumb, the deterioration of the park is proceeding despite the lack of public outcry. . . . Balboa Park's problems are due not to frogs and hot water, of course, but to the interrelated scourges of inadequate funding and disjointed management.
— *Center for City Parks Excellence, 2008*[67]

By bringing new attention to the city's largest park, preparation for the 1915 commemoration helped expose decades of city neglect. In the mid-1980s, at the park's nadir, individual museums located within its boundaries and other park institutions took the lead in funding badly needed upgrades. Their efforts spawned a number of philanthropic groups committed to supporting the park's cultural institutions. However, few efforts focused on providing funds for the operation of the park itself. In 2006, the park had received less than $700,000 in direct private support.[68]

The election of Mayor Jerry Sanders marked two important developments that contributed to the deteriorating health of Balboa Park. Elected on a platform of cutting waste and bringing the municipal budget back to balance in the aftermath of the pension fiasco, Sanders found the job far more difficult once in office. The city council opposed cuts to popular programs and the closure of neighborhood parks and libraries located in their districts. In turn, the Sanders budgets continued the practice of shorting basic maintenance and further reduced funding for less visible park department functions such as landscaping.

In addition, as the city's first "strong" mayor, Sanders took charge in restructuring the city bureaucracy previously operating under an appointed city manager rather than an elected chief executive. Under the old council-manager system, Balboa Park was managed by a department tasked with overseeing the city's entire parks inventory, including several other developed regional parks. There was no dedicated management oversight for Balboa Park. Under the Sanders reorganization, city departments were further consolidated, with park planning moved into the citywide Planning Department and maintenance delegated to its Public Works unit. The change, along with a years-long hiring freeze, contributed to a loss of staff and institutional memory.[69]

As the city effectively dismantled its structure for managing Balboa Park, it confronted a series of new challenges. A 2003 study, commissioned with a state grant, documented considerable problems related to transportation to and within the park. The study recommended a new circulation system and a complete overhaul of parking, at a cost of $500 million. With the pension crisis blocking city access to municipal bond markets, the recommendations were quietly shelved. A second analysis, commissioned by several San Diego foundations, identified nearly $250 million in needed work, including badly deferred maintenance and projects promised under the park's master plan but never funded by the city.[70]

Despite its symbolic stature among residents and visitors, the park has remained a low priority for elected officials. With most of the festering problems hidden beneath the surface, no natural electoral constituency or public official emerged to champion the park's cause. Indeed, most voters appeared oblivious to the problems. In a phone survey funded by the foundations, a surprising 95 percent of respondents rated their satisfaction with Balboa Park as either "excellent" or "good." Patrons of the park's cultural institutions remained reluctant to front their own money, fearing that it would be diverted to other parts of the city's budget. With other pressing concerns taking center stage in the political arena, the city did not seem a likely source for the park's salvation.[71]

A Going-Private Strategy

My hope would be that we would have an entity that would bring the focus and attention to the park. A nonprofit partner whose sole purpose is to champion the park would get us to where we need to be.

— *City Councilman Todd Gloria, 2009*[72]

With the city's General Fund an unlikely source of new money and no public champion making a case for increased investment in the park, foundation consultants identified several options for raising capital to fund existing Balboa Park projects and prepare for the centennial. Two strategies—seeking higher taxes and the creation of a regional park district—were largely ruled out because they would require voters to approve new property taxes or assessments. Two others—a partnership with the county and the formation of a private conservancy—were referred for further study to the city's Balboa Park Committee, a group of private citizens serving in an advisory capacity to the mayor and city council.

Echoing the consultant's findings, the committee noted that it saw "no evidence of civic or political will to increase taxes to support Balboa Park in the future." Although it encouraged the city to continue working on closer collaboration with the county, the committee noted the "financial and political impediments" that stood in the way of creating a joint-powers authority to manage the park. The county was already busy with planning its own downtown park on county-owned land located near the County Administration Building.[73]

While calling on the city to ensure that Balboa Park would remain public in perpetuity and to ensure that privatization never be allowed, the committee endorsed the creation of a nonprofit conservancy to raise private funds and, over time, to assume increased managerial responsibilities over the park. Such a conservancy, the committee argued, would encourage private benefactors interested in giving to the park but worried that their donations would be diverted for other city uses. Leveraging private funds and future city bond proceeds, the conservancy could take the lead on moving ahead with the deferred projects.

Noting the potential for cost savings, the city's committee noted that Balboa Park "might benefit from being run with business efficiency principles." However, it urged that "profit motives related to business practices should never be allowed to overshadow the general public benefit of this public resource." Ironically, the job of designing an institution to both reassure sponsors that the mismanaged city would be kept at arm's length from the park's private endowment, and ensure voters that the conservancy was serving public ends, would fall to city officials. In the short term, delegating to a conservancy would do little to provide

Balboa Park with new revenue. It would, however, free elected officials from the responsibility of identifying additional public funds to support the park and, perhaps, shield them from direct blame for having allowed it to deteriorate so dramatically.[74]

Faustian Bargains?

[E]ven in the incredible public relations efforts associated with general plan updates and environmental impact reports, the irony of popular participation is that it creates new problems calling for creative solutions that only large-scale corporate developers have the ability and interest to provide. Progressive grassroots movements for tax reform, environmental regulation, and growth control simply increase local government's dependence on the private sector.

—*Richard Hogan*, The Failure of Planning, 2003[75]

In San Diego, the process of long-range planning—designed to assist the community in agreeing on and preparing for its future—is fundamentally broken.[76] Part of the problem is that the city's residents and other civic stakeholders share no well-recognized vision for the city's future. This dissensus has only increased over the past twenty years, with the growing divergence in the quality of life and city services between voters in the newer areas of the city and those living in its older, more diverse neighborhoods. Over the same period, growing fragmentation in the business community has further weakened its ability to spearhead broad-based planning efforts, thus ceding ground to private entrepreneurs.

Equally important, since the early 1990s, the City of San Diego has lacked a coherent institutional foundation for carrying on rational planning functions. In response to a sex scandal in the city's Planning Department, tasked with charting the long-range course for the city, direct city council control over planning functions was eliminated in 1992. This change, along with sharp cutbacks in planning staff in response to the post–Cold War recession, effectively neutered the department and shifted staff focus and energy from long-range planning to serving the interests of the real estate development community.[77] Since then, the city's planning approach—dependent, in large part, on ad hoc citizen committees of civic notables, usually appointed to make the case for favored projects, not to provide an impartial analysis of them—has served the interests of its elected officials and private developers but has poorly represented its residents. Rather than professional planners, the city's priorities have been defined by special interests like Padres owner John Moores (library), hotelier Doug Manchester (convention center), and developer Ernest Hahn (city hall).

In addition, political developments since 1990 have further shifted the city's focus away from responsible planning. The advent of district elections, according to political consultant Larry Remer, has forced "growth issues to move down to the neighborhood level so they could be sorted out," empowering local groups but also taking broader planning questions off the city council agenda.[78] Community planning groups, a growing presence in city development politics over the past two decades, have taken a markedly not-in-my-backyard approach by focusing on the prevention of unwanted local development. They have, however, done little to address festering citywide issues. Partly as a result, the void has been filled by private entrepreneurs, with the capacity to sell their projects to the public, and ambitious mayors interested in legacy-building projects who have taken the lead in shaping the city's overall agenda.

The absence of agreement among San Diego's civic elite and its citizens about what the future of the city will look like and the incapacity of local planning institutions are only partly responsible for the ad hoc quality of the local development process. The process is ad hoc in the sense that growth occurs via a series of disconnected projects; when a new project conflicts with an existing planning document, the latter is the one most easily jettisoned. An equally important ingredient since the early 1990s has been a shift in emphasis among local elected officials, from a citywide and long-term to a district-based and short-term focus. District elections reward politicians who deliver benefits that are narrowly targeted, visible to voters, and attributable (i.e., a politician can readily claim credit for them). There are few incentives to maintain larger public goods, such as Balboa Park, where costs are visible to voters and benefits are less visible, widely diffused among residents, and difficult for individual politicians to credibly claim credit for.

The final element consists of post–Proposition 13 rules that require supermajority support for raising taxes. Presumably, this high bar ought to enhance the prospects of projects with widespread support among voters while diminishing those favored by small majorities or minorities. Proposition 13 did not, however, change the electoral calculus of politicians, who are reelected on the strength of bare (usually small) majorities. In practice, Proposition 13 has made it difficult, but not impossible, for San Diego's elected officials to give majorities of voters the projects they want; the same might be said of the city's dire fiscal straits. Thus, there are ample incentives to either hide the true costs of public projects or to rely on financing mechanisms that do not require voter support. Unfortunately, such mechanisms tend to be the least transparent to voters and not always consistent with sound fiscal management, let alone a rational, deliberative planning process.

6 Redevelopment, San Diego Style
The Limits of Public-Private Partnerships

[Regarding Petco Park–East Village] we have also not gotten money to pay for parks, fire stations, churches or other services downtown. There are no water fountains or public restrooms there. We are getting a privatized downtown, with laws and gates erected all over the place that say pedestrians are not welcome.

—*Bruce Henderson, former city councilman, 2007*[1]

Since the early 1980s, the City of San Diego has lavished money and other public resources on redevelopment projects in and around its downtown core. In the 1990s, public investment in downtown redevelopment accelerated even as the city's financial position deteriorated and its basic infrastructure sank into disrepair. San Diego's downtown renaissance culminated in 1998 with a mammoth redevelopment project that combined construction of Petco Park, a baseball stadium for the San Diego Padres, and ancillary development in the once-moribund East Village. The project, which involved cooperation among several public agencies and a private corporation, the Padres, is widely hailed as a public-private partnership worthy of emulation. Similarly, through two public-private partnerships (P3s) to redevelop land formerly owned by the U.S. Navy, local officials have secured much-needed private capital for transforming San Diego's waterfront.

San Diego is not the first city to tap private-sector know-how to achieve public redevelopment objectives.[2] The disappearance of federal funding for urban programs and growing fiscal austerity over the past few decades have forced cities to develop alternative means of financing redevelopment programs. Today, cities are making liberal use of business improvement districts, tax increment funds, revenue bonds, and sin and hotel taxes to finance renewal initiatives. To attract investors, businesses, residents, and visitors, San Diego and other cities have adopted entertainment-oriented redevelopment strategies, in the hopes that sports franchises, retail, and tourism will replace the jobs and revenues once supplied by manufacturing activities.

This chapter evaluates San Diego's major post-1990 downtown and bay-front redevelopment efforts featuring P3s. San Diego's approach is unique in at least two key respects. One major difference is the extensive use of public-private redevelopment partnerships that delegate substantial public resources and powers to the private sector.[3] Indeed, San Diego has used P3s more extensively and, with Petco Park, on a larger scale than is typical of cities elsewhere. These partnerships put city staff and elected officials in the unfamiliar role of negotiating convoluted contracts—spelling out each partner's rights and responsibilities—and monitoring private actors wielding expansive public powers.[4] The degree to which they have succeeded (or not) in these roles has determined the extent to which the city's redevelopment efforts have produced public, rather than private, payoffs.

A second difference lies in the decision to delegate responsibility for overseeing complex partnerships to special nonprofit corporations. In doing so, San Diego has instituted a markedly different structure for governing its redevelopment activities from that of other California cities. As quasi-independent nonprofit corporations, the city's two primary redevelopment agencies—the Centre City Development Corporation and Southeastern Economic Development Corporation—feature separate boards of directors, staffs, legal counsels, and budgets, and are responsible for managing and implementing particular programs and projects on behalf of the city. The critical question is whether such entities act as able public agents encouraging needed investment in crumbling urban cores and promoting projects of public benefit.[5]

San Diego's unique mix of institutions has succeeded in securing greater resources for redevelopment and involving the private sector in reshaping land-use patterns downtown. In a city where local residents refuse to tax themselves to pay for public benefits and prefer private-sector actors to take the lead, these are notable accomplishments. On the downside, however, these institutions have produced P3 agreements heavily weighted toward private actors. Further, by off-loading oversight responsibilities to nonprofit corporations that view downtown real estate interests, not local residents, as their core constituency, public officials have allowed private actors to renege on their promises. Were San Diego's private-sector partners as public spirited as their advertising brochures suggest, such shortcomings would cause little concern. Unfortunately, they are not, and their record of self-interested behavior shows San Diego's redevelopment regime to be as naive as it is innovative.

San Diego's Shadow Government

San Diego's redevelopment agency—established to eliminate blight and revitalize older neighborhoods—is in crisis. . . . Critics charge that redevelopment lacks public accountability and benefits influential private interests more than the public. . . . A unique problem in San Diego is how redevelopment is organized.

> —Michael Jenkins, former assistant director, City of San Diego Community and Economic Development Department, and Norma Damashek, vice president, San Diego League of Women Voters, 2007[6]

A Nonprofit Corporation Approach

Redevelopment policy in California is structured by the California Community Redevelopment Act of 1945, which gives cities and counties authority to establish redevelopment agencies to address urban decay and to apply for federal funding. In 1958, the city council established the Redevelopment Agency of the City of San Diego to reduce blight in certain areas. The agency is essentially a legal fiction. The city council serves as the board of directors. Initially, the city manager served as the agency's executive director. In 2005, voters approved a mayor-council form of government under which the mayor assumed these duties. The agency has no staff of its own but contracts with the City of San Diego for accounting, purchasing, and legal services. It also contracts with the city for redevelopment staff needed to manage eleven project areas and to provide oversight for six others managed by two nonprofit development corporations.[7]

In 1975, at the behest of Mayor Pete Wilson, the city council created the Centre City Development Corporation (CCDC) to eliminate blight and revitalize the downtown area. Initially, CCDC was assigned to manage Horton Plaza, a massive redevelopment project designed to establish a retail hub downtown. The jurisdiction of CCDC was expanded in 1976 (Columbia and Marina project areas), in 1982 (Gaslamp Quarter), and most recently in 1992 (Little Italy, Cortez Hill, and East Village). Figure 6.1 shows the location of the different project areas managed by CCDC. In 1981, the city chartered the Southeastern Economic Development Corporation (SEDC) to implement economic and redevelopment projects in southeast San Diego. Both entities are governed by boards of directors appointed by the mayor and city council.[8]

CCDC and SEDC were both created to circumvent civil service procedures that govern the hiring of outside consultants and project management staff. Both corporations are able to bypass the public contracting procedures adopted by the city. Indeed, CCDC was created precisely because local public officials believed these rules to be time consuming and cumbersome (i.e., developer unfriendly). The boards of these agencies are staffed by insiders—developers, lawyers, consultants, and activists—many of whom have a vested (and, too often, financial) interest in the projects they manage.

San Diego's redevelopment agencies are funded by a mix of tax increment funds, federal Community Development Block Grants, bond proceeds, and city loans. The tax increment forms by far the largest revenue source. For each project area, a base-year assessed valuation for purposes of taxing property is established. Tax increment revenue refers to the taxes collected annually as a result of any increase in the tax value of the property above the base-year assessment.[9] Rather than flow into the city's General Fund and to other local government agencies, the redevelopment agency keeps the tax increment. These funds are carried over from year to year and used to fund new projects.

San Diego is the only big city in California that has chosen to delegate its central redevelopment functions to nonprofit corporations.[10] The city's recent experience with these corporations, however, has raised questions about whether such arrangements protect the interests of local residents. In 2008, CCDC Executive Director Nancy Graham unexpectedly resigned amid conflict-of-interest charges related to her involvement with private developers lobbying for CCDC-backed projects downtown. Meanwhile, SEDC's Chief Executive Officer Carolyn Smith was fired over allegations of unapproved and extravagant executive compensation bonuses. Such scandals, combined with management and performance concerns raised by the San Diego County Grand Jury, have led to calls to reevaluate San Diego's shadow-government experiment.

FIGURE 6.1   Project areas of the Centre City Development Corporation
SOURCE: Centre City Development Corporation.

In fairness, until the 1970s, redevelopment agencies in other California cities, including Los Angeles and San Francisco, also resembled shadow governments. Local redevelopment officials regularly placed the concerns of businesses and real estate developers over those of existing neighborhoods and residents. Unlike San Diego, redevelopment in these cities was carried out by municipal agencies on a citywide level without spin-off corporations managing specific projects. In some cities, mayors and city councils even appointed citizen commissions to oversee redevelopment programs; however, local boosters typically dominated such boards. Other cities opted to retain redevelopment powers in the hands of elected officials.

Starting in the 1960s, popular backlash against redevelopment—expressed in lawsuits and the reassertion of mayoral and city council oversight and control—altered redevelopment efforts in Los Angeles and San Francisco. By the late 1980s, redevelopment priorities and investment in L.A. had shifted from downtown commercial projects to outlying blighted communities, with a focus on affordable housing and neighborhood revitalization. In San Francisco, the pace and scale of downtown commercial redevelopment declined with voter-approved growth-control initiatives.[11] Not so in San Diego. While other California big cities were reprioritizing redevelopment projects and investments and scaling back central city revitalization, San Diego pursued full-throttle downtown redevelopment.

Table 6.1 compares redevelopment revenues and expenditures in Los Angeles, San Francisco, and San Diego between 1990 and 2003, the year before Petco Park opened. In San Diego, CCDC directed nearly 80 percent of the city's total redevelopment investment downtown. In contrast, Los Angeles invested 61 percent and San Francisco 70 percent of redevelopment dollars downtown. Since 2003, as San Diego's downtown project areas have begun to approach their legal caps in the amount of property tax revenues that CCDC can collect, the city has worked to diversify its investments, increasing the amount of money spent in areas outside downtown. In 2010, CCDC scored a major political victory when state Assemblyman Nathan Fletcher authored legislation eliminating the ceiling on downtown redevelopment dollars, in preparation for investing potentially $500 million in a new downtown football stadium for the San Diego Chargers.[12]

TABLE 6.1   Tax increment, redevelopment revenue, and spending in Los
Angeles, San Francisco, and San Diego, 1990–2003 (millions of 2000 dollars)

City agency	Tax increment	Total revenues[a]	Total expenditures
Los Angeles Community Redevelopment Agency	1,400	2,400	3,100
Downtown[b]	975	1,500	1,900
Share of citywide total	68%	62%	61%
San Francisco Redevelopment Agency	350	1,300	2,000
Downtown[c]	243	936	1,400
Share of citywide total	69%	72%	70%
San Diego Redevelopment Agency	434	646	868
CCDC (downtown)[d]	364	556	677
Share of citywide total	84%	86%	78%
SEDC[e]	24	40	87
Share of citywide total	6%	6%	10%
City Redevelopment Division (all other)[f]	46	50	103
Share of citywide total	11%	8%	12%

SOURCES: California State Controller, *Redevelopment Agencies Annual Report*, various years.
NOTE: Adjusted to 2000 dollars using the Implicit Price Deflator.
[a]Includes some sales and transient-occupancy taxes collected in project areas, federal grants, and other forms of income.
[b]Includes Little Tokyo, City Center, Chinatown, Central Industrial, Central Business District, Council District 9/South of Santa Monica, and Bunker Hill project areas.
[c]Includes Rincon Point and South Beach; South of Market, Golden Gateway, and Federal Office Building; and Yerba Buena Center project areas.
[d]Includes Centre City, Columbia, Gaslamp Quarter, Horton Plaza, and Marina project areas.
[e]Includes Central Imperial, Dells Imperial, Gateway Center, Mount Hope, and Southcrest project areas.
[f]Includes Barrio Logan, City Heights, College Community, College Grove, Crossroads, Grantville, Linda Vista, Market Street, North Bay, North Park, Naval Training Center, San Ysidro, and San Diego State University project areas.

Delegation or Abdication?

More than most cities, San Diego has embraced redevelopment P3s as an integral downtown revitalization strategy. Indeed, CCDC was created to facilitate a redevelopment P3 between the City of San Diego and developer Ernest Hahn to build a retail center in the heart of the city's historical but dilapidated downtown. CCDC fulfilled its role, limiting public involvement and helping clear the area to make space for the mammoth project. Horton Plaza, an outdoor mall based on an Italian hill design, was completed in 1985, at a cost of $140 million, including $40 million in public funds and a timely loan from the state.

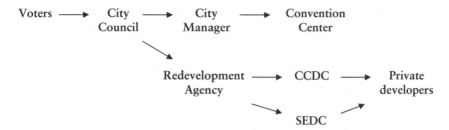

FIGURE 6.2   Nested structure of San Diego redevelopment relationships, 1990–2005

Figure 6.2 maps the complex system of nested delegations used to undertake San Diego's downtown redevelopment program up to 2005, when the strong-mayor system replaced the council-manager form of government. At each link in the chain, there is a risk of shirking by public officials and/or private developers, which allows the city's redevelopment activities to diverge from its ostensibly public mission. In particular, the link between the city council and the redevelopment agency has been fraught with legal ambiguity and institutional incapacity. Although the city council acts as the board of the redevelopment agency, it has delegated management and oversight responsibilities first to the city manager and later to the mayor.

Although city-appointed boards are supposed to manage the two development corporations on behalf of the city, a series of public controversies and recent audits has exposed deep problems within. Board members are supposed to serve fixed terms, although many routinely stay on years after their commissions expire.[13] In addition, CCDC and SEDC administrators regularly awarded bonuses and pay increases to themselves and signed no-bid contracts without the knowledge of their boards. Thus, there has been little oversight of the redevelopment agency, CCDC, or SEDC, let alone private-sector partners. The city manager had little incentive to scrutinize their activities, as criticism of them would inevitably implicate the city council. As a result, no independent reviews of the redevelopment agency, CCDC, or SEDC were conducted until recently.

In 2008, the San Diego County Grand Jury, a public watchdog group set up to investigate the operations of public agencies, concluded that the redevelopment agency had failed to exercise effective oversight over CCDC.[14] In 2009, a follow-up report cited a wholesale lack of financial and operational accountability in the relationship between the agency and its quasi-public agents. The report also found that redevelopment activities carried out by San Diego's various agencies and partners were marked by confusion in the lines of authority.[15]

Field of Schemes? Petco Park Reconsidered

We had the most extensively planned ballpark in the history of mankind. . . . I don't think most people are aware that it was the largest redevelopment program in North America.

—*Former San Diego Padres owner John Moores, 2005*[16]

Over the past ten years, downtown San Diego has been transformed by new construction supported by more than $1 billion in private investment activity.[17] A cornerstone of this latest redevelopment phase is Petco Park—a new $454 million stadium for the San Diego Padres. Most of the stadium's costs were borne by the public sector under a redevelopment P3 among the City of San Diego; the Port District; CCDC; and JMI Realty, the real estate arm of Padres owner John Moores. The structure of this P3 agreement—up-front public stadium financing in exchange for ancillary private development—cast both public- and private-sector actors in unfamiliar roles. Most peculiar were provisions that invested JMI Realty with expansive rights and authority to reshape land-use patterns within a twenty-six-block area of downtown known as East Village. Under the 1998 agreement, JMI became responsible for developing new office parks, retail centers, public open space, and affordable housing on behalf of San Diego residents.

San Diego's ballpark project has been cited by scholars and practitioners as a new redevelopment paradigm, an exception to the conventional wisdom that new sports facilities produce few economic benefits.[18] Planning scholar Tim Chapin, for example, portrays San Diego as the archetypal entrepreneurial city.[19] According to this view, local government officials assumed the lead role in cobbling together resources, marshaling public support and parlaying up-front financing into back-end profits. Proponents of this view cite the tremendous surge in private investment activity in the East Village following completion of the new stadium as evidence of San Diego's successful experiment with municipal capitalism.

This salutary account distorts the basic facts of the ballpark episode. San Diego's ambitious redevelopment P3 is a story of failed delegation, not of municipal leadership. We offer an alternative account to the conventional wisdom, detailing troubling aspects of the process leading to approval of the 1998 agreement and problems with implementation. Four years into the partnership, this "innovative" P3 was on life support, thus necessitating an overhaul of initial plans that increased public-sector costs while allowing the Padres to renegotiate the terms of the P3 to enhance private benefits. Ten years out, there is strong evidence that the bulk of the benefits from East Village revitalization have been captured by private developers, whereas many of the costs have been borne by San Diego residents. These problems are rooted in shortcomings in the P3 agreement and the institutional structures that gave rise to it.

The project's apparent strength—a contractual link between the City of San Diego's contribution to stadium construction and the team's commitment to invest significant capital in nearby neighborhoods—created perverse incentives for local elected officials. In bundling together the ballpark and much of the city's downtown redevelopment program, the arrangement gave the team substantial bargaining advantages. These were used by the Padres to renegotiate more favorable terms after work on the ballpark had begun. Initially, the project allowed elected officials to claim credit for retaining a popular sports franchise (the Padres) and achieving growth at little cost to taxpayers. Unfortunately, these officials had little motivation to protect San Diegans from the project's financial risks or to compel JMI to live up to its promises, especially if doing so threatened to grind downtown redevelopment to a halt.

San Diego's Sports Misadventures

The impetus for San Diego's downtown ballpark came in the form of a 1996 agreement between the city and its professional football franchise, the San Diego Chargers, to renovate Jack Murphy Stadium. Both the Chargers and the Padres paid rent to the city to use the stadium for home games. The city's position entering the 1996 negotiations was

decidedly weak. The Chargers were coming off their most successful season, having made it to the Super Bowl for the first time. Local officials
had previously acknowledged that the stadium's current size (sixty-one
thousand seats) and state of disrepair would require upgrades to keep it
a competitive Super Bowl site. In the final agreement, San Diego contributed $60 million for stadium improvements and offered the Chargers a
ticket guarantee of sixty thousand for all home games. If attendance were
to fall below that level, the city would reduce the team's rent to make up
the shortfall.

The 1996 agreement was a fiscal and political disaster. Renovation costs ballooned to $78 million because of the poor quality of the soil
and efforts to make the facility earthquake-proof.[20] The ticket guarantee
ended up costing far more than anticipated ($36 million between 1997
and 2004). Before signing the agreement, local officials never checked
previous attendance records, which would have revealed that a sixty
thousand threshold was wildly optimistic.[21]

The Chargers deal provided ammunition for Padres owner John
Moores's campaign for a new baseball-only stadium. Citing annual operating losses, he claimed that the team would be unable to compete with
baseball franchises playing in more modern venues. Facing the prospect of
losing the Padres, Mayor Susan Golding appointed a task force to study
the stadium issue. In response to the task force's recommendation that a
new facility be constructed, the city entered into negotiations with the
Padres. In 1997, a second ballpark task force was created to identify a site
for the new stadium and to explore alternative financing arrangements.

Bypassing City Hall

To build support for a new ballpark using public resources, city
officials opted to convene a special task force rather than work through
city government. The Task Force on Ballpark Planning, comprising seventeen private citizens drawn mostly from the business community, was
appointed in June 1997. The task force alternative offered several advantages. First, those appointed to the task force felt that local elected
officials were attempting to avoid blame should the project fail.[22] Second,
the task force route helped the mayor, who hoped to use a high-profile
deal to build her credentials for higher office, to shape the final ballpark

proposal by appointing only those sympathetic to the project to the task force. Although this made sense as a political strategy, the task force largely bypassed professional planners and other staff with redevelopment expertise.

Members of the task force worked to craft a deal that would justify the massive public investment needed to build the new stadium. Downtown was appealing, as it would enable the city to tap a variety of redevelopment funds. The East Village, located near the Gaslamp Quarter and convention center, was identified as an area that might support the hotels, retail, and office projects that local public officials envisioned. With the city formulating plans to expand the convention center, the long-ignored neighborhoods in the East Village were emerging as San Diego's most desirable real estate investment opportunity.

The task force's final report agreed with the Padres that the team could not remain financially viable at the now-renamed Qualcomm Stadium and recommended that the city pursue an agreement on a new stadium in the East Village.[23] The task force also urged the city to link public financing for a new stadium to a massive East Village redevelopment project that would create new hotels and businesses. Such ancillary development would yield new revenues that the city would need to pay off its stadium bond obligations. Linking the ballpark to private-sector investment also provided a political solution for how to sell the expensive project to local voters. The slogan offered by ballpark supporters in the campaign for voter approval for the public subsidy would be "more than a ballpark."

A Memorandum of Misunderstanding?

Once the task force had blessed the downtown site, Mayor Golding and the Padres negotiated a memorandum of understanding (MOU) that specified the division of labor and financial obligations of all parties. In addition to the City of San Diego and the Padres, the 1998 MOU involved CCDC and, later, the Port District. The basic structure of the deal was financing for a new stadium in exchange for ancillary development within a seventy-five-acre (twenty-six-block) district in the East Village. The city agreed to shoulder the costs of building the stadium. In return, the Padres assumed responsibility for revitalizing the area around the stadium. The estimated cost of the ballpark project was set at $411 million, with $267.5 million for the stadium and $143.5 million in infrastructure improvements and land acquisition.

The City of San Diego assumed primary responsibility for land acquisition in the East Village and the needed up-front financing for stadium construction. The city's initial commitment to the ballpark totaled $186.5 million. It was also on the hook for $38.5 million in land acquisition. Together, these obligations totaled $215 million. With the city already facing a budget crunch and local officials unwilling to raise taxes, the bulk of this funding would come from bonds backed by future transient-occupancy tax (TOT) revenue.[24] The city contributed another $50 million in land acquisition through CCDC, which controlled the tax increment revenue harvested from project areas downtown. The Port District stepped in at the last minute to fill a $21 million shortfall. Port District funds were slated for infrastructure upgrades, such as pedestrian bridges, wider streets, and intersections.

The Padres were asked to put up $115 million for the project, $81 million to help build the stadium and $34 million for land acquisition and infrastructure. The $115 million figure, however, is misleading. The 1998 MOU allowed the team to pay for its share of the stadium via a variety of credits, including concession revenues and naming rights to the stadium. In 2003, retail giant Petco secured the naming rights for $60 million. The city, which retained a 70 percent interest in the stadium, received none of this money. Thus, the money from concessions and the stadium marquee that went to pay for the Padres' share was essentially another subsidy given to the team.[25]

The most significant project delegation involved not resources but authority. In addition to supplying $215 million in public money, the city gave JMI a nearly free hand to redevelop a twenty-six-block area of downtown. The mix of ancillary development was to include hotels, office buildings, retail space, a park beyond the outfield walls of the stadium, and residential development, including affordable housing. The city and the team agreed on a flexible schedule for the ancillary development that would, it was hoped, result in substantial new TOT revenues that the city could tap to repay its stadium bonds. The 1998 MOU, however, gave the Padres the authority to change the precise mix of ancillary development—

as long as the changes did not reduce the value of the development or the amount of TOT revenue it would deliver:

> The Developer will have the right to fine-tune its mix of hotel, office, retail, residential and other development space within the District at any time prior to the completion of Phase 1 . . . in order for the development program to respond to market conditions. . . . The Padres/Developer shall have the right to transfer all or part of these rights and obligations to an entity reasonably acceptable to the City and [Redevelopment] Agency, and the parties recognize that market demand shall be the critical determinant in the ability of the Padres/Developer to commit by April 1, 1999 to the high level of Phase 1 development contemplated.[26]

This and other clauses gave the Padres substantial flexibility in determining the mix of ancillary development and, by implication, the extent of the ballpark project's public benefits.

From a business perspective, the 1998 MOU looked like a great deal for San Diego. It would bring a massive infusion of private investment to a blighted area. From a policy perspective, however, the problems with the MOU were legion. First, the primary beneficiary of the ballpark deal, the Padres, was a private organization whose operations had little impact on the local economy. Compared to the benefits it received, the team was asked to contribute few of its own resources. Second, the city was responsible for most of the up-front costs of land acquisition and stadium financing. These costs were fixed and immediate. The obligations of the Padres were vague and on the back end. Thus, the city, not the team, was assuming most of the up-front risk associated with the project.

Third, the language of the MOU made the interests of the Padres paramount. By allowing the team to fine-tune the ancillary development, local officials ceded control over what was built in the East Village. In effect, the MOU shaping San Diego's redevelopment P3 assumed that the team's goals would coincide with the public interest. As a result, the MOU contained minimal institutional checks and left the door open to renegotiation. Primary oversight for the project was delegated to CCDC, whose interest was to maximize the amount of new tax increment funds generated from the project, all of which would be used for further downtown development. The schedule envisioned by Mayor Golding and the

Padres suggested that several hotel projects would be completed before the stadium opened, providing new TOT revenues to repay the city's bonds, even though the largest of the planned hotels would be constructed outside of the project area under the aegis of the Port District.

Securing Voter Approval

Concerned that the ballpark project would be viewed as a backroom deal in the mold of the Chargers agreement, local officials agreed to place the MOU on the November 1998 ballot. The mayor and the Padres left few stones unturned in soliciting support for Proposition C, the ballpark project initiative. Pro-ballpark organizations spent $2.5 million, including funds for daily public-opinion tracking polls, versus roughly $25,000 spent by the opposition. The Padres marshaled support from local business groups and plied elected officials with gifts and campaign contributions. In at least one case, these gifts were improper. In 2001, Councilwoman Valerie Stallings pleaded guilty to accepting an insider stock deal from Moores, allegedly a payoff for efforts to secure approval of the ballpark agreement. Mayor Golding and the Padres also put pressure on the San Diego County Taxpayers Association, which had warned of the ballpark project's adverse impact on the city's finances.[27]

As the mayor and the Padres were whipping up enthusiasm for the ballpark project, others began finding fault with the MOU's structure. In June 1998, the San Diego County Grand Jury began looking into the ballpark deal. The grand jury issued a report in November that accused ballpark proponents, including local officials, of withholding information and failing to evaluate the project's fiscal impact. Most damaging was the finding that the project's ultimate cost, approximately $800 million over the thirty-year bond debt-service life, could not be paid for if assumptions about TOT revenues turned out to be inaccurate or the economy faltered.[28] City staff told the grand jury that they agreed that the projections were optimistic but that "the given instructions were to use and show" these estimates "and none lower than that." The report's findings were prophetic. Little of the hotel tax money materialized by the time Petco Park opened. Moreover, the TOT estimates used to sell the ballot measure to voters proved wildly optimistic within months of the vote.[29]

Unfortunately for Proposition C's opponents, the report was not released until the day voters went to the polls to decide the fate of the project. Its findings had been kept under wraps by the mayor and city attorney, under the pretext of allowing CCDC and the Port District time to respond. The ballot measure passed with 59.5 percent of the vote, a decisive victory for stadium proponents and an apparent mandate for transforming downtown. The MOU placed hundreds of millions of dollars in public financing and unprecedented legal authority in the hands of a single private-sector actor—the Padres. The fate of the project rested on the wistful hopes of local public officials and residents that the team's interests would coincide with their own.

Sufficient Assurances?

The same concerns that led to the appointment of a task force to handle ballpark planning were apparent as the city prepared to implement the largest redevelopment project in its history. Convinced that the task would be too complicated, technically and politically, for regular city staff, the city council hired Mike Madigan, vice president of a large development company, to serve as San Diego's ballpark czar. With a salary of $200,000 a year, Madigan became the most highly paid public official in San Diego. Although Madigan's credentials were impeccable, outsourcing oversight and management responsibilities to a paid consultant further limited the mayor's and the council's ability to shape the project. Madigan would eventually resign over conflict-of-interest concerns because of his own investment in East Village real estate.

Under this peculiar arrangement, the city allowed JMI Realty, the John Moores–owned real estate firm responsible for carrying out the ancillary development, to significantly underdeliver on the promises the team made in the MOU. For example, although architectural renderings circulated with the ballot measure promised a three- to four-acre public park, the "park at the park" shrank to fewer than two acres in the plans the team ultimately submitted to the city. The MOU did not specify the park's dimensions, and the Padres argued that the models voters saw were simply artistic and, thus, not binding. Similarly, although the renderings depicted a park surrounded by small six-floor buildings, the team's final plan included three high-rises, two of which exceeded twenty stories.[30]

The MOU structuring the redevelopment P3 did allow local officials to sign off on the final terms of construction. Just as the team could fine-tune its plans, the city council was required to twice certify that the Padres had made "sufficient assurances" that the team's obligations would be met when the ballpark opened. If such assurances were not forthcoming, the city could cancel the ballpark project, although doing so would entail an end to the team's redevelopment activities. Not surprisingly, local officials were reluctant to use this leverage to secure concessions, worried about shouldering the political blame for killing a popular project and wreaking havoc downtown. As April 1, 1999, approached—the date of the first certification—the team had made scant progress. JMI Realty had spent $24 million on land for the ballpark but had secured no commitments from lenders and found no tenants for its proposed office building. Its latest plans included nearly 100 fewer hotel rooms than promised, although the team said that it would generate the same amount of hotel tax revenue as the 850 rooms it originally agreed to.[31]

Privately, local officials complained that the team had not spent enough risk capital—money that would be lost if the project fell apart. Even developer-friendly CCDC refused to vote that "sufficient assurances" had been made that the project would generate the tax revenue needed to pay for the ballpark. Former ballpark proponents urged the city council to hold off until the team could produce more results. The San Diego County Taxpayers Association warned that the city would put itself out on a limb if it moved ahead when the future of the hotel projects needed to pay for the bonds remained uncertain. Despite these concerns, the city council gave in to the Padres, which argued that the public bonds were needed to make headway on the financing front. After JMI agreed to build all of the 850 hotel rooms provided in the initial agreement and to bid for another hotel project if needed, the council gave the redevelopment plan a green light.

Although the city council had certified that the team was meeting its commitments, the city failed to sell its stadium bonds by early 2000 as planned. Uncertainty over hotel tax revenues—which the city needed to pay for its bond obligation—and a series of lawsuits initiated by former Councilman Bruce Henderson, a ballpark opponent, stood in the way. With the legal challenges and hotel fiascos threatening to raise the interest rate on the bonds, thus increasing the city's expected annual costs by more than $2 million, the bond sale ran into growing opposition on the city council.[32]

The City of San Diego had lent more than $20 million to pay for construction until bond money became available. These funds had been fully spent by 2001, when public officials had to make their second "sufficient assurances" finding. JMI Realty, which had cleared the project area of existing buildings, shut down construction, leaving in the East Village an empty lot with steel ballpark beams. Not a single major hotel included in the initial agreement had begun construction. The team argued that it was not to blame for the delays. Although the agreement with the Padres was designed to insulate the city from risk, Golding's successor, Mayor Dick Murphy, warned that San Diego could not live with a hole in the East Village. Abandoning the project and standing up to the team was simply not a credible option.

Instead, Mayor Murphy devised an alternative financial plan that departed from the deal voters approved in 1998. Murphy's plan no longer included a hotel site long mired in litigation. Nor did it require the Padres' hotels to be completed by 2003, when the ballpark was originally slated to open. Although the team had secured financing for hotels, the agreements were set to expire. There was no assurance that new loans would be obtained. Rather than rely on new hotel construction, Murphy proposed that the city raid its other hotel tax revenues, earmarked for civic and cultural purposes. With several lawsuits challenging the project still on appeal, the plan would require San Diego to pay higher interest rates than initially anticipated. The city council approved the Murphy plan in November 2001.[33]

Revisiting Project Public Benefits

Four years into San Diego's "innovative" redevelopment P3, its costs and benefits to local taxpayers had altered considerably. Sold to voters as a downtown cure-all with a huge upside and no cost to local taxpayers, the ballpark project had suddenly become a drain on city revenues. JMI Realty had used its discretionary authority to eliminate aspects of the ancillary development—office parks, retail centers, open space—that were most attractive from the city's standpoint because they promised to provide public facilities and new sales tax revenue that would flow into the city's coffers. With none of the promised hotel projects materializing, the city would have to finance the project from its other, already-strained revenue sources.

Approval of Murphy's funding plan did not end the team's attempts to reshape the project to maximize profits. In 2005, JMI unveiled plans for Ballpark Village, a $1.4 billion, 7.1-acre project central to the ancillary development. The Ballpark Village project exemplified how the team was able to escape effective oversight by pitting San Diego's public agencies, labor, and housing groups against one another. The development promised to create more than 1,300 condos and apartments, office and retail space, and an additional hotel. The team's plans for the project, heralded as San Diego's Rockefeller Center, faced opposition from the Port District, which feared that new residential development would push maritime and industrial jobs out of one of the few downtown areas still zoned for industrial uses.[34]

The Padres launched an extensive lobbying campaign to convince CCDC to approve Ballpark Village. As part of the campaign, the Padres emphasized that the project would create one hundred new affordable-housing units for moderate-income residents, making it the first downtown project to actually build affordable housing. (Developers typically opt to pay in-lieu fees to the city rather than build the inclusionary units mandated by law.) On the basis of these assurances, CCDC signed off on the project.

Having received CCDC's blessing, JMI made a surprise announcement the day before the city council was to consider the project. Under a "community benefits agreement" negotiated in secret with a coalition of labor, housing, and environmental groups, JMI would convert all of its affordable housing into market-rate units. In exchange, the team promised to pay higher wages, use green building standards, and provide $18 million to build affordable housing off-site. CCDC blasted the secret deal, accusing the team of last-minute deception. Officials at CCDC called the pitting of the city's housing policy against affordable housing advocates both "unfortunate and unwarranted."[35] Despite the public's outrage over the secret deal, the city council approved the Ballpark Village project after JMI agreed to build one-third of the affordable units it had originally promised.[36]

Benchmarking Petco Park

There is no doubt that building the stadium increased downtown property values. Business activity has increased downtown, with some of it shifting from Mission Valley. . . . But the entity on the hook for paying the bond is the City's General Fund. If you add up all of the development from the ballpark district, you do not get enough revenues to service the debt. The bottom line is that the ballpark resulted in a net loss of about $10 million a year. It probably still is a net loss even if you credit the hotels built in the area since then. The Taxpayers' Association ultimately endorsed the ballpark plan. The stadium did take from the General Fund. So, from a business point of view, the stadium deal was a good deal. It was not from a fiscal point of view.

—*Scott Barnett, former executive director, San Diego County Taxpayers Association, 2007*[37]

Evaluating the success of redevelopment P3s is a difficult empirical exercise. Most redevelopment P3s are customized to fit the requirements of particular parcels as well as the capacities of public- and private-sector actors. Thus, comparative analyses of large-scale projects like Petco Park can be difficult and, in some cases, uninformative. Some experts suggest assessing the efficiency of P3s by comparing the actual cost to what a local government would have spent had it constructed the project in-house. For redevelopment P3s, however, this counterfactual is of little help. Most large-scale projects cannot be undertaken with local government resources alone. The involvement of private-sector actors, moreover, alters the ultimate character of land use and development in affected areas.

In evaluating the success of redevelopment P3s, it is necessary to assess the various impacts of a project, including its economic costs and benefits, and its contribution to the built environment and social character of downtown. It is also important to measure the relative contributions of both public- and private-sector actors and to compare these against the public benefits produced by redevelopment. Finally, one must consider the project's opportunity costs, that is, the forgone benefits of using the land, capital, and other public resources consumed by a P3 on the next best alternative.

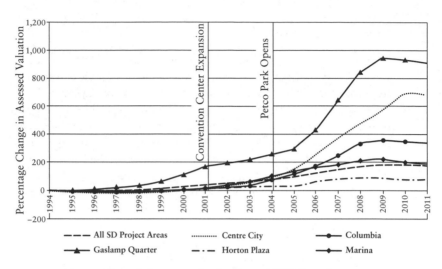

FIGURE 6.3   Growth in assessed valuation of CCDC project areas, 1994–2010

SOURCES: Office of Auditor and Controller, County of San Diego, "Property Valuations, Tax Rates, Useful Information for Taxpayers," various years.

Given the extensive public resources that San Diego provided, it is no surprise that the Petco Park project has generated substantial economic impacts that have dramatically transformed parts of downtown. Indeed, the $1 billion of private capital invested in the East Village has exceeded the expectations of its most ardent supporters. The ancillary development has been a boon for CCDC, which has seen its property tax increment funds rise by more than $10 million a year. Figure 6.3 shows changes in the assessed valuation of property in CCDC project areas between 1994 and 2010. Property values began to increase after the convention center expansion, especially in the Gaslamp Quarter. Following construction of Petco Park, property values—and thus the tax increment—increased further, with the Gaslamp and Centre City (which includes East Village) outpacing gains elsewhere.

Unfortunately, the rising property values downtown had little effect on San Diego's bottom line, because all the new tax increment has, by law, flowed into CCDC-controlled redevelopment accounts rather than the city's General Fund, from which it has had to make bond payments. All of this new revenue must be spent on other downtown bricks-and-

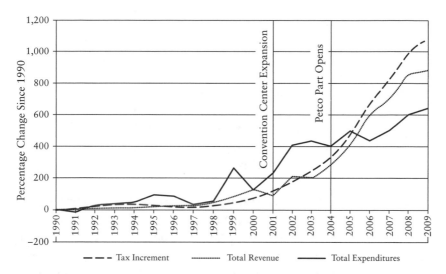

FIGURE 6.4   San Diego redevelopment expenditures and tax increment funds, 1990–2008

SOURCES: California State Controller, "Community Redevelopment Agencies Annual Report," various years.

mortar projects, including those spearheaded by JMI. Figure 6.4 tracks redevelopment revenues, expenditures, and tax increment funds between 1990 and 2008. Between 2001 and 2008, revenue collected annually by the redevelopment agency increased by nearly $150 million. Most of this growth was driven by increases in the tax increment. Interestingly, over much of this period, redevelopment expenditures were rising faster than revenues. Only in 2005 did the city receive more in tax increment funds than it put in. This figure does not include the hundreds of millions of dollars the city (i.e., non-CCDC funds) spent on Petco Park and other projects.

Although these redevelopment efforts have generated tremendous private wealth downtown, the millions invested by the city and CCDC have yielded few public benefits. The "park at the park" was the only major new open space constructed in this part of downtown over the past decade. Long-delayed efforts to open the first public school in the area or to rebuild an aging city hall have shown little progress. In addition, there is little evidence that the money invested by the redevelopment agency has improved the affordability of downtown housing, one of the agency's

TABLE 6.2   Major league baseball stadium construction costs, 1990–2003

| | % CONTRIBUTED | | $ CONTRIBUTED (MILLIONS) | |
Stadium	Public	Private	Public	Private
Petco Park	67.5	32.5	303.3	146.1[a]
MLB stadium average	70.9	29.1	242.7	102.3

SOURCE: State of Minnesota, Office of the Governor, *Stadium Screening Committee Report*, December 9, 2003.

NOTE: Costs adjusted to 2003 dollars using Urban CPI 10-Year Average.

[a]Includes $60 million from sale of naming rights.

primary mandates under state law. In 2005, a study published by the Center on Policy Initiatives found that, while the number of new housing units downtown nearly tripled between 1999 and 2005, the number of affordable housing units increased by just 65 percent, falling from 34 percent to 19 percent of new housing stock.[38] By June 2008, affordable housing had fallen to 17 percent of downtown units, barely above the minimum threshold established by state law.[39]

By 2007, three years after the ballpark opened, ancillary development had resulted in 747 completed hotel rooms—100 fewer than promised in the MOU.[40] Although TOT revenue from these rooms went to the city, it covered just a fraction of city's annual $11.3 million in payments due on the ballpark bonds and $4.1 million in operating costs for the stadium shouldered by the city.[41] In all, the ballpark project has been a net drain on the city's—though a boon for the redevelopment agency's—finances.

The exact economic impacts of the ballpark are difficult to assess, but the relative contributions of public- and private-sector actors are easy to measure. Table 6.2 reports the amount and share of funding provided by public actors and the Padres, and compares these with other baseball stadiums built between 1990 and 2003. San Diego's 67.5 percent share of ballpark costs is slightly below the average public share, although its $303 million contribution exceeds the average public cost by 25 percent. By these measures, the P3 looks no better than stadium projects pursued by other cities.

The private company JMI Realty is exempt from laws requiring disclosure of project revenues. It is, therefore, impossible to quantify the profits Moores has received from exclusive development rights in the

East Village. The new downtown ballpark has also increased the financial value of the team. In 2007, Forbes estimated that the franchise was worth $385 million. Having squeezed as much money out of the local public sector as possible, Padres owner John Moores was ready to cash out in early 2009. In March, the Padres announced the sale of the team to a group led by Arizona Diamondbacks executive Jeff Moorad. The deal, which includes an estimated $290 million in cash, $200 million in debt, and a 30 percent stake in Petco Park, reportedly values the team at $550 million.[42]

In all, San Diego's partnership with the Padres has mostly benefited two groups of actors. Padres owner John Moores took advantage of public subsidies and East Village development rights to emerge as a powerful real estate mogul. Elected officials, concerned primarily with scoring points with voters, claimed credit for keeping the Padres and revitalizing downtown without raising taxes. The fruits of these efforts were realized on Opening Day in 2004, when Mayor Susan Golding threw out the ceremonial first pitch to her successor, Mayor Dick Murphy. Because most of East Village planning took place in JMI boardrooms and CCDC board meetings, few voters were aware of how much the final product strayed from the original MOU or how few public amenities the city received for its immense investment.

San Diego taxpayers, the intended beneficiaries of the P3, have been left to absorb the fiscal fallout. Facing a severe fiscal crisis, the city has struggled to maintain its basic infrastructure—deferred maintenance has grown to nearly $1 billion.[43] Local residents watched helplessly as a woefully underequipped fire department battled wildfires that threatened to destroy local neighborhoods in 2003. The ballpark project did not cause these misfortunes, but by draining the city's already-strained fiscal resources, it has inhibited the ability of public officials to address mounting service and infrastructure challenges.

Walling Off the Bay

Here we go again with Doug Manchester, San Diego's most controversial and litigious waterfront developer, the robber baron of public coastal connections. . . . Hundreds of people have worked for some 30 years to revitalize downtown San Diego. After all that sweat and investment, we

cannot allow one developer with a questionable record to run off with the
waterfront triple crown.

—San Diego Union-Tribune *architectural critic Ann Jarmusch,*
2006[44]

The ballpark would not be San Diego's last foray into developer-
driven P3s. Just as it did decades earlier, the U.S. Navy has played a
leading role in San Diego's economic aspirations after the recession of
the early 1990s and has been a key actor in the city's redevelopment
plans. Reversing its earlier relationship with the city, this time the military would provide crucial property adjacent to downtown to fuel the
city's redevelopment dreams with two major projects on the bay front.
In both cases, San Diego's elected leaders, lacking a long-term vision
and intimidated by the cost and the complexity of the projects, would
turn for help to private developers, who would profit handsomely on
the deals.

In plotting the redevelopment of the 435-acre former Naval Training Center and the 14.5-acre waterfront Naval Broadway Complex, the
city designed public-private partnerships that promised San Diegans many
public benefits, with little or no up-front costs to the public treasury. Indeed, relying on the beneficence of the private sector was the only way
"America's cheapest city" could afford to marshal the human and capital
resources needed to plan and pay for redevelopment without abandoning
San Diego's low-tax culture. In delegating to what they hoped would be
white-horse developers, local elected officials sought to insulate themselves from the political and financial risks, which were to be borne by
the developers.

Yet in both cases, the absence of adequate monitoring by the city
and its failure to properly structure its P3 relationships meant that the
city would end up paying much more than it originally expected, both
in financial costs and in loss of access to important public resources,
while receiving fewer benefits than it was promised. As former Planning
Director Michael Stepner observed, "People believe that the private sector
can do better than the public sector. As a consequence, we often fail to
negotiate the best deal that we can. We do not provide sufficient guidance
and oversight as in other cities." As it had in the case of the downtown
ballpark, the city's delegation of authority over projects on navy-owned
land turned into virtual abdication.[45]

Corky's Porkyville

In 1993, the Base Realignment and Closure Commission (BRAC) recommended that the federal government close San Diego's Naval Training Center (NTC). Initially, the city fought efforts to decommission the base, eager to maintain its historical partnership with the U.S. Navy. However, public officials also recognized that the large property, located northwest of downtown adjacent to Lindbergh Field, offered a historical redevelopment opportunity. The old training site was located along a boat channel on the north side of San Diego Bay (see Figure 6.5). This bay-front property was eyed by civic leaders as an opportunity to build a second Balboa Park, San Diego's iconic jewel. The city followed its usual playbook, appointing a twenty-seven-member committee to study the NTC's reuse potential for public benefit and economic development.

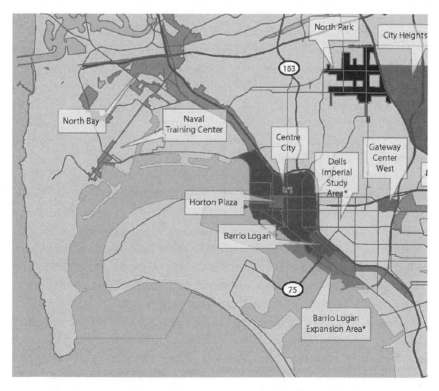

FIGURE 6.5   Naval Training Center Project Area (renamed Liberty Station)
SOURCE: City of San Diego Redevelopment Agency.

Regarding federal requirements that housing for the homeless be given priority in base reuse plans, new legislation gave the city flexibility to offer homeless support off-site.[46]

The enthusiasm of San Diego's civic boosters for the project was dampened considerably after consultants hired by the city released the price tag—an estimated $160 million—for clearing the land and installing the public infrastructure necessary to improve it. "The reuse . . . was originally considered a pot of gold for the city," one adviser explained. "But the more we go through the process, we've found that there are fewer and fewer coins in the pot." The NTC reuse committee recommended that plans for the site incorporate multiple uses, including preservation of open space; historical buildings; and a mix of education, culture, and community facilities. City officials, however, had little appetite for such an undertaking. "The city decided that our plan was beautiful on paper, but they had no money to pay for it," recalled one committee member.[47]

One committee recommendation was that 350 market-rate housing units be built on the former base. If improving the site would cost millions, city leaders argued, then a private developer would pay the cost.[48] That developer would prove to be Corky McMillin, a prominent local with close ties to the city council and the congressman whose support would be needed for the city to receive the NTC site at no cost. Under an agreement approved by the redevelopment agency in June 2000, McMillin's company was given the right to develop the entire NTC acreage, in return for a vague profit-sharing arrangement.[49]

The terms of the 2000 agreement were similar to the 1998 MOU between the city and the San Diego Padres. The city conveyed most of the 361-acre site to the company and gave the developer a free hand in determining the mix of residential, office, retail, hotel, and recreational uses. To sweeten the deal, local officials guaranteed that the company would earn at least a modest profit and keep any proceeds from the sale of residential properties. McMillin agreed to preserve some of the facility's historical structures, to invest in infrastructure improvements, and to share money from leasing commercial properties on the site. The city also expected to receive an infusion of transient occupancy taxes harvested from the site's new hotels, in addition to increased property taxes from 350 planned market-rate homes. In all, the city estimated it would receive more than $300 million over the course of forty years.[50]

In many ways, the 2000 agreement, which secured the private capital needed to redevelop the base, can be construed as a boon for San Diego. It spared the city the large expense usually associated with base closures.[51] However, under the terms of the agreement, San Diego would give up more and receive less than other California cities facing base closures during the 1990s. In San Francisco, for example, redevelopment officials extracted more than $1.2 billion in concessions, four hundred acres of parks and open space, and thousands of affordable housing units from a private developer in exchange for rights to build on a site that includes the shuttered Hunters Point naval shipyard. The NTC agreement, in contrast, left many important decisions about the final shape of the project to the private developer. As with the Padres, McMillin was allowed to fine-tune the development, as long as the city received its share of the money. McMillin exploited the vague provisions of the deal to maximize his company's take from the project. Rather than build affordable units on-site, the company opted to pay in-lieu fees—to provide affordable units elsewhere—and use the residential portion of the site for high-end housing.

In fairness, the city's historical aversion to taxes and big government left few resources and little expertise with which to undertake projects like the NTC. According to Hank Cunningham, San Diego's former head of community and economic development who oversaw the project, securing McMillin's commitment to provide hundreds of millions in up-front funding was a victory for the cash-strapped city. "McMillin advanced about $200 million in private investment capital which neither the City nor [its Redevelopment Agency] could have possibly done on its own. . . . Absent this front-end injection of capital by McMillin, NTC would today consist of abandoned building and aged, crumbling infrastructure as is the case of many, if not most, former military base re-use projects."[52]

Unfortunately for city officials, problems with the McMillin deal emerged before the ink on the agreement was dry. McMillin's plan for the site, rechristened Liberty Station, was opposed by San Diego's Save Our Heritage Organization (SOHO), the Peninsula Community Planning Board, and the city's Planning Commission. The original plan included 350 moderately priced homes (McMillin's promise to build homes that regular San Diegans could afford had been a major selling point); two hotels; an arts and culture center; and forty-six acres of parks, athletic fields, and open space. Although the development won national praise for its design, critics charged that Liberty Station was a prime example of developers' bait-and-switch tactics. At the 2001 groundbreaking, protestors carried signs that read "NTC: Corky's Porkyville."[53]

Such public relations setbacks were the least of McMillin's problems. Privately, redevelopment officials worried about the company's ability to deliver on its promises.[54] McMillin left no stone unturned in soliciting additional funds for the project. In 2001, he irked Mayor Dick Murphy by requesting $8.5 million from the city for 155 streetlights, storm drain improvements, and water lines that were not included in the original plan adopted in 1998. The next year, McMillin asked for a no-cost, thirty-month extension on his development of the hotel site. In 2005, City Attorney Michael Aguirre opposed granting McMillin's NTC Foundation $6.8 million from the city's Community Development Block Grants, a federal program targeting low-income communities, as part of an $11 million effort to rehabilitate historical buildings.[55] Having gone all in with McMillan in 2000, however, public officials were loath to see the project fail. In 2005, the council approved the sale of $16 million in public bonds for the project's waterfront park, with $5.9 million going to repay McMillin's company for improvements to nearby streets, passing on the cost of the improvements not to the company but to Liberty Station's property owners.[56]

"No city contract in modern memory aroused outrage among more San Diegans than this one," wrote veteran newspaper columnist Neil Morgan. "To some, those 349 spec homes [many purchased by McMillin company officials] seemed blasphemy on a park-like site that could have become another Balboa Park by the bay." According to historian Mike Davis, NTC was the template for projected "gentrification" of the bay, from Point Loma to Petco Park, should the city ever redevelop nearby Lindbergh Field—the region's main airport—and the Marine Corps Recruit Depot. By late 2004, work on the luxury housing section of the project was largely complete, but ground had not yet been broken on the forty-six-acre waterfront park, the arts center, or planned hotels.[57]

Following a detailed investigation in 2007, the *San Diego Union-Tribune* reported that San Diego had received few, if any, of the public benefits that were promised, whereas the developer had made an estimated $230 million from the sale of luxury homes. Because the original profit-sharing agreement between the company and the city excluded revenues generated by the sale of the homes and required McMillin to be reimbursed for any "unexpected expenses," the city had spent more than it received in new property tax increment. Further, although McMillin had promised to build affordable houses for middle-class San Diegans, a separate analysis indicated that more than one-third of the NTC units had been bought by speculators and company officials. The paper called the deal a "boom for McMillin, bust for [the] city." Former Planning Director Michael Stepner agreed that the city did not get its fair share: "Perhaps this failure to obtain a better deal is attributable to a lack of skill in city government. The Planning Department did not have people that could deal with complex public-private partnerships."[58]

Papa Doug: Bait and Switch?

Across San Diego Bay from the Naval Training Center and close to downtown lies the Embarcadero and San Diego's "front door." For years, the mostly vacant properties along this stretch of downtown waterfront have moonlighted as overflow parking. With San Diego's downtown renaissance, however, such properties have become lucrative redevelopment opportunities. None is more lucrative than the Navy Broadway Complex (NBC), a 14.5-acre site between Broadway to the north and Seaport Village to the south (see Figure 6.6). Under an agreement signed by the U.S. Navy, which owns the land, the fate of the site is controlled by private developer Doug Manchester. "Papa Doug" (as he insisted on being called) played a vital role in transforming the downtown waterfront, starting in the 1980s with the Manchester Grand Hyatt Hotel and the Marriott Hotel and Marina, whose triple towers won him enduring local enmity for walling off the harbor.

In 1992, the City of San Diego teamed up with the U.S. Navy in an effort to rebuild the navy's regional headquarters. Under the 1992 agreement, a private developer would be solicited to construct a new naval office building. The navy would receive the new building in exchange for granting the developer a long-term lease and development rights to the surrounding area. The remaining land could be used to construct waterfront retail and office space, in addition to streets and other public amenities. The navy would continue to own the land, with the city providing

FIGURE 6.6   Navy Broadway Complex
SOURCE: Centre City Development Corporation.

any necessary service upgrades. Mired in a severe recession, local officials hoped that the new construction would end downtown's economic slump and serve as a catalyst for additional projects.

The 1992 agreement also outlined broad design guidelines for the future Navy Broadway Complex but offered no implementation or regulatory role for city planning officials. Indeed, San Diego's downtown redevelopment arm, CCDC, would be allowed only to review the final plans and certify whether they were broadly consistent with the design guidelines. More important, the agreement specified no time frame for the development to occur. It provided only that the deal would expire after twenty-five years if the navy dragged its feet. Though scarcely noticed or commented on by the media and local residents, the city had just ceded its land-use authority and control over a major portion of its bay front to the navy and a yet-to-be named private developer.

The agreement began to gather dust shortly after it was signed, until another round of base closures in 2006 threatened to mothball the naval headquarters. Pointing to the 1992 agreement, the navy received a reprieve from BRAC until the end of the year to find a developer for the deal. In March 2006, the navy awarded Manchester Financial Group exclusive redevelopment rights to the eight-block site. However, much had changed in the fourteen years since the agreement was made. Downtown development had flourished as a result of the late 1990s real estate boom and public investments in the convention center and ballpark projects. Stepner, who took the lead in negotiating the 1992 agreement, agreed that it no longer met the city's needs: "In 1992, the agreement could be fairly represented as a victory for the community. Today, with the rediscovery of the waterfront, and the benefits that accrue to communities with such attractive downtown spaces, we need to look at the property differently."[59]

A looming January 2007 deadline imposed by BRAC left little time for Manchester to obtain CCDC's approval for a redevelopment plan for the site. After January 2007, the NBC site would revert to base-closure procedures, under which it could potentially be claimed by another federal agency or awarded to another developer. Fortunately for Manchester, local officials were unwilling to take that risk. Manchester's plan envisaged a nineteen-story office tower to replace existing navy offices, to be followed by a forty-story hotel, a twenty-four-story office tower, a museum, and another hotel anchoring the project's southern tip. A revised plan boosted the size of the proposed buildings from 2.8 million square feet to 3.2 million square feet. The new plan also reduced the amount of open space from six acres to four acres and proposed larger structures along Harbor Drive. A later revision also replaced a planned hotel with a condo hotel, threatening to cost the city $1.2 million in annual TOT revenues it needed to pay for increased policing and other public services.[60]

To critics, Manchester's last-minute additions looked like another example of bait and switch. Responding to a firestorm of criticism from planners and community groups, Manchester downsized his blueprint for the project. In his original proposal, Manchester promised to construct an "iconic" three-story museum. Revised plans for the site replaced this museum with a thirteen-story office and retail building, with the museum grounds now broken up into smaller spaces in other buildings. In the course of negotiations, which were temporarily stalled by a review by the city attorney, Manchester also agreed to lease the roughly half-block site of a planned 250,000-square-foot building on the site to CCDC to build a park. The city agreed to pay $20 million for the 40,000 square feet of land that some believed the public already owned.[61]

The 1992 agreement obligated the city to supply the site with expanded public services and police protection. Despite claims that the project would cost more than it would bring in, and its apparent violations of the spirit of the original design guidelines, Manchester's revised proposal received a green light from CCDC and the city council. Local officials rejected arguments from community activists, who filed a series of lawsuits challenging the project on the grounds that too much time had passed since the initial 1992 environmental assessment was completed. Instead, the city allowed Manchester to continue without completing a new environmental review, even as analysts at the California Coastal Commission raised red flags.[62]

In January 2007, the San Diego Navy Broadway Complex coalition, a community group opposed to the navy's plans for the property and the city's entire North Embarcadero Visionary Plan,[63] sued the Department of Defense. The lawsuit contended that the navy's decision to go forward with the project based on a 1990 environmental impact statement and an updated statement in 2006, left the public with little opportunity to comment on the project's environmental consequences. In June 2008, a federal judge ruled that the navy had to show its plans to the public and allow for its input on how the project will impact the surrounding environment. The lawsuit and the judge's ruling, however, have done little except delay the inevitable. With Mayor Jerry Sanders and CCDC deferring to the navy, there is little to stop Manchester from following through with his $1.7 billion plan to privatize the city's last-best bay-front redevelopment opportunity.[64]

The Leader of the Band?

We have never lacked for plans, sound and unsound, practical and fantastic. What we have lacked is unified execution.

    —*Robert Moses, 1938*[65]

Conventional accounts of San Diego's downtown redevelopment program cite the role of large public-private projects—Horton Plaza, and, more recently, Petco Park and East Village—in stabilizing downtown property values and spurring additional investment in the area. With respect to Petco Park, a public investment of roughly $300 million has helped transform a dilapidated area into a bustling tourist hub, with gleaming new condo towers, restaurants, and high-end hotels. Nonetheless, the long-term economic impact of this ambitious project is open to question. With the mix of ancillary development changing from a heavy dose of office and retail space to predominately residential and, more recently, hotel projects, the city has seen few high-paying new jobs created. Moreover, the ballpark has failed to stem the steep deterioration in the downtown housing market that began in 2005. Indeed, by subsidizing new housing construction in the area with tax breaks and zoning relief, the project contributed to the oversupply of condominiums that helped produce San Diego's housing slowdown.

Although San Diego's redevelopment program has been a success in transforming the built environment, it has done little to address other priorities identified in California redevelopment law. The state legislature has noted that the "fundamental purpose of redevelopment is to expand the supply of low and moderate-income housing, to expand employment opportunities for the jobless, underemployed, and low-income persons, and to provide an environment for social, economic, and psychological growth and well-being of all citizens."[66] On all of these measures, San Diego's redevelopment program has made little progress.[67]

Although the physical transformation brought on by San Diego's public-private partnerships has been startling, the public benefits they have yielded are far less dramatic. Over the past twenty years, the city and CCDC—its downtown redevelopment arm—have poured large sums into projects that have resulted in few high-paying new jobs. The jobs that have been created tend to be at the low end of the economic spectrum (e.g., hotel workers, security guards), and public officials have failed to provide affordable housing and services for these and other needy residents. In addition to the up-front revenues and borrowing capacity it has provided, the city has often been left on the hook on the back end for providing supporting public services and infrastructure. Despite promises that downtown redevelopment projects would pay for themselves, local taxpayers all too often have been left holding the bag.

San Diego, like many other cities, has bet heavily on the infrastructure of play. Its redevelopment strategies are not unlike those being plied across the country and overseas. Its beaches, parks, downtown ballpark, and convention center have allowed San Diego to compete with New York, San Francisco, Las Vegas, and other top destinations for tourism dollars. What is noteworthy about San Diego is how little control public officials have been willing to exercise over this process and the extent to which downtown development has served private rather than public interests. Public-improvement land uses, such as parks, libraries, and waterfront vistas, have been crowded out by new hotels, condos, and other private spaces. These latter projects help enrich a few well-positioned developers but offer few benefits to most residents. Indeed, in the Petco Park and Navy Broadway Complex episodes, the city had to step in after the fact with additional expensive inducements for developers to preserve any public space at all.

Although San Diego has succeeded in avoiding the economic pitfalls usually associated with the reuse of military facilities, it also has squandered its peace dividend by giving former military lands to private developers interested in using public resources to maximize private profits. The Naval Training Center was supposed to be a self-sustaining community with ample parks and affordable homes for working families. What residents got instead was another dense district with expensive housing. Nonetheless, the city is still on the hook for street repairs, traffic lights, and other services it failed to require in the initial P3 agreement. The Navy Broadway Complex, one of the last remaining pieces of valuable bay-front real estate, will likely be redeveloped as an overbuilt complex of private hotels and offices, walling off the bay and discouraging pedestrian traffic.

Under its current political system, San Diego remains vulnerable to poorly structured development deals. Its city council is composed of understaffed representatives who, with district elections, have little interest in directing general planning or redevelopment efforts. Term-limited council members also lack both the inclination and institutional capacity to provide oversight of shadow governments like the Centre City Development Corporation. The town's leading newspaper, largely representing downtown business interests, has failed as a civic watchdog. The few watchdog organizations that do exist (e.g., the San Diego County Taxpayers Association) are loath to take on powerful private interests.

Taken together, Petco Park and East Village, the Naval Training Center, and the Navy Broadway Complex projects constituted a historic opportunity for dramatically remaking San Diego's downtown and bay front. Redevelopment officials devoted ample public resources—land, authority, and financing—to make these projects succeed. Like many other cities, San Diego looked to developers to provide substantial public benefits in the form of parks, affordable housing, and ancillary development. With inadequate public leadership and oversight, developer-driven redevelopment projects have easily strayed from their original public purposes.

Entering the second decade of the twenty-first century, San Diego's redevelopment program faces an uncertain future. One source of uncertainty is the future of the San Diego Chargers, who have asked public officials to sign off on a new football stadium downtown. The team maintains that the city will have to come up with most of the project's estimated $800 million cost. Having provided the initial momentum for Moores's stadium gambit, the Chargers' latest campaign, backed by an implicit threat to move to Los Angeles, has brought San Diego's redevelopment story nearly full circle.[68] A second source of uncertainty is Governor Jerry Brown's proposal to eliminate local redevelopment agencies and use reclaimed property tax revenues to plug the state's budget deficit.[69] Given the lack of inclination among local officials to fix the fundamental problems with its redevelopment governance, it might take the state's own fiscal catastrophe to save San Diego from repeating the mistakes of its redevelopment past.

III   *At the Crossroads*

Regional and Binational Infrastructure
Governance Challenges and Failures

> You can call it North America's first binational city—a center of pros-
> pering manufacturing, trade and high technology, a multiracial society
> of well over 3 million people. . . . The San Diego-Tijuana citistate is all
> those things, a kind of prototype for an urbanized 21st century. If it's
> also the site of illegal border crossings, widespread smuggling, overloaded
> highways and water systems, troubled schools—well, maybe those are
> destined to be hallmarks of the next century too.
>
> —*Neal Peirce, 1997*[1]

Regional Governance Reconsidered

San Diego's governance challenges and failures extend well beyond the boundaries of the region's largest city. Consisting of San Diego
County, the metropolitan region of 3 million residents faces daunting
twenty-first-century infrastructure challenges: inadequate airport, port,
and freight-rail facilities to meet the demands of globalization; looming
water-supply shortages and sharp water price hikes caused by continued
population growth and cutbacks in once-secure, low-cost imported supplies; still-deficient local fire protection notwithstanding the disastrous
2003 and 2007 wildfires; and, with illegal immigration and post-9/11 ter-
rorism threats, a cumbersome border security regime that threatens once-
promising binational trade and economic linkages between San Diego
and Baja California. In this chapter we examine the region's failure to
provide adequate public goods, so critical to growth, public safety, and
the overall quality of life. As with the city, the region suffers from leadership, institutional, and political cultural deficiencies.

Although lack of leadership is arguably the greatest deficit, governance arrangements have also contributed to a regional infrastructure
deficit. Owing to its semi-isolated geography, San Diego County should
be a natural laboratory for innovative regional governance approaches.
The county is bounded by the Pacific Ocean to the west, Mexico to the

south, and steep mountains to the east. To the north, the U.S. Marine Corps' Camp Pendleton training facility physically separates San Diego from metropolitan Los Angeles.

In this geographic cul-de-sac, San Diego has created a host of regional single-purpose special districts for infrastructure provision. These include the San Diego County Water Authority (created in 1944), the San Diego Unified Port District (1962), and the San Diego County Regional Airport Authority (2003). Two public transit agencies provide bus and train service: the Metropolitan Transit System and the North County Transit District (1975). The San Diego Association of Governments (1966), arguably the most successful regional agency, is the metropolitan planning organization but has also been given capital planning and fare-setting powers for the county's two transit systems. However, San Diego's single-purpose special districts create serious coordination problems across policy arenas and their voting rules tend to magnify the voices of smaller communities at the expense of the central city and region.[2]

San Diego's infrastructure governance differs in critical respects from other California metropolitan areas such as Los Angeles and San Francisco, which rely heavily on central city agencies. For example, the City of Los Angeles has three powerful, semiautonomous proprietary departments managing Los Angeles and Ontario International Airports, the Port of Los Angeles, and the municipal water and power systems. As such, L.A. mayors, through agency appointments and other powers, are able to directly shape critical infrastructure decisions affecting all of Southern California. Similarly, mayors in other California cities with proprietary departments, such as San Francisco and Long Beach, have comparable powers and influence. This is not always the case for the City of San Diego. Although it is the driver of much regional policy making, the city is a minority vote on most regional boards. As such, the city lacks proprietary control over critical infrastructure decision-making regarding airports, ports, water, and energy. Even when the City of San Diego succeeds in securing the institutional capacity to make regional decisions, its representatives on these special boards do not always have the will to fight for the interests of all residents in the region.[3]

For fire protection, San Diego lacks even this problematic regional solution. Historically, San Diego has had no county fire department or regional authority. Instead, the region is served by a hodgepodge of over sixty city, rural, and volunteer fire departments and state and federal fire-fighting agencies. A small initial step was taken in 2008, when the San Diego County Regional Fire Authority was created to oversee fire protection in rural East and North Counties, previously served by six volunteer agencies and the California Department of Forestry and Fire Protection (CALFIRE).[4] Other Southern California urban areas facing similar fire threats such as L.A. and Orange County rely on well-provisioned county fire departments or regional fire authorities.

The major regional counter to centrifugal tendencies and fragmentation is the San Diego Association of Governments (SANDAG). Originally a voluntary joint-powers authority comprising the county and its eighteen cities and focused on regional transportation planning, SANDAG was given more land-use powers by legislation authored by state Assemblywoman Christine Kehoe. Signed into law in 2003, the law provided SANDAG with some of the teeth of a regional government by mandating that it "complete the process of preparing and adopting a regional comprehensive plan" monitoring "smart growth" initiatives, housing needs, and transportation project impacts. Under earlier legislation authored by state Senator Steve Peace, SANDAG was given new capital planning and construction powers for the region's light-rail and trolley systems. As the largest table in town, SANDAG is a vehicle for encouraging local cooperation. However, SANDAG is limited in its ability to set the regional policy agenda and to remedy major deficiencies such as fire protection and airport development.[5]

This chapter examines major regional and binational infrastructure and governance challenges and failures. Though not the focus here, critical social policy arenas such as the county's social service provision and K–12 school governance and policy making merit further research and examination.[6] Our analysis is divided into five sections. The first section examines trade infrastructure—the region's ports, freight-rail, airports, land ports of entry, and trade corridors. The second section examines the failure to create a new international airport at nearby Marine Corps Air Station Miramar. The third section examines regional water provision by the County Water Authority and its frequently rocky relationship with the Metropolitan Water District, the giant water wholesaler for Southern California. The fourth section analyzes the county's chronic failure to create a regionwide fire authority and to provide adequate local fire protection. The final section examines the prospects for and daunting challenges of cross-border cooperation in the post-9/11 era.

Trade Infrastructure Deficits

The airport remains a ceiling on our ambitions to integrate San Diego into the world economy.

> —*Anne Evans, chair, San Diego Regional Chamber of Commerce, 1998*[7]

Global Insulation

Throughout the late twentieth century, as other West Coast metropolitan regions like Los Angeles, the Bay Area, and Seattle expanded their trade-related infrastructure and embraced globalization, San Diego did not because its economy was not oriented toward global trade. Until the end of the Cold War, the San Diego economy relied heavily on the defense industry. Thus, the region's harbor facilities served the U.S. Navy and a once-vibrant fishing industry. As tourism grew, mostly consisting of Southern Californians and Arizonans traveling by car, new harbor development featured hotels, restaurants, and retail shops rather than cargo movement. Starting in the 1980s, San Diego's high-tech development largely featured research and development rather than manufacturing. Thus, there was little need to develop an airport system to attract more tourists from afar or to move local products to national and global markets.

As a consequence, San Diego entered the twenty-first century with a 1950s-era small niche port and a single, short-runway airport. Its major trade portal was the Otay Mesa land port of entry to Mexico. Given limited opportunities to expand its severely constrained port and airport system, San Diego continues to heavily rely on L.A.'s global gateways. More than 90 percent of the region's vessel cargo goes through the Los Angeles and Long Beach megaports. More than 25 percent of San Diego air passengers travel to airports outside the region, primarily to Los Angeles International Airport (LAX). More than 50 percent of the region's air cargo ships through L.A.'s airports—LAX and Ontario International Airport. Lacking a direct rail connection to the East, the cross-border region's freight-rail shipments are also routed through Los Angeles, which has three transcontinental lines linking its megaport complex with the rest of North America.[8] San Diego's heavy reliance on L.A.'s superior port, airport, and freight-rail facilities will remain so for the foreseeable future.

In the past, San Diego's ability to use L.A.-area infrastructure was beneficial. San Diego residents and businesses could maintain their well-publicized quality of life and enjoy relatively convenient global access while avoiding costly local facility investments and environmental burdens.[9] However, the costs and risks of this free-rider strategy are mounting. L.A.-area ports and airports are now constrained in terms of their own expansion possibilities. With growing traffic congestion, travel times to L.A.-area facilities are increasing. Thus, San Diegans are now pinning their hopes on high-speed rail service to LAX and Ontario International Airport and to other California metropolitan regions such as the Bay Area and Sacramento.[10] Alternatively, San Diego might look south to Mexico to resolve its airport and port needs. In August 2010, a proposed pedestrian bridge from Otay Mesa to the Tijuana Airport received U.S. State Department approval.

Another reason for the region's trade infrastructure deficit is that San Diego has relied on regional special districts, thus magnifying the voice of smaller communities with policy priorities other than trade promotion rather than L.A.-like city agencies that are single-mindedly focused on trade and infrastructure development. San Diego trade infrastructure investments are made by fragmented, limited-purpose special districts whose decision rules magnify the voice—and veto power—of smaller communities at the expense of the City of San Diego. Representing more than 40 percent of the county's population, the city—a permanent minority voting bloc on most of these specialized boards—confronts an uncertain global and economic future shaped by public investment decisions it cannot fully control. The central city—indeed the entire region—is also handicapped by a lack of sustained leadership on trade and infrastructure development and by long-standing "smokestacks" versus "geraniums" divisions among both residents and public officials regarding growth. Thus, both governance and leadership shortcomings have contributed to San Diego's vision and infrastructure shortfalls.

In turn, the region's infrastructure deficiencies both shape and limit its trade and development potential. Despite its favorable location,

San Diego's economy is more insulated from the global marketplace than other West Coast trade centers such as Los Angeles, the Bay Area, and Seattle-Tacoma. In 2008, only 9 percent of San Diego's gross metropolitan product came from exports ($15.5 billion), placing it sixty-seventh among the nation's top one hundred metropolitan areas.[11] Local exports are a potent generator of high-wage jobs and high value-added growth.

Although there are rosy predictions of future robust North American Free Trade Agreement trade growth with Mexico, a major question is whether San Diego can capture a larger share of local origin-and-destination activity. Rather than high-value-added trade, manufacturing, and infrastructure investments, the region has invested heavily in stable, low-value-added industries such as tourism. Despite impressive progress in developing research-and-development high-tech industries (but not manufacturing) and an advanced telecommunications infrastructure, the region's port and airport deficiencies represent a ceiling on its global and high-value growth ambitions.[12]

Port and Rail Development

Created in 1962 as a regional special district by the waterfront cities of San Diego, National City, Chula Vista, Imperial Beach, and Coronado to permit financing and development of the National City Marine Terminal, and to relieve San Diego's overcrowded Tenth Avenue terminal facility, the San Diego Unified Port District also took over Lindbergh Field—the region's major airport—because of its location on the tidelands. With the U.S. Navy, fishing industry, tourism, and recreation long dominating San Diego Bay, the newly created Port of San Diego did little to modernize when faced with the challenge of the cargo containerization revolution, which transformed maritime trade and port development around the globe.

Deriving primary revenue from waterfront property management and airport operations, the Port District in the 1980s paid the entire cost of the $140 million San Diego Convention Center while maintaining a shrinking, unprofitable maritime division. Subsequently, Port District member communities like National City and Chula Vista, which voted for the convention center financing, demanded investments in their own waterfronts to enhance their tourism and commercial appeal. As a result, until the mid-1990s, the Port District concentrated on commercial development of the waterfront—serving the tourism industry—rather than airport and port expansion.[13]

In the mid-1990s, with defense downsizing and the growth of the new high-tech economy, the Port District made airport and maritime master planning a high priority consistent with a regional trade and development orientation rather than focusing on lease revenue maximization.[14] However, the creation of the Regional Airport Authority in 2003 to operate Lindbergh Field and to develop a new international airport heightened financial pressure on the Port District. The loss of Lindbergh Field revenues—almost half its yearly income—aggravated the port's fears of further revenue loss from a possible raid by the cash-strapped State of California.

Oscillating between a strategy oriented primarily toward tourism and the cruise industry versus a maritime cargo-oriented strategy, the Port District has lagged in joining the global expansion of the cruise-ship industry, including the rise of megaliners. One problem is that cruise ships departing Los Angeles and Long Beach are barred from stopping in San Diego by the Passenger Services Act of 1886, which prohibits foreign-flag ships from picking up or dropping off passengers between U.S. ports. San Diego's attempts to obtain a legal waiver have been opposed by the maritime unions, which have feared a shift away from U.S. flagships whose crews are required by law to be made up of a majority of American citizens.[15] The more than six hundred thousand passengers a year who did embark or disembark in San Diego were poorly served by an old cruise terminal. In late 2010 the Port District opened a new cruise-ship terminal on the Broadway Pier as part of the North Embarcadero redevelopment project.

Together with Mexico's nearby Port of Ensenada, the Port of San Diego handles roughly 1 percent of the container shipments that pass through the mammoth Ports of Los Angeles and Long Beach. In 2004, San Diego port officials appeared overjoyed when labor shortages and higher-than-expected cargo volume at Long Beach led two Japanese cargo ships to off-load in San Diego rather than put up with the wait. San Diego has tried to become a niche port, specializing in imported automobiles, fruits, soda ash, tuna, and lumber. In the late 1990s, cargo gains occurred at the National City Marine Terminal, the beneficiary of most of the port's $165 million infrastructure upgrade as well as $23 million in Burlington

Northern–Santa Fe (BNSF) rail yard improvements that served as the port of entry for vehicles imported from Asia and Europe. The car maker Honda even agreed to make San Diego a primary port of entry.[16]

In contrast, the Tenth Avenue Marine Terminal (TAMT), which possesses a unique cold-storage facility but ships comparatively low volumes of bulk cargo, has been a money-losing operation responsible for the port's marine operations deficit. A $52.8 million dredging improvement program to deepen the main channel to forty-five feet to accommodate state-of-the-art container ships, which would have included major wharf improvements at TAMT, was opposed by the Army Corps of Engineers. Neither the Port District nor the Army Corps of Engineers has made the massive commitment to maritime terminal expansion and deepwater dredging needed to accommodate large container ships.[17]

In terms of rail connections, the Port of San Diego has only one first-class line, the north-south BNSF spur line. Despite San Diego's perennial dreams of becoming a railroad entrepôt, it continues to suffer from the region's lack, on both sides of the border, of adequate direct rail connections to national and international markets. San Diego freight is still shipped via the BNSF spur line to Los Angeles for transshipment, resulting in costly delays of up to three days. The Baja California maquiladora industry, currently heavily dependent on trucking, is without direct rail links to either the southeastern United States or the interior of Mexico.[18]

The San Diego and Arizona Eastern (SD&AE) Railway—a 134-mile-long rail link, 44 miles of which runs through Mexico—that was severed by torrential rains in 1983 would, if restored, provide San Diego and Tijuana with a direct freight connection to the East via the Union Pacific's Sunset Route. The SD&AE Desert Line, rechristened "the NAFTA train," has been stalled by political and legal hurdles on both sides of the border. The Transportation Equity Act for the 21st Century (TEA 21), enacted in 1998, contained $10 million to build a South Bay rail yard but nothing toward the more than $100 million required to repair and modernize SD&AE. In 2002, the Carrizo Gorge Railway committed private money to a limited restoration of the line but not enough to complete it without public funding. Restoration efforts were discouraged by a SANDAG study showing that the port couldn't handle the amount of grain and containers that the railroad could deliver.[19]

Airport Development

Regional airport development in San Diego has long been a fragmented political and institutional minefield despite repeated efforts at reform. Historically, the San Diego Association of Governments was responsible for regional airport planning and site decisions, whereas the Port District managed Lindbergh Field. The City of San Diego operates two general aviation airports—Brown Field and Montgomery Field—whereas the County of San Diego operates eight primarily general aviation airports; the county's McClellan-Palomar airport offers commercial service to LAX.

Gateway airports are critical for regions such as San Diego seeking to develop high-tech, knowledge-based economies. Research by business guru David Birch shows that knowledge-based economies rest on such pillars as a world-class research university, superior quality of life, and proximity to an international airport.[20] Where the knowledge industry is a major driver of the local economy as in San Diego, studies suggest that the relationship between information technologies and air travel is one of synergy rather than substitution. Although technology streamlines order taking, internal operations, and production, air travel still is needed to make business contacts and to close deals.[21]

San Diego lacks a gateway airport—and has no prospects for developing one in sight. Owing to its physical constraints—a single, short 9,400-foot runway and limited expansion potential—Lindbergh Field currently is not able to meet a significant share of the region's air passenger and cargo demand. The opportunity cost to the region's economy is substantial. Given limited international passenger and air cargo service (to Mexico and Canada until flights to the United Kingdom resumed in 2011), the airport generates (directly, indirectly, and induced) only 5 percent of the county's gross regional product. Compared to LAX, which accounts for nearly 10 percent of the L.A. region's much larger economy, diminutive Lindbergh Field is well behind the curve. A gateway airport like LAX also generates higher average wages and value-added activity than does Lindbergh Field.[22]

Strong cross-border opposition to building a binational airport near the border at Otay Mesa has impeded the prospects for a major new facility replacing or supplementing the current facilities of San Diego's

Lindbergh and Tijuana's Rodriguez Fields. Not-in-my-backyard sentiment and developer interests preferring more residential subdivisions on
scarce vacant land over transportation infrastructure also defeated efforts
to transform city-operated and border-adjacent Brown Field into a state-
of-the-art intermodal cargo airport and industrial center. Such a proposal
was rejected by the San Diego city council in 2001. Buzz Fink, chair of
the Brown Field advisory committee, observed: "There's simply a lack of
leadership at the city when it comes to planning for the future of the airport." He singled out the council's deference to the parochial perspective
of the member representing District 8 (where Brown Field is located) as
the main reason for deadlock.[23]

Border Trade Corridors

Although among other West Coast trade centers traffic flows primarily are east-west, San Diego–Tijuana trade flows predominantly are
north-south. Thus, for the cross-border region, the land ports of entry
and connecting highways form the backbone of the trade transportation
system. In the cross-border region itself, the most immediate transportation bottleneck is the highway system to and from the border. The California Department of Transportation has designated three major freeways
carrying global goods—I-5, I-8, and I-15—as Intermodal Corridors of
Economic Significance (ICES). They were also critical components of the
federally designated "NAFTA network" of highways and the "National
Highway System." Southern California's four commercial border crossings—Otay Mesa, Tecate, East Calexico, and Andrade—are potential
choke points whose overload threatens the smooth flow of these arteries.
Growth in cross-border trade since the advent of NAFTA in 1994 has
resulted in a dramatic increase in truck traffic, particularly through the
Otay Mesa land port of entry. Truck traffic and congestion became acute
problems on adjacent local streets because of lack of direct connections
between border crossings and the interstate highway system.

Unlike port, rail, and airport development, which are locally controlled, border trade corridor projects depend on federal and state approval and funding. Port-of-entry projects are even more complicated,
requiring Mexican government approval. Driven by trade growth and
goods-movement industry lobbying, trade corridor projects in San Diego

have become a major federal and state funding priority. San Diego enjoys a reputation of being adept at lobbying for federal and state monies at minimal cost to local taxpayers. In particular, SANDAG, the region's transportation planning agency, has a lengthy track record of building regional consensus and speaking with a unified voice in Sacramento and Washington, D.C., for local transportation project funding.

In 2008, San Diego's border infrastructure projects garnered $400 million from the state's $2 billion Trade Corridors Improvement Fund (TCIF) intended to improve infrastructure along federally designated "Trade Corridors of National Significance." This was double the amount that the region's population might warrant. Then, SANDAG assumed the lead role, with input from the Port District, in compiling a list of desired regional projects. SANDAG's board voted on a list of projects to submit to the California Transportation Commission (CTC), the state agency charged with overseeing and allocating TCIF money.

On the Mexican side of the border, there is also strong interest in improving the region's highway system and border crossings. For Baja California's maquiladoras, component parts from Asia are trucked in from the Los Angeles–Long Beach port complex. Finished products then are trucked back across the border to destinations primarily within a five-hundred-mile radius (e.g., San Diego, Los Angeles, the Bay Area, Phoenix, Las Vegas). By value, nearly 90 percent of the northbound freight that originates in Mexico is carried by trucks. Congestion is growing, particularly since the highway system and border crossings such as San Ysidro also serve Tijuana's large tourism-oriented service sector. However, in Mexico's more centralized political system, where key decisions are made in Mexico City, there is limited local authority and financing available for border-related infrastructure projects.[24]

Although highways are the key trade infrastructure component, cross-border rail facilities could be in the picture, but these have been underdeveloped. As border scholar Larry Herzog notes, Texas is much better linked to Mexico by railroads than is California. Some of this is understandable and a function of geography. However, California has put little effort into cross-border rail connections.[25]

Border infrastructure planning and development are complicated by the sheer institutional complexity of the task. This is particularly true for border ports of entry. As border economist James Gerber observes:

For example, the Otay Mesa-Mesa de Otay planning task force, under the auspices of the San Diego Association of Governments, is planning for a new border crossing. . . . A new border crossing has transportation, housing, environmental and economic development implications (in addition to security) and it is not surprising that there are a large number of stakeholders that must be consulted. . . . In addition to 30 local, state, and federal agencies in the United States and Mexico, both countries have private, non-state actors with a stake, such as environmental groups, academics, and chambers of commerce.[26]

The difficulties that SANDAG and other regional agencies face in coordinating the activities and resources of these various stakeholders is likely to continue hampering cross-border commerce in the years to come.

Gunning Down Miramar Airport

Airports stimulate great visionaries and public leaders, but also breed economic small mindedness and sycophantic civic cowards. You cannot avoid either in this quest. So, in the end, that means that you have to really want to go forward enough to stand up to the blowback that will occur.

—*San Diego attorney and civic activist Pat Shea, 2006*[27]

In 2003, the San Diego County Regional Airport Authority was created by the state to operate Lindbergh Field, to direct a comprehensive study of potential sites for a new international airport, to place on the ballot a proposed new site no later than November 2006, and to serve as the Airport Land Use Commission for the region's sixteen airports. The idea was to bring together all of the major political jurisdictions affected—the City of San Diego, the County of San Diego, the San Diego Unified Port District, SANDAG, and their Mexican counterparts in Baja California. It is governed by a nine-member board whose members are appointed by the governor; the county sheriff; and the mayors of the City of San Diego, South County, East County, and North County coastal and inland cities.

Proposition A

After an exhaustive site evaluation process, the airport authority board recommended to county voters that Marine Corps Air Station (MCAS) Miramar—formerly the U.S. Navy's "Top Gun" flight-training facility—be the new regional airport site if and when the military no longer wanted the facility. However, with the military, impacted communities, and environmental groups vehemently opposed, key public officials opposed or neutral, and the business community split, San Diego voters in November 2006 decisively rejected the plan.[28] Instead, the airport authority developed a costly proposal to renovate and rehabilitate cramped Lindbergh Field by moving the terminals and improving public transit access.

San Diego's inability to move forward with an international airport at Miramar was a combined failure of governance, regional leadership, and public will. The airport authority's enabling legislation mandated that a new airport site be placed on the county ballot by 2006. Thus, in June 2006, the San Diego Regional Airport Authority voted seven to two to put on the November ballot an "advisory" measure (Proposition A) asking county voters:

> To provide for San Diego's long-term air transportation needs, shall the Airport Authority and government officials work to obtain approximately 3,000 of 23,000 acres at MCAS Miramar by 2020 for a commercial airport, provided necessary traffic and freeway improvements are made, military readiness is maintained without expense to the military for modifying or relocating operations, no local taxes are used on the airport, overall noise impacts are reduced, and necessary Lindbergh Field improvements are completed?[29]

Under intense political pressure both from the U.S. Marines and the U.S. Navy, and their local supporters in a region where military influence remains strong, the airport authority watered down stronger language urging government officials to "make every effort to persuade Congress and the military" to hand over a portion of Miramar for civilian use by 2020. The final wording also steered clear of any reference to "joint use" with the military. The authority exposed itself to tremendous backlash by exploring what-if and out-of-the-box scenarios about what Miramar would look like without the marines—for example, by moving fighter training north to a refurbished Camp Pendleton—even though this might be the best solution for San Diego.[30]

Proponents of a new civilian airport at Miramar argued that, despite the post-9/11 dip in air traffic, Lindbergh Field—the most heavily used single-runway airport in the country, with a record 17.6 million

passengers in 2005—was back on track to exceed its maximum operational capacity of 25.6 million passengers a year within fifteen years. The
airport was already operating beyond its maximum annual cargo capacity of 140,000 tons a year. Planned infrastructure and facility improvements could ease the crunch but will not prepare cramped Lindbergh
Field—just 661 acres, one-sixth the size of LAX—to handle the new
generation of jumbo jets capable of linking San Diego directly with Tokyo
and Beijing without the addition of a twelve-thousand-foot runway. The
airport authority estimated that San Diego's economic loss by 2030 from
failure to remove constraints on regional airport capacity to be as much
as $130 billion. Although Miramar opponents disputed this estimate,
John D. Kasarda, a leading authority on airport development, affirmed
that the cost of inaction to San Diego would be astronomical in terms of
both its ability to attract tourists and to retain high-tech business.[31]

Strong Opposition Versus Weak Support

The No on Miramar Campaign, headed by Ret. Rear Admiral
Bruce Boland, U.S. Navy, denied that there was an imminent utilization
crisis at Lindbergh Field. Local academics weighed in that Lindbergh
Field, supplemented by San Diego's small commuter airports (Palomar,
Brown, Gillespie, Montgomery, and Ramona), could continue to serve
the region's aviation needs for the foreseeable future. Left unspoken was
the heavy historical reliance on metropolitan L.A.'s airport facilities,
which has served a significant share of San Diego's air passenger and
cargo needs. With not-in-my-backyard pressures forcing the City of Los
Angeles in 2005 to drastically cut back its plans for LAX modernization
by imposing a 78 million annual passenger ceiling, San Diego sooner
rather than later would have to reduce its reliance on its northern neighbor to meet its growing air transport needs.[32]

The U.S. Marines and the U.S. Navy strongly opposed the Miramar ballot measure. The military services argued on the basis of national
security in torpedoing any arrangement to share or use Miramar as a
civilian airport. Rather than stand up to the military to support the long-
term economic health of the region, Mayor Jerry Sanders and several city
council members drew back from supporting a new Miramar airport.
Only Councilman Tony Young was willing to take on the military: "We're

looking for a solution here in San Diego. We're growing up. We're not the military-only town we used to be."[33] Democratic congressional representatives Bob Filner and Susan Davis joined Republicans Daryl Issa, Brian Bilbray, and Duncan L. Hunter in lockstep behind the military in opposing the Miramar plan.

The Alliance in Support of Airport Progress in the Twenty-First Century, or ASAP21, a coalition of business and labor groups that sought to replace Lindbergh Field, organized support for Proposition A. The problem with ASAP21 was that it could not even rely on the unified backing of the San Diego Regional Chamber of Commerce that had created the group. Bowing to military pressure, the chamber's Policy Committee voted nine to four against endorsing Proposition A. In an unusual move, the entire chamber decided—by a paper-thin margin—to endorse the proposition, but without much conviction or credibility.[34]

Predictably, the split in the chamber's ranks arrayed real estate, finance, and high-tech interests against the local military-industrial complex. Having just fought to save San Diego's military installations, including MCAS Miramar, from the base realignment and closure process, the chamber found it difficult to do an abrupt about face. Of the region's business groups, only the San Diego Regional Economic Development Corporation strongly backed the Miramar proposal, but not with the alacrity with which it had endorsed SANDAG's TransNet half-cent sales tax ballot measure for regional highway and transit projects in 2004.[35]

Not surprisingly given the measure's strong opposition and weak support, San Diego County voters in November 2006 decisively rejected Proposition A by a margin of 62 percent to 38 percent. In the wake of the defeat, the airport authority chose to soldier on by focusing on Lindbergh Field improvements. Former state Senator Steve Peace, author of the authority's state-enabling legislation, said he had agreed to the creation of the airport authority—rather than a more comprehensive regional transportation and infrastructure agency—only because he believed that the voters' decision would "put that question behind us." The implication was that the airport authority should fall on its sword and solely concentrate on improvements to Lindbergh Field.[36]

Nor was this the first time that San Diego had passed on the opportunity at Miramar. "If we're going to get this stimulus to growth and importance, aviation planning must center on Miramar," read a 1953 *San*

Diego Evening Tribune editorial anticipating the new jet age. Rejecting this advice, city officials declined the military's offer in the 1950s to hand over the site for commercial airport development on the grounds that Miramar was a too-distant fourteen miles from downtown. A 1981 report also pointed to Miramar as the best option for a commercial airport, as did an advisory referendum passed narrowly by county voters in 1994.[37]

Water Provision: Megaregional Quandaries

We [San Diego County residents] are facing dramatically increasing water rates and a treated-water shortage for the next three years because the County Water Authority has been more focused on battling MWD [Metropolitan Water District] and gaining more "independence" for San Diego from L.A. than on taking care of its primary responsibility as a regional utility for reliably and affordably meeting our imported water-supply needs.

—*Anonymous San Diego County water official, 2005*[38]

San Diego is a semiarid Mediterranean-like environment. The average annual rainfall of 10.5 inches is similar to what Middle Eastern cities such as Beirut receive. The geology of San Diego is not conducive to groundwater storage, which limits the ability to use and reuse local runoff. As a result, local water supplies can support a population of only several hundred thousand, far fewer people than the 3 million residents living in the region today. For San Diego to grow and prosper, it needed to import water supplies from outside the region.

The Metropolitan Water District

Unlike Los Angeles, which developed its own imported supplies from the distant Owens Valley in the early twentieth century by financing and building an aqueduct to transport water to Los Angeles, San Diego historically lacked the leadership, regional institutions, and deep pockets to build a conveyance system for water from the Colorado River or Northern California. As with international ports and airports, San Diego early on chose to rely on Los Angeles for water provision. In 1924, the City of Los Angeles filed for 1.1 million acre-feet of water from the Colorado River. Four years later Los Angeles and its suburbs created the

Metropolitan Water District of Southern California (MWD) to finance, build, and operate an aqueduct from the Colorado River. Los Angeles transferred its Colorado River rights to the fledgling MWD.[39]

Although the City of San Diego filed for 112,000 acre-feet of Colorado River water in 1926, it was unable to finance and build an aqueduct to bring its imported supplies to the region. Conflicts among urban, suburban, and agricultural water agencies and users delayed the creation of a San Diego County Water Authority until 1944.[40] As a result of explosive growth during World War II, the region was rapidly running out of water by the war's end. At the behest of the U.S. Navy, the federal government ordered the County Water Authority to join MWD in 1946; an aqueduct connecting San Diego to MWD's system was built by the U.S. Navy and the City of San Diego surrendered its small Colorado River claims to MWD.[41]

This so-called shotgun marriage meant that late-twentieth-century San Diego would heavily rely on an L.A.-created (and, in the view of San Diego officials, L.A.-dominated) agency to furnish imported water needed for regional growth. Los Angeles, because of its early financing of the Colorado River Aqueduct, had extensive preferential rights, or claims to water during times of scarcity, that later-joining San Diego lacked. San Diego, however, was MWD's largest customer, with much of its early water supplies devoted to local agricultural use. Historically, San Diego paid much less for MWD water provision than did Los Angeles because of San Diego's low early infrastructure payments and large agricultural water discounts.

In 1982, California voters rejected a proposal for the Peripheral Canal, designed to bring more Northern California water to Southern California. This event and a lengthy drought in the late 1980s forced Southern California water agencies, particularly in San Diego, to rethink their long-term strategies to ensure the reliability of their water supplies. Of MWD's twenty-six Southern California water agencies, the San Diego County Water Authority was among the most dependent—between 85 percent and 90 percent of its total water usage—on MWD's imported supplies from the Colorado River and from the State Water Project.[42]

San Diego's pre-1990 relationship with MWD, and particularly the City of Los Angeles, one of MWD's founding members, was symptomatic of its overall philosophy of infrastructure provision. Tax-and-rate-hike-averse San Diego preferred to look to others—the federal and state governments, Los Angeles, and MWD—for needed infrastructure financing and provision. By 1990, however, this strategy had broken down. Facing the threat of drought-induced water rationing, and possible cutoffs if L.A. invoked its superior preferential rights, San Diego decided to seek a modicum of water independence from MWD and Los Angeles by diversifying its water supplies.

Imperial Valley Water-Transfer Conflicts

During the 1990s, the County Water Authority succeeded in turning a lengthy and fairly cooperative history with MWD into internecine warfare by abandoning the pursuit of regional interdependence for the quixotic goal of water independence. The County Water Authority brokered a separate deal to import some of the neighboring Imperial Valley's plentiful Colorado River supplies, first with the billionaire Bass brothers, Texas interlopers posing as California water farmers, and then directly with the Imperial Irrigation District (IID), the agency managing Imperial Valley's substantial Colorado River water allotment.[43]

To make economic sense, this strategy required the County Water Authority to convince MWD to carry in its own aqueduct San Diego's new water purchases at nominal rates. San Diego had no other way of moving the water from the Imperial Valley to its own system. MWD objected to San Diego's proposed low wheeling (or conveyance) charges, which it claimed represented a large subsidy from other MWD member agencies given MWD's substantial fixed costs, such as its State Water Project contracts. When the California courts ruled in favor of MWD's proposed wheeling charges, thereby substantially raising the end price of Imperial Valley water supplies, San Diego bought the water anyway.

Significantly, the City of San Diego, not the region as a whole, was the major force behind the drive for independence from MWD and the IID water deal. Although city leadership was displayed here, the question is whether the region's long-term interests were well served. To overcome vehement opposition to the IID deal from agricultural and suburban water agencies, the city's ten board directors moved to change the voting rules inside the County Water Authority. For most of its history, the County Water Authority operated informally on a one-agency-one-vote basis for its twenty-four member agencies. Yet the formal rules did allow for weighted voting based on member agencies' total financial contributions to the County Water Authority. With the leverage of the weighted vote, the city—with 48 percent of a weighted vote—could more or less determine the County Water Authority's decision making. The city's support would prove pivotal in the County Water Authority's approval of the IID deal. Given its new heft in local water governance, the City of San Diego was also able to craft local rate structures and other policies to minimize its own burden relative to that of other member agencies.

The city pushed through the weighted vote and installed one of its own directors, a forceful advocate of the IID water transfer, as chair of the County Water Authority board. Having done so, the Imperial Valley water deal was quickly approved. The city's delegation on the board treated the protests from member agencies in northern San Diego County—who were outraged at the deal's high price tag and the City of San Diego's strong-arm tactics—in the same high-handed fashion that it accused the MWD of treating the County Water Authority.[44]

Renewed Battles

The IID deal would prove an expensive proposition. When the costs of water purchases, wheeling charges, environmental and economic mitigation, and other payments were added up, the County Water Authority by 2010 paid nearly $1,000 per acre-foot for Imperial Valley water—significantly more than the cost of MWD water—making it the most expensive agriculture-to-urban water transfer in California, if not the nation.[45] What most irked County Water Authority officials was the high $252 per acre-foot wheeling charge payment to MWD for use of the Colorado River Aqueduct to move IID water. In exchange for hefty subsidies for local water projects, including support for a water desalination project in Carlsbad, the County Water Authority agreed not to sue MWD over its new rate structure (including wheeling charges) for five years. When the moratorium expired in mid-2010, however, the County Water Authority promptly filed a lawsuit.[46]

In an ironic twist, the County Water Authority argued that San Diego was subsidizing other MWD member agencies, including Los Angeles, under the new rate structure. In a similar vein, the County Water

Authority criticized MWD's proposed twenty-five-year strategy for stock-piling water for droughts and other emergencies. Local water officials claimed that the strategy would create huge amounts of unused "buffer" water at enormous expense, particularly for the County Water Authority, MWD's largest customer. While San Diego demanded the right to opt out of the plan, the vast majority of MWD's twenty-six member agencies praised the twenty-five-year supply plan, which they said would help develop new supplies such as desalination plants and water recycling and would also fairly allocate member agency benefits and burdens.[47]

In contrast, the County Water Authority complained about the heavy financial burdens it supposedly bore under MWD's rate structure and long-term reliability plan. At the same time, San Diego chose to ignore the substantial benefits of its MWD membership. In addition to MWD's underwriting of San Diego's phenomenal postwar growth, with large subsidies provided by founding member agencies, in particular Los Angeles, the MWD twenty-five-year supply plan heavily subsidized San Diego's ambitious water-supply diversification efforts.[48] Local member agency project initiatives, ranging from desalination facilities to conservation and reclamation, received a $250-per-acre-foot subsidy from MWD. With an ambitious desalination strategy and a host of other local projects, the County Water Authority was among MWD's more subsidized member agencies.

There was financial risk attached to the County Water Authority's 2010 lawsuit. MWD reserved the right to rescind its local project initiative subsidies should member agencies legally challenge its rate structure. Thus, the lawsuit has placed San Diego's desalination plans and other subsidized projects in jeopardy. Significantly, San Diego's diversification plans did not include reclamation. Although other Southern California agencies such as the Orange County Water District and the City of Los Angeles launched ambitious reclamation and recycling programs, the City of San Diego, led by Mayor Jerry Sanders and a strident *Union-Tribune* editorial board echoing earlier critics, denounced so-called toilet-to-tap proposals for extracting drinking water from treated wastewater. Notwithstanding city council approval of a reclaimed water pilot project, overriding the mayor's veto, San Diego seriously lagged behind other Southern California water agencies in recycling efforts.[49]

Ironically, the IID water transfer, the linchpin of San Diego's drive for water independence, was placed in legal jeopardy in early 2010 when a California court struck down a series of agreements central to the sharing of Colorado River water, including the County Water Authority's deal to buy water from the Imperial Valley. At issue was the receding Salton Sea in Imperial County, a large inland lake created by a two-year flooding of the Colorado River in 1905. San Diego's water transfers robbed the inland lake of agricultural runoff that had sustained it for years. This raised serious public health concerns as exposed wind-whipped dust from the receding lake was carried through the valley. The court ruled that there was no adequate state financing plan for mitigation and environmental restoration of the Salton Sea.[50]

The City of San Diego's leadership role in the IID deal and other policies of the County Water Authority are in contrast to its less prominent role in other regional agencies. The region's largest city was able to use the County Water Authority's voting rules to commandeer the agency for its own purposes. However, once in command, the City of San Diego did not appear to behave as a regional or megaregional steward. Instead, its actions belied a decidedly parochial approach, seeking to secure MWD water supply benefits while reducing its financial burdens and shifting the costs to other MWD member agencies and even to other County Water Authority members. With sharp local water-price hikes occurring amid a lengthy drought, the City of San Diego and the County Water Authority stepped up their efforts to make MWD and Los Angeles the chief scapegoats. In predictable lockstep fashion, the *San Diego Union-Tribune* editorial page lambasted MWD, claiming that "arrogance is in [the] water giant's DNA."[51]

To longtime observers of San Diego's water politics, none of this was surprising. As an MWD board director from Orange County observed in late 2010:

> The Water Authority's demonizing of MWD continues unabated. It's quite interesting that the devil can't be found in San Diego! All of the much higher water costs are a result of San Diego's costly penchant to somehow be independent of MWD (or, is it Los Angeles, sometimes I can't tell). It's a funny concept to me since their gambit to achieve that with the IID only works by relying on MWD infrastructure. If folks at the Authority weren't paranoid about preferential rights . . . , they could continue to buy MWD water at a much lower cost than they're going to pay with the IID transaction.[52]

Regional Fire-Preparedness: The Curse of Fragmentation

The determinations in this report underscore the fact that the region's bewildering organization of unserved areas and redundant, under-funded public agencies did not evolve spontaneously; it was encouraged and given shape by short-sighted public policy choices that were adopted without a vision of how such decisions would impact public safety.

—*San Diego Local Agency Formation Commission, 2005*[53]

With wide expanses of open space surrounding a large metropolitan area, the County of San Diego has historically faced greater wildfire dangers than other urbanized areas of California. Over the past several decades, this problem has been made worse by pro-growth policies in the unincorporated parts of the county, which have pushed dense development into rural areas with the least amount of public safety infrastructure and the greatest fire dangers, and the absence of a single, widely adopted fire and building code. Indeed, since the 1920s, San Diego County has represented 20 percent of all homes destroyed in California wildfires, although the county contains just one-tenth of the state population and a small fraction of its overall land area.[54]

Despite its acute fire dangers, however, the region has historically suffered from both inadequate resources and a fundamentally dysfunctional approach to managing fire prevention on a regional scale. As the largest county in the state without a consolidated fire department, San Diego has experienced extreme fragmentation in the provision of basic fire-fighting services. Since the 1970s, the county as a whole has relied on more than sixty different public agencies—ranging from the U.S. Forest Service and CALFIRE to municipal fire departments and fire agencies run by sovereign Native American tribes and tiny special-purpose agencies covering small regions of the county's large unincorporated area—to provide fire protection to its citizens.

Fewer than one-third of these agencies have employed professional staff, with the rest relying on poorly trained and inadequately equipped volunteers. Until very recently, nearly 1 million acres of unincorporated territory in the county remained outside of the jurisdiction of any fire protection agency. In addition, the county has made heavy use of a system of "mutual aid" that relies on other jurisdictions, including nearby counties and incorporated cities within the metropolitan area, to provide basic support for fires outside of their own boundaries.[55]

Overall, the San Diego region has faced two interrelated challenges to providing adequate fire protection within its territory to keep small wildfires from turning into major conflagrations. First, San Diego County, as a whole, has spent significantly less on firefighters, necessary equipment, and basic fire infrastructure than other California areas, including Orange County, its fiscally conservative northern neighbor.[56] In recent years, as the county has moved toward the consolidation of its disparate fire agencies, this gap has actually grown.[57] Instead, the county has chosen to free ride on state taxpayers, its cities, and nearby jurisdictions. Second, the county has spread its own meager resources too thinly across many fragmented government bodies, thus preventing the realization of significant economies of scale. Both of these problems have come about as a result of decisions made by San Diego elected officials and California voters (Proposition 13) in the 1970s; these policies have made recent efforts to reverse the growing fragmentation of fire protection doubly difficult.[58]

Humpty Dumpty's Great Fall

If two firestorms have taught San Diego anything, it is that walls of flames driven by ferocious winds respect no limits.

—San Diego Union-Tribune *editorial board, 2008*[59]

Under California law, cities and counties are not required to provide fire protection and rescue services to their constituents, who are left to fend for themselves. However, most local governments—in particular, larger and more urban jurisdictions—do include firefighting as one of their core functions. Historically, this has not been the case in San Diego County. In the 1920s, the county began providing a basic level of fire protection to its unincorporated areas through a contract with CALFIRE, a state agency charged with fighting wildfires in areas covered by dense vegetation. During fire season, the state budget pays for the cost of CALFIRE firefighters, whose primary mission is to stop wildfires from spreading rather than to protect homes and other structures. Under the agency's initial contract with San Diego, the county provided funds to retain a CALFIRE presence in unincorporated areas after the end of the fire season, when state support would come to an end.[60]

In the early 1970s, with the cost of the CALFIRE services growing quickly, county supervisors changed course, voting to eliminate all county responsibility for the provision of fire protection. Instead, the supervisors encouraged unincorporated areas to annex into nearby cities with their own fire departments or to join independent special-purpose fire protection districts, which did not rely on the county for funding. In addition, the county offered some support to areas wishing to form volunteer fire companies, pledging to provide funds for training the volunteers. These decisions greatly accelerated the fragmentation of fire services by encouraging the formation of small, independently run and managed bodies.

Voter passage of Proposition 13 in 1978 made even this patchwork approach difficult to sustain. Under the initiative's new constitutional cap on property taxes and implementing legislation passed by the state legislature, government agencies that did not receive property taxes in 1978 became ineligible to receive property tax revenue in the future. As a result, fire protection districts formed after 1978 have been left to find other sources of money. In addition, the initiative process and subsequent state legislation greatly reduced the likelihood of annexation of unincorporated areas into nearby fire districts and cities, because new areas would bring additional responsibility but few new revenues. Finally, although Proposition 13 allowed local governments to increase other types of taxes to pay for specific functions, like fire protection, it required that the taxes be affirmed by a two-thirds vote of the electorate.[61] In short, Proposition 13 further accelerated the centrifugal forces unleashed by county policy, even as it made finding sustainable funding for a decentralized fire protection system more difficult. The county government, with its own finances hurt by Proposition 13's property tax cuts, soon announced an end to its minimal financial support of volunteer fire companies.

By the early 1980s, continued fragmentation in the wake of new financing limits created a growing crisis in rural fire protection. San Diego had become a county divided between haves, fire protection districts created before 1978 and enjoying some semblance of adequate service levels, and have-nots, agencies created after the passage of Proposition 13 and forced to rely on volunteers and community fund-raisers like bake sales for financing. The clear inequities created new barriers to consolidation and annexation. Any plan to combine agencies would need to promise constituents an enhancement in service levels to convince them that consolidation would be an improvement over the status quo. At the same time, it would have to assuage concerns of wealthier districts and cities that their funds would not be used to subsidize services in other areas. In other words, after Proposition 13, revenues became the primary barrier to putting the pieces of the region's fragmented system back together again.

To address the growing crisis, county leaders unveiled a plan in 1981 to consolidate the backcountry's vast fire-fighting apparatus into a new regional fire protection district, run by independently elected directors, staffed by volunteers, and funded by a new fire assessment to be passed by a two-thirds vote. Yet the plan—in particular, the imposition of the new tax—received a frosty reception among voters, who rejected it by a two-to-one margin in the spring of 1981. Five months later, voters also rejected a scaled-down proposal, which reduced the scope of consolidation but retained the new fire assessment. In the face of unwavering voter opposition, the county supervisors eventually adopted a far less ambitious plan covering the least protected areas of the county. Funded by a voluntary revenue transfer from the county rather than a new tax, the new fire district covered more than eight hundred miles and included the majority of voluntary fire companies in southeastern San Diego County.[62]

Putting the Pieces Back Together

The biggest challenge associated with reorganization of any service delivery system is money.

—*San Diego Local Agency Formation Commission, 2007*[63]

Largely dormant through the late 1980s and early 1990s, efforts to consolidate regional fire protection programs received a new boost after the 2003 wildfires, which exposed the woeful state of the county's fire-preparedness. Lacking a sustainable funding source, many rural districts had let their engines and trucks go unmaintained and fall into disrepair. In parts of the county, needed fire stations were never built. As they worked to contain the flames, firefighters from different jurisdictions, using different radios and frequencies, struggled to communicate with one another.

With wildfires raging in other parts of the state, little additional help came by way of mutual aid in the early days of the fire. Finally, absent a single regional fire district, no individual agency wanted to pay the full cost of helicopters only to have other districts free ride on the investment. The lease on the region's only helicopter, at the City of San Diego's fire department, lapsed just days before the fire. A year earlier, Mayor Dick Murphy voted against leasing the helicopter, arguing that it was unfair for the city to bear the burden of paying for a regional resource.[64]

In the wake of the wildfires, county supervisors unveiled efforts to enhance regional coordination and increase investment in firefighting capacity. The county acquired a helicopter, placing it under the control of the Sheriff's Department. In 2005, the supervisors also created the County Fire Enhancement Program to distribute county funds to existing fire districts and help pay for the replacement of old equipment.[65] In addition, in 2004, county voters overwhelmingly approved an advisory ballot measure calling for the consolidation of backcountry fire agencies into a single, regional fire district. Fewer than one in five voters cast their ballots against the measure.

Although the 2004 measure created new political momentum for consolidation, it may also have hardened public opinion against new revenue, the glue necessary to bring disparate agencies together. By explicitly saying that the consolidated regional agency would be funded by existing revenues and would not result in new taxes, the measure reinforced expectations that fire protection could be improved without any increased costs to taxpayers.[66] Shortly after the vote, however, a fiscal analysis carried out by the San Diego Local Agency Formation Commission (LAFCO) showed that a regional fire district would require substantial new revenue, above the property tax dollars and assessments collected by existing districts. A new tax, however, was a losing cause: between 1978 and 2004, fire districts had asked voters for new or increased revenues more than seventy times; voters rejected two-thirds of these proposals.[67] Supervisors also ruled out using county revenue to help fund the new agency. County-sponsored legislation to divert property tax dollars from local school districts to fund a new regional fire district and have the state backfill the school budgets to make up the difference quickly died in the state legislature.

With few options for new revenue, consolidation efforts ground to a halt. It would take another set of wildfires in 2007, this time killing ten people and destroying 1,700 homes in the county, to bring new attention to regional fire protection and to revive efforts to reverse the forces of fragmentation. Shortly after the wildfires, a reluctant board of supervisors proposed a $52 countywide parcel tax to improve fire preparedness in the region as part of a broader consolidation proposal approved by LAFCO. However, the board of supervisors remained internally conflicted on the issue, and its members did little to campaign for the measure, which appeared on the November 2008 ballot. Supervisor Dianne Jacob, the county's leading advocate for consolidation and a LAFCO board member who represented much of the unincorporated backcountry, initially voted against placing the measure on the ballot before finally changing her mind.

Nor did the supervisors succeed in overcoming concerns from other stakeholders. Many rural residents who were already paying special taxes and assessments for their existing fire districts opposed paying a second tax. In addition, elected officials in incorporated cities, whose residents would provide the bulk of new revenue for a program designed primarily to benefit residents in unincorporated parts of the county, also expressed concern. In Encinitas and La Mesa, city councils passed resolutions opposing the increase. Only the City of San Diego, which stood to benefit from the tax by having many of the county's new reserve fire apparatus placed in city fire stations, enthusiastically endorsed the proposal, with Mayor Jerry Sanders becoming its key public face and proponent.[68]

Despite the lackluster campaign, more than 63 percent of county voters supported the tax increase in November. However, the number fell short of two-thirds, the supermajority threshold required under Proposition 13, with voters in the most fire-prone backcountry areas voting most heavily against the measure's passage. A month later, the county moved ahead with the creation of a new regional fire district. Although the supervisors agreed to increase the county's contribution to the agency above the amounts previously budgeted for the County Fire Enhancement Program, the new money provided only a fraction of the funds necessary to fully fund a regional fire department.

With little new revenue to offset their loss of autonomy, several large fire districts opted out of the new regional body. To retain the support of other members, the county greatly limited the authority of the new fire warden, a post created to run the regional department. The plan did not assign the warden any authority over the day-to-day coordination of fire and emergency response and explicitly noted that the warden would not have any operational responsibility, which would remain with the individual local fire agencies.[69]

Although the new regional district took some steps toward badly needed consolidation, it did little to create a single, unified structure to improve county fire-preparedness. More important, with the failure of the parcel tax in 2008, the new authority has had to find ways to expand existing fire services to previously unserved and underserved areas with little new money. By 2010, the county's combined fire agencies continued to spend significantly less than their neighbors to the north, investing just $152.85 per capita in fire protection, compared to $177.98 in Orange County and $217.71 in Los Angeles County, a gap that had grown from five years earlier, a period that preceded the start of the consolidation efforts.[70]

Cross-Border Conundrums

Today, globalization along the border evokes a critical debate—does the region's future lie with the perpetuation of the wall, and all that it symbolizes—national security, sovereignty, defense, and militarization— or does it reside in the propagation of a world of transparent boundaries and trans-frontier cities?
  —Border scholar Lawrence A. Herzog, 2003[71]

San Diego is the hinge of a Pacific Rim megaregion extending from Baja California to Los Angeles. It is also a border metropolis with 3 million county residents that has as its conjoined twin Baja California Norte, with more than 3 million residents (half of whom live in Tijuana). With the largest trade and debt relations, foreign investment flows, migration traffic, and production-sharing arrangements of any two countries on opposite sides of the global north-south divide, the U.S. and Mexico are uniquely implicated in a binational drama that extends beyond their common border. In the early twenty-first century, cross-border relations have been severely strained by controversies over illegal immigration, drug-related violence and drug flows, and post-9/11 border security concerns. Since 2001 there has been a seismic policy shift from a cross-border trade paradigm to a homeland security paradigm in terms of U.S. efforts and public monies spent.[72]

In this daunting environment, how well is San Diego meeting the economic and political challenges of becoming a transborder metropolis? Though still a laggard compared to other West Coast metropolises in terms of Pacific Rim trade possibilities, San Diego finally emerged by 2000 from what local newspaper columnist Neil Morgan called its "cul-de-sac" existence of ocean, desert, the navy, and defense-aerospace spending. A regional NAFTA hub, San Diego's ambitions to become a gateway to Latin America hinged on enhancing economic integration with Mexico through Tijuana.[73]

San Tijuana

Once viewed as a tawdry honky-tonk town, Tijuana began to rise in the estimation of San Diego's business leaders in the 1970s, when the trolley line between downtown San Diego and the border was built as a part of San Diego's downtown revitalization plan. But the real catalyst for the new trade-and-investment strategy reenvisioning the neighboring cities as "San Tijuana"—Siamese twins joined in a regional city-state— was the growth of the maquiladoras. These cross-border assembly plants combined Mexican labor with electronic components and producer services—management, engineering, legal, accounting, advertising, and so on—originally provided from San Diego but increasingly from around the world. They benefited from post-1983 Mexican trade liberalization and, ten years later, the advent of NAFTA.[74]

The maquiladora industry once represented the cutting edge of the two-way economic penetration between the United States and Mexico, stimulated by NAFTA and accelerated by Mexican privatization initiatives designed to entice foreign investors. This two-way trade and investment represented a growing component of the San Diego economy. Facilitating cross-border economic development, Baja California's trade infrastructure could serve San Diego's needs. Tijuana's Rodriguez Field airport, with a ten-thousand-foot runway that can handle international jet flights, and the Port of Ensenada, with growing container traffic, have supplemented San Diego's limited airport and port facilities.[75]

Beginning in the late 1980s, business, professional, and academic organizations on both sides of the border took the lead in trying to forge a cross-border consensus on transportation and development issues. In the 1990s a modicum of cross-border intergovernmental planning was achieved. The cities of San Diego and Tijuana cooperated on economic, environmental, and emergency response planning. Both SANDAG and several other Southern California agencies signed an agreement with the State of Baja California and its five municipalities to develop a joint border transportation plan. A variety of working groups were established to examine issues related to cross-border development, including the Regional Border Ports of Entry (Tijuana, Tecate, and San Diego) Council, a forum for regional and federal agencies, as well as community stakeholders, to examine opportunities to improve the management of the border crossings. It also provided a forum for considering the long-term expansion needs of the border ports of entry. There were also spillover benefits to San Diego with the establishment of an alliance among California, Baja California Norte, and Baja California Sur to tap into the $8.4 billion in federal money allotted for border environmental and infrastructure projects.[76]

Political Fences

There were sharp political barriers, however, to furthering cross-border outreach. One major challenge was illegal immigration, which exacerbated already-prevalent Anglo indifference or hostility to things Mexican. Vigilante campaigns, encouraged by local conservative radio talk-show hosts, to "light up the border" with vehicle headlights or make citizen arrests of suspicious foreigners at Lindbergh Field were extreme manifestations of prevalent public attitudes that became more common after 9/11, culminating in vigilante group attempts to interdict illegal immigrants at the border.[77]

The stakes of the immigration reform debate were high for San Diego, where an estimated 10 percent of the workforce were illegals, and even higher for Tijuana families desperately dependent on their earnings. "I do not see a solution in building more fences," said Mexican Senator Hector Osuna Jaime, a former Tijuana mayor. "You have to ask how high, what material will be used, and who will build it. We might even help you, but it's not going to solve the problem."[78]

Grassroots Anglo hostility was compounded by the political marginalization of San Diego's Latino community. Compared with neighboring Los Angeles, America's self-styled finest city has seriously lagged in achieving political integration of its Mexican-origin residents.[79] Although prominent San Diego Latinos have succeeded in winning key political offices—in 2010, the presidents of both the city council and the city's school board were Latino, as was the president of the regional chamber of commerce—the community has lacked a strong political organization and has not succeeded in building a broader rainbow coalition that includes other significant minority groups, including blacks and Asian Americans. In the absence of institutionalized leadership, Latino politics in the city and in the broader region have been dominated by competing family-based political dynasties.[80]

In San Diego, the political difficulties to transborder integration have been exacerbated by politicians motivated by populist hostility against the elite business consensus on border issues. Negative attitudes toward cross-border cooperation have been pervasive, crossing ideological and partisan lines. Congressman Duncan L. Hunter, a conservative Republican, and Congressman Bob Filner, a liberal Democrat, both opposed NAFTA and, albeit for different reasons, a binational airport. Hunter also single-handedly killed federal loan guarantees for the proposed reopening of the San Diego and Arizona Eastern railroad, on the grounds that the trains would serve as a welcome wagon for swelling hordes of illegal immigrants and drug smugglers.[81]

The Wall

Growing political opposition to illegal immigration, marked by the failure of comprehensive immigration reform under both Presidents Bush and Obama, has further complicated border politics for the region. Operation Gatekeeper, initiated in 1994 despite initial concerns over the militarization of the border, was generally credited with facilitating the flow of people and goods between San Diego and Tijuana by fostering a new level of cooperation between U.S. federal, state, and local law enforcement authorities and their Mexican counterparts. Unfortunately, fears of illegal immigration, seemingly impermeable to the fact of declining crime rates in San Diego, far outran the reality that the vast majority of undocumented workers merely passed through San Diego on the way to Los Angeles and points beyond. In 2005, these concerns took a somewhat reluctant President Bush to the Rio Grande, where he promised one thousand more agents and high-tech drone surveillance planes as additional efforts to secure the border. President Obama, an early advocate of immigration reform, largely followed in the footsteps of his predecessor in the run-up to the 2010 midterm elections, calling up National Guard troops to secure the border and pledging hundreds of millions of dollars in additional investment in border security.[82]

As part of efforts to reduce illegal immigration through deterrence, federal officials have pushed for the construction of new physical barriers along the San Diego–Tijuana border. Legislation adopted in the late 1990s required that existing barriers be replaced by a rugged triple fence along the fourteen-mile border and gave immigration officials authority to override existing state and federal environmental protections. Construction, along with enhanced security measures designed to avoid terrorist entry after 9/11, have resulted in long delays at the border, greatly increasing the transaction costs of cross-border trade, and have hampered efforts to promote closer integration on both sides of the border. San Diego's fence does indeed seem to have slowed illegal immigrant inflows—or, rather, to have apparently shifted them further east to crossings in more dangerous mountainous and desert terrain. The cost, however, has been a chilling effect on cross-border cooperative morale and goodwill in the region.[83]

Although the problems facing the City of San Diego and its underfunded pension, public services, and infrastructure systems have attracted more national attention, the challenges confronting the binational region as a whole are, if anything, as severe. Dealing with these challenges will require sustained and coordinated action—not only on the part of the city but also on the part of other municipalities, the county government, and the region's multiplicity of single-purpose agencies. Unfortunately, there is little evidence that either political leaders, who remain divided about how to address overcrowding at the region's only major airport, looming water shortages and steep water-price hikes, and the absence of comprehensive fire protection, or residents, who continue to oppose most efforts to raise taxes to pay for needed public services, have come to appreciate their linked fates or to accept the need for collective action on a regional scale. State constitutional provisions, which exacerbate a status quo bias in local institutions and provide voter minorities with veto power over most major public initiatives, make these tasks doubly difficult.

The San Diego region has done little to prepare for the major infrastructure challenges of the twenty-first century. This is most apparent in the visible failures of regional stewardship of fire protection and airport development. The searing images of wildfires burning unchecked into heavily populated areas serves as both an enduring symbol of local and regional governments' futility and a reminder of the consequences of chronic inaction. In the coming years, as these problems grow more dire, only a fundamental reform of the region's governance system and an infusion of enlightened leadership and public support can stem what many fear is the beginning of the region's downward trajectory.

It is easy to understand why qualified people would choose not to get into local government, given it is so terrible. . . . In San Diego, we have a really small group of influentials. These folks are motivated to participate in government in order to get something from it. These include developers of property and those benefiting from franchise agreements. It is [in] nobody's interest to look at the City's best interests. I call San Diego the city of happy talk. There are lots of people taking a part of the government gravy train.

—*Former mayoral candidate Pat Shea, 2007*[1]

The end of World War II was a transformative moment for American cities. Wartime industry and migration swelled urban centers, straining the facilities and capacities of local governments. The influx of poor, minority residents focused the nation's attention on the need to promote urban renewal and confront difficult questions of civil rights. By the 1960s, the crisis of urban governance was receiving attention from policy makers across the country. "The [urban] problem is the largest we have ever known," Senator Robert Kennedy noted in 1966. "And we confront an urban wilderness more frightening than the wilderness faced by the pilgrims or the pioneers." Some, like urbanist Douglas Yates, concluded that American cities were simply "ungovernable," their problems too vast and their institutions too fragmented to tackle the task.[2]

Today, cities face a different set of dilemmas arising from new social and economic forces. Many urban areas face challenges rooted in the global forces of immigration and economic globalization and the local forces of governmental fragmentation, the latter driven by increasingly restless middle-class constituents. In many ways, San Diego epitomizes the ungovernable city of the twenty-first century.

The scale of San Diego's governance challenges puts the city in a league of its own. The magnitude of its pension liability and budget deficits has few analogues in other locales. The state of disrepair of its basic infrastructure and the woeful levels of funding for core city services put San Diego at the bottom even among other cash-strapped California governments. The gaping disjunction between the grand ambitions of the city's elected officials and business community and the pressing concerns of local residents defies the common sense of most outside observers. Yet, although the extent to which San Diego has failed to address its most pressing civic problems might be unusual, the nature of the governance challenges it has faced over the past two decades are far from unique. Examining the origins of these challenges and the strategies San Diegans have chosen to tackle them offers lessons for cities confronting similar crises.

In this chapter, we retrace the key factors we believe are central to understanding both the causes of San Diego's governance challenges and the city's failure to resolve them. Although the absence of elite leadership—in the private and public sectors—has played a pivotal role, it is only part of the story. Equally important has been voters' growing distrust of local government and their reluctance to provide the resources it needs to carry out basic public functions. Changing institutional dynamics, including the increasing resort to ballot-box budgeting and reform, have exacerbated these trends. We conclude by briefly examining the policy options available to remedy past failures and by highlighting the insights that the San Diego case can provide for communities elsewhere.

Boosters, Bluejackets, and Public Entrepreneurs

When I came to San Diego, there were a few people who wielded power. Some downtown bankers and other people. That is still the case to some degree, but what has happened though is that you don't have a C. Arnholt Smith, or Bill Lynch, who owned banks. Our banks are owned by people in San Francisco, or Charlotte, or someplace else, so you don't have the same concentration of power and you certainly don't have those institutions playing a role in philanthropy, which also affects politics. There has been a diffusion of power in the business community, part of it absentee ownership and part of it more diversity.

—*Bernie Jones, former editor,* San Diego Union-Tribune, *2009*[3]

William Heath Davis arrived in San Diego from San Francisco in 1850, where he had been a merchant and shipper. Convinced that a settlement close to the waterfront would attract residents and trade to the area, Davis bought 160 acres of land, laid out plans for the city, and built a wharf and warehouse. A recession in 1851 brought a premature end to Davis's speculative venture. In 1867, however, San Francisco furniture store owner Alonzo Horton revived the venture, buying eight hundred acres of Davis's New Town for $265. Horton, a natural salesman, returned to San Francisco to advertise his properties in what would later become downtown San Diego. What lots he could not sell, he donated to churches and families that promised to build right away.

Horton was San Diego's first prominent businessman and booster. Although his scheme to use land to attract new residents and the railroad failed in the 1880s, a similar strategy would be adopted in the early twentieth century by Congressman William Kettner and the San Diego Chamber of Commerce to entice the U.S. Navy. As we recounted in Chapter 2, the success of these pre–World War I private and public actors laid the foundation for San Diego's phenomenal twentieth-century growth. In subsequent decades, the informal partnership between the business community, public officials, and the navy was instrumental in shaping land use patterns and mobilizing voters in support of bond campaigns to build water and transportation infrastructure.[4]

In addition to building houses, offices, factories, and infrastructure, San Diego's boosters and bluejackets, as they have been named by historian Abraham Shragge, contributed to its cultural life.[5] Business mogul John D. Spreckels, for example, built Spreckels Theatre, California's first commercial playhouse, and contributed to the 1915 Panama-California Exposition. George Marston, owner of San Diego's leading department store, helped found the YMCA and championed local parks. While shaping San Diego's economic and cultural development, these businessmen also became the chief stewards of its politics.[6]

In the years following World War II, the political influence of San Diego's business community was consolidated in the hands of a local power elite, led by U.S. National Bank owner C. Arnholt Smith and James S. Copley, owner of the *San Diego Union* and *San Diego Evening Tribune*. Another pillar of the local business community was the San Diego Convention and Tourism Bureau, formed in 1954 and renamed the Convention and Visitors Bureau (ConVis) in 1965. ConVis led a campaign for a publicly financed convention center. To get around the opposition of local residents, ConVis worked out a deal with Mayor Charlie Dail to finance the project with money from the city's capital outlay program and municipal employee retirement fund. The convention center opened in September 1964. In 1965, ConVis achieved "self-sufficiency" with the passage of the transient-occupancy tax—a tax levied on hotel guests that has been used to finance the city's tourism marketing efforts ever since.

Around this time, local business leaders and politicians were forging another alliance that would dramatically alter the city's development trajectory. In the late 1950s, the San Diego Downtown Association formed an ad hoc committee to study the deterioration of the city's downtown core. Downtown had languished as San Diego's suburban periphery grew; new malls and housing tracts in Linda Vista and Mission Valley had contributed to a decline in retail sales and population. In 1959, several committee members founded San Diegans Inc. (SDI), a nonprofit organization composed of sixteen of the city's leading property owners.

San Diegans Inc. resembled other executive organizations in large American cities in both its composition and its objectives. The group advocated a massive infusion of resources to spur construction downtown; it also pushed the city council to develop a citywide general plan and a master plan for downtown. The ambitious agenda of SDI was resisted by local politicians. The city council refused to seek federal funds for downtown redevelopment. When voters rejected a bond proposal to finance the Community Concourse, it was SDI officials who suggested financing the project with money borrowed from the municipal employee retirement fund.[7]

By the early 1960s, the first efforts to revitalize downtown were under way, with new skyscrapers popping up alongside San Diego's Community Concourse. These were the first large structures to be built there since the Spreckels Building in 1927. By this time, there was little daylight between the business community's pro-growth agenda and the talking points of local politicians. Under Mayor Frank Curran, the downtown civic center was completed, and voters approved a bond to build a stadium in Mission Valley for the San Diego Padres Major League Baseball expansion team. Curran's mayoralty, however, ended under a cloud when he and members of the city council were indicted for participating in a scheme to raise taxi rates in exchange for campaign contributions. The early 1970s also saw the collapse of Smith's political influence. Smith's U.S. National Bank failed in 1973 under the weight of bad loans offered to other Smith-controlled companies. Copley died the same year, marking the end of a civic strongman era.

In Chapter 2, we discussed how Mayor Pete Wilson's rise in local politics was facilitated by the vacuum created by the Yellow Cab scandal and the exodus of Smith, Copley, and other notables of the old-guard business community. Wilson, who presided over the city council under San Diego's council-manager plan, used his powers to set the legislative agenda and appoint allies to key positions. Wilson, however, had little appetite for parliamentary maneuvering. Indeed, whenever he could, he sought to move issues out of the council and into more friendly decision-making venues.[8]

Wilson's lasting institutional contribution was the Centre City Development Corporation (CCDC). Wilson rejected overtures from SDI, whose members wanted it to serve as the main planning organization for downtown. The structural details of CCDC were worked out with the local chamber of commerce. In the end, both sides got what they wanted. Wilson would get to appoint the board of the new entity and its executive director. The business community, with the advent of tax increment financing, secured a stable and dedicated source of revenue for new downtown projects.

It is tempting to read these developments as the beginning of the end of active business leadership in San Diego politics. This would make San Diego similar to other cities experiencing a decline in the local corporate presence. Urban scholar Royce Hanson has tracked the presence of Fortune 500 companies in U.S. metropolitan areas. Between 1960 and 2003, large companies were moving operations to the suburbs in Cleveland, Pittsburgh, Baltimore, and other areas. The loss of corporate talent, Hanson argues, has meant fewer opportunities to engage corporate managers in civic affairs, a more fragmented civic elite, and a corresponding loss of civic leadership capacity.[9]

As Table 8.1 shows, this characterization does not adequately describe San Diego. In 1960, San Diego was home to just one Fortune 500 firm—Ryan Aeronautical Corporation. In 2003, it was home to four—Sempra Energy, Qualcomm, Gateway, and Science Applications (by 2010, the latter two had moved their headquarters out of town). San Diego never had a large corporate presence to begin with. Indeed, as we described in Chapter 2, the city has always nurtured small proprietors

TABLE 8.1   Fortune 500 companies in metropolitan areas, 1960, 1980, and 2003

Metropolitan area	1960	1980	2003	Change 1980–2003
Washington, D.C.	0	3	16	13
Dallas	7	8	19	11
Houston	1	11	19	8
Atlanta	0	4	12	8
Minneapolis–St. Paul	7	11	17	6
San Jose	2	6	11	5
Los Angeles	13	9	14	5
Columbus	1	0	5	5
Charlotte	1	2	6	4
Kansas City	3	2	6	4
San Diego	1	0	4	4
San Francisco–Oakland	10	8	10	2
Indianapolis	2	2	4	2
Phoenix	0	3	3	0
Philadelphia	21	14	13	−1
Detroit	18	13	12	−1
Baltimore	2	4	3	−1
Hartford	2	6	4	−2
Milwaukee	7	11	8	−3
Portland	1	6	1	−4
Cleveland	15	13	7	−6
Pittsburgh	25	16	7	−9

SOURCES: Figures for California regions compiled by the authors from data provided by *Fortune* magazine. Figures for non-California regions are from table 3 in Royce Hanson, Harold Wolman, David Connolly, Katherine Pearson, and Robert McManmon, "Corporate Citizenship and Urban Problem Solving," *Journal of Urban Affairs* 32:1 (February 2010), p. 6.

and branch plants, not corporate headquarters, despite efforts to attract the latter. Big business has been a much greater presence in Los Angeles and the Bay Area. Overall, California's metropolitan regions, notwithstanding conventional wisdom, have avoided the loss of local corporate presence, each hosting more Fortune 500 companies in 2003 than in 1980.

Under Wilson, CCDC became the crucial locus of interaction between the business community and public officials. Why did Wilson prefer public planning under CCDC to private planning under SDI? In retrospect, three reasons seem apparent. First, the CCDC model enabled local politicians to exert greater control over the growth agenda. Second, CCDC helped mobilize a business community that by the 1970s lacked both organization and resources. Third, CCDC allowed Wilson and others to tap public resources efficiently, that is, without going through the city council, annual budget process, or voters.

Political control was partly achieved by eliminating the competition. Following CCDC's incorporation, the modus vivendi behind SDI and other private-sector planning initiatives was lost. By the late 1980s, SDI was largely defunct. In 1993, the group formally merged back into the San Diego Downtown Association. Political control has also been enhanced by CCDC's institutional resources. Through its discretion to fast-track projects and, more important, to distribute the tax increment, CCDC has allowed mayors to put their own stamp on land-use and development patterns downtown.

Since its reincarnation, CCDC has also been an effective tool for local elected officials to tap private-sector expertise and political support. The template was established in the early 1980s with Wilson's relationship with developer Ernest Hahn. Hahn worked closely with CCDC to secure the land and financing to build Horton Plaza. Hahn needed more than land and money, however, to make the project work. The developer pushed Wilson to build mass transit downtown, to clean up the Gaslamp Quarter, and to construct a new convention center. In fact, CCDC was instrumental in accomplishing Hahn's first two demands; the Port of San Diego, another special-purpose government, eventually achieved the third.

CCDC obviated the need for the old cumbersome process of approving and paying for large projects in San Diego. Under the old regime, local business leaders—like department store owner Guilford Whitney, Ryan Aeronautical Corporation founder Claude T. Ryan, local contractor Morley Golden, and the aforementioned Copley—provided the leadership to secure voter passage of general obligation bonds for financing large public works projects. In doing so, it was necessary to engage voters and to communicate the benefits of proposed projects. Voters generally trusted these businessmen more than elected officials.

The combination of tax increment financing and revenue bonds—a form of borrowing backed by future revenues—allowed politicians to claim that new projects would be revenue neutral. After CCDC's incorporation in 1975, there was less need to rely on general obligation bonds to pay for expensive projects. Such bond proposals have never been popular with San Diego voters and, even before Wilson's time, were difficult to get passed. Horton Plaza, the San Diego Convention Center, and Petco Park—the cornerstones of San Diego's downtown revitalization program—were all financed without general obligation bonds. Voters did sign off on conceptual proposals for the convention center in 1983 and the ballpark project in 1998, but neither required proponents to achieve high voter thresholds or to ask for tax increases.

The new downtown redevelopment regime offered few incentives for private-sector leaders to engage the public directly. With ConVis and CCDC, elements of San Diego's business community were formally incorporated into local government. Local boosterism has been institutionalized even as local proprietorship has given way to chain stores and multinational conglomerates managed from afar. Table 8.2, which lists the county's twenty largest property owners, illustrates the extent to which San Diego's business community has become the province of outsiders. Only four companies have local roots. Table 8.2 also suggests the difficulty that today's public officials face in recruiting corporate leaders to participate in civic initiatives. Three of San Diego's largest property owners are located in Los Angeles County, one is in Orange County, and fully half are owned by out-of-state entities.

The replacement of broad civic-minded business leaders with narrow project-focused developers suits the interests of public officials. Separating the tax increment from other revenues and placing it under CCDC control means that elected officials do not have to justify awarding large redevelopment subsidies even as citywide funding for libraries, parks, and roads is cut. The poster child for the new form of politics was John Moores, a software developer from Houston who breezed into San Diego in 1994 when he bought the San Diego Padres. In four short years, Moores succeeded in securing hundreds of millions of public dollars from the city's General Fund, CCDC, and the Port District. Moores lavished elected officials with campaign contributions and gifts. Having ironed out a favorable agreement with Mayor Susan Golding, Moores orchestrated a glitzy campaign to secure voter approval. After winning a narrow majority vote, he spent the following decade profiting from development rights on land near the ballpark. By 2009, Moores was ready to cash out. And then, having put down few roots in San Diego, Moores left town.

TABLE 8.2 Top twenty property owners in San Diego by taxes paid, fiscal year 2010–11

Property owner	Industry or sector	Location[a]	Amount paid	Corporate owner
San Diego Gas & Electric Co.	Energy utility	San Diego, CA	$63,455,985	Sempra Energy
Southern California Edison Co.	Energy utility	Rosemead, CA	$28,828,695	Edison International
Irvine Co.	Real estate	Newport Beach, CA	$17,761,358	
San Diego Family Housing LLC	Military housing	Dallas, TX	$14,835,726	Public-private partnership involving U.S. Navy, the Lincoln Property Co. (Dallas, TX), and Clark Realty (Bethesda, MD).
Kilroy Realty LLP	Real estate	Los Angeles, CA	$14,679,407	
Qualcomm Inc.	Semiconductor	San Diego, CA	$13,626,003	
Camp Pendleton & Quantico Housing LLC	Military housing	Dallas, TX	$11,654,352	Partnership involving Lincoln Property Co. (Dallas, TX), Hunt Building Co. (El Paso, TX), and Clark Realty (Bethesda, MD).
Pacific Bell Telephone Company	Telecom utility	San Francisco, CA	$9,708,652	AT&T
Arden Realty LLP	Real estate	Los Angeles, CA	$8,440,141	
OC/SD Holdings LLC	Real estate	Englewood, CO	$6,584,929	
Genentech Inc.	Pharmaceutical	Basel, Switzerland	$5,762,893	Roche Group
Pfizer Inc.	Pharmaceutical	New York, NY	$5,565,709	
Otay Mesa Generating Co. LLC	Energy	San Jose, CA	$5,552,753	Otay Mesa Corporation and Pacific Gas & Electric
Fashion Valley Mall LLC	Retail	Indianapolis, IN	$5,001,451	Simon Property Group
One Park Boulevard LLC (Hilton Bayfront)	Hotel	McLean, VA	$4,778,202	
SeaWorld Inc.	Theme park	Leuven, Belgium	$4,571,849	Anheuser-Busch
Prebys Conrad Trust	Real estate	San Diego, CA	$4,491,045	
CNL Hotel Del Partners LLP	Hotel	New York, NY	$4,230,007	CNL Hotels and Resorts (Morgan Stanley)
La Jolla Crossroads 1 LLC	Real estate	San Diego, CA	$4,041,928	Garden Communities LLC
Solar Turbines	Alternative energy	Peoria, IL	$3,998,150	Caterpillar Inc.

SOURCE: San Diego County Auditor and Controller.

[a]This represents the location of the corporate parent, not the subsidiary.

San Diegans Hate Their Government but Love Local Politicians

One of the problems in San Diego is that its politicians want power, but not to use it.

—Scott Barnett, former executive director, San Diego County Taxpayers Association, 2007[10]

In 2000, the Public Policy Institute of California surveyed San Diego County residents' perceptions about the quality of life and problems facing their community. The outlook of most residents was positive, with large majorities agreeing that things were headed in the right direction (66 percent). This sunny outlook was dimmed somewhat by the list of problems residents cited. Topping the list were traffic congestion, affordable housing, and the environment. Ranking fifth on the list, however, above homelessness, lack of parks, too much growth, crime, and joblessness, was "the amount of property taxes, sales taxes, and other local taxes and fees that residents have to pay." Interestingly, coming in eighth was "inadequate government funding for local services."[11]

These simultaneous impulses, San Diegans' reflexive dislike of taxes and yearning for more government services, are at the crux of a dilemma for public officials. How does one deliver public services at appropriate levels without raising taxes and thereby arousing the ire of constituents? The dilemma is exacerbated by the suspicions that voters have about local government. When asked to identify the causes of the problems facing their community, 75 percent of San Diegans in 2000 agreed that "government spending money on the wrong things" was a major cause. Indeed, far more San Diegans cited this reason than "too fast growth," "poor quality schools," the "growing gap between the rich and poor," or "too much immigration." Ranking third behind misplaced government spending priorities was "ineffective government." Also making the list of major causes were "the way government goes about allocating state and local taxes" and "greed and corruption in government."[12]

The 2000 survey offers a valuable snapshot of San Diegans' historical distrust of local government, even as they demand more from it. The survey was taken at a high point for the city, just four years after the 1996 Republican National Convention. It predates the political scandals that emerged over the following ten years, including the conviction of City Councilwoman Valerie Stallings in 2001 for accepting gifts in exchange for voting for the ballpark deal, the indictment of three council members in 2003 for accepting bribes from a local strip-club owner, and the conviction of local Congressman Randy "Duke" Cunningham in 2005 for accepting bribes in exchange for steering federal contracts to his friends. It also predates the pension scandal and the wildfires of 2003 and 2007, in which the incapacity of local government was prominently on display. Finally, it documents voters' distrust of local government a full eight years before the 2008 global economic downturn exacerbated the city's fiscal crisis, which resulted in deep cuts to local government services. In other words, the distrust that San Diegans harbor for local government predates its recent poor performance.

Although local voters' distrust did not necessarily derive from government performance, it has shaped local politics to a great extent. Public officials are quite aware that residents believe that local government ought to do as little as possible. They prefer allowing the private sector to take the lead. Residents believe that local government officials waste much of the money they receive in taxes and that government spending can be cut dramatically without consequence to the quality of public services they receive. Public officials accept voters' antipathy to tax increases at face value and have strenuously avoided putting tax measures on the ballot. Nonetheless, these same officials recognize that cuts to public services are also very unpopular.

In Chapter 5 (see Table 5.2), we documented the extent to which public officials have avoided testing voters' antipathy to tax hikes. Between 1995 and 2008 only three proposals for tax increases were put on the ballot. Two such proposals were offered in 2004 and targeted nonresident hotel occupants. The other was offered in 1996 and sought to raise the local sales tax by a quarter of a cent to pay for new branch libraries. None of the three, including a March 2004 proposal to raise hotel taxes to pay for emergency police and fire service, came close to the necessary two-thirds voter threshold.

Voters and public officials in other California cities were more successful in passing proposals for new taxes and bonds. Indeed, the data presented in Chapter 5 show San Diego to be an outlier among large cities and counties in California. Those figures may understate San Diego's anomalous fiscal behavior. Between January 2001 and March 2010, 565 local revenue measures were proposed by municipal governments in Cali-

TABLE 8.3   City of San Diego tax and bond initiatives, 1960–2009

	Proposed	Passed	% taxes and bonds passed	% voting yes (mean)
1960–69				
Taxes	2	2	100.0	60.1
Bonds	17	8	47.1	66.1
1970–79				
Taxes	3	1	33.3	42.1
Bonds	13	2	15.4	53.9
1980–89				
Taxes	0	0	—	—
Bonds	2	0	0.0	60.1
1990–99				
Taxes	1	0[a]	0.0	53.1
Bonds	2	1	50.0	56.0
2000–09				
Taxes	2	0	0.0	51.7
Bonds[b]	0	0	—	—

SOURCE: Office of the City Clerk, City of San Diego.

[a]In November 1996, city voters approved a proposition providing for a branch library endowment fund paid for by the city's share of a quarter-cent increase in the county sales tax. The proposition did not go into effect because voters failed to approve the proposed quarter-cent sales tax increase.

[b]Between 2003 and 2008, the City of San Diego had its credit rating suspended as a result of accounting irregularities involving its pension system for municipal employees.

fornia. Of the 360 measures that required a majority vote by local voters, 243 passed, for a success rate of 68 percent. Ninety-eight of the 205 measures requiring a two-thirds vote passed, for a success rate of 48 percent.[13] Passing local ballot propositions for new revenues is a difficult task in post–Proposition 13 California. But local governments do have other revenue-raising tools, and nearly every local government outside of San Diego has tried to use them.

Such was not always the case in the City of San Diego. Table 8.3 shows the number of proposals for new taxes and bonds that San Diegans voted on and approved in various decades, from 1960 to 2009. In the 1960s, public officials were highly successful in getting voters to sign off on new revenues; two tax and eight bond proposals passed. These included bonds for $23.8 million and $3.5 million, respectively, to complete facilities in Balboa Park; $15 million to upgrade the city's inadequate sewer system; and a property tax increase to provide for a public transportation system. In the 1970s, voters approved a bond to build the San Diego Wild Animal Park and, in the same June 1978 election that produced Proposition 13, signed off on a $65 million bond for open space and parks. This pattern changed abruptly in the late 1970s and 1980s. Since the passage of Proposition 13, which raised the voter threshold to two-thirds on certain local tax hikes, not a single tax increase and only one bond measure have secured voter approval.

In Chapter 1, we introduced the term *new fiscal populism* to describe a breed of public officials who flourish under conditions of voter distrust of local government. Such politicians win office by advertising their fiscal and managerial credentials. Their combination of fiscal conservatism and social liberalism appeals to voters who want to keep the costs of government low while avoiding extreme positions on social issues like affirmative action and the environment.[14] San Diego Mayor Jerry Sanders, a former police chief who pledged to play hardball with municipal employees and reversed his opposition to gay marriage, is cut from the new fiscal populist mold.

Sanders was elected in 2005 to put the city's fiscal house in order. While other candidates talked about tax increases on the one hand and bankruptcy on the other, Sanders embraced cuts to the municipal workforce, salary freezes, and other cost-cutting measures. Once in office, he worked to implement financial reforms. With City Attorney Michael Aguirre's lawsuits against the city's retirement system going nowhere, the mayor was stuck with the benefit increases granted by previous administrations. In 2008, Sanders convinced city employees to agree to a two-tiered pension system. In 2009, the city council backed the mayor's plan to unilaterally impose new labor contracts on police and blue-collar workers. But the burden of the city's burgeoning pension payments and investment losses dwarfed the modest savings the mayor achieved.

Even before the global economic downturn that began in October 2008, Sanders faced the unwholesome choice between raising taxes to cover shortfalls in the municipal budget and imposing deep cuts to public services. The recession merely hastened the inevitable showdown between San Diegans' demands for high-quality public services and their steadfast refusal to support measures to pay for them. Ever the conciliatory figure, Sanders was ill equipped to pursue either tax hikes or service cuts with much enthusiasm. Ultimately, voters in San Diego made Sanders's choice for him. In the November 2008 elections, voters ousted city attorney Aguirre and elected four new members to the city council.

One of the incoming council members was Carl DeMaio, a Republican elected from District 5. DeMaio was a relative newcomer to San Diego, having arrived in 2002 as a senior fellow for the Reason Foundation. Reason is a libertarian think tank advocating smaller government and market-friendly public policies. Ironically, the pretext for DeMaio's arrival was Reason's giving the city council an award for running the most efficient local government in California. The irony did not stop there. In 2000, DeMaio helped found the Performance Institute, a for-profit think tank specializing in training government workers in performance-based management practices. DeMaio's timing was fortuitous. With Republicans taking over the White House in 2000, DeMaio cashed in on the contacts he had made as a Republican operative in Washington, D.C. On the strength of several lucrative contracts with federal agencies, DeMaio built the Performance Institute into a multimillion-dollar enterprise.

With Aguirre's defeat and DeMaio's election, the pendulum of the new fiscal populism in San Diego swung from left to right. DeMaio's status as a self-proclaimed businessman-turned-government-watchdog is belied by his deep roots in ideological Republican politics. DeMaio got his start working with House Speaker Newt Gingrich and Virginia Thomas, former labor counsel of the U.S. Chamber of Commerce and wife of U.S. Supreme Court Justice Clarence Thomas, at the Congressional Institute. The institute was set up to coordinate planning among Republicans in the U.S. House, party insiders, and corporate lobbyists. While at the Reason Foundation, DeMaio helped author a report that called for the privatization of many federal government operations. DeMaio also wrote reports on competitive outsourcing of federal contracts.

In a further ironic twist, these reports came out as DeMaio achieved his greatest business triumph—the Performance Institute's inclusion in a special schedule of vendors that compete with one another for federal contracts and, as such, are insulated from competition with the open market. The listing paved the way for a series of federal contracts that transformed Performance into an $8.5 million company by the time DeMaio cashed out in 2007. Now ensconced in San Diego, DeMaio began working to implement his privatization and antiunion agenda at the local level.

DeMaio is not the first local politician to capitalize on San Diegans' distrust of their government. Similar antigovernment rhetoric has been used by elected officials to defeat proposals to upgrade the city's wastewater system, force residents to pay the true costs of trash collection, fund the city's library and park facilities, place municipal employee health care on a sound fiscal footing, and raise taxes to pay for police and fire protection. DeMaio's real innovation lies in his relentless efforts at self-promotion. The new councilman turned an organization ostensibly devoted to training government workers into a political machine generating ideas and campaign cash for local conservative causes.

Since 1991, not a single member of the San Diego city council has been defeated for reelection.[15] Four council members who voted to underfund the municipal retirement system in 2002 were subsequently returned to office by their constituents in 2004. Even Mayor Dick Murphy, who presided over the pension scandal, was narrowly reelected in 2004. What explains the electoral success of individual politicians in a setting where the large majority of residents distrust their government? The secret lies in these officials' ability to deliver benefits to the subpopulations of residents who control their electoral fates and to avoid controversial positions on divisive issues like taxes.

On certain occasions, mayors and council members have also used the strategy of running against local government to great effect. In the immediate aftermath of the pension scandal, the strategy was used successfully by political outsiders Michael Aguirre and Donna Frye. These progressives promised to end the backroom deals that contributed to the city's fiscal morass and to increase government accountability. Ultimately, however, conservatives like Sanders and DeMaio became the true masters of antigovernment rhetoric. By holding up municipal employees as local bogeymen, these politicians succeeded in mobilizing voter distrust in the service of conservative causes like privatization and increased executive authority. Unfortunately, they have failed to lead the city out of its fiscal woes and have managed to further polarize San Diego's divided electorate.

Changing Institutions, Changing Politics

Paradoxically, the further the initiative process goes, the more difficult and problematic effective citizenship becomes. California has not just seen a sharp decline in the quality of public services—education, public parks, highways, water projects—that were once regarded as models for the nation. It has also seen the evolution of an increasingly unmanageable and incomprehensible structure of state and local government that exacerbates the same public disaffection and alienation that have brought it on, thus creating a vicious cycle of reform and frustration.

—*Peter Schrag,* Paradise Lost, *1998*[16]

In Chapter 4, we explained how the two-constituencies problem contributes to disagreements between mayors and city councils in San Diego. Conflict springs from differences in the constituencies of the mayor, who represents voters, and members of the city council, each of whom represents a subset of the city's residents. The problem is exacerbated by the self-sorting of residents into local neighborhoods according to race, ethnicity, and class, and it is magnified by disparities in voter registration and turnout. But the two-constituencies problem transcends such battles between the two branches. Indeed, the most important two-constituencies problem involves the city council, which controls spending for local programs and services, and voters citywide, who must approve most measures to increase revenues. Under state law, a majority of voters must sign off on new taxes for general government purposes. If a proposed tax is earmarked for a special purpose (e.g., for libraries, fire protection, or other services), two-thirds of voters must give their approval.

The differences between the coalition needed to increase expenditures for local programs and services (a council majority) and the coalition needed to increase revenues to pay for them (a citywide voter majority or supermajority) are at the root of the dilemmas of the new fiscal populism, San Diego style. Over the past twenty years, the council has voted to increase spending on libraries, municipal pensions, downtown redevelopment, and other programs. However, voters citywide have consistently rejected efforts to increase revenues to pay for what their elected representatives have voted for. Table 8.4A shows how San Diegans voted on three revenue measures designed to increase funding for public services. The first was an attempt in 1996 to raise money for branch libraries. In November 1996, a majority of voters approved a plan to use the city's share of a proposed quarter-cent increase in the sales tax for branch libraries. Proposition C passed with 53 percent of the vote. Only District 5 failed to return a majority. However, the measure failed because an

TABLE 8.4A   City and county voting results for selected local revenue measures

District	1996 QUARTER-CENT SALES TAX FOR LIBRARY PURPOSES				2004 2.5% HOTEL TAX INCREASE			2008 FIRE SERVICES PARCEL TAX		
	Reg. voters	Turnout (%)	Prop C Yes (%)	Prop A[a] Yes (%)	Reg. voters	Turnout (%)	Prop C[a] Yes (%)	Reg. voters	Turnout (%)	Prop A[a] Yes (%)
1	94,628	71.9	54.0	60.7	92,208	47.1	61.3	111,696	78.5	66.3
2	89,182	62.3	58.2	66.2	92,582	41.4	60.4	100,160	74.6	64.0
3	76,045	57.7	59.6	69.2	68,893	40.7	65.6	76,458	73.6	70.2
4	65,225	53.3	52.2	67.6	56,227	31.4	63.5	62,522	66.4	72.1
5	91,254	69.0	47.7	55.2	82,507	45.3	61.6	88,819	79.0	66.6
6	87,724	67.5	50.1	58.1	77,623	46.3	59.8	84,100	77.1	63.1
7	82,530	66.6	51.3	59.5	71,960	45.2	61.1	77,066	74.9	65.3
8	47,146	48.7	54.6	70.0	44,671	28.7	64.3	53,996	66.0	71.1
City	633,734	63.5	53.1	62.1	586,671	42.0	61.8	654,817	74.6	66.7
Non-city	753,791	67.0		56.7				833,340	76.7	61.2
County	1,387,525	65.4		59.1				1,488,157	75.8	63.6

SOURCES: San Diego County, Office of the Registrar, various years.

[a]Required two-thirds vote for passage.

insufficient number of voters in San Diego and the rest of the county voted for the sales tax increase. The measure succeeded in winning the necessary two-thirds in four council districts. Unfortunately, three of these four districts were those with the fewest voters and the lowest voter turnout.

Similar setbacks were experienced in 2004 and 2008. In March 2004, voters narrowly rejected a measure to increase hotel taxes to fund police and fire emergency services. Support for the measure, Proposition C, was highest in San Diego's three poorest districts and lowest in the affluent coastal and suburban districts. As with the 1996 vote on libraries, support for new revenues happened to be highest in areas with the lowest voter registration and turnout.[17] In 2008, voters defeated an attempt to implement a countywide property parcel tax to increase funding for regional fire protection services. The measure, Proposition A, received more than two-thirds support in five of eight council districts, including more than 70 percent in Districts 3, 4, and 8. Unfortunately, high support in these districts was offset by greater opposition in vote-rich Districts 2 and 6 and other parts of the county. The 2004 and 2008 measures both failed less than a year removed from disastrous wildfires that exposed the serious inadequacies of the region's existing fire protection services.

Conflicts between the city's subpopulations have been especially apparent on efforts to reform the city's governance arrangements in the wake of the pension scandal. In addition to considering proposals to increase local revenues, local voters have been asked to weigh in on proposals to change the city's institutional makeup. Table 8.4B describes the pattern of voting on four selected charter changes between 2004 and 2010. The first two, Propositions F and G, passed with narrow citywide majorities. Proposition F changed the city's form of government from a council-manager to a mayor-council plan. Proposition G sought to impose a fifteen-year schedule for repaying the city's pension liability, a vote later ruled to be advisory. The short repayment schedule would have necessitated even deeper cuts to public services than the twenty-year schedule adopted in 2007.

Table 8.4B shows that the same discrepancies in registration and turnout that shaped the outcome of the 2004 and 2005 mayoral elections (see Chapter 4, Tables 4.3A and 4.3B) were equally decisive here. Proposition F passed on the strength of comfortable margins in vote-rich Districts 1 and 5. Majorities of voters in three districts opposed the switch

TABLE 8.4B City voting results for selected local reform measures

District	2004 STRONG MAYOR AND PENSION REFORM				2006 CONTRACT OUT SERVICES			2010 STRONG MAYOR PERMANENT		
	Reg. voters	Turnout (%)[a]	Prop F Yes (%)	Prop G Yes (%)	Reg. voters	Turnout (%)	Prop C Yes (%)	Reg. voters	Turnout (%)	Prop D Yes (%)
1	106,009	65.3	53.1	58.0	98,848	56.9	67.4	104,858	33.3	58.0
2	109,336	58.2	50.0	53.6	95,102	49.4	62.7	91,986	32.6	55.5
3	79,994	58.7	45.6	45.9	69,502	49.4	50.3	71,527	30.7	48.5
4	64,084	54.0	50.8	49.2	56,983	40.0	46.9	58,369	26.0	51.4
5	91,072	65.6	57.2	58.0	84,296	56.6	67.0	84,126	35.9	60.2
6	88,335	64.0	48.9	53.1	80,594	53.6	59.3	79,408	36.6	52.8
7	81,214	60.9	52.1	55.8	72,056	52.5	60.6	71,362	35.2	56.3
8	52,155	53.1	52.8	48.8	46,795	39.7	53.5	51,053	24.9	52.3
City	672,199	60.7	51.4	53.6	604,176	50.9	60.4	612,689	32.5	55.1

SOURCES: San Diego County, Office of the Registrar, various years.

[a]Turnout percentages reflect votes on Prop F (strong mayor). Turnout percentages for Prop G (pension reform) were similar but slightly lower because of roll-off.

and one other, District 4, passed it by the slimmest of margins. Without significant majorities in the most affluent areas of the city, San Diego would have retained its council-manager plan. The vote shares for Proposition D in 2010, which made permanent the strong-mayor form of government, suggest that support for the reform has not changed much since 2004. Similarly, Proposition G received its greatest support in Districts 1 and 5. Majorities of voters in the city's three poorest districts, where minority group voters are most prevalent, opposed the austere fifteen-year repayment schedule.

The 2006 vote on Proposition C, which allowed the City of San Diego to contract out services traditionally performed by city employees to private-sector organizations, illustrates the decisiveness of affluent white voters in citywide elections. Proposition C was a reform pushed by Mayor Sanders. Local labor organizations fought hard against Proposition C. As Table 8.4B illustrates, this defeat was driven by the same coalition that elected Sanders in 2005. Districts 1, 2, 5, and 7 delivered large majorities in favor of managed competition. Majorities of voters in Districts 4 and 8 opposed the measure. The measure passed in District 3 by the narrowest of margins. Nonetheless, because of weak registration and turnout, opposition in these areas counted for much less than support in more mobilized areas.

This brief review of recent initiative contests underscores four essential points about the nature of local politics and how it has changed since 1990. First, San Diegans remain divided on whether new revenues are needed to improve deficiencies in public services as well as on what institutional changes would best address the problems exposed by the pension scandal in 2003. Second, these and other divisions have been institutionalized with the implementation of district elections and, more recently, the strong-mayor form of government. Third, disagreements between the mayor and city council, and discrepancies between what is approved by the city council compared to the citywide electorate that participates in the initiative process, are driven by differences in their respective constituencies. Finally, the outcomes of mayoral elections and initiative campaigns have been heavily influenced by disparities in registration and turnout among San Diego's various subpopulations. These disparities have ensured that the preferences of San Diego's affluent white voters continue to be decisive.

Thus, the new fiscal populism in San Diego has institutional foundations. The power to determine the level of expenditures for local programs and services lies with the city council. Since 1990, council members have been elected by district. Democrats enjoy a registration advantage in three districts; Democratic candidates frequently do well in others (Barack Obama won majorities in all eight districts in 2008). Since 2002, Democrats have enjoyed a majority on the city council and have used this to resist cuts to popular public services and, on occasion, have voted to increase expenditures. They have successfully stalled efforts to implement managed competition. The power to raise revenues to fund public services, however, lies with local voters. When given the chance in 1996, 2004, and 2008 to increase revenues to pay for libraries and police and fire protection services, voters refused.

That the new fiscal populism has institutional foundations does not mean that institutions are determinative. It means that the path of least resistance is to forgo asking voters to dip into their own pockets to pay for public services and to oppose initiatives that would require them to do so. The most effective line of attack is to tap into voters' long-standing distrust of local government. In recent years, such different figures as City Attorney Michael Aguirre, Mayor Sanders, and Councilman Carl DeMaio have won office by running against local government. Each offered a platform whereby voters would be asked to, in the words of then-local columnist Gerry Braun, do nothing and be congratulated for doing it.

Fighting against such powerful tides requires leadership. In San Diego, leadership has been sorely lacking. In the private sector, few local business leaders have stepped up to the plate to offer concrete solutions for fixing obvious revenue problems and institutional deficiencies. The local chamber of commerce has generally sat on the sidelines in the city's and region's most critical policy debates. In the public sector, elected officials have scarcely done better. Mayor Sanders has resisted measures to increase revenues and offered only halfhearted support for a 2010 sales tax hike measure to close the city's budget deficit. Recognizing the high bar to securing tax increases, members of the council voted to underfund the pension and for other shortsighted schemes to balance the budget.

The evidence suggests that San Diego's voters, though less inclined to support new revenues than voters in other California cities and typically regarding local government with a wary eye, are not immovable. Each of the revenue measures analyzed here was supported by a majority of San Diego voters. The level of support, however, was insufficient to meet the two-thirds threshold for special taxes. A recent survey by the independent budget analyst similarly found that San Diego residents were willing to pay more to maintain public services at current levels. Survey respondents voiced a preference for increased user fees and charges over higher sales and property taxes. Nonetheless, the survey demonstrated that residents can appreciate the relationship between revenues and services. San Diego's political leaders have simply failed to make the same connection.

The Crisis of San Diego Politics

At the end of the day, there's going to be Armageddon in the city.
—*Firefighters' union president Frank De Clercq, 2010*[18]

As we discussed in Chapter 3, San Diego's pension scandal unleashed a series of institutional reforms, pushed through by an unusual alliance of civic leaders from both sides of the ideological spectrum. However, the city has found no similar consensus on efforts to close its chronic budget deficit, which has only grown larger in recent years. The three factors discussed here—the absence of civic leadership, voter tax aversion and distrust in government, and adverse institutional constraints—have prevented the city from putting its finances on a more solid footing.

In 2010, the city still lacked a coherent strategy to close the gap. Mayor Sanders's plan to reap significant savings through outsourcing of city services remained mired in labor negotiations. While another ad hoc panel, the Citizens Revenue Review and Economic Competitiveness Commission appointed in 2009, identified potential sources of new funds, all required either a vote of the people or extensive cost studies that would significantly delay implementation.[19] Among immediately available revenues, a labor-funded poll showed only a half-penny sales tax increase attracting support from voters likely to participate in a low-turnout midterm election in 2010.[20]

Quietly, Sanders approached the city council about a potential deal to link a sales tax increase on the November 2010 ballot with progress on key city reforms, including outsourcing of services. However, when word of the negotiations reached business leaders, who were inclined to oppose all tax increases, Sanders quickly disavowed the proposal.[21] In a statement, the mayor's office refused to acknowledge that Sanders had floated a compromise plan and said that the weak economy meant that it "was not the proper time" to consider raising taxes.[22]

Proposition D

For five years, my efforts to build consensus on cost controls were held back by the argument that San Diegans would rather raise taxes than reduce services. That notion got a fair hearing, and it's now been laid to rest.
    —Mayor Jerry Sanders, state-of-the-city address, 2011

Many political observers advocated a compromise measure—combining cost-cutting and benefit reductions with new revenue—as a way to end the standoff. However, the sequencing of cuts and tax increases would require trust on both sides, something neither labor nor business leaders were willing to provide. Labor leaders feared that concessions on employee benefits would reduce immediate pressure on the budget, thereby reducing support for higher taxes. Business leaders worried that raising taxes would eliminate their leverage for additional benefit cuts. The absence of strong leaders—individuals with long-term investment in the city and enough reputational capital to guarantee that any deal made would not unravel over the passage of time—made the task of overcoming distrust on both sides doubly difficult.

With just days left ahead of the deadline to place measures on the November 2010 ballot, council members Donna Frye and Todd Gloria unveiled a sales tax proposal incorporating many of the elements Sanders had originally suggested. Under the Frye-Gloria plan, voters would be asked to approve a temporary, five-year sales tax hike. Before new revenues could be collected, however, the measure would require certification from the city auditor that a series of ten cost-cutting reforms had been completed by the council. The required reforms included higher employee contributions into the pension system, a reduction in retiree health-care benefits, and the completion of the formal guide necessary to begin outsourcing city services.[23] Reversing himself yet again, Sanders announced his support for the measure, which would appear as Proposition D on the fall election ballot.

Proposition D quickly won the endorsement of organized labor, which pledged to financially back the campaign on its behalf. A divided chamber of commerce and the Regional Economic Development Corporation, two business umbrella organizations, also came out in support, though neither group offered significant financial backing. However, the business community did not speak with one voice. Realtors, car dealers, and restaurant owners all opposed the sales tax increase and threw their weight behind Republican Councilmen Kevin Faulconer and DeMaio, who spoke out vehemently against raising taxes.

By September 2010, labor leaders signed off on the city's managed competition guide, and the city council adopted several of the promised reforms. However, the progress did not satisfy DeMaio and Faulconer. The two Republicans had begun calling Proposition D a "pension tax"— a familiar tactic borrowed from the campaigns against the 2004 tax measures—and had captured media attention with new reports purporting to document waste and abuse in city government.

Their message clearly resonated with the voters. On Election Day, Proposition D received just 38 percent of the vote, far short of the simple majority needed for passage. The measure failed to garner a majority in any of the eight city council districts. Consistent with the voting patterns on previous tax initiatives, however, support for the sales tax was highest in District 3 (49.9 percent) and lowest in District 5 (31.1 percent). Once again, turnout was lowest in areas where poor and minority residents were most concentrated.

Financing Redevelopment

The campaign over Proposition D was overshadowed by another development with important implications for the city budget. Earlier in the year, the city council and CCDC began efforts to extend the life of various redevelopment project areas downtown. Without the extension, the city would need to wind down redevelopment activity by the early 2020s, when it would hit the $3 billion cap set by state law.

Lifting the redevelopment cap was central to the construction of a new Chargers football stadium adjacent to Petco Park, a project avidly endorsed by Sanders and the downtown business community. Without redevelopment dollars, the city would have no way to pay the estimated $500 million to $600 million the Chargers were seeking from local government for a new stadium. However, extending the life of redevelopment areas would also exacerbate the city's budget deficit, by continuing to divert scarce tax dollars into dedicated redevelopment accounts, where they would not be available to pay for basic city services. Officials estimated that lifting the cap would deprive the city budget of nearly $300 million in property taxes over the course of the following three decades.[24] Although redevelopment boosters argued that this loss would be offset by economic development spurred by redevelopment, there is little doubt that extending downtown redevelopment would produce significant short-term costs for the city budget.[25]

With several good-government and neighborhood groups opposed to shifting more tax dollars downtown, Sanders and CCDC worked behind the scenes to lobby state lawmakers for an exemption to the state redevelopment law—allowing the city to raise the redevelopment cap without completing the necessary studies. Doing so would also sidestep a vote of the city council, which was increasingly skeptical about downtown redevelopment, and avoid a likely lawsuit from the county, which was worried about losing its own property tax dollars to redevelopment.

In early October, the backroom bargaining bore fruit. As part of all-night negotiations over the state's overdue budget, a provision extending the life of San Diego's downtown redevelopment areas was slipped into a budget trailer bill by Assemblyman Nathan Fletcher. A rising star in the Republican Party, Fletcher was seen by many as a potential successor to Sanders, whose second term was to end in 2012. With little debate and limited public notice, the bill was quickly approved.[26] Although Fletcher was hailed by downtown business groups, the move was decried by many San Diegans. Members of the city council, the governing body for the city's redevelopment agency, knew nothing about the ongoing negotiations and lashed out at Sanders and CCDC. "I feel as though we've been betrayed," Councilwoman Marti Emerald complained angrily. Despite their outrage, council members refrained from asking the governor to veto the legislation.

In addition to the financial cost to the city budget, the redevelopment deal created a new headache for supporters of Proposition D. DeMaio, usually an ally of downtown business groups and a redevelopment supporter, argued that the move illustrated the duplicity of San Diego's elected officials and undermined their pledge to carry out necessary budget reforms. Linking the redevelopment deal to the sales tax increase, DeMaio told the press: "The whole public process has been completely disregarded in favor of an 11th hour closed-door, politician to politician deal. . . . That's what [the public] got in this deal. That's what they're going to get on Prop. D."[27] Coming just a day after the chamber of commerce endorsed Proposition D, the passage of the redevelopment bill further undermined the city's effort to convince voters to approve the sales tax increase.

Looking Forward

We presented the public with a choice. That choice has now been made by the voters. I'll work with the City Council to keep us on the path of reform and fiscal responsibility, but make no mistake there'll be tough cuts coming ahead.

—*San Diego Mayor Jerry Sanders, 2010*[28]

Given the scale of San Diego's fiscal and governance problems, it is unlikely that any single set of political institutions or policies can reverse several decades' worth of errors, misjudgments, and general absence of political will. Nor is it likely that, in the absence of greater civic leadership and higher rates of participation and engagement from local residents, San Diego's elected officials will be able to close the widening gap between city revenues and expenditures and reconcile competing budgetary pressures in a coherent way. Nevertheless, there do exist significant opportunities for institutional and economic reforms that can begin to mend San Diego's chronic policy dysfunctions. In this section, we review a variety of proposals that have been offered and assess their potential for addressing the city's financial and governance challenges.

Revenue Enhancements: A Lost Cause?

San Diego's financial crisis has its origins in inadequate city revenues, not excessive spending. The revenue problem is twofold. First, San Diego's overall tax receipts lag far behind other major California cities, a fact ably documented by multiple city-commissioned studies.[29] Second, despite the city's low revenue base, San Diego must use its regular budget to pay for services supported by separate, dedicated revenue streams elsewhere. San Diego is one of the only major cities in California to provide residential garbage collection free of charge. Its storm-water fees cover a fraction of the total cost for pollution prevention and the maintenance of storm drain infrastructure. The rest of the bill is picked up by the city's General Fund. For years, city leaders also dragged their feet on reviewing other user fee–supported services, failing to ensure that their charges recovered the full cost of service provision.[30]

Increasing revenues to achieve parity with other cities, however, requires the city to seek the consent of its voters—consent that recent history suggests San Diego voters are not likely to give. Although trash collection fees are expressly exempt from these procedural hurdles, free refuse collection is guaranteed by the San Diego city charter, which can be amended only by a vote of city residents. Given the failure of Proposition D, the city is unlikely to succeed in persuading its fiscally conservative voters to approve higher taxes and fees, at least not in the near future.

In short, state institutions' and residents' aversion to taxes take most forms of new revenue off the table. However, San Diego has several other strategies for increasing the funds available to the city budget. During the early years of the city's redevelopment program, elected officials provided significant start-up capital to finance San Diego's redevelopment projects. This money represented loans from the city's budget, although a recent federal audit noted that the city failed to ensure for the repayment of outstanding redevelopment loans. At present, the outstanding balance approaches $270 million, and the city currently has no long-term plan for its repayment.[31] Initiating the repayment of the debt using tax increment dollars can provide significant new short-term revenues for the city budget, though not a long-term solution to San Diego's structural budget deficit.

In addition, residents can relieve the pressure on the city's day-to-day budget by passing a general obligation bond to pay for upgrades of aging infrastructure, including repaving potholed roads. Between 2004 and 2010, for example, San Diego spent more than $130 million on street resurfacing. Recent estimates by the city auditor suggest that the bill for outstanding repairs approaches $400 million.[32] A bond could also support the construction of new libraries and other capital facilities currently funded directly through the General Fund or bonds that borrow money against future General Fund revenues.

Despite the failure of recent tax proposals, there is reason to believe that a bond measure, which would require a two-thirds vote, could be designed to attract support from San Diego residents. In 1998 and again in 2008, San Diego voters overwhelmingly approved two major school bonds to improve facilities at the city's schools, administered by a separate agency. By earmarking bond proceeds to specific construction projects, city leaders could allocate projects to each council district to build a citywide majority. A bond measure would likely receive support from the construction industry, a powerful voice in San Diego's business community, and by limiting funding to capital projects could overcome voter concerns that new revenues would be used to pay for pensions for city workers.

Retiree Benefits: Little Room for Reform

At the start of fiscal year 2010, San Diego's outstanding debt for retiree benefits totaled nearly $3.5 billion—dwarfing all other city liabilities. The figure includes a deficit of more than $2.1 billion in the city's retirement system and an unfunded liability of approximately $1.4 billion for retiree health care.[33] In 2010, San Diego was contributing more than 40 percent of its total payroll into the pension system, and it had only taken tentative steps to begin prefunding the health-care liability. Collectively, the annual bill for retiree benefits has continued to grow—even as the overall size of the budget has shrunk as a result of declining revenues.

Both debts have similar historical origins. In 1982, Mayor Pete Wilson persuaded city employees to voluntarily withdraw from the federal Social Security system, in a move designed to save the city money by reducing its payroll taxes. In exchange, Wilson promised employees that taxpayers would provide them with city-funded health care for life. However, neither Wilson nor his successors ever put aside the funds necessary to pay for this commitment. For most of its recent history, the city paid its annual health-care bill from surplus pension earnings. Nor did the city take steps to prefund the future liability.[34]

In recent years, city leaders have attempted to reduce these debts, with little luck. Most new employees hired after June 2009 have received significantly lower pension benefits under a two-tier system.[35] Workers hired since July 2009 have also received a much stingier retiree health guarantee. In addition, most workers have increased their own pension contributions. These changes, which will produce significant savings over the next several decades, have made only a small dent in the city's existing retiree debts.

The problem is that the outstanding liabilities are driven almost exclusively by benefits already earned by current and former employees, whereas reforms designed to reduce retirement benefits target new employees. California's constitution, which prohibits public agencies from backsliding on concessions won by workers through good-faith negotiations, does not allow the city to impose retroactive pension benefit cuts, the only policy that would result in a serious reduction of the pension debt. Even proposals like the elimination of the defined-benefit pension for new city workers and the creation of 401(k)-style plans would do little to significantly lower the pension liability.

Municipal Bankruptcy: An Uncharted Path

Given voters' unwillingness to raise taxes and strict legal limits on the city's ability to unilaterally and retroactively reduce retiree benefits, some local observers, including former city attorney Mike Aguirre, have argued that San Diego has reached the point of insolvency. Aguirre and others have urged the city to seek protection under Chapter 9 of the federal bankruptcy code, a law written at the height of the Great Depression to provide an orderly process to restructure municipal debts.

The dearth of legal precedent addressing the legal reach of municipal bankruptcy makes it difficult to predict whether the city could successfully use the bankruptcy process to reduce retiree benefits despite state and local laws that usually make these benefits out of reach.[36] To date, no municipality has ever succeeded in reducing its pension liability through the bankruptcy courts, although growing questions about the soundness of public pensions in cities and states across the country suggest that many more are likely to try in the coming years.

What is clear, however, is that San Diego is likely to face significant challenges in any future effort to seek bankruptcy protection. Unlike other parts of the federal bankruptcy code, Chapter 9 is designed to make municipal bankruptcy the avenue of last resort, including a requirement that local governments prove that they are insolvent.[37] Given the unwillingness of San Diego voters to raise taxes to levels in place in other California cities, it is a hurdle the city is unlikely to clear. In a widely cited 1940 decision, a federal appellate court rejected a bankruptcy petition from a small California irrigation district on the grounds that it had not exhausted its taxing powers. The court ruled that "we are unable to find any reason why the tax rate should not have been increased sufficiently to meet the District's obligations, or why it can be said that the plan is 'equitable' and 'fair' and for the 'best interest of the creditors' with no sufficient showing that the taxing power was inadequate to raise the taxes to pay for them."[38]

In short, bankruptcy remains a highly speculative and uncertain option for San Diego. A successful filing would likely provide significant fiscal relief but only after years of litigation. In the short term, bankruptcy will bring significant costs—in the form of legal fees and higher borrowing costs—that will make the challenge of balancing the budget only more harrowing.

Managed Competition: Privatizing Government

Perhaps the most promising proposal offered by Councilman De-Maio, from the point of view of political viability and potential for immediate cost savings, is the implementation of San Diego's managed competition program. In 2006, San Diego voters approved an amendment to the city charter allowing for the outsourcing of key city services to the private sector. Since then, local support for outsourcing has only grown. Until recently, opposition from organized labor has blocked city efforts to solicit private-sector bids for the delivery of city services. Ahead of the public vote on Proposition D, however, city unions gave their blessing to the city's managed competition guide, paving the way for full implementation of outsourcing. DeMaio has estimated that having private-sector firms compete with city workers for the delivery of municipal services can achieve annual savings of between $10 million and $20 million.

Independent research has generally confirmed that outsourcing public-service provision to the private sector has the potential to reduce taxpayer costs.[39] One problem with such academic analyses, however, is that they focus almost exclusively on municipalities that have successfully carried out outsourcing efforts. Because local governments should accept private-sector bids only when these produce actual cost savings, and should keep in-house service provision when private firms fail to do so, limiting the analyses to successful cases of outsourcing produces significant selection bias that overestimates the likely benefits of outsourcing. More comprehensive analyses, in contrast, paint a more equivocal picture. A 1996 review found that contracting out actually led to an increase in public-sector costs in more than a quarter of the cases studied.[40] In a 2007 survey of local governments, nearly a quarter of responding municipalities reported reversing outsourcing efforts by bringing the responsibility for services previously delivered by the private sector back in-house. Among local governments that reported reversing their decision to contract out service provision, more than half cited insufficient cost savings as a factor in their decision.[41]

In general, scholars agree that the success of specific outsourcing efforts depends on the nature of the service being contracted out, the quality of the contract governing the relationship between the government entity and its private-sector vendor, and the capacity for effective oversight by local government officials. Given San Diego's dearth of effective civic watchdogs, the city's troubled political history, and the consistent failure of the city council to ensure that private-sector redevelopment efforts produce significant public benefits, there is ample reason to be skeptical that the city's political institutions are currently set up to deliver the oversight necessary to make outsourcing succeed. Unlike local government bodies, government contractors are exempt from the transparency requirements of California's open-meeting and public-record laws, which makes the monitoring task for citizens even harder.

The Land of Oz in the New Millennium

You call some place paradise—kiss it goodbye.
        —The Eagles, "The Last Resort," 1976

L. Frank Baum, author of *The Wonderful Wizard of Oz*, was already an acclaimed writer when he came to San Diego from Hollywood in the first decade of the twentieth century. His purpose in visiting the area was leisure rather than business. Baum adored the seaside enclave, especially the Hotel del Coronado, located across the bay from downtown. The Del was not the original inspiration for the Emerald City of Oz, but its striking features influenced Baum's description of it in subsequent installments of the Oz series. Trot, the child heroine of Baum's *The Sea Fairies*, *Sky Island*, and *The Scarecrow of Oz*, lives in a cottage overlooking the Pacific Ocean, near a small village and sea caves that serve as the antechamber to Oz.[42] The setting bears a striking resemblance to La Jolla—which Baum visited between 1904 and 1911.

For Baum, a refugee from upstate New York, Chicago, and South Dakota, San Diego was an earthly fairyland. In a poem published in the *San Diego Union* titled "Coronado: The Queen of Fairyland," Baum celebrated the area's physical beauty, which he believed could regenerate the weary:

> And mortals whisper, wondering:
> "Indeed, 'tis Fairyland!
> For where is joy without alloy
> Enchantment strange and grand."
> And tired eyes grow bright again,
> And careworn faces smile;
> And dreams are sweet and moments fleet,
> And hearts are free from guile.[43]

The Emerald City of Oz shares many of these features. Oz is wealthy and prosperous, with abundant fields and farms, a mirror image of economically depressed Kansas. In *The Wonderful Wizard of Oz*, those who enter the city wear green-tinted glasses to protect their eyes from its glory and brightness.

From his cozy perch on Coronado, Baum would have been able to gaze across San Diego Bay to Davis's New Town, a patchwork of houses, wharfs, and warehouses still struggling to take shape. On the morning of October 21, 2007, a passerby similarly situated would have been able to take in a much grander vista. San Diego's downtown skyline looks more like the Emerald City of Baum's imagination. Its landmarks include One America Plaza, owned by the Irvine Company and at thirty-four stories the city's tallest building. (Outsiders can recognize the building by its rooftop, which resembles a Phillips-head screwdriver.) There are the two towers of the Manchester Grand Hyatt, built by Douglas Manchester, which at 497 feet are the tallest buildings along the waterfront on the West Coast. Also on the water is the San Diego Convention Center, with Petco Park visible directly behind. Finally, there is Emerald Plaza, marked by six hexagonal towers ringed at night with green neon lights.

San Diego's boosters have cultivated an Oz-like civic image of the city—a prosperous place replete with boutique shops, upscale restaurants, luxury hotels, outdoor recreation, professional sports, and "authentic" attractions celebrating the city's martial and nautical history. Not unlike other "revitalized" American downtowns, one can walk the streets of downtown San Diego without encountering a poor person, tripping over uneven streets and potholes, or seeing boarded-up shops and residences. Like the Emerald City of Oz, this experience, carefully choreographed by local leaders, is an illusion.

The illusion exploded late in the day on October 21, 2007. From across the bay, a megacloud of smoke was visible above America's Potemkin village. Oz was burning. This time, there were multiple conflagrations. The largest was the Witch Creek Fire, which began in northeast San Diego County and spread quickly to the suburban communities of Ramona, Rancho Bernardo, Poway, and Escondido. With strong Santa Ana winds pushing the fire toward the coast, county officials worried that the damage would exceed that from the fires four years earlier. Even more spectacular was the Harris Fire, whose towering flames were visible above Mount San Miguel from downtown. The Harris Fire began in south San Diego County near the Mexican border and burned perilously close to Chula Vista, a suburban community southeast of the City of San Diego.

By the time the last of the fires was contained by San Diego's undermanned, beleaguered, and heroic firefighters nineteen days later, the combined toll did exceed the damage exacted by the 2003 Cedar Fire. At one point, five hundred thousand of the region's residents were under mandatory orders to evacuate—more, according to the county sheriff, than evacuated from New Orleans during Hurricane Katrina. All told, more than three hundred thousand acres burned, 1,500 homes were lost, and 700 other buildings were destroyed. As with the 2003 fire, the region was woefully unprepared for the disaster. This time, critics argued, San Diego ought to have known better.

In November, U.S. Senator Dianne Feinstein convened a hearing in San Diego on the wildfires. She took local officials to task for their systematic underfunding of fire protection services. The star of the hearing was former Fire Chief Jeff Bowman, who had resigned in 2006 out of frustration at the Cassandra-like treatment he was receiving from local officials. "It's déjà vu," Bowman told the subcommittee. "The recommendations get made, and nothing happens." City officials pointed to two failed attempts at increasing taxes to pay for better fire-preparedness. But Bowman was right. San Diego had done little to prepare for the wildfires of 2007. Senator Feinstein wistfully hoped that the third time would be the charm.[44] It was not. In November 2008, nearly four in ten county voters decided they would rather brave future infernos than pay more taxes. The mayor and city council responded by further cutting funding for fire protection, which resulted in rolling fire-engine brownouts and reduced response times.

San Diego's sad record in the area of fire protection services illustrates the vexing analytical problem facing urban scholars and the intractable political difficulty facing practitioners. Paradise is being plundered, but there are no barbarians at the gates. Who is responsible for the San Diego wildfires of 2007? Contributing factors include droughtlike conditions in Southern California, warm weather, and Santa Ana winds exceeding eighty-five miles per hour. Some of the fires were initially sparked by downed power lines. One was deliberately started by a suspect whom police fatally shot, another by a ten-year-old boy playing with matches. The underfunding cited by Feinstein meant that fewer firefighters were available, that fewer homes were ultimately saved. But the underfunding goes back decades and implicates a long list of business leaders and public officials, not to mention an unidentifiable number of local residents.

Perhaps the more important question is, Who is responsible for the San Diego wildfires of tomorrow? Currently, fire protection ranks among San Diego's most critical governance failures. With two recent episodes of raging wildfires seared in San Diego's collective consciousness, the consequences of inaction are as predictable as they are dire. Unfortunately, civic leaders and voters alike have abdicated. Voters have abdicated by succumbing to antigovernment populism and failing to support responsible revenue measures designed to increase resources. Prominent members of San Diego's civic elite opposed these same measures and have supported further cuts in services even as they sponsor schemes to divert local revenues to grandiose public works projects.

Unfortunately, the locus of San Diego's governance failures reaches beyond the shameful state of its fire protection services. Over the previous chapters, we documented the extent of these failures, which encompass fiscal policy, wastewater systems, parks, libraries and other services, urban planning, downtown redevelopment, and regional water and transportation infrastructure. We also attempted to describe the forces, actors, and institutions that contributed to San Diego's difficult present circumstances. Collectively, deficiencies in San Diego's civic leadership, political culture, and political institutions have created a setting where, to paraphrase the former journalist and author Peter Schrag, "nobody is responsible and nothing gets done." Reversing these trends will require the focus, determination, and good faith of all members of the San Diego community.

Notes

Preface

1. Quoted in Rick Cole, "Cities of Bell & Vernon Expose Governance Failures," *Planning Report* 24:9 (December–January 2011), p. 10.

2. "Futureville," *Economist*, February 3, 1996, p. 20; John M. Broder, "Sunny San Diego Finds Itself Being Viewed as a Kind of Enron-by-the-Sea," *New York Times*, September 2004.

Chapter 1

1. San Diego Convention and Visitors Bureau, *San Diego Neighborhood Guide* (n.d.).

2. Regarding "sunshine" marketing claims, see San Diego Convention and Visitors Bureau, *About San Diego, San Diego Beach Guide—San Diego's Best Beaches, The San Diego Golfer's Guide to Smiling through the Rough Stuff*, and *Research and Reports*. For contrasting noir views of San Diego, see Mike Davis, Kelly Mayhew, and Jim Miller, *Under the Perfect Sun: The San Diego Tourists Never See* (New York: New Press, 2003); Susan G. Davis, *Spectacular Nature: Corporate Culture and the Sea World Experience* (Berkeley: University of California Press, 1997).

3. A Potemkin village is "an impressive facade or show designed to hide an undesirable fact or condition." The term comes from the Russian minister Grigori Potemkin, who "supposedly built impressive fake villages along a route Catherine the Great was to travel." *Merriam-Webster's Collegiate Dictionary*, 11th ed., s.v. "Potemkin village."

4. Interview with Norma Damashek, president, San Diego League of Women Voters, 2009.

5. Gerry Braun, "SeaWorld Coaster: Did They Take Us for a Ride?" *San Diego Union-Tribune*, December 9, 2007.

6. See Saguaro Seminar, *2000 Social Capital Community Benchmark Survey*, Roper Center Public Opinion Archives, University of Connecticut, 2010. San Diego, one of forty-two communities surveyed, has lower social capital than its socioeconomic profile would predict. In particular, San Diego residents score especially low on political capital as measured by how many people are registered to vote, actually vote, express interest in politics, are knowledgeable about political affairs, and read newspapers regularly.

7. From the 1980s onward, the number of local television and radio stations covering city hall declined noticeably. In 1992, the *San Diego Union* and the *San Diego Tribune* merged. In the early 1990s, the *Los Angeles Times'* San Diego edition folded. In the wake of the pension scandal, the *Union-Tribune* ramped up its watchdog news stories and then ramped down when the paper was sold in 2009.

8. Interview with former San Diego City Councilman Bruce Henderson, 2007; interview with Erik Bruvold, president, National University System Institute for Policy Research, 2009. On the relationships among social capital, civic capacity, and government performance, see Robert D. Putnam, "Bowling Alone: America's Declining Social Capital," *Journal of Democracy* 6:1 (January 1995), pp. 65–78; Sheri Berman, "Civil Society and the Collapse of the Weimar Republic," *World Politics* 49:3 (April 1997), pp. 401–29; Robert W. Jackman and Ross A. Miller, "Social Capital and Politics," *Annual Review of Political Science* 1 (1998), pp. 47–73; Rhys Andrews, "Civic Culture and Public Service Failure: An Empirical Exploration," *Urban Studies* 44:4 (April 2007), pp. 845–63; Margit Travis, "Making Democracy Work More? Exploring the Linkage between Social Capital and Government Performance," *Political Research Quarterly* 59:2 (June 2006), pp. 211–25.

9. "Futureville," *Economist*, February 3, 1996, p. 20.

10. Adam Lashinsky, "Stay Classy, San Diego! It's Wealthy, Sunny, Beautiful—and Possibly the Most Dysfunctional Big City in America. Can a New Mayor Fix It?" *Fortune*, November 16, 2005.

11. Paul Peterson, *City Limits* (Chicago: University of Chicago Press, 1981).

12. Richard Florida, *The Rise of the Creative Class: And How It's Transforming Work, Leisure, Community and Everyday Life* (New York: Basic Books, 2002). Florida later downgraded San Diego because of the high cost of housing.

13. See San Diego Downtown Partnership, "Paradise in Progress," http://www.ccdc.com/programs/paradise-in-progress/overview.html.

14. Tim Chapin, "Beyond the Entrepreneurial City: Municipal Capitalism in San Diego," *Journal of Urban Affairs* 24:5 (Winter 2002), pp. 565–81.

15. Steven P. Erie, Vladimir Kogan, and Scott A. MacKenzie, "Redevelopment, San Diego Style: The Limits of Public-Private Partnerships," *Urban Affairs Review* 45:5 (May 2010), pp. 644–78.

16. When San Diego tried to shift enterprise funds into the city's General Fund, civic watchdogs became unglued, worried that such shifts would result in fee increases, such as for water and sewer charges, and thus represent a "hidden" tax.

17. Murtaza H. Baxamusa, *The Bottom Line: Solutions for San Diego's Budget Crisis—A Comparative Analysis of California's Largest Cities* (San Diego: Center on Policy Initiatives, April 2005).

18. David Zahniser and Phil Willon, "L.A. Seeks to Scale Back Pensions," *Los Angeles Times*, January 6, 2010, p. A3. On a per capita basis, Los Angeles's budget deficit is much smaller than San Diego's.

19. In 2000, *Governing* magazine gave the City of San Diego a B+ for its financial management and a B for overall performance. However, the report card did express concern about the city's reliance on onetime revenues to balance its budget and San Diego's split between bureaucratic haves (e.g., agencies with borrowing power or independent funding sources) and have-nots (those dependent on the General Fund). See *The Government Performance Project 2000—Report Card*, http://www.governing.com/gpp2000/gp0sand.htm (accessed March 2009).

20. "Futureville," *Economist*, February 3, 1996.

21. Joel Kotkin, "San Diego: The Model GOP City," *Los Angeles Times*, August 11, 1996.

22. Kotkin, "San Diego: The Model GOP City."

23. Joel Kotkin, "San Diego: A City for the New Millennium," *City Journal* 7:1 (Winter 1997).

24. John M. Broder, "Sunny San Diego Finds Itself Being Viewed as a Kind of Enron-by-the-Sea," *New York Times*, September 7, 2004; Alan Greenblatt, "Paradise Insolvent," *Governing* (November 2005).

25. Lashinsky, "Stay Classy, San Diego!"

26. Amy Argetsinger, "Three Mayors, One Bad Week," *Washington Post*, July 22, 2005.

27. Maria L. La Ganga and Tony Perry, "Its Ego Bruised, San Diego Asks: 'What Next?'" *Los Angeles Times*, April 29, 2005.

28. Greenblatt, "Paradise Insolvent."

29. San Diego City Employees' Retirement System, *June 30, 2009 Actuarial Valuation for the City of San Diego* (Cheiron, January 2010), table 1.1, p. i.

30. Karen Brandon, "This Is Their Kind of Town . . . San Diego Is. Scandals Cause 3rd Mayor Vote in Months," *Chicago Tribune*, July 24, 2005.

31. Lori Weisberg and David Washburn, "America's Cheapest City: Residents' Love of Services, Hatred of Higher Taxes Have Helped Contribute to San Diego's Financial Chaos," *San Diego Union-Tribune*, August 28, 2005.

32. See Richard Louv, "The Eight Wonders of San Diego," *San Diego Union-Tribune*, July 4, 2004.

33. See TRIP, "Future Mobility in California: The Condition, Use and Funding of California's Roads, Bridges and Transit System" (Washington, D.C.: TRIP, December 2009).

34. See Richard C. Feiock, ed., *Metropolitan Governance: Conflict, Competition, and Cooperation* (Washington, D.C.: Georgetown University Press, 2004); Jon Pierre, "Models of Urban Governance: The Institutional Dimension of Urban Politics," *Urban Affairs Review* 34:3 (January 1999), pp. 372–96.

35. Marion E. Orr and Gerry Stoker, "Urban Regimes and Leadership in Detroit," *Urban Affairs Review* 30:1 (September 1994), pp. 48–73.

36. Clarence N. Stone, *Regime Politics: Governing Atlanta* (Lawrence: University Press of Kansas, 1987). See also Clarence N. Stone, "Urban Regimes and the Capacity to Govern: A Political Economy Approach," *Journal of Urban Affairs* 15:1 (March 1993), pp. 1–28.

37. Gerry Stoker, "Regime Theory and Urban Politics," in *Theories of Urban Politics*, ed. David Judge, Gerry Stoker, and Harold Wolman (Thousand Oaks, Calif.: Sage Publications, 1995), pp. 54–71.

38. Royce Hanson, *Civic Culture and Urban Change: Governing Dallas* (Detroit: Wayne State University Press, 2003). The term *logic of appropriateness* comes from James G. March and Johan P. Olsen, *Rediscovering Institutions: The Organizational Basis of Politics* (New York: Free Press, 1989).

39. For one example of such an account, see Peterson, *City Limits*.

40. Stephen L. Elkin, *City and Regime in the American Republic* (Chicago: University of Chicago Press, 1987), pp. 98–99.

41. Mancur Olson, *Power and Prosperity: Outgrowing Communist and Capitalist Dictatorships* (New York: Basic Books, 2000).

42. Stone, *Regime Politics*.

43. See James Austin and Arthur McCaffrey, "Business Leadership Coalitions and Public-Private Partnerships in American Cities: A Business Perspective on Regime Theory," *Journal of Urban Affairs* 24:1 (Spring 2002), pp. 35–54; Royce Hanson, Harold Wolman, David Connolly, Katherine Pearson, and Robert

McManmon, "Corporate Citizenship and Urban Problem Solving: The Changing Civic Role of Business Leaders in American Cities," *Journal of Urban Affairs* 32:1 (February 2010), pp. 1–23.

44. This argument is consistent with the more general changes observed by Elizabeth Strom, "Rethinking the Politics of Downtown Development," *Journal of Urban Affairs* 30:1 (February 2008), pp. 37–61.

45. Transformative leadership is where "one or more persons engage with each other in such a way that leaders and followers raise one another to higher levels of motivation and morality." See James MacGregor Burns, *Leadership* (New York: Harper and Row, 1978).

46. National Center for Veterans Analysis and Statistics, *VetPop2007* (Washington, D.C.: U.S. Department of Veterans Affairs).

47. Jeremy M. Teigen, "Veterans' Party Identification, Candidate Affect, and Vote Choice in the 2004 U.S. Presidential Election," *Armed Forces and Society* 33:3 (April 2007), pp. 414–37.

48. Daniel Romer, Kate Kenski, Kenneth Winneg, Christopher Adasiewicz, and Kathleen Hall Jamieson, *Capturing Campaign Dynamics, 2000 and 2004: The National Annenberg Election Survey* (Philadelphia: University of Pennsylvania Press, 2006). But see E. M. Schreiber, "Enduring Effects of Military Service? Opinion Differences between U.S. Veterans and Nonveterans," *Social Forces* 57:3 (March 1979), pp. 824–39.

49. See, for example, James S. Coleman, *Foundations of Social Theory* (Cambridge, Mass.: Belknap Press of Harvard University Press, 1990); Robert D. Putnam, *Making Democracy Work: Civic Tradition in Modern Italy* (Princeton, N.J.: Princeton University Press, 1993); John Brehm and Wendy Rahn, "Individual-Level Evidence for the Causes and Consequences of Social Capital," *American Journal of Political Science* 41:3 (July 1997), pp. 999–1023. There is ample disagreement among scholars about the precise definition of social capital, and a convincing case can be made that its effects on politics are endogenous. See Robert W. Jackman and Ross A. Miller, "Social Capital and Politics," *Annual Review of Political Science* 1 (1998), pp. 47–73.

50. Francis Fukuyama, *Trust: The Social Virtues and the Creation of Prosperity* (New York: Free Press, 1995).

51. Mark Baldassare, *When Government Fails: The Orange County Bankruptcy* (Berkeley: University of California Press, 1998). See also David O. Sears and Jack Citrin, *Tax Revolt: Something for Nothing in California* (Cambridge, Mass.: Harvard University Press, 1985).

52. Terry Nichols Clark and Lorna Crowley Ferguson, *City Money: Political Processes, Fiscal Strain, and Retrenchment* (New York: Columbia University Press, 1983).

53. Robert Stoker makes a similar point about such shadow governments in "Baltimore: The Self-Evaluating City?" in *The Politics of Urban Development*, ed. Clarence Stone and Heywood Sanders (Lawrence: University Press of Kansas, 1987), pp. 244–68.

54. Indeed, these institutions provide incentives for elected officials to act like public-sector analogues to the roving bandits in San Diego's private sector.

55. Quoted in Roger Lowenstein, *While America Aged* (New York: Penguin Press, 2008), p. 155.

56. Hanson et al., "Corporate Citizenship and Urban Problem Solving."

57. Adam J. McGlynn and Dari E. Sylvester, "Assessing the Effects of Municipal Term Limits on Fiscal Policy in the U.S. Cities," *State and Local Government Review* 42:2 (August 2010), pp. 118–32.

58. Advisory Commission on Intergovernmental Relations, *Tax and Expenditure Limits on Local Governments* (Washington, D.C.: U.S. Advisory Commission on Intergovernmental Relations, 1994).

59. See *Examining the Retirement Security of State and Local Government Employees* (Washington, D.C.: Government Printing Office, 2006), Serial No. 109-54, a Field Hearing before the Subcommittee on Employer-Employee Relations of the Committee on Education and the Workforce, U.S. House of Representatives, August 30, 2006; Mary Williams Walsh and David W. Chen, "Big Deficit Seen in New Jersey Pension Fund," *New York Times*, March 16, 2007.

60. Davis et al., *Under the Perfect Sun*, p. 5.

61. There is a dearth of research on San Diego politics, planning, and policy making. Notable exceptions are David Greenstone's *A Report on Politics in San Diego* (Cambridge, Mass.: Joint Center for Urban Studies of the Massachusetts Institute of Technology and Harvard University, 1962) and, more recently, Davis et al., *Under the Perfect Sun*, which tells the sordid history of elite "private governments" and of labor resistance and community activism from below. Their story, however, ends in 2000—before the city's pension scandal and fiscal crisis fully unfolded. Otherwise, the topic is confined to (1) chapters in histories of the city and region, such as Iris Engstrand's *San Diego: California's Cornerstone* (San Diego: Sunbelt Publications, 2005), Roger Showley's *San Diego: Perfecting Paradise* (Carlsbad, Calif.: Heritage Media Group, 1999), and Richard Pourade's now-dated *The History of San Diego* (San Diego: Copley Books, 1960–1977); (2) chapters in histories of California, such as Kevin Starr's epic California Dream series and Roger Lotchin's *Fortress California, 1910–1961: From Warfare to Welfare* (New York: Oxford University Press, 1992); and (3) accounts of Sunbelt and Southwestern urban history and politics, such as Anthony W. Corso, "San Diego: The Anti-City," in *Sunbelt Cities: Politics and Growth since World War II*, ed. Richard Bernard and Bradley Rice (Austin: University of Texas Press, 1983),

pp. 328–43, Carl Abbott, *The New Urban America: Growth and Politics in Sunbelt Cities*, rev. ed. (Chapel Hill: University of North Carolina Press, 1987), and Amy Bridges, *Morning Glories: Municipal Reform in the Southwest* (Princeton, N.J.: Princeton University Press, 1997).

62. There are stirrings of relevant research. With San Diego's civic troubles commanding national interest and attention, journalists have produced insightful analyses of the city's pension debacle. San Diego represents an important case study in Lowenstein's *While America Aged*, pp. 153–219. Regarding the bribery and corruption scandal involving former local congressman Randy "Duke" Cunningham, see Marcus Stern, Jerry Kammer, Dean Calbreath, and George E. Condon Jr., *The Wrong Stuff: The Extraordinary Saga of Randy "Duke" Cunningham, the Most Corrupt Congressman Ever Caught* (New York: Public Affairs, 2007). One planning scholar has deemed San Diego's regional planning a failure, whereas another has hailed the downtown ballpark district as a "new model for public/private partnerships of shared risk and returns." See Richard Hogan, *The Failure of Planning: Permitting Sprawl in San Diego Suburbs, 1970–1999* (Columbus: Ohio State University Press, 2003); and Mark S. Rosentraub, *Major League Winners: Using Sports and Cultural Centers as Tools for Economic Development* (New York: CRC Press, 2010), pp. 99–128. For studies of the historical geography, natural environment, and social development of San Diego, see Philip R. Pryde, *San Diego: An Introduction to the Region*, 4th ed. (San Diego: Sunbelt Publications, 2004); and Larry R. Ford, *Metropolitan San Diego: How Geography and Lifestyle Shape a New Urban Environment* (Philadelphia: University of Pennsylvania Press, 2005).

63. Steven P. Erie has been actively involved in the region's public service and infrastructure debates involving fire-preparedness and water, airport, and port development, and he has participated in the writing and implementation of San Diego's so-called strong-mayor governance experiment. Vladimir Kogan, a former reporter for the *Voice of San Diego*, has been involved in San Diego's redevelopment, pension, and fiscal policy debates. Scott A. MacKenzie has been involved in the region's airport debates.

64. Kevin Lynch and Donald Appleyard, *Temporary Paradise? A Look at the Special Landscape of the San Diego Region* (Report to the City of San Diego, September 1974), p. 3.

Chapter 2

1. Richard F. Pourade, *The History of San Diego* (San Diego: Copley Books, 1960–1977), vol. 3, p. 243.

2. John Emerich Edward, *First Baron Acton: Lectures on Modern History* (London: MacMillan and Co., 1906), p. 317.

3. On this approach, see Clifford Geertz, *The Interpretation of Cultures* (New York: Basic Books, 1973).

4. Harold Keen, "Stampede," *San Diego Magazine* (November 1963), p. 49.

5. Edward J. Soja, "It All Comes Together in Los Angeles," in *Postmodern Geographies: The Reassertion of Space in Critical Social Theory* (London: Verso, 1989), pp. 190–221.

6. Pourade, *History of San Diego*, vol. 1, pp. 49, 143; vol. 2, p. 19; Iris Engstrand, "The Legal Heritage of Spanish California," *Southern California Quarterly* 75:3–4 (Fall–Winter 1993), pp. 210–14. In 1769, the Spanish set up San Diego as the capital of a vast military district extending from L.A. to Tijuana, but San Diego's predominance would be short lived. See Roger Showley, "When S.D. Looks Around It Sees L.A.," *San Diego Union*, January 8, 1989, p. F1.

7. Pourade, *History of San Diego*, vol. 2, pp. 20–28, 50–51, 74, 83, 171–72; vol. 3, p. 21; vol. 4, pp. 178–79; Iris Engstrand, *San Diego: California's Cornerstone* (Tulsa, Okla.: Continental Heritage Press, 1980), pp. 22, 25.

8. Pourade, *History of San Diego*, vol. 2, p. 234; vol. 3, pp. 159–60; vol. 4, p. 28; Leonard Pitt, *The Decline of the Californios: A Social History of Spanish-Speaking Californians, 1846–1890* (Berkeley: University of California Press, 1971), pp. 110–11.

9. Donovan Lewis, *The Pioneers of California: True Stories of Early Settlers in the Golden State* (San Francisco: Scottwall Associates, 1993), pp. 141–43; Pourade, *History of San Diego*, vol. 3, pp. 203, 243; vol. 4, p. 23.

10. Pourade, *History of San Diego*, vol. 3, pp. 3, 160–61, 171–72; vol. 4, pp. 70–72, 232–34; Robert Fogelson, *The Fragmented Metropolis: Los Angeles, 1850–1930* (Berkeley: University of California Press, 1967), pp. 46, 50, 54–55, 59–61; Glenn S. Dumke, *The Boom of the Eighties in Southern California* (San Marino, Calif.: Huntington Library, 1966), p. 135; Abraham Shragge, "Boosters and Bluejackets: The Civic Culture of Militarism in San Diego, California, 1900–1945" (Ph.D. diss., University of California, San Diego, 1998), pp. 95–97.

11. Dumke, *Boom of the Eighties*, pp. 137–38, 142; Engstrand, *San Diego*, p. 64.

12. James N. Price, "The Railroad Stations of San Diego County: Then and Now," *Journal of San Diego History* 34:2 (Spring 1988); Robert M. Hanft, *San Diego & Arizona: The Impossible Railroad* (Glendale, Calif.: Trans-Anglo Books, 1984).

13. Hanft, *San Diego & Arizona*, pp. 49–52. Ironically, Spreckels in San Francisco had generally opposed the Southern Pacific "machine" and aligned his newspaper, the *Call*, with the reformers. See Walton Bean, *Boss Ruef's San Francisco* (Berkeley: University of California Press, 1967), pp. 10, 293.

14. Pourade, *History of San Diego*, vol. 4, pp. 8, 23, 50, 70, 102; Fogelson, *Fragmented Metropolis*, pp. 51, 307n32.

15. Pourade, *History of San Diego*, vol. 4, p. 24; Steven P. Erie, "How the Urban West Was Won: The Local State and Economic Growth in Los Angeles, 1880–1932," *Urban Affairs Quarterly* 27:4 (June 1992), pp. 519–54.

16. Pourade, *History of San Diego*, vol. 4, p. 105.

17. Dumke, *Boom of the Eighties*, p. 136; Irene Phillips, *The Railroad Story of San Diego County* (National City, Calif.: South Bay Press, 1956), p. 9.

18. William F. Deverell, "The Los Angeles 'Free Harbor Fight,'" *California History* 70 (1991), pp. 12–29; Deverell, *Railroad Crossing: Californians and the Railroad, 1850–1910* (Berkeley: University of California Press, 1994), pp. 93–122; Engstrand, *San Diego*, pp. 47, 64.

19. Pourade, *History of San Diego*, vol. 4, pp. 88–92; Fogelson, *Fragmented Metropolis*, p. 117; Engstrand, *San Diego*, pp. 47, 64.

20. Pourade, *History of San Diego*, vol. 4, pp. 80, 237–39; Theodore Anthony Stratham, "'Dream of a Big City': Water Politics and San Diego County Growth, 1910–1947" (Ph.D. diss., University of California, San Diego, 2005), pp. 51–52; Gregg R. Hennessey, "The Politics of Water in San Diego, 1895–1897," *Journal of San Diego History* 24:3 (Summer 1978).

21. Pourade, *History of San Diego*, vol. 4, p. 180.

22. Earl Pomeroy, *The Pacific Slope* (Seattle: University of Washington Press, 1965), pp. 151, 261; H. Austin Adams, *The Man, John D. Spreckels* (San Diego: Press of Frye and Smith, 1924).

23. Mike Davis, Kelly Mayhew, and Jim Miller, *Under the Perfect Sun: The San Diego Tourists Never See* (New York: New Press, 2003), pp. 28–29; George Mowry, *The California Progressives* (1951; repr., Chicago: Quadrangle Books, 1976), p. 213; Iris Engstrand and Kathleen Crawford, *Reflections: A History of San Diego Gas & Electric Company, 1881–1991* (San Diego: San Diego Historical Society, 1991), p. 17.

24. Grace Louise Miller, "The San Diego Progressive Movement, 1900–1920" (Ph.D. diss., University of California, Santa Barbara, 1976), pp. 45, 129, 147; Amy Bridges, *Morning Glories: Municipal Reform in the Southwest* (Princeton, N.J.: Princeton University Press, 1997), pp. 58, 78–79; Pourade, *History of San Diego*, vol. 5, pp. 34, 41–42; Roger Showley, "San Diego Has Long History of Tumultuous Votes," *San Diego Union-Tribune*, May 31, 1998, p. H6.

25. Uldis Allen Ports, "George White Marston and the San Diego Progressives, 1913–1917" (master's thesis, San Diego State University, 1976); Matthew F. Bokovoy, *The San Diego World's Fairs and Southwestern Memory, 1880–1940* (Albuquerque: University of New Mexico Press, 2005), pp. 50–57, 60, 68–69; Gregory Montes, "San Diego's City Park 1902–1910: From Parsons to Balboa,"

Journal of San Diego History 25:1 (Winter 1979); Alice Blankfort, "Urban Planning in San Diego" (master's thesis, San Diego State University, 1969), p. 47.

26. Bokovoy, *San Diego World's Fairs*, pp. 17–18, 20–23, 60, 132–34; Roger Showley, "Expo Started as Hype and Turned into a Gem," *San Diego Union*, February 4, 1990, p. F1.

27. Kevin Starr, *Americans and the California Dream, 1850–1915* (Santa Barbara, Calif.: Peregrine Smith, 1981), pp. 396–404; Bokovoy, *San Diego World's Fairs*, pp. 55–59; Showley, "San Diego Has Long History of Tumultuous Votes."

28. Gregory Montes, "Balboa Park, 1909–1911: The Rise and Fall of the Olmsted Plan," *Journal of San Diego History* 28:1 (Winter 1982); Bokovoy, *San Diego World's Fairs*, pp. 17–18, 55–59.

29. Fogelson, *Fragmented Metropolis*, pp. 216–18; Davis et al., *Under the Perfect Sun*, pp. 31, 42; Gregg R. Hennessey, "George White Marston and Conservative Reform in San Diego," *Journal of San Diego History* 32:4 (Fall 1986).

30. Pourade, *History of San Diego*, vol. 5, pp. 193, 199, 218; Uldis Allen Ports, "Geraniums vs. Smokestacks: San Diego's Mayoralty Campaign of 1917," *Journal of San Diego History* 21:3 (Summer 1975).

31. Pourade, *History of San Diego*, vol. 5, pp. 195, 199, 236–37, 264; vol. 6, p. 39; Bokovoy, *San Diego World's Fairs*, pp. 147–48, 222–25; Engstrand, *San Diego*, pp. 72, 91, 94, 98; Gregg R. Hennessey, "Creating a Monument, Re-Creating History: Junípero Serra Museum and Presidio Park," *Journal of San Diego History* 45:3 (Summer 1999), pp. 136–63.

32. Pourade, *History of San Diego*, vol. 4, p. 87; Steven P. Erie, *Globalizing L.A.: Trade, Infrastructure, and Regional Development* (Stanford, Calif.: Stanford University Press, 2004), pp. 54–55.

33. Stratham, "'Dream of a Big City,'" pp. 119–20, 154–55, 159–60, 210–13, 280; Robert E. Melbourne, "San Diego County's Water Crusader, Fred A. Heilbron," *Journal of San Diego History* 32:4 (Fall 1986); Norris Hundley Jr., *The Great Thirst: Californians and Water, 1770s–1990s* (Berkeley: University of California Press, 1992), pp. 49–50, 107–10.

34. William L. Kahrl, *Water and Power* (Berkeley: University of California Press, 1982), pp. 263, 270, 348–49; Hundley, *Great Thirst*, pp. 49–50, 107–10; Shragge, "Boosters and Bluejackets," p. 484.

35. William Wagner, *Reuben Fleet and the Story of Consolidated Aircraft* (Fallbrook, Calif.: Aero Publishers, 1976), p. 181.

36. Shragge, "Boosters and Bluejackets," pp. 129, 282, 313–19, 408, 432; Pourade, *History of San Diego*, vol. 4, pp. 28, 244–45; vol. 5, pp. 174, 263.

37. Roger Lotchin, *Fortress California, 1910–1961: From Warfare to Welfare* (New York: Oxford University Press, 1992), pp. 30, 50; Shragge, "Boosters and Bluejackets," p. 140.

38. Shragge, "Boosters and Bluejackets," pp. 389–90; Pourade, *History of San Diego*, vol. 4, pp. 197–98, 222–32.

39. Pourade, *History of San Diego*, vol. 6, pp. 9, 31, 83, 122, 237, 248–49; Gregg R. Hennessey, "San Diego, the U.S. Navy, and Urban Development: West Coast City Building, 1912–1929," *California History* 72 (Summer 1993), pp. 129–49; Lotchin, *Fortress California*, p. 37; Shragge, "Boosters and Bluejackets," pp. 76, 88–91, 111.

40. Shragge, "Boosters and Bluejackets," p. 519; Davis et al., *Under the Perfect Sun*, pp. 60–61; Pourade, *History of San Diego*, vol. 7, pp. 7–9.

41. Gerald D. Nash, *The American West Transformed: The Impact of the Second World War* (Bloomington: Indiana University Press, 1985), p. 59; Carl Abbott, *The New Urban America: Growth and Politics in Sunbelt Cities* (Chapel Hill: University of North Carolina Press, 1981), p. 104; Christine Killory, "Temporary Suburbs: The Lost Opportunities of San Diego's National Defense Housing Projects," *Journal of San Diego History* 39:1–2 (Winter–Spring 1993); Iris Engstrand and Paul Campuzano, *Harley Eugene Knox: San Diego's Mayor for the People, 1943–1951* (San Diego: San Diego Historical Society, 2002), pp. 41, 47; Shragge, "Boosters and Bluejackets," pp. 507–8; Pourade, *History of San Diego*, vol. 7, pp. 9, 38, 41, 43.

42. Pourade, *History of San Diego*, vol. 7, pp. 8, 32–33, 40–48; Abbott, *The New Urban America*, p. 115; Joseph O. McClintic, "California's Local Revenue Problem," *Annals of the American Academy of Political and Social Science* 248 (November 1946), pp. 260–67; Roger W. Lotchin, *The Bad City in the Good War: San Francisco, Los Angeles, Oakland, and San Diego* (Bloomington: Indiana University Press, 2003), pp. 64, 186, 200–232.

43. Pourade, *History of San Diego*, vol. 7, pp. 188–89.

44. Pourade, *History of San Diego*, vol. 7, pp. 32–33, 179, 252; Engstrand, *San Diego*, pp. 116, 126. Long-serving City Planning Director Glenn Rick pushed the Mission Bay Park plan from the 1930s through the early 1950s. See Glenn A. Rick, *San Diego, 1927–1955: Reflections of a City Planner* (San Diego: Glenn A. Rick, 1977), pp. 9–15, 31–40; William B. Rick, "Mission Bay: An Engineer's Vision Come True," *Journal of San Diego History* 48:1 (Winter 2002). For an analysis of 1950s-era San Diego's political, social, and economic development, see David Greenstone, *A Report on Politics in San Diego* (Cambridge, Mass.: Joint Center for Urban Studies of the Massachusetts Institute of Technology and Harvard University, 1962).

45. Davis, Mayhew, and Miller, *Under the Perfect Sun*, pp. 67–69, 81; Engstrand, *San Diego*, pp. 187–89; Frederick L. Ryan, "Economic Growth: The San Diego Case," *Land Economics* 36:3 (August 1960), p. 290; James L. Clayton, "Defense Spending: Key to California's Growth," *Western Political Quarterly* 15:2 (June 1962), pp. 280–93.

46. G. William Domhoff, *Who Rules America?* (New York: Prentice Hall, 1967); Allen Pred, *City Systems in Advanced Economies: Past Growth, Present Processes and Future Development Options* (New York: John Wiley and Sons, 1977); Roger Friedland, "Park Place and Main Street: Business and the Urban Power Structure," *American Review of Sociology* 10 (1984), pp. 402–3.

47. Engstrand, *San Diego*, pp. 128, 214; Davis et al., *Under the Perfect Sun*, pp. 71–73.

48. Davis et al., *Under the Perfect Sun*, pp. 77–80; Pourade, *History of San Diego*, vol. 7, pp. 163, 197–99; Keen, "Stampede," pp. 48–49, 134.

49. Keen, "Stampede," pp. 48, 135–36.

50. Pourade, *History of San Diego*, vol. 7, pp. 158, 187, 206, 214–15; Rick, *San Diego*, pp. 98–101; Engstrand, *San Diego*, pp. 124–25, 130–31; Bernard J. Frieden and Lynne B. Sagalyn, *Downtown, Inc.: How American Cities Rebuild* (Cambridge: Massachusetts Institute of Technology Press, 1989), p. 123.

51. Pourade, *History of San Diego*, vol. 7, pp. 206, 214, 252; Harold Keen, "Curran and His Critics," *San Diego Magazine* (January 1965), pp. 73, 97–98; Harold Keen, "San Diego's Racial Powder Keg," *San Diego Magazine* (July 1963), pp. 66–67, 90–91; Harold Keen, "The Crises That Broke Walter Hahn," *San Diego Magazine* (December 1971), p. 107; Roger M. Showley, *San Diego: Perfecting Paradise* (Carlsbad, Calif.: Heritage Media Corp., 1999), p. 134.

52. Pourade, *History of San Diego*, vol. 7, pp. 102, 148–49, 204–6; Davis et al., *Under the Perfect Sun*, pp. 73–77.

53. Dan Berger, Peter Jensen, and Margaret C. Berg, *San Diego: Where Tomorrow Begins* (Northridge, Calif.: Windsor Publications, 1987), p. 61; Engstrand, *San Diego*, pp. 120–23, 128; Harold Keen, "Politics, Planning, and Personal Vendettas," *San Diego Magazine* (February 1968), pp. 35–36; Harold Keen, "A City Led Down the Garden Path," *San Diego Magazine* (May 1968), pp. 51–52, 97; Keen, "The Crises That Broke Walter Hahn," pp. 69–71, 102.

54. Davis et al., *Under the Perfect Sun*, pp. 81–82; Pourade, *History of San Diego*, vol. 7, pp. 116, 225, 242–43; Harold Keen, "The City Dumped," *San Diego Magazine* (June 1972), p. 85; Showley, *San Diego*, p. 130.

55. Showley, *San Diego*, p. 137; Davis et al., *Under the Perfect Sun*, pp. 96, 101–2; Harold Keen, "Tom Fletcher's Five-Year Plan," *San Diego Magazine* (December 1966), p. 49; Mary Harrington Hall, "Who Runs San Diego?" *San Diego Magazine* (July 1961), p. 41; interview with Jim Mills, former California state senator and Senate president pro tem, 2007.

56. Keen, "Curran and His Critics," pp. 95, 97; Harold Keen, "A Classical and Crucial D.A. Primary," *San Diego Magazine* (May 1970), pp. 50–51; Harold Keen, "City on Trial," *San Diego Magazine* (December 1970), pp. 70–75;

Harold Keen, "The Financial Power Structure: A New Ball Game," *San Diego Magazine* (January 1974), pp. 58–60.

57. Davis et al., *Under the Perfect Sun*, pp. 84–89, 104; Keen, "The Crises That Broke Walter Hahn," p. 108; Harold Keen, "Post Mortems: The Trials," *San Diego Magazine* (April 1971), pp. 33–35, 128–29.

58. Interview with Mike Madigan, former assistant to Mayor Pete Wilson for program and policy development, 2007.

59. Interview with Michael Stepner, former City of San Diego acting planning director and city architect, 2007.

60. Harold Keen, "The Wilson Era: San Diego's New Power Structure," *San Diego Magazine* (May 1973), p. 77; Davis et al., *Under the Perfect Sun*, p. 91.

61. Interview with former City Councilman Bruce Henderson, 2007; Davis et al., *Under the Perfect Sun*, pp. 102–4, 108, 110; Harold Keen, "A War without Proper Sides: The Death of Old Line Politics in San Diego," *San Diego Magazine* (October 1976), p. 45; Keen, "The Wilson Era," pp. 83, 124.

62. Keen, "The Wilson Era," pp. 80, 85; Harold Keen, "The Wilson Era: Phase Two," *San Diego Magazine* (September 1973), pp. 90–91; Keen, "A War without Proper Sides," p. 47; Davis et al., *Under the Perfect Sun*, pp. 108–9; Keen, "The City Dumped," pp. 81–87; Madigan interview.

63. The formula adopted by state officials for returning property taxes to local governments after the passage of Proposition 13 was based on preexisting tax rates. Thus, fiscally conservative San Diego, which had lowered its tax rate, suffered relative to Los Angeles and other cities with higher rates; interview with former city firefighters' union president Ron Saathoff, 2007.

64. Stepner interview.

65. San Diego City Planning Department, *The San Diego General Plan Study* (San Diego: City Planning Department, December 1961).

66. Madigan interview.

67. Madigan interview.

68. Mills interview. Also see Laura A. Schiesl, "Problems in Paradise: Citizen Activism and Rapid Growth in San Diego, 1970–1990," *Southern California Quarterly* 83:2 (Summer 2001), pp. 181–220.

69. Harold Keen, "Would You Invest in This Town?" *San Diego Magazine* (January 1977), pp. 87, 147; Madigan interview.

70. Frieden and Sagalyn, *Downtown, Inc.*, pp. 123–26; Berger et al., *San Diego*, pp. 63, 65; Engstrand, *San Diego*, pp. 142–43; Harold Keen, "Change at the Top," *San Diego Magazine* (January 1973), p. 90; Paul S. Grogan and Tony Proscio, *Comeback Cities: A Blueprint for Urban Neighborhood Revival* (Boulder, Colo.: Westview Press, 2000), p. 280.

71. Keen, "Would You Invest in This Town?" pp. 79–81; Showley, *San Diego*, pp. 144–52.

72. Davis et al., *Under the Perfect Sun*, pp. 105–7; Harold Keen, "The Pete Paradox," *San Diego Magazine* (November 1979), pp. 314, 327, 329–30.

73. Madigan interview.

74. Mills interview.

75. Showley, *San Diego*, pp. 158–59, 163–65; Mills interview.

76. Keen, "The Pete Paradox," pp. 127, 129–30, 314; Keen, "The Financial Power Structure," pp. 60–61; Keen, "A War without Proper Sides," p. 48.

77. Davis et al., *Under the Perfect Sun*, pp. 112–13; Keen, "The Pete Paradox," pp. 313–16.

78. Davis et al., *Under the Perfect Sun*, pp. 116–18.

79. Showley, *San Diego*, p. 161; Berger et al., *San Diego*, p. 85.

80. Davis et al., *Under the Perfect Sun*, pp. 118–19, 124.

81. Abbott, *Metropolitan Frontier*, p. 179; Davis et al., *Under the Perfect Sun*, pp. 125–27; Showley, *San Diego*, pp. 163, 174–75; Berger et al., *San Diego*, p. 74.

82. Joel Kotkin, *The New Geography: How the Digital Revolution Is Reshaping the American Landscape* (New York: Random House, 2000), p. 41; Dennis McDougal, *Privileged Son: Otis Chandler and the Rise and Fall of the L.A. Times Dynasty* (Cambridge, Mass.: Da Capo Press, 2001), pp. 336, 394.

83. Kevin Starr, *Coast of Dreams: California on the Edge, 1990–2003* (New York: Alfred A. Knopf, 2004), pp. 371–76; Showley, *San Diego*, pp. 162–63.

84. Showley, "When S.D. Looks Around It Sees L.A."; see also Engstrand and Crawford, *Reflections*.

85. The more things change, the more they stay the same.

86. Henderson interview.

87. Regarding San Diego's business community political prowess, see Arnold Klaus, "History of the San Diego Chamber of Commerce" (unpublished manuscript, 1967).

Chapter 3

1. Interview with former City Attorney Mike Aguirre, 2009.

2. Ester R. Fuchs, *Mayors and Money: Fiscal Policy in New York and Chicago* (Chicago: University of Chicago Press, 1992), p. 11.

3. See Katharine L. Bradbury, "Structural Fiscal Distress in Cities—Causes and Consequences," *New England Economic Review* (January–February 1983), pp. 32–43.

4. See, for example, Helen F. Ladd and John Yinger, *America's Ailing Cities: Fiscal Health and the Design of Urban Policy* (Baltimore: Johns Hopkins University Press, 1989); Terry Nichols Clark and Lorna Crowley Ferguson, *City Money: Political Processes, Fiscal Strain and Retrenchment* (New York: Columbia University Press, 1983); Roger E. Alcaly and David Mermelstein, eds., *The Fiscal Crisis of American Cities: Essays on the Political Economy of Urban America with Special Reference to New York* (New York: Vintage Books, 1977).

5. Larry C. Ledebur and William R. Barnes, *City Distress: Metropolitan Disparities and Economic Growth* (Washington, D.C.: National League of Cities, 1991); M. Gottdiener and A. P. Lagopoulos, eds., *Cities in Stress: A New Look at the Urban Crisis* (Beverly Hills, Calif.: Sage Publications, 1986); Michael A. Pagano, *City Fiscal Conditions in 2002: A Research Report on America's Cities* (Washington, D.C.: National League of Cities, 2002).

6. Most studies of urban financial crises are case studies. On New York, see Ester Fuchs, *Mayors and Money*; Martin Shefter, *Political Crisis/Fiscal Crisis: The Collapse and Revival of New York City* (New York: Basic Books, 1985); Ken Auletta, *The Streets Were Paved with Gold* (New York: Vintage Books, 1980). On Cleveland, see Todd Swanstrom, *The Crisis of Growth Politics: Cleveland, Kucinich, and the Challenge of Urban Populism* (Philadelphia: Temple University Press, 1985). On Philadelphia, see Robert P. Inman, "How to Have a Fiscal Crisis: Lessons from Philadelphia," *American Economic Review* 85:2 (1995), pp. 378–83. On Orange County, see Mark Baldassare, *When Government Fails: The Orange County Bankruptcy* (Berkeley: University of California Press, 1998). On Miami, see Milan J. Dluhy and Howard A. Frank, *The Miami Fiscal Crisis: Can a Poor City Regain Prosperity?* (Westport, Conn.: Praeger Publishers, 2002).

7. Interview with former City Manager Jack McGrory, 2007.

8. Quoted in Alan Greenblatt, "Paradise Insolvent," *Governing* (November 2005), p. 41.

9. Interview with Erik Bruvold, president, National University System Institute for Policy Research, 2009.

10. Interview with Jack McGrory; interview with Mike Madigan, former assistant to Mayor Pete Wilson for program and policy development, 2007.

11. In fiscal year 1999–2000, San Diego received 17.1 percent of the 1 percent property tax base. By contrast, Oakland received 33.2 percent, Los Angeles collected 28.9 percent, Sacramento collected 28.1 percent, and Fresno received 24.6 percent. Other cities, including San Jose, Santa Barbara, Anaheim, and Irvine received a smaller portion of the property tax base than San Diego. Kelling, Northcross, and Nobriga, *City of San Diego Facilities Financing Study* (San Diego, Calif.: April 12, 2002).

12. San Francisco, a consolidated city-county government, is excluded from the analysis.

13. California State Controller, *Financial Transactions Concerning Cities of California* (Sacramento, Calif.: various years). Specifically, the measure required a public vote on any local tax imposed to pay for specific governmental programs. Proposition 218, adopted in 1996, also required a majority vote on any nondedicated tax increase.

14. Jeffrey I. Chapman, *Proposition 13: Some Unintended Consequences* (San Francisco: Public Policy Institute of California, 1998), p. 15.

15. Chapman, *Proposition 13*; Gregory D. Saxton, Christopher W. Hoene, and Steven P. Erie, "Fiscal Constraints and the Loss of Home Rule: The Long-Term Impacts of California's Post-Proposition 13 Fiscal Regime," *American Review of Public Administration* 32:4 (December 2002), pp. 423–54; Kelling et al., *City of San Diego Facilities Financing Study*.

16. In a 2009 report, the San Diego County Grand Jury argued that the absence of trash collection fees for homeowners prevented the city from encouraging recycling among residents and was largely unfair to apartment residents, who must pay for trash disposal.

17. Interview with Jack McGrory.

18. First, in 1982, Mayor Wilson opted to drop out of the federal Social Security and Medicare systems, moving city workers over to a local plan with benefits comparable to what the federal government provided. To fund health care, Wilson chose a pay-as-you-go plan rather than putting the costs on a sound actuarial footing. Second, Wilson used his influence with SDCERS to tap retirement assets for local projects. Fund assets, for example, were used to construct a downtown parking garage, which was leased back to the city and then sold for a nominal price. Technically, leases did not count as municipal debt, thus enabling local officials to avoid public votes. In selling properties for less than their value, however, the fund was accepting lower returns than it was entitled to. Interview with former city firefighters union President Ron Saathoff, 2007.

19. If investment returns dipped below 8 percent, no checks would be issued. See Arthur Levitt Jr., Lynn E. Turner, and Troy A. Dahlberg, *Report of the Audit Committee of the City of San Diego: Investigation into the San Diego City Employees' Retirement System and the City of San Diego Sewer Rate Structure*, "Statement of Facts" (San Diego, Calif.: Kroll, August 8, 2006), pp. 32–34.

20. Interview with Ron Saathoff.

21. The thirteen-member board comprised the city manager, the city treasurer and city auditor, two members representing firefighter and police unions, three members elected from the city workforce, one from retired workers, and four selected by the mayor and city council.

22. Interview with Scott Barnett, former executive director, San Diego County Taxpayers Association, 2007.

23. Saxton et al., "Fiscal Constraints and the Loss of Home Rule"; interview with Jack McGrory.

24. On the policy implications of district elections, see Susan Welch and Timothy Bledsoe, *Urban Reform and Its Consequences* (Chicago: University of Chicago Press, 1988).

25. Susan Golding, "The Door to Our Future," 1993 state-of-the-city address; Mike Davis, Kelly Mayhew, and Jim Miller, *Under the Perfect Sun: The San Diego Tourists Never See* (New York: Verso Press, 2003), pp. 126–27, 134–41.

26. Interview with Scott Barnett.

27. Former City Manager McGrory disputes this claim. He contends, "Somehow I think the 10 percent hold back on budgets is confused with mid-year budget freezes in years when our revenues weren't coming in on budget or when the state was raiding our treasury—I certainly didn't have a secret reserve—although I was very aggressive in trying to prevent the [city] council from raiding whatever reserves we had for emergency purposes." Interview with Jack McGrory.

28. Interview with former City Councilman Bruce Henderson, 2007; Gerry Braun, "The Smooth Operator: Jack McGrory Led City Hall before the Storm Hit. Did He Lead It into Trouble?" *San Diego Union-Tribune*, December 18, 2008, p. A1.

29. Braun, "The Smooth Operator."

30. "Former San Diego City Manager Jack McGrory Deconstructs City's Governance Crisis," *Metro Investment Report*, December–January 2005; interview with Jack McGrory.

31. Interview with Ron Saathoff.

32. Under a formula of 2 percent at age fifty-five, for example, employees would receive 2 percent of their average monthly wage—usually based on the salary at the end of their career—for each year of service if they retired at age fifty-five or later.

33. Levitt et al., *Report of the Audit Committee of the City of San Diego*, "Statement of Facts," pp. 34–38; interview with Jack McGrory.

34. Interview with Jack McGrory.

35. From 1.48 percent to 2 percent times number of years of service.

36. Levitt et al., *Report of the Audit Committee of the City of San Diego*, "Statement of Facts," pp. 38–43; interview with Jack McGrory; Philip J. LaVelle, "Pension Trustees OK Parts of Plan to Ease City's Ills," *San Diego Union-Tribune*, June 22, 1996, p. A1; interview with Mike Aguirre.

37. Levitt et al., *Report of the Audit Committee of the City of San Diego*, "Interview with Rick Roeder." Regarding MP-1, former City Manager Jack McGrory argues that "the employees also made for a significant part of the MP-1 benefit improvements which should be pointed out. I would still maintain that MP-1 by itself would not have created the situation the city found itself in. The latter two rounds of benefit improvements [e.g., MP-2] without any real accounting for them just blew away the MP-1 plan." Interview with Jack McGrory.

38. Levitt et al., *Report of the Audit Committee of the City of San Diego*, "Statement of Facts," pp. 43–46, 59–66.

39. Levitt et al., *Report of the Audit Committee of the City of San Diego*, "Statement of Facts," pp. 49–52.

40. Interview with Bruce Henderson.

41. Roger Lowenstein, *While America Aged* (New York: Penguin Press, 2008), pp. 175–94; Levitt et al., *Report of the Audit Committee of the City of San Diego*, "Statement of Facts," pp. 52–59; *Blue Ribbon Committee Report on City of San Diego Finances* (San Diego: Blue Ribbon Committee on City of San Diego, February 2002).

42. Levitt et al., *Report of the Audit Committee of the City of San Diego*, "Statement of Facts," pp. 61–64.

43. The proposal increased the multiplier from 2.25 percent to 2.5 percent and used a retiree's highest one-year salary as the base.

44. Levitt et al., *Report of the Audit Committee of the City of San Diego*, "Statement of Facts," pp. 66–79.

45. Levitt et al., *Report of the Audit Committee of the City of San Diego*, "Statement of Facts," pp. 66–79.

46. Lowenstein, *While America Aged*, pp. 175–94.

47. Levitt et al., *Report of the Audit Committee of the City of San Diego*, "Statement of Facts," pp. 66–79; Lowenstein, *While America Aged*, pp. 175–94.

48. E-mail from Terri Webster to pension board member Ray Garnica, March 18, 2002; Philip J. LaVelle, "Financial Realities Come Crashing Down on San Diego Pension Fund," *San Diego Union-Tribune*, December 21, 2002, p. A1.

49. Philip J. LaVelle, "City Pension System Seen under Siege, Under-Funded," *San Diego Union-Tribune*, February 12, 2003, p. A1; Philip J. LaVelle, "Pension Fund Could Face $2 Billion Deficit by 2009," *San Diego Union-Tribune*, May 10, 2003, p. A1.

50. Lowenstein, *While America Aged*, pp. 195–219; Philip J. LaVelle, "Troubles Continue for San Diego's Pension Fund," *San Diego Union-Tribune*, December 20, 2003, p. B1.

51. Philip J. LaVelle, "City Pension Woes Called 'Significant,'" *San Diego Union-Tribune*, February 4, 2004, p. B1; Philip J. LaVelle, "Mayor Warns

of Dire Ways to Cut Pension Deficit," *San Diego Union-Tribune*, February 5, 2004, p. A1.

52. Levitt et al., *Report of the Audit Committee of the City of San Diego*, "Statement of Facts," pp. 81–83.

53. Interview with Mike Madigan.

54. Philip J. LaVelle, "Pension Report Slams City Hall," *San Diego Union-Tribune*, September 17, 2004, p. A1.

55. Matthew T. Hall, "City Adopts Borrowing Plan to Fix Pension Gap," *San Diego Union-Tribune*, October 6, 2004, p. B1; Philip J. LaVelle, "Pension Fund Crises Fueling Mayoral Duel," *San Diego Union-Tribune*, October 11, 2004, p. A1.

56. Philip J. LaVelle, "Pension Whistle-Blower Sees 'Sinister' Ouster Plot," *San Diego Union-Tribune*, December 14, 2004, p. A1.

57. Office of the City Attorney of San Diego, *Interim Report No. 1 regarding Possible Abuse, Fraud, and Illegal Acts by San Diego City Officials and Employees* (San Diego: Office of the City Attorney, January 14, 2005); interview with Mike Aguirre.

58. Jonathan Heller and Jennifer Vigil, "Aguirre's Suit Seeks Cutback in Pension," *San Diego Union-Tribune*, July 8, 2005, p. A1.

59. Office of the City Attorney of San Diego, *Interim Report No. 2 regarding Possible Abuse, Illegal Acts or Fraud by City of San Diego Officials* (San Diego: Office of the City Attorney, February 9, 2005); Scott H. Peters, "San Diego Is Taking Steps to Correct Pension Woes," *San Diego Union-Tribune*, February 20, 2005, p. G6.

60. Matthew T. Hall, "Pension Board Refuses to Co-operate in Deficit Inquiry," *San Diego Union-Tribune*, February 19, 2005, p. B3.

61. Lewis died before the trial began.

62. A judge later dismissed the charges against Zucchet.

63. Jennifer Vigil and Jonathan Heller, "Pension Trustees Delay Decision," *San Diego Union-Tribune*, May 21, 2005, p. B3; Jonathan Heller, "Pension Fallout: City Hit with Bill," *San Diego Union-Tribune*, June 17, 2005, p. B1.

64. Office of the City Attorney of San Diego, *Interim Report No. 3 regarding Violations of State and Local Laws as Related to the SDCERS Pension Fund* (San Diego: Office of the City Attorney, April 9, 2005); Office of the City Attorney of San Diego, *Interim Report No. 4 regarding Additional Funding for Outside Professionals Reviewing Alleged Illegal Acts* (San Diego: Office of the City Attorney, May 9, 2005).

65. Jonathan Heller and Jennifer Vigil, "Pension Board's Budget Held Up," *San Diego Union-Tribune*, June 15, 2005, p. B1; Jennifer Vigil and Ron Powell, "Pension Board Urged to Fire Consultant," *San Diego Union-Tribune*,

June 8, 2005, p. B1; Jonathan Heller, "Pension Board Fails to Act on Request for Documents," *San Diego Union-Tribune*, July 6, 2005, p. B2; Jennifer Vigil, "Aguirre Sues to Shift Control of Pension System," *San Diego Union-Tribune*, July 9, 2005, p. B1; Jonathan Heller and Jennifer Vigil, "Aguirre's Suit Seeks Cutback in Pensions," *San Diego Union-Tribune*, July 8, 2005, p. A1.

66. Interview with former mayoral candidate Pat Shea, 2009.

67. Matthew T. Hall and Jennifer Vigil, "Aguirre Urges City to Admit Errors and Follow His Plan," *San Diego Union-Tribune*, August 17, 2005, p. A1.

68. Jennifer Vigil, "Aguirre's Pension Suit Dismissed," *San Diego Union-Tribune*, October 1, 2005, p. B1; Jennifer Vigil, "Judge Rebuffs Aguirre Again," *San Diego Union-Tribune*, March 7, 2006, p. B3.

69. "Reality Check," *San Diego Union-Tribune*, October 7, 2005, p. B8; Philip J. LaVelle, "Plan Touted by Frye, Aguirre," *San Diego Union-Tribune*, October 11, 2005, p. B1; Philip J. LaVelle, "Candidates Question Each Other's Pension Benefits," *San Diego Union-Tribune*, October 15, 2005, p. B3; "Cutting Costs," *San Diego Union-Tribune*, October 28, 2005, p. B8.

70. Quoted in Matthew T. Hall and Jennifer Vigil, "Meeting to Reveal S.D. Pension Deficit," *San Diego Union-Tribune*, March 17, 2006, p. B1.

71. Matthew T. Hall, "Investors Buy Bonds to Boost Pension System," *San Diego Union-Tribune*, June 16, 2006, p. B2.

72. Matthew T. Hall, "Sanders Unveils Borrowing Plan," *San Diego Union-Tribune*, April 11, 2006, p. B1.

73. Independent Budget Analyst, "Mayor's Proposed Fiscal Year 2007 Budget," Report No. 06-18, April 28, 2006.

74. Jennifer Vigil, "Pension Report Finds Laws Were Violated," *San Diego Union-Tribune*, January 21, 2006, p. A1; Navigant Consulting, "Investigation for the Board of Administration of the San Diego City Employees' Retirement System," January 20, 2006.

75. Office of the City Attorney of San Diego, *Interim Report No. 18: The Adverse Domination of the Government of the City of San Diego* (San Diego: Office of the City Attorney, August 30, 2007); Jennifer Vigil, "Sanders Seeks to Sideline Aguirre," *San Diego Union-Tribune*, September 27, 2007, p. B1; Alex Roth, "Aguirre's War on Expenses Getting Expensive," *San Diego Union-Tribune*, October 7, 2007, p. A1.

76. City of San Diego, Office of Mayor Jerry Sanders, published letter to Mike Aguirre, city attorney, September 28, 2007.

77. Independent Budget Analyst, *IBA Matrix for Kroll Recommendations*, November 2006; Matthew T. Hall, "Pension Deficit's Size Gets Clearer," *San Diego Union-Tribune*, October 8, 2006, p. B1.

78. Craig Gustafson and Matthew T. Hall, "SEC Slams City on Pension Debt," *San Diego Union-Tribune*, November 15, 2006, p. A1; City of San Diego, *Five-Year Financial Outlook, Fiscal Years 2008–2012* (San Diego: Office of the Mayor, November 29, 2006).

79. Jennifer Vigil, "Sanders Changing Pension Blueprint," *San Diego Union-Tribune*, March 4, 2008, p. B1; Craig Gustafson, "Unions OK Pension Trims for City's Future Workers," *San Diego Union-Tribune*, July 23, 2008, p. A1.

80. "San Diego Returns to Bond Market," *San Diego Union-Tribune*, January 13, 2009.

81. San Diego City Employees' Retirement System, "June 30, 2009 Actuarial Valuation for the City of San Diego," January 2010.

82. Andrea Tevlin, "City of San Diego Structural Budget Deficit," Office of the Independent Budget Analyst, Report No. 08-14, February 14, 2008.

83. Jerry Sanders, "State of the City," speech, January 12, 2006.

84. Jerry Sanders and Jay M. Goldstone, "City of San Diego 2010–2014 Five-Year Financial Outlook," November 2008.

85. Jay M. Goldstone and Mary Lewis, "Mayor's May Revision for the Fiscal Year 2010 Proposed Budget," May 18, 2009.

86. Interview with attorney Pat Shea.

87. Joe Nation, "The Funding Status of Independent Public Employee Pension Systems in California," Stanford Institute for Economic Policy Research, November 2010.

88. Although voters adopted the fifteen-year amortization schedule as part of a package of city-charter reforms approved in 2004, the vote was later ruled to be advisory by the state attorney general.

89. Interview with former City Comptroller Greg Levin, 2009; Jerry Sanders, Jay M. Goldstone, Mary Lewis, and Mark Leonard, "City of San Diego FY2012–2016 Five-Year Outlook," February 1, 2011.

90. City of San Diego, *Comprehensive Annual Financial Report . . .* June 30, 2009.

91. Murtaza H. Baxamusa, "The Bottom Line: Solutions for San Diego's Budget Crisis," Center on Policy Initiatives, April 2005; Thad Kousser, "Is San Diego a Low Tax City?" unpublished paper prepared for the 2005 San Diego mayoral debate; Kelling et al., *City of San Diego Facilities Financing Study*; Tevlin, "City of San Diego Structural Budget Deficit."

92. Interview with former City Councilman Scott Peters, 2009.

93. "No on Prop. J," *San Diego Union-Tribune*, September 30, 2005, p. B12.

94. "Trash This Idea," *San Diego Union-Tribune*, April 10, 2009.

95. Rani Gupta, "Council Stuns with Votes to Impose Contracts," *Voiceofsandiego.org*, April 15, 2009.

96. In May 2010, the San Diego District Attorney's Office abandoned its case against Ron Saathoff for violating state conflict-of-interest laws. The state supreme court had thrown out charges against five other members of the retirement board in January. Liam Dillon, "DA's Charges against Saathoff Dropped," *Voiceofsandiego.org*, May 5, 2010. In September 2010, the U.S. Attorney's Office in San Diego decided not to appeal a federal district judge's decision to throw out the indictment against five former members of the pension system, including Ron Saathoff. Greg Moran, "Feds Drop Appeal in San Diego Pension Case," *San Diego Union-Tribune*, September 14, 2010.

Chapter 4

1. "Deal with It," *San Diego Union-Tribune*, December 9, 2009, p. B6.

2. Jennifer Vigil, "Mayor: Deficits Remain Big Part of Fiscal Future," *San Diego Union-Tribune*, January 12, 2008, p. B1.

3. San Francisco, a consolidated city-county, is excluded.

4. Carl DeMaio, "Six-Figure Salaries Soar in the City Work Force," *San Diego Union-Tribune*, March 12, 2006, p. G1.

5. Steve Schmidt and Danielle Cervantes, "City Caught in a Payroll Vise," *San Diego Union-Tribune*, December 11, 2005, p. A1.

6. The head of San Diego's managed competition program, Mark Patzman, did carry out an informal comparison of city pay practices with those of the private sector. He concluded that the city's blue-collar workers earned more than the prevailing wages in the area, whereas its white-collar employees made less. Interview with former managed competition Program Manager Mark Patzman, 2009.

7. The payroll expenditures are adjusted for growth in California income derived from annual data from the California Franchise Tax Board and are presented in 2007 dollars.

8. San Diego City Employees' Retirement System, "Comprehensive Annual Financial Report for Fiscal Year Ended June 30, 2009."

9. These figures include the city's total pension contribution. About 80 percent of the payment is made from the General Fund.

10. Liam Dillon, "Council Passes Mayor's Budget," *Voiceofsandiego.org*, December 9, 2009.

11. Jay M. Goldstone, "Fiscal Year 2010 Mid-Year Budget Monitoring Report," Report to the City Council, No. 10-021, February 24, 2010.

12. Jerry Sanders, "Preserving the Quality of Life in San Diego," *San Diego Union-Tribune*, April 12, 2009, p. F2.

13. Andrew Donohue, "Mayoral Race Resumes with Calls for Resignation," *Voiceofsandiego.org*, September 9, 2005.

14. Jennifer Vigil, "S.D. Bankruptcy Talk Lingers, but It's Down to Whisper," *San Diego Union-Tribune*, June 19, 2006, p. A1.

15. Evan McLaughlin, "Layoffs Didn't Eject Workers from City's Rolls," *Voiceofsandiego.org*, December 5, 2007.

16. Penni Takade, "Authorization Process and Policy for Current Year Budget Changes," Office of the Independent Budget Analyst, Report 06-48, October 13, 2006.

17. Implementing a two-thirds veto override would have required creating a ninth city council district, thus necessitating a middecade redistricting. The redistricting made the idea unpopular with the city council. Interview with City Club of San Diego President George Mitrovich, 2009.

18. Craig Gustafson, "Mayor Has First, Last, Only Word in City Info," *San Diego Union-Tribune*, November 12, 2006, p. A1.

19. Interview with former San Diego City Comptroller Greg Levin, 2009.

20. Angela Means, "In the Matter of Blue Level Swim Program," Office of the Independent Budget Analyst, Report 06-44, October 12, 2006; Tom Haynes, "In the Matter of the Take Back the Streets Program Contracts," Office of the Independent Budget Analyst, Report 06-43, October 12, 2006.

21. Stacey LoMedico and Ted Martinez, "Blue Level Swim Program," Report to the City Council, No. 06-152, October 13, 2006.

22. Haynes, "In the Matter of the Take Back the Streets Program Contracts."

23. Craig Gustafson, "Council, Sanders in Power Struggle," *San Diego Union-Tribune*, October 18, 2006, p. B1.

24. Evan McLaughlin, "Council Reins in Budget Control," *Voiceofsan diego.org*, February 6, 2007.

25. Evan McLaughlin, "Mayor, Council Strike Compromise on Cuts," *Voiceofsandiego.org*, March 2, 2007.

26. Interview with Jerry Butkiewicz, secretary-treasurer, San Diego and Imperial Counties Labor Council, 2008.

27. Research by scholars of urban politics has found that district elections tend to reinforce a focus on service delivery, rather than broad policy deliberation, among elected officials. See Susan Welch and Timothy Bledsoe, *Urban Reform and Its Consequences: A Study of Representation* (Chicago: University of Chicago Press, 1988), chapter 5.

28. Interview with former City Manager Jack McGrory, 2007.

29. Bruce E. Cain, "Epilogue: Seeking Consensus among Conflicting Electorates," in *Governing California: Politics, Government, and Public Policy in the Golden State*, ed. Gerald C. Lubenow and Bruce E. Cain (Berkeley: Institute of Governmental Studies Press, 1997), pp. 337–40.

30. Zoltan L. Hajnal and Paul G. Lewis, "Municipal Institutions and Voter Turnout in Local Elections," *Urban Affairs Review* 38:5 (May 2003), pp. 645–68.

31. Support Center and Executive Service Corps, "Zero-Based Management Review of the San Diego Public Library," presentation to the city manager, September 4, 1998.

32. Anna Tatár, "Library System Building Program," City Manager, Report No. 01-234, October 26, 2001.

33. Support Center and Executive Services Corps, "Zero-Based Management Review."

34. Support Center and Executive Services Corps, "Zero-Based Management Review."

35. San Diego City Council Policy 100-19, "Annual Appropriation for Library Operation and Maintenance."

36. Support Center and Executive Service Corps, "Zero-Based Management Review."

37. "Expanding San Diego's Library System," *San Diego Union-Tribune*, July 28, 2002, p. G4.

38. Nader Tirandazi, Mary Lewis, and Angela Colton, "Fiscal Year 2009 Year-End Budget Monitoring," Report to the City Council, No. 09-058, May 1, 2009.

39. Jeff Bowman, "Cedar Fire 2003 after Action Report," June 2004.

40. Bowman, "Cedar Fire 2003 after Action Report"; City of San Diego, "Public Safety Needs Assessment," City Manager, Report No. 04-057, March 17, 2004.

41. Philip J. LaVelle, "Fire Chief Says Mayor Was Aware of Deficiencies," *San Diego Union-Tribune*, November 20, 2005, p. B8.

42. Commission on Fire Accreditation International, "San Diego Fire Rescue Department Standards of Response Coverage," February 2005, p. 4.

43. Commission on Fire Accreditation International, "San Diego Fire Rescue Department Standards of Response Coverage"; Rob Davis, "As San Diego Grew, Firefighting Didn't Keep Up," *Voiceofsandiego.org*, November 9, 2007.

44. Commission on Fire Accreditation International, "San Diego Fire Rescue Department Standards of Response Coverage"; Davis, "As San Diego Grew, Firefighting Didn't Keep Up"; Rob Davis, "The Fire Station Plan That Isn't," *Voiceofsandiego.org*, November 30, 2007.

45. Will Carless, "Wildfire-Preparedness Still Shows Shortcomings," *Voiceofsandiego.org*, July 19, 2007; Commission on Fire Accreditation International, "San Diego Fire Rescue Department Standards of Response Coverage"; Keegan Kyle, "Fact Check: Fewer Firefighters Than Other Cities," *Voiceofsan diego.org*, August 19, 2010.

46. Commission on Fire Accreditation International, "San Diego Fire Rescue Department Standards of Response Coverage"; Tracy Jarman and Jill Olen, "Fire-Rescue Business Process Reengineering Report," Report to the City Council, No. 08-077, May 9, 2008.

47. Tony Manolatos, "As Fire Chief Departs, Uncertainty Smolders," *San Diego Union-Tribune*, June 2, 2006, p. A1.

48. Jeff Bowman and William Lansdowne, "Comprehensive Public Safety Needs Assessment," City Manager's Report, No. 04-057, March 17, 2004.

49. Carless, "Wildfire-Preparedness Still Shows Shortcomings."

50. "Bowman Departs," *San Diego Union-Tribune*, April 9, 2006, p. G2.

51. Tracy Jarman and Jay Goldstone, "Fire-Rescue Standards of Cover Report to PS&NS," Report to the City Council, February 27, 2009; Javier Mainar, "Fire-Rescue Department Engine Brownout Plan and Lifeguard Reductions Update," Report to Public Safety and Neighborhood Services Committee, July 28, 2010.

52. Keegan Kyle, "Fire Chief: Brownouts Slowed Response to Choking Child," *Voiceofsandiego.org*, July 21, 2010.

53. Taken from Brewster's remarks explaining his June 1991 decision to defer accepting an accord between the City of San Diego and the federal Environmental Protection Agency. See Philip J. LaVelle, "U.S. Judge Defers Huge Sewage Plan," *San Diego Union*, June 6, 1991, p. A1.

54. Mike Lee, "More Rate Hikes," *San Diego Union-Tribune*, September 8, 2006.

55. Neither substance can exceed thirty milligrams per liter.

56. Kathryn Balint, "City OKs Billions in New Sewer Works," *San Diego Tribune*, November 1, 1989, p. B1.

57. Kathryn Balint, "Council Reverses Course on Sewage; Seeks Waiver to Avoid Cost of Secondary Treatment," *San Diego Tribune*, October 3, 1990, p. A1.

58. Kathryn Balint, "Many Area Waterways on EPA 'Polluted' List," *San Diego Tribune*, December 29, 1990, p. A1; Kathryn Balint and Steve LaRue, "Wilson Helps, Storm Hurts as Sewage Flows," *San Diego Union-Tribune*, February 7, 1992, p. A1.

59. LaVelle, "U.S. Judge Defers Huge Sewage Plan."

60. Kathryn Balint, "More Sewage-System Options Sought," *San Diego Union-Tribune*, May 5, 1992, p. B2; Steve LaRue, "Council Stands by Sewage Proposal," *San Diego Union-Tribune*, May 27, 1992, p. B1.

61. Derrick DePledge, "Clinton Helps San Diego Try for Sewage Treatment Waiver," *San Diego Union-Tribune*, November 1, 1994, p. B3.

62. The $1 million application contained studies that showed that discharges from Point Loma did not adversely affect marine life.

63. Stephen Green and Kathryn Balint, "Good News from EPA on Sewage," *San Diego Union-Tribune*, June 13, 1995, p. A1; Kathryn Balint, "Sewage-Treatment War Comes to Peaceful End," *San Diego Union-Tribune*, September 14, 1996, p. A1.

64. Interview with Jack McGrory.

65. Terry Rodgers, "San Diego Wins Sewage Waiver Renewal," *San Diego Union-Tribune*, September 10, 2002, p. A1.

66. Bruce Reznick and Marco Gonzalez, "Refusing to Come Clean," *San Diego Union-Tribune*, February 6, 2002, p. B7.

67. City of San Diego, *City of San Diego Water Reuse Study* (San Diego: City of San Diego, March 2006). The $700 million estimate assumes that the city can acquire twenty-eight to thirty acres of navy land next to the Point Loma facility. Without the land, the cost of implementation increases to $1 billion. The navy has so far declined to make the land available to the city.

68. Office of the City Attorney of San Diego, *Interim Report No. 13: The Case for Proposed Adjustments to Water and Wastewater Rates in the City of San Diego* (San Diego: Office of the City Attorney, 2007).

69. Indeed, these delays cost the city an opportunity to apply for federal funding from the stimulus package to pay for the program. Angela Lau, "Wastewater to Tap Water?" *San Diego Union-Tribune*, January 23, 2009; Mike Lee, "City Didn't Seek Federal Aid for Water Project," *San Diego Union-Tribune*, July 8, 2009, p. A1. On the city's failure to comply with legal settlements regarding reclaimed water, see San Diego County Grand Jury, *Water for the City of San Diego Revisited* (San Diego: San Diego County Grand Jury, May 2007).

70. Mike Lee, "Officials Seek Third Sewage Waiver," *San Diego Union-Tribune*, November 21, 2007, p. B1.

71. Office of the City Attorney, *Interim Report No. 13*.

72. Annual figures provided by the City of San Diego, Metropolitan Wastewater Department.

73. City of San Diego, Independent Rates Oversight Committee, *Annual Report on the San Diego Water Department (SDWD) and Metropolitan Wastewater Department (MWWD) for the Fiscal Year Ended June 30, 2008* (San Diego: City of San Diego, 2008).

74. Interview with Greg Levin.

75. Interview with Greg Levin.

76. "The Case against Prop. D," *San Diego Union-Tribune*, September 12, 2010.

Chapter 5

1. Nico Calavita, Roger Caves, and Kathleen Ferrier, "The Challenges of Smart Growth: The San Diego Case," in *Revitalizing the City: Strategies to Contain Sprawl and Revive the Core*, ed. Fritz W. Wagner, Timothy E. Joder, Anthony J. Mumphrey Jr., Krishna M. Akundi, and Alan F. J. Artibise (New York: M. E. Sharpe, 2005), pp. 41–67.

2. "City of San Diego General Plan Executive Summary," March 10, 2008, p. ii.

3. Paul G. Lewis and Max Neiman, *Custodians of Place: Governing the Growth and Development of Cities* (Washington, D.C.: Georgetown University Press, 2009).

4. In late 2010, Qualcomm founder Irwin Jacobs announced an ambitious effort to divert cars from Balboa Park's Plaza de Panama. However, there has been little interest in the park's other, and arguably more serious, infrastructure needs.

5. Roger M. Showley, "It's Time to Pour Pride into a New City Hall," *San Diego Union-Tribune*, September 17, 1995, p. H1.

6. California State Controller, *Cities Annual Report, Fiscal Year 2007–08* (Sacramento: California State Controller, April 2010).

7. We exclude San Francisco from this analysis because of its unique status as both county and city. Its inclusion would only skew the numbers further.

8. John Nolen, *San Diego: A Comprehensive Plan for Its Improvement* (Boston: Geo. H. Ellis Co. Printers, 1908).

9. Nico Calavita, "Growth Machines and Ballot Box Planning: The San Diego Case," *Journal of Urban Affairs* 14:1 (March 1992), pp. 1–24.

10. City Council of San Diego, "Strategic Framework Element," Res. R-297230, adopted October 22, 2002.

11. Randi F. Coopersmith, Richard L. Miller, and Christopher J. Morrow, "Growth Management in the City of San Diego: Planning the Future Now," *Journal of Urban Planning and Development* 119:3 (September 1993), pp. 116–24.

12. Coopersmith et al., "Growth Management in the City of San Diego."

13. Calavita et al., "The Challenges of Smart Growth."

14. The city did not adopt a development-impact fee program for public facilities in urbanized communities until 1987.

15. Gail Goldberg, "Strategic Framework Element Program," City Manager's Report, No. 02-200, September 18, 2002; City of San Diego, "General Plan Monitoring Report," July 2004; interview with former City Council President Scott Peters, 2009.

16. While the city estimated that 10 percent of all trips within villages would be made using transit, walking, or biking, an environmental impact analysis concluded that the plan would do little to ease traffic.

17. Roger M. Showley, "'City of Villages' on Tap: Council Set to Debate Renewal of San Diego," *San Diego Union-Tribune*, September 22, 2002, p. B1.

18. Lori Weisberg and Susan Gembrowski, "Planners Say It Takes Villages to Grow a City," *San Diego Union-Tribune*, January 6, 2002, p. B1.

19. Lori Weisberg, "'City of Villages' Heads toward Future," *San Diego Union-Tribune*, January 30, 2004, p. B2.

20. Lisa Ross, "Murphy's City of Villages: A Never-Never Land Kind of Idea," *San Diego Union-Tribune*, January 10, 2002, p. B11.

21. Community Planners Committee, Resolution No. 08-2002, adopted June 25, 2002.

22. Goldberg, "Strategic Framework Element Program"; City Council of San Diego, "Strategic Framework Element," Resolution R-297230.

23. Lori Weisberg, "Increased Densities Out of the City of Villages Plan," *San Diego Union-Tribune*, October 23, 2002, p. B1.

24. Roger M. Showley, "Pilot Error: Turbulence Ahead for City of Villages," *San Diego Union-Tribune*, May 4, 2003, p. I1.

25. Kelly Bennett, "Taking Years to Raise a Village," *Voiceofsandiego .org*, September 17, 2007.

26. Interview with former Director of Community and Economic Development Hank Cunningham, 2010.

27. Evan McLaughlin, "In Otay Mesa, Builders Push Hard to Convert Land," *Voiceofsandiego.org*, February 20, 2007.

28. Martin Stolz, "Community Plan Update Still on Hold," *San Diego Union-Tribune*, December 5, 2005.

29. Roger M. Showley, "Competing Architects Detail Strategies for Library," *San Diego Union-Tribune*, June 23, 1996, p. B3.

30. Neil Morgan, "Best Chance to End Feuds over Library Is Regional," *San Diego Union-Tribune*, December 13, 1998, p. A3.

31. Roger M. Showley, "Local Libraries Loved, New Tax Is Not, Poll Says," *San Diego Union-Tribune*, February 23, 1996, p. B1.

32. Pat Flynn and Steven Schmidt, "Mayor Calls for Charter Convention, New Library," *San Diego Union*, January 15, 1991, p. A1.

33. Roger M. Showley, "Library Bond Plan Focuses on Branches," *San Diego Union-Tribune*, September 19, 1995, p. B1.

34. Roger M. Showley, "Props. A, C Would Help Branch Libraries," *San Diego Union-Tribune*, October 18, 1996, p. B6; Samuel Autman, "Proposition L Loses," *San Diego Union-Tribune*, March 3, 1999, p. A1.

35. Roger M. Showley, "Idea of Domed Library Applauded, but Cost May Be Out of Reach," *San Diego Union-Tribune*, November 23, 1997, p. B3.

36. Roger M. Showley, "Library in Area of Ballpark Suggested," *San Diego Union-Tribune*, October 9, 1998, p. A1.

37. Roger M. Showley, "Board Wants New Library North of Rail Depot," *San Diego Union-Tribune*, April 10, 1999, p. B1; Don Bauder, "A Library Near a Ballpark? Let's Balk at That Squeeze Play," *San Diego Union-Tribune*, May 13, 1999, p. C1.

38. Anna Tatár, "Library Department Facility Improvements," City Manager's Report, No. 02-159, July 10, 2002; "Expanding San Diego's Library System," *San Diego Union-Tribune*, July 28, 2002, p. G4.

39. Bruce Herring, "Library System Improvements Program," City Manager's Report, No. 02-264, November 8, 2002.

40. Ray Huard, "Council OKs Library Financing Proposal," *San Diego Union-Tribune*, November 19, 2002, p. B1; Helen Gao, "Library Budget Fails to Meet Goals," *San Diego Union Tribune*, July 27, 2009.

41. Scott Lewis, "In Mel and Judith We Trust," *Voiceofsandiego.org*, July 2, 2010.

42. Roger M. Showley, "It's Time to Pour Pride into a New City Hall," *San Diego Union-Tribune*, September 17, 1995, p. H1.

43. Roger M. Showley, "A New City Hall Again?" *San Diego Union*, September 4, 1988, p. F1.

44. Showley, "A New City Hall Again?"

45. Sharon L. Jones, "Panel Reaffirms Its Choice of Site for a City Complex," *San Diego Tribune*, April 12, 1991, p. B11.

46. Robert Lichter and Wayne Raffesberger, "Spruce Up City Hall, Don't Move It," *San Diego Union-Tribune*, August 22, 1991, p. B13.

47. Ray Huard, "San Diego OKs Air System Upgrade," *San Diego Union-Tribune*, June 6, 2001, p. B2.

48. Matthew T. Hall, "Sanders' Hall Plan Is Grist for Critics," *San Diego Union-Tribune*, January 15, 2007, p. B1.

49. Although a second firm had initially expressed interest, it declined to submit a bid for the project.

50. Jeanette Steele and Brooke Williams, "Questions Raised on Hired PR for New City Hall," *San Diego Union-Tribune*, May 17, 2009, p. A1.

51. R. B. Brenner, "Convention Center Pact Is Awarded," *San Diego Union*, March 4, 1987, p. A1.

52. Although just fifty thousand square feet larger than the old center, the new convention center was a significant upgrade over the old center in that the exhibition and meetings spaces were consolidated in a single structure designed to handle modern convention meetings.

53. Ken Hudson, "Convention Center Size Cut by 20%," *San Diego Union*, January 25, 1984, p. A1.

54. Alison DaRosa, "Convention Center Plans Shaken," *San Diego Tribune*, January 25, 1984, p. A1.

55. James Richardson, "Chamber, Mayor Differ with FPPC," *San Diego Union*, October 25, 1984, p. B1. Hedgecock was not convicted on any of the charges related to the convention center project.

56. Sanford R. Goodkin, "Convention Center: Reflection of San Diego's Spirit," *San Diego Union*, December 1, 1989, p. F2.

57. Mark Arner and Pat Flynn, "Port Rejects City Request for $4.5 Million," *San Diego Union-Tribune*, June 23, 1993, p. B1.

58. Dana Wilkie, "Barely Open, Center in Line for Expansion?" *San Diego Tribune*, December 5, 1989, p. B1; Frank Green, "Golding to Push Addition to Center," *San Diego Union-Tribune*, January 30, 1993, p. C1.

59. In fact, the GOP chose Texas as the site for its convention in large part for political reasons. Democrat Ann Richards had just won the gubernatorial election there, and the party hoped to use the convention to shore up political support in the state.

60. Dana Wilkie, "Convention Center Board Plans to Study Expansion," *San Diego Tribune*, January 21, 1991, p. B1; Mark Arner, "Port District to Help Expand Convention Center," *San Diego Union-Tribune*, April 27, 1994, p. B1.

61. Green, "Golding to Push Addition to Center"; Mark Arner, "Council to Tackle Finance Question," *San Diego Union-Tribune*, February 19, 1996, p. B1.

62. Philip J. LaVelle, "Backers Outspend Foes on Convention Center Expansion Measure," *San Diego Union-Tribune*, May 23, 1998, p. B1.

63. Jeanette Steele, "Convention Center Plan Puts Bayfront at Forefront," *San Diego Union-Tribune*, September 24, 2008, p. C1.

64. Heywood Sanders, "Space Available: The Realities of Convention Centers as Economic Development Strategy," Brookings Institution Research Brief, January 2005.

65. Center for City Parks Excellence, *Keeping Balboa Park Magnificent in Its Second Century: A Look at Management, Fundraising, and Private Partnerships at Five Other Major U.S. City Parks* (Washington, D.C.: Trust for Public Land, April 2006).

66. Balboa Park's East Mesa had served as the site of the city's old landfill.

67. Center for City Parks Excellence, *The Soul of San Diego: Keeping Balboa Park Magnificent in Its Second Century* (Washington, D.C.: Trust for Public Land, January 2008).

68. Center for City Parks Excellence, *Keeping Balboa Park Magnificent.*

69. San Diego Balboa Park Committee, "The Future of Balboa Park: Funding, Management and Governance," Final Report to the Mayor and City Council, December 18, 2008.

70. Center for City Parks Excellence, *The Soul of San Diego.*

71. Center for City Parks Excellence, *The Soul of San Diego.*

72. Jeanette Steele, "City Moves Forward on Fundraising Panel," *San Diego Union-Tribune*, October 12, 2009, p. B1.

73. San Diego Balboa Park Committee, "The Future of Balboa Park."

74. San Diego Balboa Park Committee, "The Future of Balboa Park."

75. Richard Hogan, *The Failure of Planning: Permitting Sprawl in San Diego Suburbs, 1990–1999* (Columbus: Ohio State University Press, 2003), p. xiv.

76. There is debate in the planning literature about whether planning should be a process-oriented enterprise—planners as umpires who call balls and strikes while stakeholder groups hash out a consensus about their vision—or outcome oriented, with planners acting as "trustees" who, independently, seek to maximize the long-term welfare of the city. See Susan S. Fainstein, "New Directions in Planning Theory," *Urban Affairs Review* 35:4 (March 2000), pp. 451–78. Although we lean toward the latter view, it suffices to say that San Diego's planning regime has produced neither a fair process nor defensible outcomes.

77. Lori Weisberg, "City Names New Boss of Troubled Division," *San Diego Union-Tribune*, May 29, 1992, p. B1.

78. Interview with political consultant Larry Remer, 2009.

Chapter 6

Portions of an earlier version of this chapter appeared in "Redevelopment, San Diego Style: The Limits of Public-Private Partnerships," *Urban Affairs Review* 45:5 (May 2010), pp. 644–78, doi: 10.1177/1078087409359760.

1. Interview with former San Diego City Councilman Bruce Henderson, 2007.

2. See Lynne B. Sagalyn, "Public/Private Development," *Journal of the American Planning Association* 75:1 (March 2007), pp. 7–22; Bernard J. Frieden and Lynne B. Sagalyn, *Downtown Inc.: How America Rebuilds Cities* (Cambridge: Massachusetts Institute of Technology Press, 1989).

3. For a positive spin on such partnerships, see National Council for Public-Private Partnerships, *For the Good of the People: Using Public/Private Partnerships to Meet America's Essential Needs* (Washington, D.C.: National Council for Public-Private Partnerships, 2002); Jon Pierre, ed., *Debating Governance: Authority, Steering, and Democracy* (Oxford: Oxford University Press, 2002); Pauline Vaillancourt Rosenau, ed., *Public-Private Policy Partnerships* (Cambridge: Massachusetts Institute of Technology Press, 2000). A less flattering view is provided by Louise Jezierski, "Neighborhoods and Public-Private Partnerships in Pittsburgh," *Urban Affairs Quarterly* 26:2 (December 1990), pp. 217–40. Also see Jon Pierre, ed., *Partnerships in Urban Governance: European and American Experience* (New York: St. Martin's Press, 1998).

4. Public-private partnerships set up a classic principal-agent relationship whereby a local government entity (the principal) delegates resources and authority to one or more nonpublic organizations (agents). Because of diverging preferences and the often superior information possessed by agents but denied to the principal, these relationships risk agency loss—the extent to which the agent's activities depart from the principal's objectives. See Gary J. Miller, "The Political Evolution of Principal-Agent Models," *Annual Review of Political Science* 8 (2005), pp. 203–25.

5. Other redevelopment efforts deserve mention. In the once-blighted midcity area, City Heights, a public-private partnership between the city and the Price Foundation, has yielded substantial public benefits, including affordable housing, schools, libraries, and parks. Absent a public-spirited philanthropist such as the Price Foundation, the City Heights model is difficult to replicate. Little Italy, a once-decaying small-business district adjacent to downtown, has also been cited as a redevelopment model. However, Little Italy's commercial and residential revitalization can be attributed at least as much to the role of local special assessments—including the creation of business improvement and community benefit districts—as to city-sponsored efforts.

6. Michael Jenkins and Norma Damashek, "Redevelopment, San Diego Style," *San Diego Union-Tribune*, October 12, 2007.

7. Currently, redevelopment staff consists of approximately twenty-eight employees of the Redevelopment Division of the Department of Community Planning and Investment. The division's budget for the 2007–08 fiscal year was $86.9 million—funded by the redevelopment agency. San Diego County Grand Jury, *CCDC: What Does It Develop and with Whose Money?* (San Diego: County of San Diego, 2008).

8. The SEDC is staffed by approximately fifteen individuals who are not city employees. The SEDC's budget for the 2007–08 fiscal year was $32.5 million—funded by the redevelopment agency. The CCDC currently has a staff of

fifty-five individuals who are not city employees; its budget for the 2007–08 fiscal year was $217.5 million—also funded by the redevelopment agency. San Diego County Grand Jury, *CCDC: What Does It Develop and with Whose Money?*

9. The workings of tax increment financing can be illustrated using the example of the downtown Gaslamp Quarter: "The Gaslamp Quarter was established as a project area in 1982, which also was established as the base year for assessed values of all parcels in that area. For example, a parcel was assessed at $100,000 in 1982. Its property tax would be approximately 1% or $1,000 of which 17.7% or about $177 would accrue to the general fund of the City of San Diego. After the same parcel was redeveloped in 2002, it might be reassessed at a value of $1 million, an increase of $900,000. The gross tax increment of 1% or $9,000 would accrue to the Redevelopment Agency while the City's general fund would still be allocated the tax on the parcel's 1982 value, adjusted for inflation at no more than 2% annually. The Redevelopment Agency could continue to collect the tax increment for the balance of the fifty-year period dating from the inception of the project area." San Diego County Grand Jury, *CCDC: What Does It Develop and with Whose Money?*, p. 5.

10. Andrew Donohue, "SD Unique in Redevelopment," *Voiceofsan diego.org*, August 12, 2008.

11. On Los Angeles, see Mara Marks, "Shifting Ground: The Rise and Fall of the Los Angeles Community Redevelopment Agency," *Southern California Quarterly* 86:3 (Fall 2004), pp. 241–90. On San Francisco, see John H. Mollenkopf, *The Contested City* (Princeton, N.J.: Princeton University Press, 1983); Richard DeLeon, *Left Coast City: Progressive Politics in San Francisco, 1973–1991* (Lawrence: University Press of Kansas, 1992).

12. However, the newly elected governor Jerry Brown soon proposed dissolving local government redevelopment agencies, putting the future of CCDC—and the new Chargers stadium—in doubt.

13. Andrew Donohue, "Terms Expired, Board Members Remain for Years," *Voiceofsandiego.org*, December 20, 2006.

14. San Diego County Grand Jury, *CCDC: What Does It Develop and with Whose Money?*

15. San Diego County Grand Jury, *Redevelopment in the City of San Diego—A Call for Transparency* (San Diego: County of San Diego, 2009).

16. Tim McCain, "John Moores Solos on Petco Park's First Anniversary," *San Diego Magazine* (April 2005).

17. The $1 billion estimate comes from the City of San Diego. In 2007, CCDC estimated that private investment in the area totaled $3.99 billion, although it is unclear how much of the funds can be directly attributed to the ballpark project. Jeanette Steele, "Ballpark, as Catalyst, Is Batting .500," *San Diego*

Union-Tribune, April 6, 2009; Centre City Development Corporation, *Ballpark Scorecard: More Than a Ballpark* (San Diego: CCDC, 2007).

18. The limited capacity of stadium projects as economic catalysts has been amply demonstrated by Roger G. Noll and Andrew Zimbalist, eds., *Sports, Jobs, and Taxes: The Economic Impact of Sports Teams and Stadiums* (Washington, D.C.: Brookings Institution, 1997).

19. Tim Chapin, "Beyond the Entrepreneurial City: Municipal Capitalism in San Diego," *Journal of Urban Affairs* 24:5 (Winter 2002), pp. 565–81.

20. The city made up the difference by selling the naming rights of the stadium to the local telecommunications giant Qualcomm.

21. The city council adopted the agreement ten minutes after it was presented on the basis of assurances from the City Manager Jack McGrory that the guarantee was worth no more than $10 million. When attendance dropped in the late 1990s, the ticket guarantee began to eat up much of the rent the city received. See Gerry Braun, "The Smooth Operator: Jack McGrory Led City Hall before the Storm Hit—Did He Lead It into Trouble?" *San Diego Union-Tribune*, December 18, 2005, p. A1; interview with Bruce Henderson.

22. Interview with Pat Shea, former chair, Task Force on Ballpark Planning, 2007.

23. See Task Force on Ballpark Planning, "Report of the City of San Diego Task Force on Ballpark Planning," 1998.

24. Transient-occupancy taxes are applied to individuals occupying rooms in a hotel, inn, house, motel, or other lodging for a short period of time (usually thirty days or less).

25. Such naming rights agreements are not uncommon among recent stadium projects. However, as Table 6.2 indicates, the City of San Diego was already contributing far more in absolute dollars than other cities were. Thus, allowing the Padres to keep all revenue from the sale of the naming rights added to an already-large public subsidy.

26. "Memorandum of Understanding between the City of San Diego, the Redevelopment Agency of the City of San Diego, the Centre City Development Corporation, and Padres L.P. concerning a Ballpark District, Construction of a Baseball Park, and a Redevelopment Project," 1998, http://www.sandiego.gov/petcopark/.

27. In 1999, these and other accusations were the subject of a grand jury investigation. The final report accused the mayor of colluding with other city officials to influence the vote outcome. See Philip J. LaVelle, "Grand Jury Rips Golding over Efforts for Ballpark," *San Diego Union-Tribune*, June 5, 1999, p. B1.

28. San Diego County Grand Jury, "Standards of Disclosure Re: Ballpark Financing Project," Interim Report No. 2 to San Diego City Council, 1998.

29. Interview with Scott Barnett, former executive director, San Diego County Taxpayers Association, 2007.

30. The city eventually forced the team to abandon one of the three high-rises and ultimately paid the team $4 million to expand the park to cover two acres.

31. Lori Weisberg, "Padres Unveil Details about Development," *San Diego Union-Tribune*, March 13, 1999, p. B1.

32. Philip J. LaVelle, "Padres Avoid Tough Financial Questions in PR Campaign," *San Diego Union-Tribune*, January 10, 2000, p. B1.

33. See Office of the City Manager, "Offering Document, Continuing Disclosure Agreement, Contract of Purchase and Certain Other Actions in Connection with the City's Ballpark and Redevelopment Project," Report No. 01-239, November 14, 2001.

34. Martin Stolz, "Critics Take Swing at JMI's Pitch for Ballpark Village," *San Diego Union-Tribune*, May 31, 2005, p. B1.

35. Martin Stolz, "Panel Calls Ballpark Village Deal Presentation Misleading," *San Diego Union-Tribune*, October 2, 2005, p. B7.

36. In 2007, JMI Realty attempted to renege on the project labor agreement it signed with affordable housing, labor, and community organizations downtown. After promising to build some affordable units alongside condominiums and retail space on the site, the team circulated plans for a mammoth convention hotel instead. The project was abandoned in 2008, a casualty of turbulence in the financial markets and a conflict-of-interest scandal at CCDC.

37. Interview with Scott Barnett.

38. David Karjanen, *Priced Out: An Analysis of Housing in Downtown San Diego* (San Diego: Center on Policy Initiatives, 2005).

39. Office of the City Auditor, *Performance Audit of the Centre City Development Corporation* (San Diego: City of San Diego, 2009).

40. Centre City Development Corporation, *Ballpark Scorecard*.

41. Since the ballpark opened, the terms of the MOU have ensured that the city's share of the operating expenses have risen every year, whereas the team's has fallen. See Jeanette Steele, "Ballpark, as Catalyst, Is Batting .500."

42. Dan Hayes, "Moorad Closer to Full Owner," *North County Times*, March 24, 2010. Moores originally bought the team for $80 million in 1994.

43. City of San Diego, *2011–2015 Five-Year Financial Outlook* (San Diego: City of San Diego, 2009).

44. Ann Jarmusch, "Triple Ploy; Manchester Holds Cards in Trio of Waterfront Developments," *San Diego Union-Tribune*, July 23, 2006, p. I1.

45. Interview with Michael Stepner, former City of San Diego acting planning director and city architect, 2007.

46. Interview with Wayne Raffesberger, former member, NTC Reuse Committee, and vice chair, Citizens' NTC Oversight Committee, 2009.

47. Interview with Wayne Raffesberger.

48. Ronald W. Powell, "Deciding Best Uses for NTC a Challenge," *San Diego Union-Tribune*, August 5, 1996, p. B1; "What's NTC Coming To? A New City or the Old?" *San Diego Union-Tribune*, July 28, 1998, p. A3.

49. The reuse committee originally recommended that Lennar Corporation, a national builder, be given the job, but the mayor and city council overruled the recommendation.

50. Ronald W. Powell, "Nothing Is Simple in Deal for NTC; Who Pays, Who Benefits Remains Contentious," *San Diego Union-Tribune*, July 22, 2001, p. B1; Ronald W. Powell, "Much of NTC Has Changed in Past Years," *San Diego Union-Tribune*, December 5, 2004, p. B7.

51. Tadlock Cowan and Baird Webel, "Military Base Closures: Socioeconomic Impacts," Congressional Research Service, Report for Congress, 2005.

52. Interview with Hank Cunningham, former City of San Diego director of community and economic development, 2009.

53. Ronald W. Powell, "The Old NTC Is Officially Liberty Station Now; Protesters Shout at Groundbreaking," *San Diego Union-Tribune*, February 27, 2001, p. B1.

54. Interview with Wayne Raffesberger.

55. Preston Turegano, "Buy a Brick, Help Restore NTC Buildings," *San Diego Union-Tribune*, June 27, 2004, p. F8; Roger M. Showley, "Next Port: Liberty Station," *San Diego Union-Tribune*, September 8, 2002; Ronald W. Powell, "Aguirre Questions Low-Income Status; Group Faces Challenge as It Seeks Funds for Naval Training Center Renovation," *San Diego Union-Tribune*, November 20, 2005, p. B1.

56. Powell, "Much of NTC Has Changed in Past Years"; Ronald W. Powell, "Developer Faces Opposition in Getting 30-Month Hotel Extension," *San Diego Union-Tribune*, May 19, 2003, p. B3; Ronald W. Powell, "Fast Track for Waterfront Park Plan; Council Approves Selling of Bonds," *San Diego Union-Tribune*, May 25, 2005, p. B2; Ray Huard, "Council, McMillin Deadlock over NTC Project; Dispute Centers on Maintenance Fees," *San Diego Union-Tribune*, May 7, 2003, p. B3.

57. Neil Morgan, "Corkytown," *Voiceofsandiego.org*, March 28, 2005.

58. Brooke Williams, Agustin Armendariz, and Maureen Magee, "Boom for McMillin, Bust for City," *San Diego Union-Tribune*, March 3, 2007, p. A1; Brooke Williams, Agustin Armendariz, and Maureen Magee, "Million-Dollar

Middle America?" *San Diego Union-Tribune*, March 4, 2007, p. A1; interview with Michael Stepner.

59. Evan McLaughlin, "All Crosshairs, No Bullets," *Voiceofsandiego .org*, August 11, 2006; Mike Freeman, "High-Rises to Anchor Navy Project; Hotel and Office Tower Planned by Manchester," *San Diego Union-Tribune*, April 4, 2006, p. C1; James B. Kelleher, "He Covers the Waterfront," *San Diego Magazine* (September 1999); Martin Stolz, "Navy's Secrecy about Development Criticized," *San Diego Union-Tribune*, March 12, 2006, p. B1; Lawrence A. Herzog, "The Future of San Diego; Can Naval Planning Become Urban Planning?" *San Diego Union-Tribune*, April 12, 2006, p. B7.

60. Freeman, "High-Rises to Anchor Navy Project"; Ann Jarmusch, "Bay-Front Plans Awash with Ideas, Possibilities; Proposal Could Use Major Tweaking," *San Diego Union-Tribune*, September 18, 2006, p. D1; Mike Freeman, "Officials Criticize Bayfront Revisions," *San Diego Union Tribune*, May 25, 2006, p. A1.

61. Freeman, "Officials Criticize Bayfront Revisions"; "Think Greatness; City's Front Porch Should Maximize Vision," *San Diego Union-Tribune*, April 16, 2006, p. G2; Dani Dodge, "Parkland Agreement Is Reached Downtown," *San Diego Union-Tribune*, December 20, 2006, p. B1.

62. Eric Wolff, "Court Rules against Navy on Navy Broadway Complex Case, Demands More Public Hearings," *San Diego CityBeat*, June 26, 2008.

63. The North Embarcadero Visionary Plan is a joint effort by the Port of San Diego, the Centre City Development Corporation, and the City of San Diego to redevelop parts of San Diego's downtown waterfront.

64. Wolff, "Court Rules against Navy on Navy Broadway Complex Case."

65. Quoted in David C. Perry, "Urban Tourism and Privatizing Discourses of Public Infrastructure," in *The Infrastructure of Play: Building the Tourist City*, ed. Dennis R. Judd (New York: M. E. Sharpe, 2002), p. 27.

66. California Health and Safety Code § 33071.

67. An independent performance audit, commissioned by the city, noted: "There appears to be little disagreement that CCDC has met and often exceeded expectations related to facilitating infrastructure improvements. . . . However, it does not appear that CCDC has promoted economic development or social service delivery to the extent that CCDC's peers have—this represents one of the most cited concerns by community stakeholders groups, which at times expressed criticisms that CCDC is primarily oriented to facilitate development and thus caters to developers" (pp. 18–19). Office of the City Auditor, *Performance Audit of the Centre City Development Corporation* (San Diego: City of San Diego, 2009).

68. As of June 2010, CCDC had spent all but $350 million of the $2.9 billion in tax increment funds authorized by a cap set in 1992. Funding a new downtown stadium for the Chargers would likely take CCDC above the cap. The agency initially considered asking the city council to raise its cap, which would divert even more money from the city's General Fund to downtown redevelopment. However, Fletcher's legislation circumvented the city council and changed state redevelopment law to eliminate the cap.

69. Matthew T. Hall and Roger Showley, "Ending Redevelopment Would Hit 16 Local Cities," *San Diego Union-Tribune*, January 21, 2011.

Chapter 7

1. Neal R. Peirce, "Taking a Look at North America's Binational Citistate," *New Orleans Times-Picayune*, May 26, 1997, p. B7.

2. For a general discussion of metropolitan governance arrangements and public goods and service provision, see Vincent Ostrom, Charles M. Tiebout, and Robert Warren, "The Organization of Government in Metropolitan Areas: A Theoretical Inquiry," *American Political Science Review* 55:4 (1961), pp. 831–42.

3. Steven P. Erie, *Globalizing L.A.: Trade, Infrastructure, and Regional Development* (Stanford, Calif.: Stanford University Press, 2004).

4. However, the consolidation only provided a new chief to oversee the authority and no new equipment or firefighters.

5. Steven P. Erie, *Toward a Trade Infrastructure Strategy for the San Diego-Tijuana Region* (San Diego: San Diego Dialogue, 1999); Carolyn Chase, "Plan before Power," *Earth Times*, October 2002.

6. On the deficiencies in San Diego County's social safety net, see Kelly Bennett and Dagny Salas, "San Diego's Safety Net: Riddled with Gaps," *Voiceofsandiego.org*, January 31, 2010; Kelly Bennett and Dagny Salas, "County Government Resents Bearing Safety Net's Burden," *Voiceofsandiego.org*, February 1, 2010.

7. Anne Evans, "1998 Was a Good Year for San Diego," *San Diego Union-Tribune*, December 30, 1998.

8. Erie, *Globalizing L.A.*, pp. 13, 226; Erie, *Toward a Trade Infrastructure Strategy*.

9. Steven P. Erie and Charles Nathanson, *The Challenges of Developing the Cross-Border Region's Trade Infrastructure* (San Diego: San Diego Dialogue, May 2000).

10. Robert J. Hawkins, "Airport Solution: High-Speed Rail?" *San Diego Union-Tribune*, January 30, 2011, p. B1.

11. Emilia Istrate, Jonathan Rothwell, and Bruce Katz, *Export Nation: How U.S. Metros Lead National Export Growth and Boost Competitiveness* (Washington, D.C.: Brookings Institution, July 2010), appendix B, p. 32; Dean Calbreath, "County Missing Out on Important Exports," *San Diego Union-Tribune*, July 27, 2010, p. C1.

12. Richard Feinberg, with Gretchen Schuck, *San Diego, Baja California and Globalization: Coming from Behind* (Los Angeles: Pacific Council on International Policy, October 2001); San Diego Dialogue Forum *Fronterizo, the Global Engagement of San Diego/Baja California: Final Report* (San Diego: San Diego Dialogue, November 2000).

13. See Steven Erie, "At Competitive Disadvantage: San Diego's Infrastructure," *Metro Investment Report* 2:11 (April 1995), pp. 1, 12, 13; Janine Zuniga, "National City's Ship Finally Comes In," *San Diego Union-Tribune*, July 19, 2010, p. A1.

14. Erie and Nathanson, *The Challenges of Developing the Cross-Border Region's Trade Infrastructure.*

15. Erie, *Toward a Trade Infrastructure Strategy.*

16. Ronald W. Powell, "S.D. Easing Cargo Backup; Ships Are Unloading Here to Avoid Long Beach Wait," *San Diego Union-Tribune*, October 29, 2004, p. C1.

17. Erie, *Toward a Trade Infrastructure Strategy.*

18. Erie, *Toward a Trade Infrastructure Strategy.*

19. Diane Lindquist, "NAFTA Rail Network Is Sought for Region," *San Diego Union-Tribune*, February 23, 1996, p. C2; Matthew T. Hall, "Deal Reached to Repair, Run Rail Link; Train Service to Imperial County Could Be Resumed within Two Years," *San Diego Union-Tribune*, May 10, 2002, p. B1.

20. David L. Birch, "The Q Factor," *National Civic Review* 76:4 (July–August 1987).

21. Erie, *Toward a Trade Infrastructure Strategy.*

22. Erie, *Toward a Trade Infrastructure Strategy*, p. 18.

23. Jeff McDonald and David Hasemyer, "Runway Paved with Neglect: Brown Field Has Deteriorated under San Diego's Ownership, and Mistakes Have Been Costly," *San Diego Union-Tribune*, September 25, 2005, p. A1.

24. Erie, *Toward a Trade Infrastructure Strategy.*

25. Lawrence A. Herzog, *Global Crossroads: Planning and Infrastructure for the California-Baja California Border Region* (San Diego: Trans-Border Institute/University Readers, 2009).

26. James Gerber, "Developing the U.S.-Mexico Border Region for a Prosperous and Secure Relationship: Human and Physical Infrastructure along

the U.S. Border with Mexico," Binational Research Paper (Houston, Tex.: James A. Baker III Institute for Public Policy, 2009), p. 22.

27. Pat Shea, "Put a New Airport in the Desert," *Voiceofsandiego.org*, March 20, 2006.

28. See Steven Erie, "San Diego Rejects Proposal for New Airport, Faces Few Options to Ease Burden on Lindbergh," *Metro Investment Report* 14:3 (December–January 2006–07), pp. 21–22.

29. Jeff Ristine, "Turbulent Fight Expected over Airport Site: Miramar Measure to Appear on Ballot," *San Diego Union-Tribune*, June 6, 2006.

30. Rob Davis, "Business Leaders Try to Tweak Miramar Proposal," *Voiceofsandiego.org*, July 11, 2006; Ristine, "Turbulent Fight Expected over Airport Site."

31. Alliance in Support of Airport Progress in the 21st Century (ASAP21), "Eight Reasons Why San Diego County Needs a Bigger Airport," http://www.asap21.net/index.php.

32. Richard Carson, "Overlooking the Lindbergh Option," *San Diego Union-Tribune*, September 7, 2006; Rob Davis, "Airport Supporters Take Aim at 'That Budding Rockstar,'" *Voiceofsandiego.org*, August 24, 2006.

33. Jeff Ristine, "Joint Airport on a Base Will Not Fly, Military Says," *San Diego Union-Tribune*, March 16, 2006; Andrew Donohue and Rob Davis, "Sanders Neutral in Airport War," *Voiceofsandiego.org*, May 25, 2006; Rob Davis, "Economics: It's Miramar," *Voiceofsandiego.org*, September 8, 2006.

34. Jeff Ristine, "Chamber Group's Board Votes to Support Miramar Airport Plan," *San Diego Union-Tribune*, July 27, 2006.

35. Evan McLaughlin and Daniel Strumpf, "San Diego Wrestles with Military Past as It Looks to Future," *Voiceofsandiego.org*, September 26, 2006.

36. Jeff Ristine, "Is Prop. A Last Word on Site for Airport? Despite 'Advisory' Label, Voters Treating It That Way," *San Diego Union-Tribune*, October 15, 2006; Jim Panknin, "The Region Can Use Lindbergh," *Voiceofsandiego.org*, April 7, 2006.

37. Rob Davis, "Lindbergh: Is the Wolf Here?" *Voiceofsandiego.org*, October 23, 2006.

38. Anonymous San Diego water official, in private correspondence with authors, 2005.

39. Steven P. Erie, *Beyond 'Chinatown': The Metropolitan Water District, Growth, and the Environment in Southern California* (Stanford, Calif.: Stanford University Press, 2006).

40. The Water Authority now comprises twenty-four member agencies, including the City of San Diego.

41. On the early history of San Diego water development, see Theodore Andrew Strathman, "'Dream of a Big City': Water Politics and San Diego County Growth, 1910–1947" (Ph.D. diss., University of California, San Diego, 2005).

42. Approved by the state's voters in a 1960 bond measure, the State Water Project (SWP) is the world's largest publicly built and operated water and power development and conveyance system. Consisting of the California Aqueduct, as well as dams and reservoirs, the SWP provides Northern California water for agricultural use in the San Joaquin Valley and for urban use in Southern California.

43. Because of an early filing for a large water claim, the Imperial Irrigation District has claims to roughly three-quarters of California's yearly allotment of 4.4 million acre-feet of Colorado River water.

44. Erie, *Beyond 'Chinatown'*, pp. 97–132.

45. An acre-foot is equivalent to 326,000 gallons of water, which with conservation meets the yearly needs of two average families of four individuals.

46. Michael Burge and Michael Gardner, "County Water Board to Sue Wholesaler, *San Diego Union-Tribune*, June 11, 2010, p. B3.

47. Mike Lee, "San Diego Subsidizing Rates for Other Areas, Local Agency Says," *San Diego Union-Tribune*, September 17, 2010.

48. On L.A.'s large historical subsidy of San Diego water provision, see Steven P. Erie, Greg Freeman, and Pascale Joassart-Marcelli, "W(h)ither Sprawl? Have Southern California Water Policies Subsidized Suburban Development?" in *Up against the Sprawl? Public Policy and the Making of Southern California*, ed. Jennifer Wolch, Manuel Pastor Jr., and Peter Dreier (Minneapolis: University of Minnesota Press, 2004), pp. 45–70.

49. Mike Lee, "Sanders against Sending Treated Wastewater to Tap," *San Diego Union-Tribune*, July 20, 2006, p. A1; "Yuck! San Diego Should Flush 'Toilet to Tap' Plan," *San Diego Union-Tribune*, July 24, 2006, p. B6; Mike Lee and Jennifer Vigil, "Council Beats Veto on Water Recycling," *San Diego Union-Tribune*, December 4, 2007, p. A1.

50. Michael Gardner, "Water Source for S.D. Region Put in Jeopardy," *San Diego Union-Tribune*, January 15, 2010, p. A1.

51. "MWD: Arrogance Is in Water Giant's DNA," *San Diego Union-Tribune*, September 30, 2010, p. B6.

52. Anonymous MWD board director, in personal correspondence with authors, September 2010.

53. San Diego Local Agency Formation Commission (LAFCO), "Fire Protection and Emergency Service Review," February 7, 2005.

54. San Diego LAFCO, "Fire Protection and Emergency Service Review"; Gary L. Pryor, "Conceptual Reorganization of San Diego County Fire Services," January 22, 2007.

55. San Diego LAFCO, "Fire Protection and Emergency Service Review."

56. W. Erik Bruvold, "Investments in Fire and EMS in San Diego, Los Angeles, and Orange Counties: An Update," National University System Institute for Policy Research, September 1, 2010.

57. Jeff Bowman and W. Erik Bruvold, "San Diego County Falls Further Behind: An Update on Fire Protection Investment in Southern California and an Analysis of Recommendations Made in Response to 2003 and 2007 Wildfires," National University System Institute for Policy Research, September 2009.

58. San Diego LAFCO, "Funding Fire Protection: An Overview of Funding Issues Facing Fire Protection Districts," November 2003.

59. *San Diego Union-Tribune*, "Regional Fire Plan," April 28, 2008, p. B6.

60. San Diego LAFCO, "Micro Report: Reorganization of Structural Fire Protection and Emergency Medical Services," January 31, 2007.

61. San Diego LAFCO, "Funding Fire Protection: An Overview of Funding Issues Facing Fire Protection Districts"; San Diego LAFCO, "Micro Report."

62. San Diego LAFCO, "Micro Report."

63. Michael D. Ott and Shirley Anderson, "Reorganization of Structural Fire Protection and Emergency Medical Services in Unincorporated San Diego County," San Diego LAFCO, May 7, 2007.

64. Philip J. LaVelle, "'Critical' Fire Upgrade Pleas Deleted from Chief's Report," *San Diego Union-Tribune*, November 19, 2003, p. A1.

65. Ott and Anderson, "Reorganization of Structural Fire Protection and Emergency Medical Services in Unincorporated San Diego County."

66. San Diego LAFCO, "Fire Protection and Emergency Medical Services Review."

67. San Diego LAFCO, "Fire Protection and Emergency Medical Services Review."

68. Tony Manolatos, Craig Gustafson, and Agustin Armendariz, "Fire-Prone, Tax-Wary," *San Diego Union-Tribune*, November 23, 2008, p. A1.

69. Citygate Associates, "Regional Fire Services Deployment Study for the County of San Diego Office of Emergency Services," May 5, 2010.

70. Bruvold, "Investments in Fire and EMS in San Diego, Los Angeles, and Orange Counties: An Update."

71. Lawrence A. Herzog, "Global Tijuana: Exploring Its Seven Ecologies," *TBI Bulletin* (December 4, 2003).

72. Herzog, *Global Crossroads*.

73. Lawrence A. Herzog, *Return to the Center: Culture, Public Space, and City Building in a Global Era* (Austin: University of Texas Press, 2006), p. 197.

74. Leslie Sklair, "The Maquila Industry and the Creation of a Transnational Capitalist Class in the United States-Mexico Border Region," in *Changing Boundaries in the Americas: New Perspectives on the U.S.-Mexican, Central American, and South American Borders* (San Diego: University of California, San Diego Center for U.S. Mexican Studies, 1992), pp. 69–88.

75. San Diego Dialogue, *Who Crosses the Border: A View of the San Diego/Tijuana Metropolitan Region* (San Diego: University of California, San Diego, Extended Studies and Public Programs, April 1994), p. 20; San Diego Dialogue, *The San Diego/Tijuana Binational Region* (San Diego University of California, San Diego, Extended Studies and Public Programs, 1996).

76. Diane Lindquist, "Building Good Will," *San Diego Union-Tribune*, February 16, 1997, p. I1; California Trade and Commerce Agency, "Memorandum: Major Policy Initiatives," August 30, 1997; City of San Diego, Mayor's Office, "Mayors Golding and Osuna Millan to Preside over Binational Committee Meeting," press release, February 27, 1997.

77. John Freeman, "Frontline: Go Back to Mexico!," June 7, 1994, *San Diego Union-Tribune*, p. E1; Leonel Sanchez, "Latinos Denounce U.S. Citizen Patrol," *San Diego Union-Tribune*, May 22, 1996, p. B1.

78. Diane Lindquist, "San Diego's Stake in the Debate over Immigration," *San Diego Union-Tribune*, June 15, 2006, p. C1.

79. In 2005, when Los Angeles Mayor Antonio Villaraigosa was inaugurated, Latinos also held the positions of city council president, city attorney, Los Angeles Unified School District board president, chair of the county board of supervisors, county sheriff, and chair of the Los Angeles County Metropolitan Transportation Authority.

80. See Liam Dillon, "In City Council Race, a Family Affair," *Voiceofsandiego.org*, April 13, 2010.

81. Jim Miller, "In Need of a Sea Change," *San Diego Union-Tribune*, March 16, 1997, p. I1.

82. San Diego Dialogue, *Enforcement and Facilitation: An Analysis of the San Ysidro Port of Entry and the Implementation of Gatekeeper Phase II* (San Diego: University of California, San Diego, Extended Studies and Public Programs, January 1996), p. A10; Allen Bersin, "Reinventing the U.S.-Mexico Border," *San Diego Union-Tribune*, August 25, 1996, p. G3; Peter Nicholas, "Obama Seeks Border Funds; the $600 Million Plan Would Add More Than 1,000 Agents and Two Drones," *Los Angeles Times*, June 23, 2010, p. A1.

83. Blas Nunez-Neto and Michael John Garcia, "Border Security: The San Diego Fence," Congressional Research Service, May 23, 2007; Sandra Dibble, "Tijuana Striving for Better Days," *San Diego Union-Tribune*, October 7, 2010, p. A1; Richard Marosi, "A Harsher Border Crossing; Improved Security along the U.S.-Mexico Frontier Makes for an Increasingly Difficult Journey for Older and Less-Fit Migrants," *Los Angeles Times*, August 20, 2006, p. B1.

Chapter 8

1. Interview with former mayoral candidate Pat Shea, 2007.

2. Douglas Yates, *The Ungovernable City: The Politics of Urban Problems and Policy Making* (Cambridge: Massachusetts Institute of Technology Press, 1977), p. 1 (Kennedy quote).

3. Interview with former editor of the *San Diego Union-Tribune* Bernie Jones, 2009.

4. Bruce Linder, "Rear Admiral Roger Welles—San Diego's First 'Navy Mayor,'" *Journal of San Diego History* 49:2 (Spring 2003).

5. Abraham Shragge, "Boosters and Bluejackets: The Civic Culture of Militarism in San Diego, California, 1900–1945" (Ph.D. diss., University of California, San Diego, 1998).

6. Ray Brandes, "The Politics and History of William Kettner," *Journal of San Diego History* 11:3 (June 1995).

7. Reinar M. Hof, "San Diegans, Inc.: The Formative Years, 1958–63," *Journal of San Diego History* 36:1 (Winter 1990).

8. Interview with Mike Madigan, former assistant to Mayor Pete Wilson for program and policy development, 2007.

9. Royce Hanson, Harold Wolman, David Connolly, Katherine Pearson, and Robert McManmon, "Corporate Citizenship and Urban Problem Solving: The Changing Civic Role of Business Leaders in American Cities," *Journal of Urban Affairs* 32:1 (February 2010), pp. 1–23.

10. Interview with Scott Barnett, former executive director, San Diego County Taxpayers Association, 2007.

11. Public Policy Institute of California, *PPIC Statewide Survey: Special Survey of San Diego County* (Sacramento: Public Policy Institute of California, July 2000).

12. Public Policy Institute of California, *PPIC Statewide Survey*.

13. "An Overview of Local Revenue Measures in California since 2001," *California Local Government and Finance Almanac*, March 2010, *http://www.californiacityfinance.com/LocalMeasuresSince01.pdf*.

14. Terry Nichols Clark and Lorna Crowley Ferguson, *City Money: Political Processes, Fiscal Strain, and Retrenchment* (New York: Columbia University Press, 1983).

15. Bruce Henderson was the last incumbent city council member to be defeated, losing to Valerie Stallings in District 6 in 1991. Another council member, Linda Bernhardt, was recalled in 1991 in District 5 following an acrimonious dispute over redistricting.

16. Peter Schrag, *Paradise Lost* (Berkeley: University of California Press, 1998).

17. A slightly revised measure, Proposition J, which would have increased hotel taxes for general government purposes, was also defeated in November 2004.

18. Liam Dillon and Emily Alpert, "Sales Tax Fails after Frye Won't Back It," *Voiceofsandiego.org*, July 26, 2010.

19. Melinda Nickelberry, Tom Haynes, Elaine DuVal, Jeff Kawar, Lisa Byrne, Dominika Bukalova, and Brittany Coppage, "Revenue Options for the City of San Diego," Office of the Independent Budget Analyst Report No. 10-29, March 22, 2010.

20. Fairbank, Maslin, Maulin, Metz & Associates, "City of San Diego Ballot Measure Issue Survey," June 11–15, 2010.

21. Word of the talks was apparently leaked by Republican Councilman Kevin Faulconer, who was grooming himself for a mayoral run in 2012.

22. Liam Dillon, "Under Pressure, Mayor Bows Out without a Fight," *Voiceofsandiego.org*, July 21, 2010.

23. Donna Frye and Todd Gloria, "Reform and Revenue Ballot Measure," City of San Diego memorandum, July 29, 2010.

24. Tom Haynes, "Preliminary Actions in Preparation of a Proposed Amendment to the Centre City Redevelopment Plan (Cap Increase)," Office of the Independent Budget Analyst, Report No. 10-36, April 23, 2010.

25. Tom Haynes, "Additional Analysis Regarding an Increase to CCDC Tax Increment Limit," Office of the Independent Budget Analyst, Report No. 10-54, June 18, 2010.

26. Scott Lewis, "Downtown Chargers Stadium Boosted by State Legislators," *Voiceofsandiego.org*, October 8, 2010.

27. Liam Dillon, "How the Big Redevelopment Deal Affects Prop. D," *Voiceofsandiego.org*, October 27, 2010.

28. Craig Gustafson, "Voters Roundly Reject Prop. D," *San Diego Union-Tribune*, November 2, 2010.

29. Lisa Celaya, Elaine Duval, Tom Haynes, Jeff Kawar, Jeffrey Sturak, Dominika Bukalova, Brittany Coppage, Penni Takade, and Andrea Tevlin,

"Review of Five-Year Financial Outlook and Budget Balancing Scenarios," Office of the Independent Budget Analyst, Report No. 09-2, January 15, 2009.

30. Andrea Tevlin, "Need for Comprehensive Annual User Fee Review Process as Part of the Annual Budget," Office of the Independent Budget Analyst, Report No. 08-20, February 28, 2008.

31. Janice L. Weinrick and William Anderson, "Educational Revenue Augmentation Fund Payments, Proposed Fiscal Year 2010 San Diego Redevelopment Agency Budget Amendments, Agency Debt to the City and Community Development Block Grant Proposed Repayment Terms," Redevelopment Agency, Report No. 10-11, February 17, 2010; Tom Haynes and Andrea Tevlin, "Redevelopment Agency ERAF, CDBG Repayment, and Debt to the City," Office of the Independent Budget Analyst, Report No. 10-17, February 19, 2010.

32. Office of the City Auditor, "Street Maintenance: City Needs to Improve Planning, Coordination, and Oversight to Effectively Manage Transportation Assets," Report No. 11-009, November 2010.

33. Cheiron, "San Diego City Employees' Retirement System June 30, 2009 Actuarial Valuation," July 2010; City of San Diego, "Study by the Joint Committee on Retiree Health," September 7, 2010.

34. City of San Diego, "Study by the Joint Committee on Retiree Health."

35. Until recently, the two-tier pension system covered police and general employees but not the city's firefighters. However, the firefighters' union agreed to institute a similar two-tier plan in its latest contract with the city.

36. Carol W. Lewis, "Municipal Bankruptcy and the States: Authorization to File under Chapter 9," *Urban Affairs Review* 30:7 (September 1994), pp. 3–26.

37. Michael W. McConnell and Randal C. Picker, "When Cities Go Broke: A Conceptual Introduction to Municipal Bankruptcy," *University of Chicago Law Review* (Spring 1993), pp. 425–95.

38. Quoted in Lewis, "Municipal Bankruptcy and the States," p. 18.

39. Simon Domberger and Paul Jensen, "Contracting Out by the Public Sector: Theory, Evidence, Prospects," *Oxford Review of Economic Policy* (Fall 1997), pp. 53–66.

40. Australia Industry Commission, "Competitive Tendering and Contracting by Public Sector Agencies," Report No. 48, January 24, 1996.

41. International City-County Management Association, "Profile of Local Government Service Delivery Choices, 2007."

42. Bard C. Cosman, "L. Frank Baum's La Jolla," *Journal of San Diego History* 44:4 (Fall 1998).

43. Cosman, "L. Frank Baum's La Jolla."

44. Tony Perry, "San Diego Must Boost Fire Spending, Feinstein Says," *Los Angeles Times*, November 28, 2007.

Index